HEURISTIC INQUIRY

To the memory of Clark Moustakas (1923–2012)
And to the memory of Eugene Gendlin (1926–2017)

HEURISTIC INQUIRY
Researching Human Experience Holistically

Nevine Sultan

University of St. Thomas

Los Angeles | London | New Delhi
Singapore | Washington DC | Melbourne

Sara Miller McCune founded SAGE Publishing in 1965 to support the dissemination of usable knowledge and educate a global community. SAGE publishes more than 1000 journals and over 800 new books each year, spanning a wide range of subject areas. Our growing selection of library products includes archives, data, case studies and video. SAGE remains majority owned by our founder and after her lifetime will become owned by a charitable trust that secures the company's continued independence.

Los Angeles | London | New Delhi | Singapore | Washington DC | Melbourne

• Praise for the Book •

"This book presents a valuable introduction to heuristic inquiry that is at the same time sophisticated and accessible. This is an important resource for those seeking to explore lived experience in a rigorous and reflexive way. It addresses a significant gap by presenting a refreshing, easy-to-follow introduction to this methodological approach without compromising in rigor and sophistication."

—Gerardo Blanco Ramirez, *University of Massachusetts, Boston*

"This text creatively integrates research methods, therapeutic processes, and the arts all in an insightful exploration of the human condition. It invites readers to reflect, meditate, and think deeply about how to internalize the heuristic research process in order to uncover the truth of people's living experiences. Consequently, heuristic research opens our minds to new realms and possibilities for human inquiry."

—Claire Michele Rice, *Nova Southeastern University*

"This text provides a valuable service to novice and experienced researchers through its straightforward, yet complex and nuanced, approach to heuristic inquiry."

—Joseph McNabb, *Northeastern University*

"This book offers a comprehensive overview of heuristic inquiry and provides an engaging, focused discussion of the methodological issues involved throughout all phases of the research process. Sultan provides an accessible and comprehensive guide for those designing and conducting heuristic inquiries."

—Angela Eckhoff, *Old Dominion University*

"Nevine Sultan has produced a work of remarkable depth, richness, and vitality. Drawing on her own research, Sultan speaks with authenticity, clarity, and rigor regarding the challenges and rewards of coming to grips with phenomena through co-creative processes. This text fills the long methodological void that has haunted the field since Moustakas's *Heuristic Research*. A must-read for anyone interested in qualitative research."

—Graham Bright, *York St John University, UK*

FOR INFORMATION:

SAGE Publications, Inc.
2455 Teller Road
Thousand Oaks, California 91320
E-mail: order@sagepub.com

SAGE Publications Ltd.
1 Oliver's Yard
55 City Road
London, EC1Y 1SP
United Kingdom

SAGE Publications India Pvt. Ltd.
B 1/I 1 Mohan Cooperative Industrial Area
Mathura Road, New Delhi 110 044
India

SAGE Publications Asia-Pacific Pte. Ltd.
3 Church Street
#10-04 Samsung Hub
Singapore 049483

Copyright © 2019 by SAGE Publications, Inc.

All rights reserved. No part of this book may be reproduced or utilized in any form or by any means, electronic or mechanical, including photocopying, recording, or by any information storage and retrieval system, without permission in writing from the publisher.

Printed in the United States of America

ISBN: 978-1-5063-5548-1

This book is printed on acid-free paper.

Acquisitions Editor: Helen Salmon
Editorial Assistant: Megan O'Heffernan
Production Editor: Jane Haenel
Copy Editor: Meg Granger
Typesetter: Hurix Digital
Proofreader: Caryne Brown
Indexer: Michael Ferreira
Cover Designer: Candice Harman
Marketing Manager: Susannah Goldes

18 19 20 21 22 10 9 8 7 6 5 4 3 2 1

• Brief Contents •

Preface		**xiv**
Acknowledgments		**xxv**
About the Author		**xxvii**
Chapter 1 •	What Is Heuristic Inquiry, Anyway?	1
Chapter 2 •	Locating Heuristic Inquiry Within Contemporary Qualitative Research	23
Chapter 3 •	Philosophical and Theoretical Foundations of Heuristic Inquiry	41
Chapter 4 •	Heuristic Processes and Phases	78
Chapter 5 •	Heuristic Research Design	104
Chapter 6 •	Heuristic Data Collection, Organization, and Analysis	121
Chapter 7 •	Relationality, Reflexivity, and Meaning-Making	157
Chapter 8 •	Evaluating the Research: A Collaborative Process	177
Chapter 9 •	Writing a Living Manuscript: An Embodied Relational Approach	191
Chapter 10 •	Ethics of Heuristic Research	210
Chapter 11 •	Universal Applications of Heuristic Inquiry: Bridging Research and Living Experience	229
Chapter 12 •	An Ending∞Beginning	241
Appendices		**244**
Glossary		**260**
References		**265**
Index		**281**

• Detailed Contents •

Preface	xiv
Acknowledgments	xxv
About the Author	xxvii

Chapter 1 • What Is Heuristic Inquiry, Anyway? — 1

A Brief Recent History	2
The Purpose of Heuristic Inquiry	9
Essential Features	10
• Exercise 1.1. Sensing Into and Expressing a Rough Understanding of Heuristic Inquiry	16
Processes and Phases	17
Limitations of Heuristic Inquiry	19
Closing Reflections	21

Chapter 2 • Locating Heuristic Inquiry Within Contemporary Qualitative Research — 23

Relationship to Phenomenology	24
Bricolaging With Similar Qualitative Approaches	29
Grounded Theory	30
Essential and Distinguishing Features	30
Bricolaging Grounded Theory With Heuristic Inquiry	32
Narrative Research	33
Essential and Distinguishing Features	33
Bricolaging Narrative Research With Heuristic Inquiry	34
Feminist Research	36
Essential and Distinguishing Features	36
Bricolaging Feminist Research With Heuristic Inquiry	36
Closing Reflections	38
• Exercise 2.1. Exploring the Labyrinth	38

Chapter 3 • Philosophical and Theoretical Foundations of Heuristic Inquiry — 41

Why Do We Learn About Theory?	42
Heuristic Inquiry as an Empirical Process	46
• Exercise 3.1. Exploring the Subjectivity∞Objectivity Continuum	49

Heuristic Inquiry as Qualitative Research	50
Heuristic Inquiry as Social Constructivism	53
Ontological Assumptions	55
Epistemological Assumptions	56
Axiological Assumptions	57
Methodological Assumptions	58
Rhetorical Assumptions	58
Heuristic Inquiry as "Phenomenologically Aligned"	60
Philosophers Whose Work Inspired Heuristic Inquiry	63
Edmund Husserl	63
Martin Buber	65
Carl Rogers	66
Abraham Maslow	69
Michael Polanyi	70
Eugene Gendlin	72
Maurice Merleau-Ponty	73
Closing Reflections	76
• Exercise 3.2. Exploring Other Ways of Being and of Knowing	77

Chapter 4 • Heuristic Processes and Phases   78

The Seven Processes of Heuristic Inquiry	81
Identifying With the Focus of Inquiry	81
• Exercise 4.1. An Empty Chair Experiment to Facilitate Identifying With the Focus of Inquiry	83
Self-Dialogue	85
Tacit Knowing	87
Intuition	89
Indwelling	90
Focusing	91
The Internal Frame of Reference	92
• Exercise 4.2. Six-Step Focusing Exercise to Clear an Inner Space	93
The Six Phases of Heuristic Inquiry	94
Initial Engagement	94
Immersion	95
Incubation	96
Illumination	97
Explication	98
Creative Synthesis	99
The Heuristic Phases in Action	99
Maintaining a Heuristic Attitude During the Research Journey	100
• Exercise 4.3. Needs Self-Assessment Exercise	101
Closing Reflections	102

Chapter 5 • Heuristic Research Design — 104

- Becoming Aware of a Topic and Formulating the Research Question(s) — 105
- Conducting the Literature Review — 108
  - Timing Your Literature Review — 109
  - Reviewing the Literature — 110
- Preparing for the Study — 111
  - Writing a Heuristic-Friendly IRB Proposal — 111
  - Creating a Set of Guidelines for the Study — 114
  - Creating Generic Content and Forms — 114
  - Selecting, Inviting, and Securing Co-Researchers — 115
    - *General Sampling Considerations* — 115
    - *Sample Size* — 117
    - *Building Rapport and Trust* — 118
- Closing Reflections — 120

Chapter 6 • Heuristic Data Collection, Organization, and Analysis — 121

- Data Collection — 122
  - Interviews — 123
    - *Preparing for the Interviews* — 123
    - *Embodied Relational Interviewing* — 124
    - *Disruptions in Flow* — 131
    - *Time and Structure Considerations* — 131
    - *Where and How* — 133
  - Researcher and Co-Researcher Artifacts — 134
  - Researcher Journals — 136
- Winding Down Data Collection — 140
- Data Organization and Management — 140
  - Immersion∞Incubation∞Reflexivity — 140
  - Creating Verbatim Transcripts — 141
- Data Analysis: Theme Illumination and Identification — 145
  - Following Clear Procedures — 145
  - Honoring Content and Context — 146
  - Deciphering Potential Themes — 147
  - Organizing Themes According to Research Questions — 149
  - Maintaining Discipline — 149
- Data Analysis: Theme Explication — 151
  - Individual Depictions — 151
  - Composite Depictions — 152
  - Exemplary Portraits — 153
  - Creative Synthesis — 154
- Closing Reflections — 156

Chapter 7 • Relationality, Reflexivity, and Meaning-Making — 157

- Relationality — 158
  - Shared Experiential Learning — 159
  - Connecting, Disconnecting, and Reconnecting — 160
    - *Empathy, Resonance, and Intersubjectivity* — 160
    - *Honoring Difference and Conflict* — 163
    - *Negotiating Power and Privilege* — 165
    - *Advancing Empowerment, Agency, and Social Justice* — 167
- Reflexivity — 168
  - Approaching Reflexivity Holistically — 169
  - Evaluating Values, Beliefs, Biases, and Attitudes — 169
    - • Exercise 7.1. Exploring Our Own and Others' Values — 171
  - Locating Oneself Within the Research Process — 172
  - Demystifying the Role of the Researcher — 172
  - Using the Journal as a Reflexive Tool — 173
- Meaning-Making — 174
  - • Exercise 7.2. Exploring a Personal Dilemma Using the Reflexive Journal — 175
- Closing Reflections — 176

Chapter 8 • Evaluating the Research: A Collaborative Process — 177

- A Primer on Heuristic Evaluation — 178
- Defining Rigor and Trustworthiness/Goodness — 179
- Evaluation Criteria — 180
  - Credibility — 180
  - Transferability — 181
  - Dependability — 181
  - Confirmability — 181
- Evaluation Strategies — 182
- Evaluating the Integrity of Your Heuristic Study — 182
- Heuristic Evaluation as a Shared Experience — 187
- The Importance of Reflexive Leadership in Evaluation — 189
- Closing Reflections — 190

Chapter 9 • Writing a Living Manuscript: An Embodied Relational Approach — 191

- Components of a Heuristic Manuscript — 192
  - Title — 193
  - Abstract — 193
  - Keywords — 193
  - Introduction and Clear Articulation of Topic and Research Questions — 194

Theoretical Framework 194
Rationale for the Study 194
Comprehensive but Concise Literature Review 194
Method 195
Co-Researchers 195
Materials and Procedure 195
Data Collection and Analysis 196
Findings 196
Discussion 196
Limitations 197
Conclusions and Future Directions 197
Embodied Relational Writing: Balancing Rigor With Intriguing Writing Style 198
- Exercise 9.1. Experimenting With Embodied Relational Writing 204
Promoting Social Justice, Action, and Transformation 205
Writing a Publishable Heuristic Manuscript 207
Closing Reflections 209

Chapter 10 • Ethics of Heuristic Research 210

Understanding Ethics 211
Core Ethical Principles and Codes 211
Facets of a Heuristic Study That May Prompt Ethical Concerns 213
Informed Consent 214
Research Methodology and Design 217
Relational Boundaries With Co-Researchers 218
Transparency 220
Researcher Competence 220
Addressing Emergent Ethical Dilemmas 220
Consulting Discipline-Related Ethical Codes 221
Using an Ethical Decision-Making Model 221
Engaging Researcher Reflexivity 222
- Exercise 10.1. Exploring and Addressing Emergent Ethical Dilemmas in Heuristic Research 224
The Perils of Researching Sensitive Topics: Maintaining Researcher Well-Being 225
Closing Reflections 228

Chapter 11 • Universal Applications of Heuristic Inquiry: Bridging Research and Living Experience 229

Using Heuristic Inquiry Formally in Various Disciplines 230
Education 231
Political Science and Government 232

Health Care	234
Conflict Transformation	235
Counseling and Psychotherapy	236
Engaging Heuristic Inquiry Informally	239
Closing Reflections	240

Chapter 12 • An Ending∞Beginning — 241

Appendices

Appendix A: Sample Cover/Invitation Letter	244
Appendix B: Sample Demographic Information Form	247
Appendix C: Sample Informed Consent Form	248
Appendix D: Sample Instructions for Interview Meeting	250
Appendix E: Sample Semi-Structured Interview Protocol	251
Appendix F: Sample Semi-Structured Interview Protocol With Examples	253
Appendix G: Preparing for and Recording Interviews (Sample)	256
Appendix H: Open-Ended Relational Probing and Prompting	258

Glossary — 260
References — 265
Index — 281

• Preface •

The evolution of qualitative research over the past three decades has provoked a flurry of newly minted inductive approaches that, previously, would have been frowned upon. This progression has also triggered enthusiastic efforts to reconstruct a number of already well-established qualitative methodologies. The process of reenvisioning a traditional research approach does not necessarily mean that the original processes by which it was conducted were amiss. Hardly! It means only that we qualitative researchers are cognizant of the changing world around us and, in our commitment to competent research practice and its dissemination, are also committed to active participation in the movement, expansion, and growth of our research orientation and research methods in general.

Purpose and Rationale

In 1990, SAGE published Clark Moustakas's *Heuristic Research: Design, Methodology, and Applications*, a slim volume that outlined a method for conducting qualitative research that, while it was disciplined and systematic, was also imaginative and highly experiential. Since the original publication of Moustakas's groundbreaking classic book, the heuristic approach has been essentially "lost" due to lack of precision and detailed description of the underlying processes. Additionally, Moustakas's small, modest volume is in dire need of revision and revitalization to acknowledge the dramatic evolution of qualitative inquiry during the past few decades and to more efficiently meet the needs of the 21st century researcher. Today's qualitative research resides at the highly complex intersection of human experience, perception, memory, language, history, culture and other social systems, relational interactions, and social justice. In that sense, engaging in qualitative research in today's world is an act of hope and resilience and a quest for deliverance and reimagination. This book takes heuristic inquiry as we know it and stretches it to more efficiently address this vibrant diversity.

Having the capacity to expand traditional research approaches, data representation, and manuscript writing as we know and practice them enables us to formulate research questions and engage our topics of inquiry from an innovative and inventive stance. No longer are we held hostage to a predetermined, fixed research agenda that, though it may align with our overall purpose, may or may not suit fundamental details within our process of inquiry. The idea, here, is not to abandon or reject the foundations of how we do empirical research and share findings with our colleagues and the general public, nor is it to undermine rigor. Instead, the aim is to ground our research process in real life by giving a voice—through relational and empathic dialogue—to those who have shared the experiences we are researching. In addition, we hope to represent our findings in such a manner as to connect with as many readers as possible and to inspire in them novel and productive ways of interacting with phenomena that they, too, may have experienced. This attitude allows us to unfilter the clinical and opaque gaze from which we tend to approach our topics of inquiry, with the understanding that the scientific stance is but one dimension from which we may examine and explore. It invites us to transcend the dichotomous view of research as either scientific or nonscientific and to engage in inquiry within the continuum of art and science. It enables us to take the work we do as researchers beyond the walls and halls of academia and to invite genuine dialogue with people in the real world, transcending the act of collecting information pretentiously and maximizing our potential to collapse boundaries between research and practice without compromising rigor.

Focused on exploring human experience from a holistic perspective, this book presents heuristic inquiry as a unique phenomenologically aligned, experiential, creative, and reflexive–relational approach to qualitative research that is also rigorous and evidence-based. In this book, I expand some of the distinctive attributes of this unique research approach to explore questions of interest that emerge from deeply personal human experiences with social, cultural, and potentially universal implications. I describe a newly distinguishing perspective of this methodology that views and treats participants not as passive subjects of research but rather as active co-researchers and partners in a contextually embedded exploratory process of inquiry marked by genuineness and intersubjectivity. Hence, in the interest of reconstituting how we contextualize our shared journey, the term *participants* is replaced with *co-researchers* or *research partners* throughout the text. Additionally, I offer and use the term **research team** to describe the collective group of researcher and research partners.

Likewise, I expand the parameters of heuristic inquiry in its original form, in which a primary focus was on the inner experience of the researcher. I propose a heuristic approach that supports the interweaving of inner and outer—intrapersonal and interpersonal, individual and collective, personal and professional—experience, one in which, together with our co-researchers, we either discover or encounter new knowledge and jointly create freshly elaborated meanings and understandings of it. From this social constructivist perspective, *discovery* and *encounter* are used interchangeably throughout the narrative, and the personhood of researcher and co-researchers is integrated and honored within the greater social context.

In keeping with the theme of interweaving various dimensions of experience, I use the labyrinth as a metaphor for the heuristic inquiry research journey. **Labyrinths** are ancient, archetypal symbols constituted of a series of winding spirals that form a circle representing a whole that is greater than the sum of its parts. Unlike a maze, in a labyrinth, there is one path that leads toward the center and another path that leads toward the exit. In a manner of speaking (and to use a worn cliché), the only way out is through. However, what matters is not the path that is followed but the nature of the journey itself, as the researcher intuits, asks, reflects, shares, learns, connects, and integrates in an ultimate search for knowledge and meaning. Labyrinths provide opportunities for both inner and outer processes; while researchers may sometimes *feel* lost as they walk a labyrinth's circuitous path, they will not actually *get* lost. Due to their holistic nature, labyrinths engage all of our many dimensions: the cognitive, the emotional, the sensory∞kinesthetic, the perceptual, the spiritual, and the social∞relational. As such, labyrinths have been used throughout history to symbolize the many transformative journeys (Archive for Research in Archetypal Symbolism, 2010) in human life that may lead to growth, well-being, and wholeness.

Similarly, the theme of interrelationship and nonlinearity is prevalent throughout this text. This is not unusual when considering the fluid nature of heuristic inquiry and the philosophical traditions from which it emerged. Thus, the **infinity symbol** (∞) will be used often to represent such nondual, fluid relationships. This symbol has its recorded beginnings in the mathematical concept of the largest sum possible. Throughout history, however, the infinity symbol has come to represent a number of different themes, including spirituality, eternity, the interrelationship of endings and beginnings, and empowerment. As you read this book, you will be able to identify the significance of this symbol to some of these ideas and to heuristic research.

Most important, and as we reenvision heuristic inquiry to suit the needs of contemporary researchers and research teams, I offer a new take on a traditional perspective. Let me explain. Phenomenological and phenomenologically aligned methods of research have traditionally been branded as the study of **lived experience**, as though past life events are now "over" and ought to be conceptualized in the past tense. I take this traditional description and give it a linguistic and foundational turn that attributes to heuristic inquiry the broader and deeper vision of researching **living experience**. This new paradigm, while it acknowledges multiple episodes of human experience within a single life, more accurately ascribes to human experience a continual, homogenous, interconnected spirit. Within this framework, any and all episodes are not isolated entities with clearly delineated beginnings, middles, and ends but are interrelated and bonded as part of a single, continuing process that is always unfolding in the present moment. Past experience is not something that occurred in history with no bearing on one's present moment in time but is a living, breathing part of one's here-and-now way of being in the world. Hence, heuristic inquiry is the exploration of living experience.

Finally, through the use of real-life samples and examples illustrating the various processes of heuristic research, I offer a construction of the approach that is straightforward and informal yet honors its creative, intuitive, and polydimensional nature. I also provide a number of pedagogical features to facilitate the comprehension and application of this approach, including reflection questions at the beginning of each chapter; a variety of activities; journaling tips and prompts; contemplative and meditative exercises; thematic boxes; artwork, photos, and illustrations of researcher and participant artifacts; and other features designed to facilitate the reader's interaction with the material being presented. I close each chapter with a "Closing Reflections" section that synopsizes some of the core themes of the chapter.

Audience

This book is intended for graduate students, advanced undergraduate students, early career researchers, and professionals in the fields of education, leadership, social sciences, mental health and human services, health sciences, and other related fields due to its remarkable inclusion of the researcher's experience as a key element in the process of inquiry, with equal significance to that of co-researchers'. It is also a unique resource for seasoned qualitative researchers with a dynamic interest in infusing color and variety into research approaches they may have exhausted. Additionally, I would recommend this book for the general public as it describes an intuitive process of inquiry to which many who are not professional researchers can easily relate. May I also go out on a limb and say that this book offers an exceptional opportunity for quantitative researchers to dabble in the world of inductive inquiry without the confines imposed by some of the more highly structured qualitative models and experiment with reenvisioned meanings for *rigor* and *empiricism*? It does! After all, who made the rules defining what is *rigorous* and what is *empirical* in the world of research? And why do we blindly conform to these rules rather than creatively explore other avenues of research? By the way, I am not opposed to quantitative research or scientific knowledge acquisition as it is traditionally understood. I have both conducted and participated in my fair share of quantitative studies, and I acknowledge their role and their necessity. On the other hand, attempting to apply the rules of quantitative research to exploring phenomena that are ambiguous, complex, and highly personal in nature comes with challenges. One size does not fit all!

Speaking of rules, I would like to stress that while this text does propose a systematic and highly detailed description of the heuristic research process and various avenues for approaching and applying it, it does not offer an absolute or fixed blueprint for conducting the "perfect" heuristic study. To do so would be oxymoronic, as it would undermine the autobiographical, creative, and highly process- and content-oriented nature of this qualitative research approach. Heuristic inquiry is a spontaneous and intuitive methodology that embraces the individuality of researcher and co-researchers, the topic of inquiry, and the findings that are ultimately illuminated, all within the framework of relationship and collaboration. It is a collage of processes and phases that invites those who have shared (or are sharing) a similar experience on a communal journey through which new meaning and knowledge will be collectively elucidated and through which transformation may take place. In that sense, and quite paradoxically, heuristic research is best engaged as a nonsequential, open-ended process. This enhances its potential to offer us a valid and trustworthy universal representation of a highly personal phenomenon elaborated through individual voices using rich, textured narratives and other forms of creative self-expression.

Organization

Chapter 1. What Is Heuristic Inquiry, Anyway?

In this opening chapter, I explore and describe the nature of heuristic inquiry. I begin with a brief recent history of the development of this approach. I define some of the purposes of conducting heuristic studies. I include a description of the essential features of heuristic inquiry and also briefly outline the numerous phases and processes involved in the heuristic approach. I conclude with a description of some of the limitations of this methodology and ways to approach the challenges they pose for researchers.

Chapter 2. Locating Heuristic Inquiry Within Contemporary Qualitative Research

This chapter pays special attention to how heuristic inquiry is similar to other qualitative methods and also how it is quite different. I compare and contrast heuristic inquiry with grounded theory, narrative research, and feminist research. I identify ways that aspects of heuristic inquiry may be bricolaged with and embedded within some of these approaches, thereby establishing avenues for interdisciplinary alliances and situating heuristic inquiry in the larger landscape of contemporary qualitative research.

Chapter 3. Philosophical and Theoretical Foundations of Heuristic Inquiry

In this chapter, I discuss the value of heuristic research as an empirical, qualitative, and social constructivist approach grounded in the exploration of rich and complex phenomena. I offer an overview of the philosophical foundations of heuristic inquiry as a means for exploring questions and making sense of human experience and the world. This begins with Edmund Husserl and includes discussion of contributions by Martin Buber, Carl Rogers, Abraham Maslow, Michael Polanyi, Eugene Gendlin, and Maurice Merleau-Ponty. I describe a variety of ways of *being* and ways of *knowing* within the context of heuristic research, as well as the axiological, methodological, and rhetorical facets of the methodology. I illustrate heuristic inquiry's playful though disciplined focus on curiosity and openness; the personal, autobiographical nature of the research question; the importance of recognizing and establishing connections between the research question and theory and all other aspects of the research process; the creative, intuitive, nonlinear spirit of this process of inquiry; the organic nature of the acquisition and emergence of original knowledge; the honoring of personal attunement, felt sense, and tacit knowing; and the researcher's personal experience and perceptions. This includes the interaction between observation and measurement of behavior and participation within and between interpersonal and intrapersonal engagement. I also address what I view as the continua of subjective∞objective experience and emergence∞discovery.

Chapter 4. Heuristic Processes and Phases

In this chapter, I describe the various processes and phases involved in heuristic research, many of which may be used in sequential or nonsequential fashion (or both). I describe how identifying with the focus of inquiry, self-dialogue, tacit knowing, intuition, indwelling, focusing, and engaging one's internal frame of reference underlie the six phases of heuristic research, which are initial engagement, immersion, incubation, illumination, explication, and creative synthesis. I illustrate various examples of how each of these processes and phases might unfold. I focus on the how-to practicalities of the methodology while underlining its highly subjective, process-oriented nature.

Chapter 5. Heuristic Research Design

This chapter serves as an outline for conducting a heuristic research study in an organized and disciplined manner while not losing sight of the importance of maintaining the fluid spirit of this unique methodology. I begin with the researcher's awareness of a salient issue, topic, or problem. I then address processes for formulating the central research question with an understanding of its foundational role to the process of inquiry; conducting a review of the professional literature; preparing for the study (writing a proposal, preparing invitation letters and informed consent forms, etc.); and purposively selecting co-researchers.

Chapter 6. Heuristic Data Collection, Organization, and Analysis

In this chapter, I address heuristic approaches to data collection using a variety of methods (with a focus on interviewing), organizing and managing the data in multiple ways, identifying themes, and creating co-researcher depictions. I clarify how researchers may represent their illuminated findings through individual depictions, composite depictions, exemplary portraits, and creative syntheses. I highlight several unique heuristic studies of questions/issues undertaken by a variety of authors from multiple disciplines on a number of different experiences, including internalized racism, spirituality, yoga and well-being, ecological writing, and embodiment. Recognizing that heuristic inquiry is very open-ended research, I address the issue of being realistic about time and other practical parameters without compromising the integrity of a study.

Chapter 7. Relationality, Reflexivity, and Meaning-Making

Here, I dig deeper into the myriad ways of doing this type of inquiry. I focus on the relational dimensions that view participants as co-researchers and partners in a shared learning and transformational experience. Taking the relational aspects further, I address ways of honoring difference and uniqueness among co-researchers, and I discuss some of the many ways personal and universal dimensions of experience are interconnected. I examine how researchers may address issues of personal and collective meaning; construction and reconstruction/renegotiation of narratives; power and privilege; personal and collective empowerment and agency; and advocacy and social justice, all of which are both personally and culturally embedded. I highlight the importance of engaging researcher reflexivity and locating oneself within and throughout the process of inquiry with a mind to clarify the role of the researcher in a manner that honors its vitality and its potential to enhance rigor and trustworthiness. This leads into a discussion of the impact of heuristic inquiry on the researcher, research partners, and readers of the findings, and the potential for growth and transformation.

Chapter 8. Evaluating the Research: A Collaborative Process

In this chapter, I present a number of approaches for evaluating the findings of a heuristic study for rigor and trustworthiness. This includes a variety of traditional evaluation criteria and strategies, as well as approaches designed specifically to evaluate a heuristic study for alignment with the heuristic methodology and for integrity. I describe how the role of the co-researchers is equally influential to that of the researcher in the evaluation and how using a collaborative evaluation process enriches its relational and emancipatory value and allows for integration of the research experience and the personal experience(s) from which the research question(s) emerged. I also shed some light on the importance of the primary researcher taking a reflexive leadership role in the evaluation process.

Chapter 9. Writing a Living Manuscript: An Embodied Relational Approach

The focus of this chapter is on ideas for writing a manuscript that honors the holistic and intuitive nature of heuristic inquiry by using structurally and texturally nuanced narrative, with the intention of maintaining the integrity and richness of human experience and promoting higher resonance within readers of the findings. I address the importance of writing a living manuscript, one that honors the balance between maintaining rigor and writing in an intriguing manner that keeps readers engaged beyond the reading event. I attend to some of the social justice dimensions of manuscript writing, such as the use of non-academic language to reach as diverse a readership as possible and to be as inclusive as is reasonable.

Chapter 10. Ethics of Heuristic Research

In this critical chapter, I outline facets of ethics to consider when using heuristic inquiry as a research method. This includes gaining an understanding of ethics and some of its core principles and recognizing ethical dilemmas that may emerge in a heuristic study surrounding issues such as relational boundaries between researcher and research partners, informed consent, and transparency. It also involves learning how to apply ethical codes and decision-making models that meet and transcend the requirements of research review boards, with a focus on maintaining rigor while remaining flexible to the emergent nature of heuristic inquiry. Due to the demanding nature of engaging in research that holds personal meaning to the researcher, I dedicate a section of the chapter to the potential perils of vicarious/secondary experiences during the data collection, organization, and analysis processes and to the importance of embracing a self-care regimen during the research journey.

Chapter 11. Universal Applications of Heuristic Inquiry: Bridging Research and Living Experience

In this final full chapter, I profile a number of disciplines and practices in which heuristic inquiry may be engaged as an approach for exploring human experience and advancing knowledge. These include but are not limited to education, political science and government, health care, conflict transformation, and counseling and psychotherapy. I address how heuristic inquiry may be applied both formally and informally, paving ways for integrating past experience and new knowledge and for bridging research and living experience. Again, I underscore some heuristic studies of issues explored by researchers from various disciplines on a variety of topics and propose ideas for studies in other disciplines, some of which do not appear to have any heuristic research history and for which the heuristic approach may be appropriate.

Chapter 12. An Ending∞Beginning

In this brief closing note, I acknowledge and reflect on the end of our shared journey in this book and invite you to begin your own process of heuristic inquiry.

Locating Myself in This Process

It is my personal premise that knowledge is, generally speaking, acquired subjectively and is ultimately understood within a self-in-relation framework: self in relation to self, self in relation to other, and self in relation to the world.

That is, knowledge begins with a personal, inner inquiry surrounding a topic of interest that has manifested in one's experience in the world and that emerges and matures through one's inner and outer interactions with the topic in context. This is also the premise of phenomenological (and phenomenologically aligned), social constructivist, and qualitative research approaches in general and is one of the key factors distinguishing qualitative inquiry from the more objective and measurement-oriented character of quantitative approaches. One of the primary tasks of the heuristic researcher is to *locate herself* within the research task—that is, to describe her role as the researcher. In keeping with this spirit of transparency (which is but one of many intriguing facets of the heuristic approach) it is important that I disclose my personal interests, motives, biases, values, and goals as I undertook the task of writing this book.

I am a qualitative, social constructivist, and heuristic researcher. I am also a counselor educator, a licensed mental health practitioner, and a poet. Relationships, dialogue, and meaning-making are critical to my way of being in this world. As a professional counselor, educator, and researcher, I truly believe that only through immersion in a warm, empathic, nonjudgmental, and genuine relationship with oneself, with others, and with the world can authentic interaction flow and knowledge be shared. As a relational body-centered gestalt psychotherapist, I do not view dialogue and discourse as exclusive to the verbal domain; communication also happens nonverbally. There are spoken and written exchanges, and there are exchanges that are communicated through other, non-languaged forms of expression.

This book was inspired by my personal experience using the heuristic inquiry approach for my dissertation study, in which I explored the embodied experiences of body-centered psychotherapists in the therapeutic process. The very journey of selecting a research approach for my study was highly heuristic, emerging at the junction of my personal experience of embodiment in the clinical setting and my embodied way of being in the world. As a body-centered psychotherapist, I experienced my own embodiment as a place through which my clients and I could connect and from which I could elaborate therapeutic work with highly meaningful and lasting impact on both my clients and myself. While this was my own deeply felt experience, my sense was that other counselors and psychotherapists also experience somatic phenomena while working with clients. My research question emerged from my curiosity about the legitimacy of my assumption and my keen desire to learn more about other body-oriented mental health practitioners' embodied experiences. The heuristic approach allowed me to explore a phenomenon that, while deeply personal, may have universal significance among other similarly oriented psychotherapists. Likewise, the experience of designing the study was heuristic, as were the processes of seeking co-researchers, collecting and analyzing the data, evaluating the findings, writing the manuscript, and discussing the findings, in both social and professional settings, imbued as these processes were with self-dialogue, immersion, incubation, focusing, illumination, and other heuristic approaches.

One thing of which I was unaware (but of which I became aware quite quickly and abruptly) was the dearth of professional literature either describing or explaining the processes involved in conducting this type of research or presenting the findings of already completed heuristic studies. In my search for information, I came across a few articles depicting studies that had made use of the heuristic approach. What was confusing for me, at the time, was that while each study seemed to conform to the foundational phases and processes of the heuristic approach, the researcher of each study had also taken considerable creative license in both the execution of the research and its presentation. My primary (and only truly reliable) resources were thus the single book written about heuristic inquiry by Clark Moustakas (1990)—the man who originated the heuristic inquiry approach—and an article Moustakas coauthored with Douglass (1985). With so few resources, I essentially took what I could and then used my imagination to invent my own path. It did not take me long to realize that my predecessors had likely done the same, thereby explaining some of the marked differences evident among the manuscripts of those studies. As I went about my dissertation research, I encountered a number of stumbling blocks in the research process that, with much patience and determination, I was able to work through. Nevertheless, as I dug deeper into my research process, the need for a comprehensive text describing heuristic inquiry became more and more apparent. Thus began a new heuristic process through which I playfully explored the idea of writing this book, even as I was closing out my dissertation study.

My journey with heuristic inquiry did not begin with my dissertation work, however. I have been a heuristic researcher, informally, my entire life and have used the heuristic approach throughout my life's journey to make sense of a number of phenomena that I personally experienced, each of which captured me with such force as to impact every interaction I had with both my inner and outer worlds. In such moments, I felt compelled to acquire a deeper understanding by dialoguing with myself and others who had experienced the same or similar phenomena. I have explored, within myself and with others, and written about the nature of human darkness and how we can use our own darkness to enhance resilience. This project resulted in creative synthesis in the form of a poetry chapbook (Sultan, 2014). I have studied the phenomenon of stuckness, largely inspired by my experiences of being physically stuck in the womb and delivered by forceps three weeks past my due date and being psychologically stuck in the hamster wheels—time and again—of unfavorable situations and damaging relationships. I have delved into perfectionism—its harms, its benefits, and its multifaceted manifestations—in both personal and professional settings. Because I am a poet, a natural outcome of these explorations was that the creative syntheses emerged in the form of poetry.

Additionally, I have spoken with many clinical colleagues and journaled about our shared narratives of embodied intersubjectivity and somatic resonance in the psychotherapy encounter. My doctoral dissertation study (Sultan, 2015) was a heuristic inquiry in which I explored therapist embodiment, a deeply personal experience that was (and continues to be) a critical component of my clinical work with psychotherapy clients and of which I wished to arrive at a deeper understanding and create some meaning. In fact, each of these explorations was inspired by my deeply felt personal experience of the topic, which makes locating myself within the research process essential. After all, how do we hope to understand what we are researching if we fail—or *refuse*—to identify our connection to it?

The importance of the researcher's role has been minimized, diminished, and shamed for too long. We cannot possibly extract ourselves (or be extracted) from what we experience and what we research. As professional researchers, we cannot—*should* not—pretend we are not an integral part of the topics we investigate and explore. The very idea of value-free research is pure fantasy! Accordingly, it is our ethical obligation, and our duty as explorers of human experience and advancers of scientific inquiry and knowledge, to be transparent about our personal agendas. Contrary to a dated belief that any personal investment or inclination in a research endeavor on the part of the researcher compromises its validity, it has been my personal experience that identifying and clarifying the role of the researcher lends a study credibility and trustworthiness.

Finally, I view the research endeavor as a journey or quest for an unknown that is eagerly awaiting an opportunity to emerge into the light. A safe emergence of that unknown takes place within a cocreated, experiential, genuine *how* and *what* habitat of inquiry that is open and ready to unconditionally receive whatever materializes from whichever source. This requires a great deal of flexibility, creativity, and openness on the part of the research team. It demands, too, that all who are traveling the research labyrinth interact with the often-present ambiguity and confusion with curiosity, imagination, and nonjudgment; trust the process; and remain committed to seeing the journey through to its end, knowing that the end may be just another beginning!

Closing Reflections

As we journey together through this narrative, I invite you to allow yourself to be alert to words, phrases, exercises, symbols, or images that resonate with all dimensions of your being—that is, the cognitive, the emotional, the sensory∞kinesthetic, the perceptual, the spiritual, and the social∞relational. When you find them, pause and take a moment to attune to this experiencing gateway and to explore multiple discourses between and among your various perspectives. This not only gives you a flavor of some of the processes you will be using as a heuristic researcher but inspires you to create your own relationships with those processes. I also invite you, in genuine heuristic style, to release any attachment to a specified expectation or goal, to question and sit with those elements of content that feel confusing, to trust and own your reading and learning journey, and to immerse yourself fully and holistically in this process. Shall we?

• Acknowledgments •

Forget safety.
Live where you fear to live.

~ Jalaluddin Rumi

Writing this book has been a life-transforming journey for me, and an exquisite one at that. This journey has also demanded of me one daring leap of faith after another—faith in myself, faith in my world, and faith in a number of gracious and generous beings who accompanied me, persistently and unfalteringly.

I am deeply grateful for the limitless support of the editorial team at SAGE. To Helen Salmon, my editor: Your trust in this process and in me was deeply affirming, and your backing of reenvisioning heuristic inquiry through this textbook was more encouraging than you will ever know. To Chelsea Neve and Megan O'Heffernan, Helen's editorial assistants: Your tireless attention to detail and precision was both graciously challenging and refreshing. It was a joy and an honor to work with both of you. Additionally, thanks to Meg Granger, copy editor, and Jane Haenel, production editor, for your tireless work editing the manuscript.

A great thank-you to the reviewers of my book. I am especially grateful to Graham Bright of York St. John University in the United Kingdom: Your constructive and gentle feedback was instrumental and invaluable. A very special thank-you to all members of the Clinical Mental Health Counseling Department and the School of Education and Human Services at the University of St. Thomas—especially to Elizabeth Maynard and Higinia Torres-Rimbau—for your support. Thanks, also, to Jeffrey Kottler: Your encouragement to me to follow my own path was heartening and invigorating.

I would like to thank my former instructors and mentors Ray Wooten, Melanie Harper, Dana Comstock, Julie Strentzsch, and Dan Ratliff: I've learned so much about research, teaching, and counseling from all of you. I am also very grateful to my students and my counseling clients: You keep me grounded—every day and every moment—in what really matters. I owe a special debt of gratitude to my former co-researchers: Our research journeys together have fortified and enriched my knowledge and my being. Thanks, also, to my friends and colleagues Arline Didier, Regina Stowers, Donna Kapinus, Renee Turner, Fiorella Ventura, Cremilde de Oliveira, and Maureen Jones, for your priceless words, thoughts, and presence.

I wish to thank, from the bottom of my heart, my husband and best friend, Vincent Sanchez. We have been on so many life journeys together, from beginning to end . . . to new beginning. Thank you for the quiet sacrifices and the tremendous emotional support you gave throughout this journey and give so generously every day. Thank you, also, for believing in me, and for accepting me and loving me just as I am.

The author and SAGE Publishing would like to thank the following reviewers for their feedback during the development process:

Graham Bright, York St. John University

Angela Eckhoff, Old Dominion University

Tera R. Jordan, Iowa State University

Joseph W. McNabb, Northeastern University

Gerardo Blanco Ramirez, University of Massachusetts, Boston

Claire Michele Rice, Nova Southeastern University

• About the Author •

Nevine Sultan is assistant professor of Clinical Mental Health Counseling at the University of St. Thomas in Houston, Texas. She is also a licensed professional counselor in private practice, specializing in complex trauma, dissociative disorders, and grief. Nevine embraces an embodied phenomenological approach to research, education, and counseling/psychotherapy to enhance awareness and intersubjectivity and to support the integration of living experience and the creation of meaning. She is especially passionate about the relationally shared experience between researcher and co-researchers, instructor and student, and therapist and client, and the impact of embodied awareness on empathic presence and creative resilience. Her recent publications can be found in the *Journal of Humanistic Counseling* and the *Journal of Creativity in Mental Health*. She currently teaches graduate courses on human diversity; counseling theories; human growth and development; addictions and recovery; ethical, legal, and professional issues in counseling; and social justice. She is an avid meditator and creative writer.

What Is Heuristic Inquiry, Anyway?

What in your life is calling you,
When all the noise is silenced,
The meetings adjourned,
The lists laid aside,
And the wild iris blooms
By itself
In the dark forest . . .
What still pulls on your soul?

~ **Jalaluddin Rumi**

Questions for Reflection

1. Why do I research human experience?
2. What is my role as a heuristic researcher?
3. What tools can heuristic inquiry offer me and my research needs?

At first glance, the words of Rumi appear as a question. Yet as we dwell with the essence of the words, we find, held within them, both an inquiry and a most tantalizing invitation to self-reflection, self-discovery, and self-transformation. Such is the domain of heuristic inquiry, which summons us to linger in silence and solitude, even as we are magnetized by the pull of life and the richness of the dark forest, and as we seek—both within and without—knowledge, meaning, and growth. Before we begin our journey of learning how to unravel the essential nature of human phenomena, however, it's crucial that we take a brief step back and connect with the origins of heuristic inquiry. We will then discuss the essential nature of this particular methodology, as well as its purpose, some of its defining characteristics, and some limitations and considerations to keep in mind when using this approach.

A Brief Recent History

Heuristic research started out more as an informal process of assessing and meaning-making than as a research approach. Clark Moustakas (1923–2012), the originator of heuristic inquiry, stated that the approach came to him as he searched for a proper word to meaningfully represent certain processes he felt were foundational to explorations of everyday human experience (1990). The methodology itself was introduced in a more formalized manner to the world of research methods with the publication of Moustakas's book *Loneliness* (1961), in which he depicted his experience of that phenomenon as he dwelled with a decision tied to his daughter's need for heart surgery. Moustakas used his personal knowledge of and relationship with loneliness as a foundation for exploring the phenomenon in others.

While this may seem like a biased or "non-empirical" way of engaging a research topic in some research traditions, we now have rejuvenated understandings of empiricism that, while they actually date back to the most primitive attempts to operationalize the exploration of human experience, are reemerging due to their relevance to the needs of contemporary research. We will delve into this topic in greater detail in Chapter 3, but for now, we can say that much of formalized research includes a deeply felt conscious or unconscious personal interest in a particular topic the researcher has experienced in one or more contexts, and a communion between what the researcher already knows about the topic and what he is out to learn or discover about it from others who have also experienced it. As American philosopher David Abram (1996) reminds us, "The scientist does not randomly choose a specific discipline or specialty, but is drawn to a particular field by a complex of subjective experiences and encounters, many of which unfold far from the laboratory and its rarefied atmosphere" (p. 33). Research is, thus, regardless of its paradigm or orientation, a multicultural, contextual, intersubjective, and embodied act.

If we give it some thought, we may see that we are all engaging in various heuristic practices even if we do not formally name what we are doing *heuristic inquiry*. We are immersed in heuristic processes beginning with our very first efforts to learn—our preverbal experiences as infants—and continuing until the present moment of our lives. We are ceaselessly assessing what and how we sense, feel, and think about certain phenomena, while checking in with others to learn if they are experiencing them in different, similar, or the same ways, and then returning to ourselves to process all this information toward a more cohesive understanding. Heuristic inquiry acknowledges these experiences and includes them in the research process, making for a very personal and communal journey of discovery that

- includes a systematic though flexible research framework;
- engages self-searching and reflexive self-dialoguing;
- honors felt sense (Gendlin, 1981, 1996);
- stresses relationality, intersubjectivity, and "betweenness" (Buber, 1923/1970); and
- fosters integration.

In that sense, heuristic research is both art and science.

The term *heuristic* comes from the ancient Greek word *heuriskein*, "meaning to discover or to find" (Moustakas, 1990, p. 9). Moustakas described **heuristic inquiry*** as a qualitative, social constructivist, and phenomenologically aligned research model (1990, 1994). In the context of social science and educational research, heuristic inquiry has also been identified as an autobiographical approach to qualitative research (Moustakas, 1990). Other descriptors and characterizations of heuristic inquiry that are not highly elaborated in the professional literature include the following:

- Exploratory, serendipitous, and discovery-oriented
- Process- and content-focused
- Intuitive, introspective, and reflexive
- Experiential, embodied, and holistic
- Existential and humanistic
- Culturally embedded and emancipatory
- Relational, authentic, and participatory
- Imaginative and creative
- Nonlinear, fluid, and flexible

---

*The definitions of bold terms can be found in the Glossary at the end of this volume.

Finally, a novel characteristic of heuristic inquiry that emerged from my dissertation research process is that it is the study of **living experience** (i.e., interrelated, interconnected, continuing experience) rather than the study of **lived experience**, which describes all phenomenological approaches and implies that human experiences are intermittent events that are disconnected from one another and that, once they are completed, are history (Sultan, 2015). Please see Table 1.1 for brief descriptions of the general characteristics and leanings of heuristic inquiry, all of which will be more fully explored throughout the text.

As a method for investigating and exploring human living experience, heuristic inquiry was inspired by a number of theories and knowledge bases, including those advanced by Abraham Maslow (1956, 1966, 1971), Martin Buber (1923/1970), and Edmund Husserl (1900/2001). It was especially influenced by Michael Polanyi (1958, 1966, 1969), whose writings stress tacit knowledge as the basis for all other forms of knowledge; Carl Rogers (1961, 1980, 1985), whose theories and approaches greatly inspired and informed the fields of psychotherapy and humanistic psychology due to their intensely relational and awareness-oriented dimensions; and Eugene Gendlin (1962), whose focusing body psychotherapy modality stresses the inner felt sense experience that is a significant component of heuristic research. In this newly revised approach to heuristic inquiry, the work of Martin Buber is brought into deeper focus as his explorations into the necessity of an I–Thou (versus an I–It) intersubjective approach to human relationships informs this volume's enhanced emphasis on the pivotal role of the relationship between researcher and research partners. The phenomenology of perception elaborated by Maurice Merleau-Ponty (1945/2013) also links quite seamlessly with this heuristic approach through its emphasis on human interaction and meaning-making as temporal, embodied, and perceptual acts.

These historical figures and theories made a prominent contribution to the knowledge base of how we are in the world and how we understand both our individual and shared experiences through embodiment, perception, self-exploration, self-knowledge, and self-actualization. Hence, the self of the researcher and the researcher's perceptual field are key dynamics in the heuristic approach. "In its purest form, heuristics is a passionate and discerning personal involvement in problem solving, an effort to know the essence of some aspect of life through the internal pathways of the self" (Douglass & Moustakas, 1985, p. 39). So what might distinguish heuristic inquiry from, say, autoethnography? Well, in autoethnography the search for understanding the essence of a topic of inquiry through the self is focused on *one* self—that of the primary researcher. In a heuristic study, however, self-research is but one dimension of the study. Focus on individual experience is a Eurocentric lens on research and may not address advancement and movement from the personal toward the universal. Thus, heuristic researchers explore their own internal pathways, as well as those of the selves of others, as we radiate from the personal domain of experiencing a phenomenon into the realm of the

TABLE 1.1 ● **General Characteristics and Leanings of Heuristic Inquiry**

Qualitative	Exploratory and emergent. Questions focus on the *what* and *how* of the topic of inquiry (Creswell, 2009; Finlay, 2011; Krathwohl, 2009). Takes into account and is influenced by the experiences and perceptions of the researcher (Moustakas, 1990; Sultan, 2015), who is considered the key instrument of data collection and interpretation (Creswell, 2013; Porter, 2010).
Social constructivist	Assumes reality is relative and is constructed based on one's contextual and subjective meaning-making of personal experience (Ponterotto, 2005). Adopts a first-person, personalized approach to presenting the findings, acknowledging the researcher's biases, values, and attitudes, and the impact of these on the research. Relies on research partners' views of the topic of inquiry.
Phenomenologically aligned	Attempts to make sense of experience as it is perceived (Krathwohl, 2009) to allow for the illumination of deep understandings and meanings (Christensen & Brumfield, 2010). Views perception as the primary source of knowledge (Merleau-Ponty, 1945/2013) informing the constituents of one's lifeworld (Ashworth, 2003). Invites researchers to slow down, focus on the topic of inquiry, immerse themselves in it, and dwell with it while engaging empathy, acceptance, and creativity (Creswell, 2013; Finlay, 2011; Moustakas, 1990; Sultan, 2015; Wertz, 2005).
Autobiographical	Originates within the self. Includes personal history, memory, imagination, and perception, fusing past, present, and future (Moustakas, 1994; Sultan, 2015) into the here and now.
Exploratory, serendipitous, and discovery-oriented	Embraces an attitude of wonder (Wertz, 2005), openness, and curiosity (Moustakas, 1990; Sultan, 2015) toward purposive and systematic inquiry that is marked by spontaneity and either prearranged or accidental discovery (Stebbins, 2008) or emergence.
Process- and content-focused	Emphasizes the process of inquiry and its dynamics, versus a predetermined outcome. Keeps researchers close to the data that are emerging (Creswell, 2013; Krathwohl, 2009). Honors all elaborations of process and content, including dialogue and discourse, and various types of artifacts, such as writing samples, journal entries, poetry, artwork, musical compositions, photos, and symbols.

(Continued)

TABLE 1.1 ● (Continued)

Intuitive, introspective, and reflexive	Honors and acknowledges *tacit knowing*—that is, implicit knowledge or understanding (Polanyi, 1958, 1966, 1969). Informed by the process of focusing on one's *felt sense*— the rightness of feeling in one's gut (Gendlin, 1981, 1996)—which allows words, phrases, images, memories, symbols, or novel understandings representing a topic to come to the surface. Supported by the researcher's ability to reflectively and reflexively attend to both her own and her research partners' experience (Moustakas, 1990, 2015), and the interweaving of both experiences (Merleau-Ponty, 1945/2013), to attain deeper levels of awareness.
Experiential, embodied, and holistic	Views subjective human experience—the here-and-now relationship between one's body and oneself and one's body and the world—reciprocity, and perception (Merleau-Ponty, 1945/2013) as pivotal to informing the research process. Focuses on multiple facets of human experience: cognitive, emotional, sensory∞kinesthetic, perceptual, spiritual, social∞relational, and their integration (Sultan, 2015). Honors both verbal and nonverbal experience. Operates at the intersection of *being* and *knowing*.
Existential and humanistic	Underlines human perception—that is, how individuals *know* their world (Johnson, 2008)—as well as human limitations and aspirations. Emphasizes one's tendency toward meaning-making, authenticity, and self-actualization (Maslow, 1968, 1976; Rogers, 1961). Characterized by subjectivity (Douglass & Moustakas, 1985), personal involvement, and full engagement with the topic of inquiry (Rogers, 1961).
Culturally embedded and emancipatory	Includes consideration of the social context and issues related to diversity, such as gender, age, ethnicity, religion, social class, ability, and sexuality, toward social justice (Miller, 2008a). Enhances one's ability to reconstitute one's understanding of reality in a manner that embraces new perceptions and does not conflict with personal views (McGettigan, 2008a), with wide implications for social change.
Relational, authentic, and participatory	Informed by the dynamic flow of presence, self- and other-awareness, empathy (Rogers, 1961), and intersubjectivity (Buber, 1923/1970) through which researcher and co-researchers experience the confluences of betweenness and witness in their shared encounter (Sultan, 2015). Used to enhance trust and deeper exploration.

	May transform the researcher (Douglass & Moustakas, 1985) and co-researchers by providing opportunities for intense personal contact, joint self-disclosure, and creation and meaning-making of shared subjective experience (Finlay, 2011). Inclusive, equitable, empowering, awareness-enhancing, and action-oriented (Lincoln, Lynham, & Guba, 2011).
Imaginative and creative	Refers to the emergence of novelty at the intersection of a person's uniqueness with people, events, and circumstances in life (Rogers, 1961). Marked by the ability to experience "the fresh, the raw, the concrete, the idiographic, as well as the generic, the abstract, the rubricized, the categorized, and the classified" (Maslow, 1976, p. 88). Stresses freedom, spontaneity, self-acceptance, and integration. Demonstrates nontraditional approaches to data collection, organization, and analysis. Allows for nonliteral representations of perceived reality (Patton, 2008).
Nonlinear, fluid, and flexible	Informed by openness to and awareness of multiple experiences at once (Rogers, 1961), versus experiencing and perceiving in predetermined ways. Characterized by tolerance for ambiguity and the unknown, and nonattachment to specified outcomes—that is, willingness "to conduct one's research on behalf of the phenomenon" (Dahlberg, Dahlberg, & Nyström, 2008, p. 98). Adaptable to meet the needs of researchers within diverse disciplines working with phenomena that are vague or difficult to observe, measure, or document.
Living versus lived	Acknowledges all human experience as interconnected and interrelated, and thus as one continuing, enduring cycle rather than a series of discrete, disconnected historical events. Views research as the exploration of present-moment, ongoing, *living* human experience, even when exploring past experiences. Resonates with the rich, textured descriptions and voices of those who have experienced the topic of inquiry.

universal. With that, while such internal pathways may not always be clearly outlined, there is the inevitable moment of knowing one has arrived at the center of the labyrinth one is journeying and has attained illumination, only to begin a newly inspired heuristic journey. Figure 1.1 is a photo of a naturally etched environmental expression of the labyrinth. Figure 1.2 is a photo of the entrance of the walking labyrinth (a replica of the labyrinth of the Chartres Cathedral) located on the grounds of the University of St. Thomas in Houston, Texas, where I work.

FIGURE 1.1 ● **A Knot in a Plank of Wood: A Labyrinth Carved by Nature, Upon Nature**

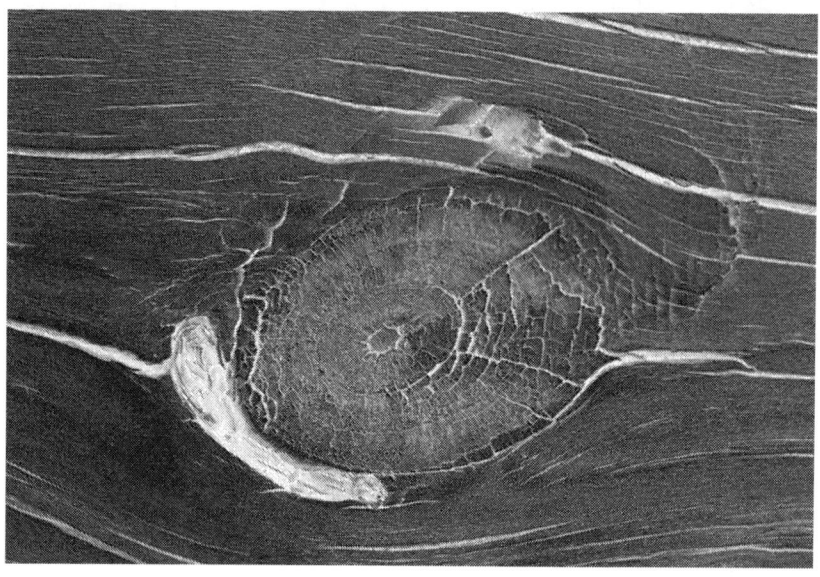

FIGURE 1.2 ● **The Entrance of the Labyrinth at the University of St. Thomas in Houston, Texas: A Replica of the Labyrinth at the Chartres Cathedral**

The Purpose of Heuristic Inquiry

Heuristic inquiry involves exploring the subjective experience of a particular phenomenon within a purposive sample of individuals. Heuristic researchers do not separate the individual from the experience but rather focus their exploration on the essential nature of the relationship or interaction between both. The central question asked by any heuristic research study is: *What is the experience of . . . ?* A secondary question of focus in a heuristic study may be: *How do I/you experience this phenomenon?* As evident, both questions are open-ended, inviting further discourse and elaboration rather than confining co-researchers to specific, predetermined responses. As an example, the central topic of inquiry in the heuristic study I conducted for my dissertation (Sultan, 2015) was the experience of embodiment in psychotherapists. The core questions I asked of my research partners, all of whom were body-centered psychotherapists with a personal experience of embodiment, were as follows:

1. What does it mean for you to be embodied?
2. How do you use your embodiment within the therapeutic process?
3. Can you share some clinical examples of how you use your embodiment in the therapeutic encounter?
4. What is your perception of the impact of your embodiment on the clients you work with?

Such questions demonstrate the central premise of heuristic inquiry—self- and other-exploration toward shared understanding of the essential nature of the core phenomenon, how it is sensed and experienced, and its significance to oneself, to others, and to the world.

You might be thinking, *I can ask these very same questions within a grounded theory study. So why heuristic inquiry and not grounded theory?* My simple response is that while we may ask the same or similar questions in studies conducted across various qualitative methodologies, the findings will vary (more on this in Chapter 2). For example, in a grounded theory study, the idea is to identify a theoretical understanding of a phenomenon through a group of themes that assimilate around a core theme, whereas in a heuristic study, the idea is to identify nonhierarchical themes that help us understand the essential nature of the phenomenon. Additionally, grounded theory and heuristic inquiry each follow their own unique process of inquiry that both informs and is informed by the research question(s). Finally, due to heuristic inquiry's humanistic background, it embraces a unique focus on holism and personhood—essentially, on what it means to be human.

Please see Box 1.1, which lists a number of heuristic inquiry research studies demonstrating the applicability of this singular research method across multiple disciplines. Some of these studies will be explored in greater depth in

> **BOX 1.1**
>
> **EXAMPLES OF HEURISTIC RESEARCH STUDIES**
>
> Alsobrook, R. F. (2015). *Yoga and emotional well-being: A heuristic inquiry into the experience of women with a yoga practice.* Unpublished doctoral dissertation, Harold Abel School of Social and Behavioral Sciences, Capella University.
>
> Green, C. (2012). *The wild writer: A heuristic inquiry into the ecological writer's experience of nature.* Unpublished master's thesis, Prescott College, Prescott, AZ.
>
> Holt-Waldo, N. Y. (2011). *The lived experience of being a holistic nurse educator: A heuristic inquiry.* Unpublished doctoral dissertation, Capella University.
>
> Leiby, J. C. (2014). *Windows to the soul: A heuristic inquiry in the use of the eyes as portals to innate presence.* Unpublished doctoral dissertation, Sofia University, Palo Alto, CA.
>
> Madden, E. M. (2015). *The lived experience of being spiritual for an atheist.* Unpublished doctoral dissertation, Harold Abel School of Social and Behavioral Science, Capella University.
>
> Moustakas, C. E. (1961). *Loneliness.* Englewood Cliffs, NJ: Prentice-Hall.
>
> Pogge, S. M. (2013). *The experience of living with chronic illness: A heuristic study.* Unpublished doctoral dissertation, Department of Psychology and Philosophy, College of Arts and Sciences, Texas Woman's University, Denton, TX.
>
> Sultan, N. (2015). *A heuristic inquiry of the embodied experiences of body psychotherapists in the therapeutic encounter.* Unpublished doctoral dissertation, Department of Counseling and Human Services, St. Mary's University, San Antonio, TX.
>
> Whatley, R. J. (2015). *Pulling the arrows out of our hearts: An heuristic inquiry into the lived experience of internalized racism of African American women.* Unpublished doctoral dissertation, Institute of Transpersonal Psychology, Palo Alto, CA.

later chapters. In the meantime, I recommend looking up some of these studies and exploring the unique features that emerge through use of the heuristic methodology.

Essential Features

Apart from any altruistic or professional motives, heuristic studies are grounded in our personal experience and embedded within our personhood. Heuristic inquiry emerges from the researcher's **initial engagement**, or first encounter, with a topic of extreme interest through an autobiographical experience that, though it is internal and personal to you (the researcher), is potentially of social and universal significance. The experience is so deeply felt that it arouses one central question you are unable to ignore. In a manner of speaking, the general topic of inquiry chooses you, which is quite a departure from many traditional approaches to research whereby you go about a rather methodical selection and "pruning" of the research topic. This deeply felt phenomenon or experience becomes a point of encounter between your internal world and the external world in which the phenomenon is playing out and in which the research is taking place. In a way, the research question and the process of exploring it become a calling, a sort of invitation to enter the labyrinth and embrace the journey.

What does this mean for you? Once the question is found, your urge to find an answer must be set aside so you can embody and live the question fully. While it requires some degree of patience and engagement with the actual research process, this practice of **immersion** allows for the ambiguity that is a central aspect of the heuristic approach while releasing any attachment to a specified goal, finding, or outcome. It also lays the foundation for the central question or topic of inquiry to embody you and thereby inform the process of inquiry and discovery. Thus, we heuristic researchers adopt the attitude of *learner* versus *expert* as we connect fully with the phenomenon being explored. We bring passion, curiosity, imagination, and vulnerability as we allow ourselves to be drawn into the rich banquet of the unknown, even while living it in all dimensions of our experience: in sleeping, in waking, in going about our day, in our interactions with others, in our dialogue with ourselves, and in any other encounters we may have. We open up our senses, our intuition, our thoughts, our feelings, and our awareness in our search for the qualities, conditions, and relationships that motivate our research question (Moustakas, 1990). We experience our entire way of being in the world—and are connected to ourselves, to others, and to the world—through the lens of our topic of inquiry. As Moustakas (1990, 2015) described it, the research question becomes a "lingering presence" (Moustakas, 2015, p. 309) as the researcher interacts with and encounters or cocreates new knowledge. See Figure 1.3 for a visual representation of this.

As you connect with varying dimensions of your experience (including interest, curiosity, openness, fascination, reflection, and various versions of the research question) and acquire novel information, you may need to step away every once in a while to allow this knowledge to incubate. **Incubation** is a process of care, cultivation, and growth that enhances and encourages insight, understanding, and integration. Paradoxically, then, to fully connect with this tacit, implicit dimension and what it holds about the topic of inquiry, you must be willing to sometimes surrender your intimate relationship with the topic of inquiry and your attachment to rigid time schedules. As Moustakas (2015) notes, "The heuristic process is rooted in experiential time, not clock time" (p. 318). Again, this calls for your willingness to be flexible with regard to a specific timeline or outcome (more on how to do this realistically in Chapter 6) as you allow yourself to move back and forth between intimacy with and distance from the research question.

FIGURE 1.3 • Topic of Inquiry/Research Question as a Lens for Being, Relating, and Knowing

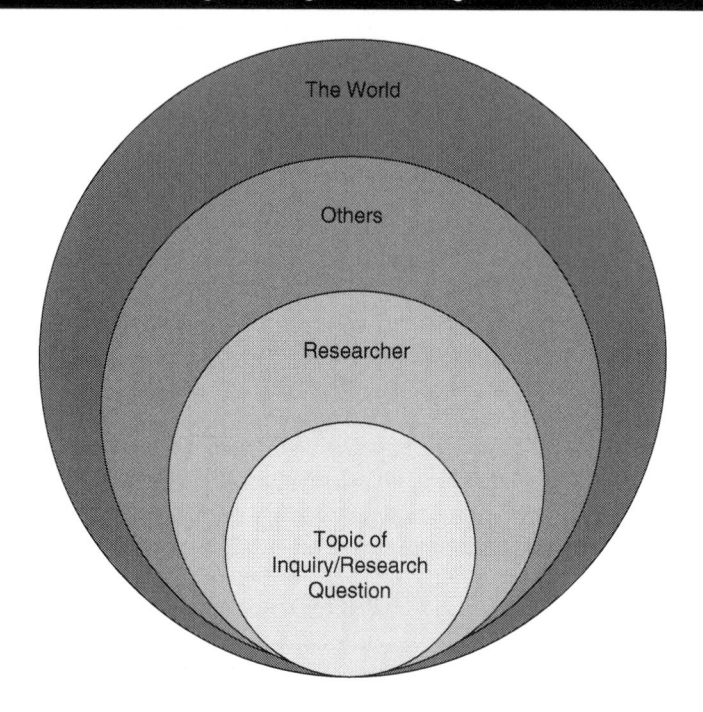

- The World
- Others
- Researcher
- Topic of Inquiry/Research Question

This can be quite scary and confusing, evoking a significant amount of fear and anxiety as you come face-to-face with uncertainty. On the other hand, if you are willing to truly surrender to the research process, there is the enormous and ever fascinating reward of being with whatever emerges serendipitously, as unexpected as it may be. In that respect, this process involves a high level of innate artistry in which you, the primary researcher, balance engagement and detachment, proximity and distance, tension and release, while remaining cautious not to become stuck on either end of these spectra. Throughout the course of the study, you go back and forth in a rhythmic dance between the processes of immersion and incubation, within and between a variety of contexts that nurture the knowledge that is about to emerge. In essence, you surrender to the labyrinth, with all its twists and turns, knowing that there is no right or wrong way to pursue that path. This flexibility of movement is guided by your internal subjective experience and in turn guides the research endeavor and the organic emergence of new knowledge throughout various phases of the inquiry, with the deeply felt question itself holding the capacity to inspire discovery, profound understanding, and transformation within all who come into contact with it.

The heuristic approach emphasizes the unraveling of the essential nature and meaning of a unique phenomenon through engagement in a number of internal processes in nonsequential fashion, including self-exploration and self-reflection toward **illumination**—that is, awareness, discovery, and deeper knowledge and understanding (Douglass & Moustakas, 1985; Sultan, 2015). It thus encourages the researcher's continued immersion and focused attention, and may evoke "the opening of wounds and passionate concerns" (Moustakas, 1990, p. 14) as you pursue a creative, existential journey that, while it originates within the self, has the potential for both personal and communal transformation.

Along similar lines, the heuristic approach demands engagement in external processes that involve dialoguing, interacting, and collaborating with others who have shared comparable or similar experiences toward jointly constructing new understandings of those experiences. This creative and relational process supports a healthy blending of boundaries and the formation of confluent spaces in which may emerge and linger exchanges with universal themes. Some qualitative methodologies stress the importance of story in this data collection phase. However, story implies the necessity of a beginning, a middle, and an end. In heuristic inquiry, although the organization of experience into a cohesive whole is critical, we researchers tend to relax expectations about arriving at a particular truth or destination. Heuristic researchers are involved in an ongoing, nonlinear process of questioning, seeking, waiting, incubating, and receiving. When a moment of encounter occurs, the researcher is inspired with more curiosity, wonder, and questions, and the process resumes. Hence, the focus in heuristic inquiry is on relational, intersubjective, empathic discourse—both verbal and nonverbal, both personal and shared. This underscores ongoing communication and conversation, even past the publication of the manuscript, as readers from diverse backgrounds interact with the findings and engage in their own heuristic process.

Underlying all this are the individual and collective beliefs, values, and assumptions of the researcher, co-researchers, and readers of the findings, which are linked by cultural norms and practices, language, and other social structures. By this token, discovery is not created only through a structured, goal-oriented objective stance, but through the scintillating hope of empathic relationships that enable new knowledge to emerge uninhibited and uncensored, or even serendipitously. In this respect, heuristic inquiry fosters the possibility of community and communion and, through those constructs (paradoxically), the validation of personal experience and identity. Heuristic inquiry thus involves working with various dimensions of the psyche such as sensing, perceiving, imagining, remembering, intuiting, feeling, thinking, and judging (Churchill, 2005) within the here and now while highlighting unique personal experiences with universal significance.

All this being said, it is important to note that in heuristic inquiry, transformation happens because the researcher is the primary instrument for data collection and thus has direct access to and intimate involvement with whatever is emerging throughout the course of the study. This includes not only the content of the data collected but the process of collecting the data, collaborating and interacting relationally with co-researchers, reorganizing previously held knowledge, and cocreating new meanings and representations. This means of engaging the process of inquiry shields the research process from becoming an automated and disembodied exercise of collecting information. It also involves openness and receptivity to data gathered through your own senses, and consideration of and responsiveness to verbal as well as nonverbal experience (Guba & Lincoln, 1989). In fact, what Polanyi (1958, 1966, 1969) refers to as **tacit knowing**—that is, implicit knowing, or knowing that lies beyond what may be readily observed or articulated—is a highly valued concept of the heuristic approach (more on tacit knowing in Chapter 4). Consequently, heuristic inquiry is a nonreductionist, holistic research approach that concerns itself more with meanings than with measurements, with essence than with appearance, with quality than with quantity, and with experience than with behavior (Douglass & Moustakas, 1985). Please see Box 1.2 for a summative description of the heuristic approach in Moustakas's (1990) own words.

Figure 1.4 illustrates the interplay of some of the many processes that go into heuristic research.

Box 1.2

A SUMMATIVE DESCRIPTION OF THE HEURISTIC APPROACH IN MOUSTAKAS'S (1990) WORDS

- "A process of internal search through which one discovers the nature and meaning of experience and develops methods and procedures for further investigation and analysis. The self of the researcher is present throughout the process and, while understanding the phenomenon with increasing depth, the researcher also experiences growing self-awareness and self-knowledge" (p. 9).

- "The heuristic process is a way of being informed, a way of knowing. Whatever presents itself in the consciousness of the investigator as perception, sense, intuition, or knowledge represents an invitation for further elucidation. What appears, what shows itself as itself, casts a light that enables one to come to know more fully what something is and means. In such a process not only is knowledge extended but the self of the researcher is illuminated" (pp. 10–11).

- "From the beginning and throughout an investigation, heuristic research involves self-search, self-dialogue, and self-discovery; the research question and methodology flow out of inner awareness, meaning, and inspiration" (p. 11).

- "I begin the heuristic investigation with my own self-awareness and explicate that awareness with reference to a question or problem until an essential insight is achieved, one that will throw a beginning light onto a critical human experience" (p. 11).

- "In heuristic investigations, I may be entranced by visions, images, and dreams that connect me to my quest. I may come into touch with new regions of myself, and discover revealing connections with others. Through the guides of a heuristic design, I am able to see and understand in a different way" (p. 11).

- "In heuristics, an unshakable connection exists between what is out there, in its appearance and reality, and what is within me in reflective thought, feeling, and awareness" (p. 12).

- "I begin the heuristic journey with something that has called to me from within my life experience, something to which I have associations and fleeting awarenesses but whose nature is largely unknown. In such an odyssey, I know little of the territory through which I must travel. But one thing is certain, the mystery summons me and lures me to let go of the known and swim in an unknown current" (p. 13).

- "Heuristics is a way of engaging in scientific search through methods and processes aimed at discovery; a way of self-inquiry and dialogue with others aimed at finding the underlying meanings of important human experiences. . . . This requires a passionate, disciplined commitment to remain with a question intensely and continuously until it is illuminated or answered" (p. 15).

FIGURE 1.4 ● The Heuristic Research Process

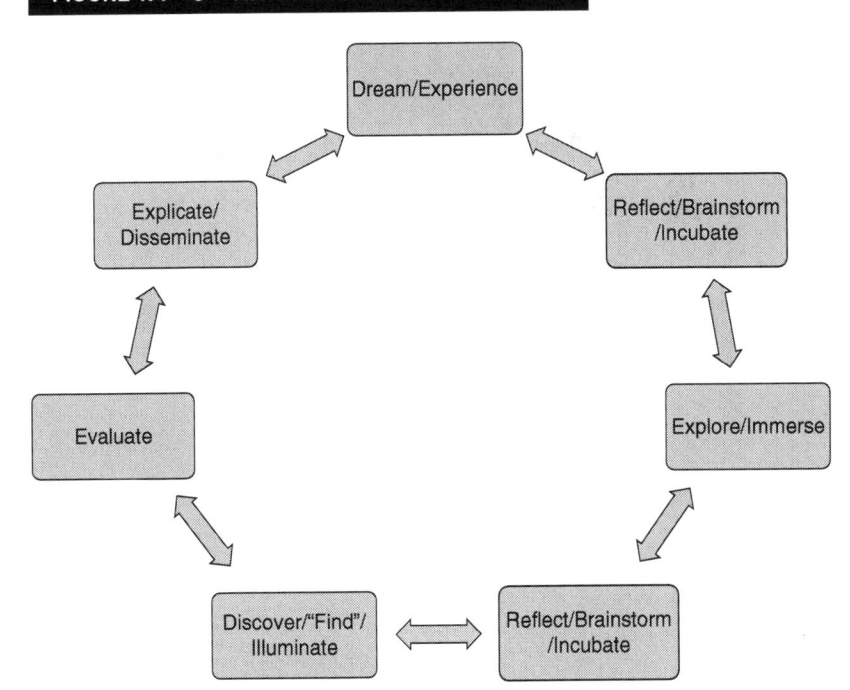

Dream/Experience → Reflect/Brainstorm/Incubate → Explore/Immerse → Reflect/Brainstorm/Incubate → Discover/"Find"/Illuminate → Evaluate → Explicate/Disseminate → Dream/Experience

I also invite you to try out Exercise 1.1, which allows you to sense into and express your current understanding of heuristic inquiry.

EXERCISE 1.1
SENSING INTO AND EXPRESSING A ROUGH UNDERSTANDING OF HEURISTIC INQUIRY

- Find a composition notebook or sketchpad to use as a journal as you read this book; journaling is a key practice embedded within the heuristic approach.
- Take a deep, conscious breath. Exhale slowly and fully. Repeat this. Take your time.
- Find your center of gravity and connect with it. Take another deep, conscious breath.
- Without looking back at Chapter 1 or ahead to any of the other chapters, and without setting a time limit to your process, write as many words, phrases, or concepts, as you can generate that are associated with heuristic inquiry.
- Also note or draw any symbols or doodles that come into your awareness.
- Write and draw without censoring your thoughts, feelings, or body sensations. Allow these experiences in your process. Do this until you feel you have exhausted your source.
- Look at all the words and phrases on your page. Read them aloud while attending consciously to the experience of speaking the words and hearing your voice. What do you experience as you articulate those words?
- Look at the symbols and doodles. What is it like to see them? Using the tips of your fingers, trace each symbol. What do you experience as you do this?
- Bring your awareness to any thoughts, emotions, or body sensations that emerge. Make note of each of your experiences—again, without censoring or judging.
- Are you able to bring an attitude of curiosity, openness, and nonjudgment to your experiences?

Example of thoughts:	I wonder where that doodle came from; what does it mean?
Examples of feelings:	sadness, anger, joy
Examples of body sensations:	tight chest, trembling hands

Processes and Phases

Moustakas (1990) outlined seven concepts and processes involved in the researcher's journey of arriving at a deeper understanding of the central question through heuristic inquiry:

- Identifying with the focus of inquiry
- Self-dialogue
- Tacit knowing
- Intuition
- Indwelling
- Focusing
- Internal frame of reference

In addition to these processes, there are six phases of heuristic inquiry that are curiously similar to Graham Wallas's (1976) stages of the creative process:

- Initial engagement
- Immersion
- Incubation
- Illumination
- Explication
- Creative synthesis

These processes and phases will be described in greater detail in Chapter 4.

As is evident from the processes and phases engaged in this unique research approach, heuristic inquiry encourages the reduction of deliberate, forced effort designed to arrive at absolute truths. It instead highlights the importance of taking a holistic and creative approach to the process of inquiry and engaging in it with genuine curiosity, openness, tolerance for ambiguity and the unknown, patience, and non-attachment to specified outcomes. This supports a fluid and flexible form and structure in all dimensions and stages of a research study that is consequently highly process- and content-oriented and that supports dialogical interaction between preexisting knowledge of the topic of inquiry and new information emerging from connecting with research partners and content on a profoundly relational and experiential level.

Because the phenomenon being explored in a heuristic inquiry emerges from the autobiographical and often intensely personal experience of the primary researcher, during the evolution of the heuristic inquiry phases and throughout the course of the study, it is your ethical responsibility to reflect on and process your experience through reflexive and reflective exercises such as journaling, artwork, meditation, role-playing, body movement, and poetry, or through consultation with peers and/or supervisors (more on this in Chapter 10). Many qualitative approaches discuss the concept of reflexive **bracketing** of the researcher's experience throughout the course of a study. Bracketing of personal experience is highly regarded in qualitative research circles, as it helps researchers critically assess, recognize, and suspend or set aside some of their personal motives and values, with the objective being to minimize the imposition of such values on the research process. This is critical, as bringing our assumptions or preexisting theories into any process of inquiry may compromise it as we attempt to confirm what we already *know* to satisfy a particular hypothesis or the need to be right. Entering into a research endeavor with a preestablished idea about the findings is an egotistic trap in which we may get caught as we attempt to protect the false edifice of our knowledge. As Tulku (1987) stated, "The *attitudes* we adopt in carrying out our investigation shape the *attributes* we find in the world we investigate" (p. 307).

While heuristic inquiry appreciates the significance and noble rationale behind bracketing, it also underscores that bracketing should not result in elimination of researcher values, with the understanding that the elimination of value biases is a fallacy (Ponterotto, 2005), especially in such a personally motivated research endeavor as that undertaken through a heuristic process. Additionally, given that heuristic inquiry is inspired, in the first place, by an autobiographical experience, it seems unrealistic to even pretend engaging in the elimination of personal values. Essentially, you experience what you perceive to be an extraordinary and captivating phenomenon and seek to create what meaning you can of it through both internal and external discourse. Heuristic inquiry enables you to do this.

Heuristic research values your personal interest and stresses the importance of the topic of inquiry being internally located versus attempting to satisfy the traditional requirements of empiricism by identifying the researcher as an unbiased, unconcerned observer. In fact, trying to embrace the role of a distant and detached bystander in heuristic research may create opportunities for you to dabble in your bias within the safety of your professed detachment. To what end? Thus, in heuristic inquiry, the purpose of bracketing and reflexivity is not to abstract the researcher from the research but instead to enhance researcher awareness as to *how* to approach the research question and process of inquiry. The idea is to allow researchers to honor and take ownership of their personal experience, to invite researchers to challenge and explore what they think they know, to extend transparency and minimize deception, and to enhance the trustworthiness of the research. In essence, as a heuristic researcher, I do not bracket myself *out of* my research studies. Instead, I bracket myself *into* the process of inquiry. As I *out* my personal interests, motivations, and agenda, I *in* myself within the study. Along those lines, I am able to bring my authentic embodied self into the research process to be present with the authentic embodied selves of the co-researchers as both process and outcome are co-constructed. New knowledge is jointly created as a shared embodied experience between me and my co-researchers. Thus, as the primary researcher, I pay particular attention to the dynamics of privileging one perspective over others and to potentially losing sight of the fact that each contribution is of worth as a bearer of knowledge and a living experience.

The rigor of the heuristic approach is generated through observation of and dialoguing with self and others, especially through in-depth interviewing (Moustakas, 1990, 2015), usually of a **purposive sample**—that is, one that targets a particular group of people based on their experience of the phenomenon being explored. In addition to interviewing, heuristic inquiry invites the inclusion of artifacts such as journal entries, artwork, musical compositions, photos, and other forms of creative expression, from both the researcher and research partners. Through openness to the experience itself and to new ways of viewing it, **indwelling** (turning inward) and intuition, shared intensity of the experience with co-researchers, and shared inquiry and reflection with co-researchers, the researcher arrives at insight into the central phenomenon (Moustakas, 1990; Patton, 2002). This creates a sense of connectedness as researcher and research partners collaborate to illuminate the nature and essence of the topic of inquiry (Patton, 2002).

Limitations of Heuristic Inquiry

Like all other research approaches, heuristic inquiry has its strengths and its limitations. The many strengths and unique characteristics of heuristic inquiry have been outlined both implicitly and explicitly, thus far, and will be highlighted throughout this text. However, in the interest of fostering ethical and rigorous qualitative research, it is also important to note some of the limitations of heuristic inquiry and to address some ways to mitigate potential negative impacts on the research process. As a holistic researcher and person, I view the fact that heuristic inquiry has limitations as a sign of its intrinsic health. I also view the limitations not as a deterrent to successful research but as an instrument the researcher, co-researchers, and readers of the findings may use to enhance their creative interaction with the information they are processing. Working creatively and intuitively with challenges may, in and of itself, yield powerful and transformative experiences. So then . . . limitations:

- *Heuristic research is not for objective folks, nor is it for those who are not creative.* First of all, we are all creative beings. We all enjoy some spirit of imagination and love for the original. If you have ever daydreamed, you are creative. If you have tried your hand at another resolution to a problem that seemed to have only one way out, you are creative. If you have to survive, on a day-by-day basis, in this world, you are creative. You get the picture. As for the objectivity piece, heuristic inquiry invites both nearness and distance, both intimacy and detachment.

Remember, it's all about maintaining the flow of the dance between the seeming polarities of experience.

- *Researchers may experience roadblocks as they try to define or refine their research question.* This will happen! I am not saying it *may* happen but that it *will*. This is a natural consequence of your personal engagement, on an intense level, with the phenomenon being explored. As you attempt to understand your experience, questions saturate both your inner and outer landscapes, as well as everything in between. Once again, I remind you to open yourself up to the sheer deluge of stimuli and to allow yourself to become immersed in it while using your self-awareness to recognize when it is time to step away and let things incubate. I also would like to caution that we researchers know precisely what it is we want to explore. However, we may taint our desire with self-doubt, social conformity, and fear of failure. Embrace all of this, I say! Eventually, the true question that burns within you slow and blue will emerge into your awareness, fully and forcefully.

- *Researchers may, during the process of immersion in the data, feel lost and never attain illumination.* Heuristic researchers often feel lost. So do other quantitative and qualitative researchers as we travel our research journeys. You are both permitted and encouraged to feel lost while acknowledging that this sense of loss of direction is but an ornament that embellishes the research process and makes it richer. Feeling lost means that we must seek other ways to get back on track. In your search for your correct path, sometimes you will come upon hidden trails you never would have dreamed of finding otherwise.

- *The final findings or manuscript may not yield any new or definitive information.* True. However, how do we define what is definitive and what is not? Whether or not something is definitive is quite subjective, as is whether or not something is new. Additionally, your topic of inquiry will hardly ever be an anomaly. Someone has already asked the very questions you are asking, although perhaps within a different context. Thus, individuals who come into contact with the findings will go through their own exploratory process of how they experience the findings and what those findings mean for them, expanding the horizons of every heuristic study into the present-moment way of being of those who interact with it. This speaks to the living process and universal significance that characterize both heuristic inquiry and human experience.

- *Some researchers, research partners, or readers of the findings may feel more perplexed after their participation or reading experience than before it.* Absolutely. On the other hand, one of the finest qualities of heuristic inquiry is its invitation to open ourselves up to the confusion that may emerge as part of both the participation and the reading experience. Remember the last time you felt confused about something and, rather than continuing to fight it until it drove you nuts, you decided to just let it go? What happened next? You remember. Remain dedicated to working your way through the labyrinth. Eventually, you will reach the center and work your way back out.

- *The heuristic research process may reveal more differences than similarities.* Agreed. Then again, heuristic inquiry celebrates difference. If it did not, heuristic researchers would direct their eyes only to their bellies and accept whatever "truths" emerged from that process as The Truth. In fact, more heuristic researchers than not like to include research partners in their studies. Take a look at the list of heuristic studies I have included in Box 1.1 and you will see what I mean. Honoring difference allows us to highlight similarity.

- *The research findings may not be easily generalizable due to the small number of research partners.* I'd like to remind you about finding the universal within the particular and vice versa. A parallel concept is finding the typical within the singular and vice versa. Finally, as a psychotherapist who is often exposed to vicariously shared experiences with my clients, I cannot help impressing on you that many dimensions of what you share with readers will resonate and arouse within them questions, thoughts, feelings, and sensations that will inspire them toward their own new directions and horizons. This, too, is part of the fluid nature of heuristic inquiry and human experience.

- *The research findings may not result in any social action or change.* This particular limitation evokes the question, *How do we define social action and change?* Many of us imagine advocacy and social action as conduct that both demands and produces decisive social transformation. On the other hand, solid and enduring change often requires time and happens in small chunks, while change that takes place rapidly may be short-lived. In that vein, if even one person is transformed in some small way by either participating in the research process or interacting with the findings, then the wheels of lasting change are in motion.

I can keep going on about the limitations of heuristic inquiry. But I think you probably see how my experiencing process works and how I embrace a good challenge. I invite you to engage a similar process with some of the challenges you will likely face as you carry out any type of research, be it qualitative or quantitative, heuristic or otherwise. Embrace your creative self and make sure that part of you stays anchored to you, around you, inside you—always!

Closing Reflections

Moustakas (1990, 2015) reminds us of the open-endedness of heuristic research, asserting that each research journey should be allowed to emerge in its own unique way. The flexibility of the heuristic approach makes it highly adaptable and, thus, ideal for researching a diversity of topics across disciplines, and phenomena that are vague or difficult to observe, measure, or document. Going about heuristic research using a rigid step-by-step outline would fly in the face of its fluid and inventive nature and undermine its spontaneity. The beauty of the heuristic approach lies in its systematic but improvisational method of conducting scientific inquiry while incorporating the self of the researcher, thereby allowing us to explore our most meaningful and significant life experiences without succumbing to the inhibitions and structures imposed upon traditional empirical research methodologies. It invites any and all manifestations of the topic of inquiry: within the researcher; within individual co-researchers; in the shared experience between and among one, the other, and the world; in journal entries, artwork, poetry, or other forms of creative expression; in letters, photos, or other artifacts; in previously published findings; in the content of dreams or other altered states; and in verbal and nonverbal discourse. It welcomes questions that have been shunned, neglected, or avoided in research (and in society) and embraces populations that have been oppressed, discriminated against, or marginalized.

Through its existential and humanistic philosophical foundations, heuristic research views human experience as embodied and relational, and acknowledges the human potential for self-actualization. It thus creates a space for the magic that happens when researcher and co-researchers come together in shared curiosity and open ourselves up to becoming enchanted and transformed, not only by findings embedded in real-life experience but by the pull of the process itself on our souls. As we inch closer to the singular, living features of a person, place, or phenomenon, the universal—ever so tenderly—unfolds!

2

Locating Heuristic Inquiry Within Contemporary Qualitative Research

You will come to a place where the streets are not marked.
Some windows are lighted, but mostly they're darked.
A place you could sprain both your elbow and chin!
Do you dare to stay out? Do you dare to go in?
How much can you lose? How much can you win?

~ **Dr. Seuss**

Questions for Reflection

1. How is heuristic inquiry related to phenomenological research?
2. How is heuristic inquiry discrete from phenomenology?
3. What makes heuristic inquiry unique from other qualitative approaches?

I have been an avid fan of Dr. Seuss's wisdom since my earliest years. The man had so many insights and sage perceptions, it's no wonder his books continue to capture the interest of readers well past their childhood years. The words above are from one of my favorites, *Oh, the Places You'll Go!* They invite and entice the reader to enter a liminal space of discernment between darkness and light and a host of other implicitly suggested polarities. At the same time, they challenge us to consider what we may gain or lose should we not accept the dare. But then, those words are so filled with the essence of exploration and adventure, how does one not take the plunge into the colorful spectrum held within them and there linger with the delicious confusion that comes with surveying all the tantalizing possibilities? Such is the spirit with which one embarks on a journey to explore the essential nature of a particular phenomenon. Such is the spirit with which one enters the labyrinth of heuristic research!

Now that we've covered the essential characteristics of heuristic inquiry, and before you begin your heuristic journey, it might be helpful to understand how heuristic inquiry shares some characteristics with phenomenological research and how it is also quite distinctive from phenomenology. Likewise, heuristic inquiry sits quite comfortably alongside a number of qualitative research methodologies such as grounded theory and narrative research, and approaches such as feminist research and transpersonal methods. More important, heuristic inquiry is an extremely versatile research methodology with numerous creative practices that may be used to incorporate unique angles from which to approach the research process. With that in mind, it is useful to know how heuristic inquiry may be bricolaged with some of these inductive approaches to enhance qualitative researchers' processes of inquiry. I will focus particularly on bridges between heuristic inquiry and grounded theory, narrative research, and feminist research.

Relationship to Phenomenology

Heuristic inquiry is, at its heart, a phenomenologically aligned research approach in that it views the process of inquiry as a synthesis of science and art, and perception as the primary source of knowledge and truth (Merleau-Ponty, 1945/2013) that cannot be doubted (Moustakas, 1994). In fact, Merleau-Ponty viewed phenomenology primarily as a way of being. Wertz (2005) added, "Phenomenology is a low-hovering, in-dwelling, meditative philosophy that glories in the concreteness of person-world relations and accords lived experience, with all its indeterminacy and ambiguity, primacy over the known" (p. 175). As a qualitative research methodology, phenomenology is concerned with uncovering the essential nature of a phenomenon and representing it using rich, layered, deep, and evocative narratives to capture the complexity of the phenomenon being explored. Likewise with heuristic inquiry, in which a central catalyst is the constant relationship between the researchers' internal perceptions, judgments, and memories and their external perceptions of reality. Hence, the phenomenon being observed is recognized only through the subjective experience of the person observing it—that is, through the researcher's and/or co-researchers' perception. In such a fluid and personal process of inquiry, truth is relative and there are no fixed outcomes or meanings (Merleau-Ponty, 1945/2013). Such a process honors previous knowledge through the understanding that the topic of inquiry is not an aberration; it's possible that someone else has asked a similar question before. However, the unique circumstances involved in the current research project inform that process of inquiry and influence all outcomes. Curiosity and wonder saturate the research process as emergent perceptions bring into awareness novel perspectives uniting past, present, and future and deepening "what something is and means" (Moustakas, 1994, p. 54). First-person narratives and creative expression are the ideal methods for presenting the research findings.

Phenomenology is a complex approach to qualitative research, and a number of different methods of applying and using it have emerged as researchers have attempted to refine research processes aimed at meeting the needs of their topics of inquiry. Finlay (2011) outlined six approaches of phenomenological research:

1. *Descriptive/empirical,* based on Husserl's (1900/2001) philosophy; includes the method developed by Giorgi (2009); describes, using a generally scientific approach to data collection and analysis, the essence of an experience.

2. *Hermeneutic/interpretive,* based on philosophies by Heidegger (1927/2008) and Gadamer (1960/2013); includes methods developed by van Manen (1990) and Todres (2007); evokes lived experience through a philosophical, linguistic, and literary lens.

3. *Lifeworld,* based on philosophies by Heidegger (1927/2008) and Merleau-Ponty (1945/2013); includes a method developed by Dahlberg, Dahlberg, and Nyström (2008) and Ashworth (2003); explores an everyday experience as it manifests in the time–space continuum and in relation to others.

4. *Interpretative phenomenological analysis,* based on philosophies of Husserl (1900/2001) and Heidegger (1927/2008); includes a method developed by Smith (2004); focuses on individual perceptions and meaning-making of an experience.

5. *First-person,* based on Husserl's (1900/2001) philosophy; includes a wide range of methods such as narrative research, feminist research, and ecological research.

6. *Reflexive-relational,* based on various philosophies, especially those of Buber (1923/1970), Gendlin (1962), and Merleau-Ponty (1945/2013); includes the heuristic approach developed by Moustakas (1990); allows for the emergence and cocreation of data through the dialogical encounters between members of the research team.

Although heuristic inquiry has its foundations in phenomenology, Douglass and Moustakas (1985) distinguished it from phenomenology in the following ways:

- Heuristic inquiry honors relationship, while phenomenology stresses a certain degree of detachment.
- Heuristic inquiry invites creative elaboration of the findings as articulated through poetry, artwork, music, or other forms of creative expression, while phenomenology focuses on the distillation of experience.
- Heuristic inquiry embraces personal meaning, while phenomenology prefers structured experience.
- Heuristic inquiry highlights co-researcher essence, wholeness, and visibility, while phenomenology may lose research participants in the distillation of experience.

One further distinction between heuristic inquiry and phenomenology—and a rather critical one—is that in phenomenology it is not necessary that the researcher have had a direct personal encounter with the topic of inquiry, while in heuristic research this factor is essential.

A heuristic research journey is grounded in the researcher's intense personal relationship with the research phenomenon, and embodied attunement to and engagement with the process of inquiry. Thus, from an embodied perspective, heuristic inquiry involves six core perspectives from which the researcher engages the central question:

- Sensory∞kinesthetic
- Perceptual
- Social∞relational
- Emotional
- Cognitive
- Spiritual

These dimensions are inseparable from one another, as one's sensory∞kinesthetic experience, for example, impacts how one feels about, thinks about, and interacts/relates with a particular occurrence. Additionally, other playful facets for interacting with the research question include intuiting, imagining, anticipating, believing, and remembering (Ray, 1994). This dynamic, holistic approach transcends the usual and preferred (though highly fragmenting and marginalizing) dualistic Cartesian mind-over-body method, in which detached observation is privileged over all other ways of knowing or is viewed as the only way of knowing. Thus—and along the lines of Merleau-Ponty's (1945/2013) embodied perceptual phenomenology—we both influence and are influenced by all of what happens within and around us. Through such an intentional process of inquiry, we become active agents in the creation of meaning and being versus receivers of others' modes. In that vein, heuristic inquiry is an emancipatory methodology (more on this in Chapter 7).

It is imperative to note that while some heuristic studies may take a self-research direction, heuristic inquiry is not necessarily or exclusively a self-research approach. It is also important to recognize that self-research is all about exploring subjective experience from a single perspective or lens—that of the researcher. There is nothing wrong with that, but that is not necessarily the perspective or vision of heuristic inquiry. Moustakas (1990) asserted that although it is feasible to conduct heuristic research with only one person, studies will attain deeper, more varied meanings when they include the experiences of others. To imagine otherwise is, I daresay, leaning toward the arrogant, as it assumes that only the experience of the researcher is valid, which is dismissive of others' experiences of a potentially universal phenomenon. The purpose of this research approach is to describe the essential nature of a particular experience, with the idea of moving from the unique to the universal. Keeping with this logic, how is it possible to identify the universal nature of an experience when one is exploring it exclusively from one's own perspective?

Similarly, heuristic research is not intended to be self-centered, self-indulgent, or narcissistic, nor should it be used to impose the researcher's experience on co-researchers or readers of the findings. Doing so would constitute a denial of the existence of the world around us and its impact on how we organize and make sense of experience, shattering the philosophical foundation on which heuristic inquiry is erected. Rather, heuristic research includes the self of the researcher as a necessary constituent of the process of inquiry in open acknowledgment of the researcher's personal experience of the phenomenon being explored and his pivotal role in the process of inquiry. As Patton (2002) explains it, the heuristic approach "epitomizes the phenomenological emphasis on meanings and knowing through personal experience" (p. 109), personalizing the process of inquiry and placing the researchers' experiences and insights at the center of the research endeavor.

Nevertheless, the researcher is never viewed as omniscient, as other sources of knowledge include research partners, the social context, and the multiple systems within which the phenomenon is taking place. One can say, rather, that the researcher's experience acts as a frame of reference for co-creating novel understandings of the living experience that is being explored (Moustakas, 2015), with the main purpose being to comprehend it profoundly and holistically. Hence, although there is no explicit emphasis on advocacy or social action in the heuristic method outlined by Moustakas (1990), heuristic inquiry honors the intersection of the personal with the mutual and of the mutual with the social context. See Figure 2.1 for a visual representation of this experience.

FIGURE 2.1 • Heuristic Inquiry Lies at the Intersection of the Personal, the Mutual, and the Social Context

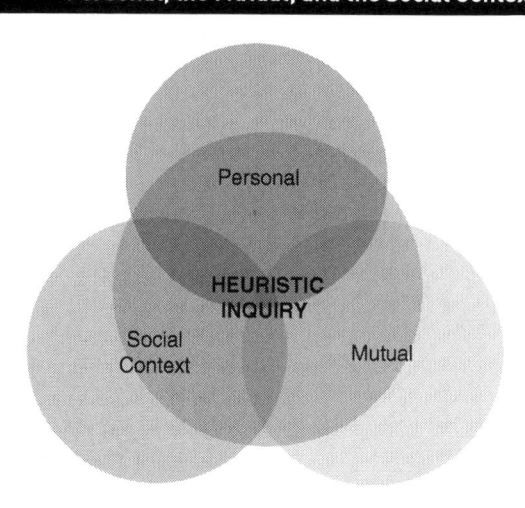

Venn diagram showing three overlapping circles labeled "Personal," "Social Context," and "Mutual," with "HEURISTIC INQUIRY" at their intersection.

TABLE 2.1 • Comparing Phenomenology and Heuristic Inquiry

Phenomenology	Heuristic Inquiry
Detached subjectivity toward the topic of inquiry and participants	Full immersion within the topic of inquiry and collaboration with research partners
Bracketing to set aside researcher values	Bracketing to identify the role of researcher values
Distillation of lived experience	Identification of essential meaning(s) of living experience articulated through creative expression
Participants superseded by the distilled elements of the topic of inquiry.	Co-researchers or research partners remain visible and whole within the essential meaning(s) of the topic of inquiry.
Somewhat linear research process	Nonlinear research process
Focus on structured experience	Focus on personal meaning
Personal experience with topic of inquiry is not required.	Personal experience with topic of inquiry is essential.

Source: Adapted from Douglass & Moustakas, 1985.

Ultimately, heuristic inquiry allows us to transcend the specifics of personal experience and move toward the universally shared essential meanings of the topic of inquiry while maintaining the wholeness of what was shared within the research process, as well as the wholeness of those individuals who shared it. In Chapter 3, I elaborate further on the phenomenological foundations of heuristic inquiry. See Table 2.1 for a side-by-side comparison of phenomenology and heuristic inquiry.

Bricolaging With Similar Qualitative Approaches

I speak four languages fluently. Thinking and communicating using a variety of languages opens, for me, multiple windows from which to view a single landscape. How I conceptualize a certain issue or question in English, for example, is quite different from how I conceptualize it in Arabic. Language is discourse embedded in and informed by culture, society, history, nature, and the body. Language also informs each of these entities. Additionally, language transcends verbal communication. Along the same lines, I am a true believer in the inclusion of all dimensions of human experience (cognitive, emotional, sensory∞kinesthetic, perceptual, spiritual, and social∞relational) toward understanding and integrating the living world. I have learned to interweave my various perspectives not only that they may enhance one another but also to synthesize all of them to arrive at a cohesive perspective that represents and honors my polydimensional, quadrilingual self. From this angle, quantity may foster diversity. On the other hand, quantity may also foster confusion. Given the myriad qualitative methods currently accessible to both novice and seasoned researchers, it is no wonder that researchers often find themselves lost at the crossroads of which method to adopt for their research, especially considering the many similarities among these methods. Additionally, the shifting perspectives, within qualitative research, on the permeability of qualitative research methodologies and the potential to borrow and exchange approaches are opening doors to explore old questions from novel angles.

With an eye on the current turn in qualitative research to **bricolage**—or piece together—multiple perspectives, practices, techniques, or tools (Denzin & Lincoln, 2011), following are brief individual descriptions of grounded theory, narrative research, and feminist research, along with accompanying discussions of how heuristic inquiry both is distinct from and may be used in conjunction with each approach to advance more flexible and fluid qualitative research paradigms that address the needs of specific topics of inquiry. Naturally, heuristic inquiry may be bricolaged with a variety of other research approaches and methodologies; however, to attempt to address all these is beyond the scope of this text. It is my hope that the qualitative approaches I have focused on will provide some inspiration and ideas for bricolaging with other qualitative approaches. My aim here is to underline the exceptional contribution of heuristic inquiry not only as a research methodology but also as a process of discernment (Hiles, 2008b) and to highlight how various components of heuristic research may be used to enhance or inform each of these other qualitative processes of inquiry. This is done with the understanding that your topic of inquiry and your central research question will facilitate your selection of an appropriate research methodology. Your central research question is the center of your labyrinth and your guiding light!

Grounded Theory
Essential and Distinguishing Features

Grounded theory is a qualitative methodology for developing a theoretical understanding of the topic of inquiry directly from the data from which it is emerging, rather than through preformulated ideas (Corbin & Strauss, 2015). In that sense, grounded theory "refers simultaneously to a method of qualitative inquiry and the products of that inquiry" (Charmaz & Bryant, 2008, p. 375). Data are collected in systematic but flexible form (Charmaz & Bryant, 2008) through interviews or observation, as well as in the form of various artifacts, including journals, artwork, and historical records (Corbin & Strauss, 2015). This format is similar to the data-collection process used in heuristic inquiry. In heuristic inquiry, data collection and analysis intertwine within a confluent process completed for one co-researcher at a time as researchers immerse themselves in each individual data set to acquire an intimate knowledge and understanding of it. Similarly, in grounded theory, the data-collection and analysis processes are conducted simultaneously and inform and influence one another throughout the course of the study in a process of *constant comparison*. Kathy Charmaz (2014) eloquently described the process thus:

> Grounded theory methods consist of systematic, yet flexible guidelines for collecting and analyzing qualitative data to construct theories from the data themselves. . . . Grounded theory begins with inductive data, invokes iterative strategies of going back and forth between data and analysis, uses comparative methods, and keeps you interacting and involved with your data and emerging analysis. (p. 1)

Whereas the heuristic approach developed in the discipline of humanistic psychology, and in response to a question regarding the nature of the specific autobiographical experience of loneliness (Moustakas, 1961, 1990, 2015), the grounded theory approach, originated by Glaser and Strauss (1967), developed in the discipline of sociology to explore the awareness of dying (Glaser & Strauss, 1965) and as a contest to the formality of separating the data collection and analysis phases of a research process. Additionally, grounded theory presented a challenge to the quantitative bent that seemed to create barriers between theory and research (Charmaz & Bryant, 2008) rather than integrating those constructs. As with heuristic inquiry, special emphasis in grounded theory was placed on multiple perspectives, inductive approaches, and emergent processes.

A number of features distinguish grounded theory as a qualitative approach, the most important of which is its focus on using the emergent data to inform the research sample and to both inform and saturate theoretical categories, which are then assimilated around a core category that represents the major theme of the study (Charmaz & Bryant, 2008). This is a departure from other qualitative forms of inquiry, in which the research sample is usually predetermined (unless snowball sampling or something similar is used for specific reasons) and in which saturation occurs when new data that are gathered provide no further insight (Creswell, 2013; Strauss & Corbin, 1998). It is also a marked difference from heuristic inquiry, in which purposive selection of a maximum variation sample is a preferred sampling method, the aim being to select individuals who have an intimate relationship with the topic of inquiry (Wertz, 2005) while allowing for identification of common themes that transcend co-researcher differences (Creswell, 2013). Another notable difference is grounded theory's use of a hierarchical structure for organizing the various categories of data that have been critically analyzed, interpreted, and coded. In heuristic inquiry, there are no hierarchies; all data are attributed equal value, with some data serving, perhaps, as constituents of other data while retaining equal importance. Additionally, the heuristic researcher generally refrains from using critical analysis or interpretation, as the main focus is to identify from the data the holistic essence of the phenomenon being explored. Likewise, **coding**, a popular method for categorizing data in grounded theory studies, is generally not used in heuristic inquiry, as the overall essential features of the phenomenon emerge through the researcher's focused immersion in the data and use of intuitive processes toward theme identification of the essential meaning of the experience.

Corbin and Strauss (2015) shared several descriptions of grounded theory inspired by their students' experience of this research methodology:

- Enjoyment of the mental challenge
- Openness and flexibility
- Relevance beyond academia
- Absorption in the work

As you read this book, you will recognize how some of these descriptors also apply to heuristic inquiry. While older versions of grounded theory viewed the researcher as fairly unobtrusive, newer models have been articulated—including *constructivist grounded theory* (Charmaz, 2007), which, not unlike heuristic inquiry, highlights the researcher's role in the process of inquiry, and *situational analysis* (Clarke, 2005), which combines constructivist concepts with postmodern ideas. Likewise, novel treatments of grounded theory (Charmaz, 2011) are similar to this reenvisioned version of heuristic inquiry in their inclusion of a focus on advancing social justice.

Bricolaging Grounded Theory With Heuristic Inquiry

What are some unique features of heuristic inquiry that may be infused into grounded theory to supplement it? One of the core characteristics of heuristic inquiry is its view of knowledge and reality as cocreated by researcher and research partners through a context-based understanding of their inner and outer experience of the topic of inquiry. This shared subjective attitude can provide a fresh perspective to grounded theory's traditional tendency to view reality as something outside of or separate from the researcher. Bringing the ideas of tacit knowing and felt sense into grounded theory allows for the infusion of higher subjectivity, providing an additional source of information with which to inform the process of inquiry. Grounded theory researchers may or may not elect to use any information gathered through their intuitive process. On the other hand, allowing that dimension to be present provides, once again, another source of knowledge acquisition and avoids fragmenting the research experience into various compartments with no apparent cohesion. Similarly, actively including the researcher's experience and encouraging researcher immersion in the data collection and analysis processes may mitigate the objective stance of the grounded theory researcher as detached explorer and enhance the rigor of the research process and findings.

Another key facet of heuristic inquiry that may balance the playing field in grounded theory is heuristics' inclusion of all aspects of the research experience as data, including artifacts from both researcher and co-researchers and whatever emerges during the data collection, organization, and analysis phases. Using this may balance the tendency of grounded theory toward abstraction, which can often marginalize particular dimensions of what is being explored, treating them as secondary variables or leaving them out of the knowledge pool altogether. Additionally, allowing every member of the research team to be a contributor means that understanding and meaning of the topic of inquiry emerge from the shared experience of all parties involved, without privileging either researcher or research partners. Grounded theory may also benefit from heuristic inquiry's lack of focus on identifying or constructing a theoretical model. While it is clearly the central goal of grounded theory to generate theory, it may be helpful for grounded theory researchers to temporarily release this goal-oriented perspective and attend to the actual process of inquiry, with an eye on the broader landscape and wholeness of the phenomenon being explored and on its character as a unified and integrated entity (or at least as one that is working toward integration through the process of inquiry) to gain a different angle before returning to the main task of generating theory. This, again, provides information from another perspective, which the grounded theory researcher is then free to either include or not include. Finally, viewing all aspects of the research process within the various systems and contexts in which they are unfolding may complement grounded theory's recent interest in attending to social justice issues, unifying the multiple dimensions of both topic and process of inquiry.

Narrative Research
Essential and Distinguishing Features

Narrative research, not unlike many types of phenomenology, is about lived experience. The focus of narrative inquiry, however, is on the construction of reality through *stories* (Creswell, 2013) that are told, usually verbally, by research partners describing their individual experiences of the topic of inquiry within their life context. While heuristic inquiry actively includes stories or accounts of the phenomenon of inquiry, the focus in heuristic research is on the continuing verbal *and* nonverbal dialogue or discourse, both with and surrounding the topic being explored, in an effort to create meaning of the experience itself, rather than to reframe an existing narrative. Another core premise of narrative research is that reality is *individually* constructed through the narration of stories (Lichtman, 2014). Again, there is a similarity, between narrative and heuristic inquiry, in the social construction of experience, with a core difference being the stress on the individual nature of that social construction from the perspective of narrative research, despite the collaborative nature of the research process.

In essence, in narrative research, knowledge and meaning of a lived experience are illuminated through the recounting and interpretation of stories not unlike those written in the literary discipline. Butler-Kisber (2010) described the narrative structure as having six elements that are quite similar to the five elements of story used to describe the phases of plot in the literary tradition:

- Abstract (summary of the story)
- Orientation (time, place, participants)
- Complicating action(s) (stability-breaking event)
- Evaluation (meaning-making)
- Resolution (what happened)
- Coda (return to the present)

This is not unusual, as plot is very necessary to narrative research and, in a sense, narrative research does view human experience as already lived.

Like grounded theory, narrative inquiry has its beginnings in sociology and anthropology (Chase, 2011; Kohler Riessman, 2008), in the collection and adaptation of the life histories and experiences of a variety of social groups. As with heuristic inquiry, narrative data is collected primarily through interviews and is supplemented by other documents and artifacts (Butler-Kisber, 2010). In fact, the heuristic interview is somewhat of a narrative interview, although it is but one part of a continuing conversation and is not necessarily privileged as the superlative source of data, as the interview is in narrative research. Like heuristic researchers, narrative researchers engage in a journaling process to facilitate examination of their assumptions, attitudes, and values (Chase, 2011). Unlike heuristic inquiry, however, though much in the manner of grounded theory, narrative research involves coding of categories in the data analysis phase. Due to the relational nature of the research process, and as with heuristic inquiry, the ethical considerations are quite critical, and narrative researchers are expected throughout the course of their research journey to remain alert and self-aware (Chase, 2011) so as not to compromise ethical standards. Additionally, and parallel to narrative research's focus on change, social justice is increasingly becoming a critical facet.

Narrative research, as mentioned earlier, tends toward interpretation by the researcher, whereas in heuristic inquiry, any meanings attributed to concepts or themes emerging from the research process are jointly constructed with co-researchers. The narrative researcher is usually in a position of authority, and this may tip the balance of equity in the research process. Additionally, narrative research honors the individual story (Chase, 2011), while heuristic inquiry views any individual contribution (including the researcher's) as but one exemplar of the topic of inquiry. Speaking of including the researcher, Kim (2016) named multiple approaches to narrative inquiry:

- *Autobiographical narrative inquiry*, in which the researcher's personal experience is the central topic of the study
- *Biographical narrative inquiry*, in which the focus is on stories about others
- *Arts-based narrative inquiry*, in which the findings are expressed in nonacademic form
- *Literary-based narrative inquiry*, which is written creatively or imaginatively
- *Visual-based narrative inquiry*, which uses visuals such as photos, collages, or paintings

Any and all of these models of narrative inquiry are not only acceptable but also necessary methods of heuristic inquiry and are readily included in all aspects of the heuristic research process as narratives, art, creativity, visuals, and other artifacts and sources of information are used to inform the study. For example, in heuristic inquiry, artifacts and the content of interviews have equal bearing as sources of data. Various forms of creative expression are used by the researcher to engage in reflexivity and to synthesize and explicate the co-constructed essential nature of the topic of inquiry.

Bricolaging Narrative Research With Heuristic Inquiry

While a number of core similarities exist between narrative research and heuristic inquiry, there are also some areas of divergence, as previously mentioned. A number of heuristic processes may be included in any narrative study, not with the purpose of modifying the nature, essence, or goal of narrative inquiry but to dabble with a variety of other approaches to enhance narrative data collection and analysis. One way of doing this is to view research participants more as partners or co-researchers. From this perspective, the relational subtleties of the research team are not open to interpretation but are honored as a prominent dynamic in the research process. Likewise, research partners are actively involved in all phases of the study and any tension created by perceived differences in power is mitigated. This empowers individuals to take ownership of their behaviors, thoughts, emotions, stories, and other dimensions of their experience and to take responsibility for their own change process. This is increasingly important as narrative research takes a more active interest in extending social justice (Chase, 2011). Another approach is to continue to honor co-researchers' narratives while also attending to nonverbal narratives as additional sources of information. Nonverbals can include not only some of the other methods of collecting data previously mentioned (artifacts such as journal entries, artwork, etc.) but also nonverbal behaviors of co-researchers such as tone of voice, gestures, posture, movement, and incongruent behavior as they share their experiences throughout the research process. These nuances offer critical information, in addition to the information shared through the verbal narratives.

Along similar lines, balancing the weight of the narrative interview with other data sources helps the research team access and connect with multiple iterations of the topic of inquiry and extends social justice efforts beyond the parameters of co-researchers' personal narratives. Other data sources, again, may include writing samples, memos, photos, poetry, journal entries, drawings or other artwork, and musical compositions, all of which are also part of research partner experiences. Including such data sources enables both the research team and readers of the findings to connect with the topic of inquiry through individual and collective interpretation of the material, rather than having others' socially constructed narratives imposed on them, many aspects of which may or may not fit with their own stories or experiences. This opens the doors for co-construction of reality whereby the research team offers multiple sources of knowledge regarding the topic of inquiry and their collective understanding of its essential nature, and readers of the findings interpret and establish connections with their own experiences of it. Finally, because interpreting others' information can be a slippery slope, why not expand efforts to jointly attribute meaning to co-researcher narratives and other forms of verbal and nonverbal expression, even during the data collection phase? In fact, narrative research can borrow from heuristic inquiry's humanistic and existential foundations that highlight positive growth and self-actualization to approach the entire research process as an exercise in reenvisioning narratives toward personal transformation, with a caution to researchers not to impose predetermined social justice agendas on their research partners. Again, this highlights heuristic inquiry's humanistic-existential attention to empowering others toward self-advocacy and self-growth.

Feminist Research

Essential and Distinguishing Features

Feminist research is more a research approach than an actual methodology with step-by-step phases or processes. It uses gender as a lens through which to view social issues (Hesse-Biber, 2014), with the primary aim being to unravel power structures and struggles (Giroux, 1982; Lincoln, Lynham, & Guba, 2011; Olesen, 2011) to motivate marginalized and oppressed populations to evaluate their lives and take action toward social change. Thus, while the primary focus of heuristic inquiry is to illuminate the essential nature of an experience, the core aim of feminist research is to illuminate social injustices, particularly as built on the foundation of male value systems (Gilligan, 1982). Due to the nature of the focus of inquiry, feminist researchers, not unlike heuristic researchers, embrace flexible research paradigms that may produce various forms of data. However, in feminist research, gender is a primary category of inquiry (Hesse-Biber, 2008, 2014; Lather, 1991), and its intersection and interaction with other elements of culture (such as ethnicity, race, ability, and socioeconomic status) are explored as researchers seek to highlight issues of power and authority, not only within the structure of the topic of inquiry but also within the research process. Like heuristic inquiry, feminist research uses the practice of reflexivity to shed light on the role of power and authority between the researcher and co-researchers.

Feminist research is evaluated based on its ability to generate action toward positive social change. Thus, while the research process is important, it does not play as critical a role as in heuristic inquiry. Instead, in feminist research the success of the research is determined by the outcome. In that vein, feminist researchers adopt either qualitative or quantitative methodologies (Hesse-Biber, 2008, 2014), depending on the needs of the research and the anticipated and/or hoped-for outcomes. Throughout the research process, both narrative and discourse are taken into consideration as aspects of lived experience. More recently, traditional notions of empiricism that were previously lauded in feminist research are being criticized in some applications that value the role of emotions, breaking down some of the positivist dualism that seemed to characterize it. Newer models of feminist research (Harding, 2004; Smith, 1990) tend to reject the adoption of single ways of seeing the world (Holzman, 2011), highlight lived experience as the basis for knowledge (Hesse-Biber, 2014), and explore the dynamics of difference, including such issues as sexual orientation, ethnicity, ability/disability, and geographic location (Olesen, 2011).

Bricolaging Feminist Research With Heuristic Inquiry

There is no doubt of the noble and dignifying intentions of feminist research. However, every research approach has limitations. In the spirit of bricolaging qualitative research methods toward enhancing the quality, rigor, and trustworthiness of all research efforts, following are a number of suggestions for complementing feminist research with some heuristic processes. Given that a primary area of focus for feminist researchers is the advancement of social justice, it is important for researchers to pay particular attention to the ethical considerations of practicing action and advocacy toward social change and transformation. One of the characteristics of heuristic inquiry is authenticity. Authentic research is inclusive and equitable. Feminist researchers, like all other researchers, are motivated by personal needs and wants. To keep the research process authentic and balanced, special attention must be given to the feminist researcher's agenda and personal investment in the topic of inquiry, the research process, and the expected or desired outcomes. Thus, the focus on researcher reflexivity should be highlighted as feminist researchers examine their values, beliefs, and biases in the interest of not imposing any advocacy and/or social justice agendas on their participants. Failure to identify a hidden agenda motivated by personal interests is potentially dangerous and unethical (more on this in Chapter 10).

Speaking of participants, while feminist researchers give special consideration to issues of power and authority between themselves and their participants, co-researchers are still referred to as *participants* rather than as *co-researchers* or *research partners*. Changing the words we use in our research efforts also changes how we embody the research process and experience it. That is, when I name individuals who are commonly referred to in the research tradition as *research participants* my *co-researchers* or *research partners*, my brain and body eventually begin to experience them as such. I no longer view them as objects or as vessels of experience from which I am seeking knowledge but as living, breathing humans with a holistic way of being in the world. Along similar lines, feminist research may benefit from the holistic approach adopted by heuristic researchers, as inequity, power, and marginalization are explored not only as social∞relational experiences but also as cognitive, emotional, sensory∞kinesthetic, perceptual, and spiritual experiences. Taking this holistic perspective moves feminist research away from its own brand of marginalization that privileges the social∞relational self and allows for a more equitable research process that engages all dimensions of human experience.

Finally, with their attention to the outcome of the research, some feminist inquirers may get caught up in attaining their goal while losing sight of the potentially empowering nature of the very process and content of the research for all individuals involved. With this in mind, feminist researchers can borrow from heuristic inquiry's intimacy with the research process and content, the quality of the dialogue and discourse between researcher and co-researchers, and any and all types of data as they emerge on their own, rather than following a predetermined trail to acquire prescribed knowledge aimed at adopting or justifying a particular stance.

Closing Reflections

Heuristic inquiry invites us to explore closely some of our most meaningful experiences as humans and, thus, promotes growth and transformation. This is also the premise of most other qualitative research methodologies. In this contemporary research environment, qualitative researchers' vision is now more focused on how best to create research processes that allow space for all possible dimensions of exploring various topics of inquiry. Oftentimes, one research approach may not have all that is required to make this happen. This is when qualitative researchers are invited to use their creative abilities to weave together multiple research methods that open hidden windows and doors to exploration. As you travel your research journey and explore your labyrinth's path (see Exercise 2.1 to try on the experience of exploring a labyrinth), heuristic research offers a colorful variety of processes that may be interwoven with other qualitative methodologies to illuminate novel pathways of inquiry. Oh, the places you can go! The possibilities are really quite endless.

EXERCISE 2.1
EXPLORING THE LABYRINTH

This finger labyrinth exercise is designed to substitute for the experience of a walking labyrinth. Texturized finger labyrinths may be purchased online. If a walking labyrinth is accessible to you, you may also use this exercise within that context. Before you begin this exercise, remember that labyrinths are not designed to trick you. A labyrinth provides one path from the entrance to the center and the same path from the center to what becomes the exit. Your path is never invisible to you, and you can always see both the center and entrance/exit of the labyrinth, as well as the labyrinth in its entirety. This facilitates releasing the need to engage in overthinking or to control your direction or goal while allowing you to focus on the richness and depth of the process. In fact, as you follow the path both inward and outward, you will notice that some moments will bring you quite close to the center of the labyrinth only to take you abruptly back to its outermost edges. The labyrinth is a holistic metaphor for the winding journey of life and, in your case, also for the heuristic research journey, both of which are saturated with opportunities for transformation.

Chapter 2 • Locating Heuristic Inquiry Within Contemporary Qualitative Research **39**

The journey inward is filled with twists and turns that mirror the many negotiations we must make as we navigate our existence and our research process. Being at the center of the labyrinth provides an opportunity for pausing, reflection and reflexivity, and the emergence or cocreation of new knowledge in our search for the essential nature of a specific phenomenon. The journey outward, dappled with similar bends and curves, is a time for integrating the new knowledge received and giving oneself the chance to be transformed by it. Whether you are traveling alone or with the company of your research team, navigating a labyrinth is a "felt" experience and, thus, a powerful catalyst for being in the here and now and learning based on the present moment. Thus, the labyrinth journey (as with the heuristic research journey) is not about the outcome but about the process. Are you ready?

- Go to Figure 2.2. Look at the image for a few moments and allow yourself to view it in its wholeness while keeping the center in your focus (recall that the center of the labyrinth is a metaphor for your central guiding question, both as inquiry and as discovery/emergence).

FIGURE 2.2 ● The Chartres Labyrinth

Source: The Chartres Labyrinth, Ssolbergj.

(*Continued*)

(Continued)

- Allow a question or topic that has been in your awareness for some time, and that you wish to explore more deeply, to come to you. For now, it is not necessary that this question be related to your intentions for a formalized research study; it can be about anything you have personally experienced and that is meaningful to you.
- Give your mind permission to become quiet, and place your index finger at the point of entrance on the labyrinth image.
- With your finger, begin to trace your way slowly and intentionally through the spiraling path.
- Keep your question close to you by engaging your emotions and body sensations. If you feel as if you are getting stuck with your experience or you are becoming confused, allow yourself to be in this stuck and confused place. It is important that you not become distracted by your thoughts and judgments and that you not rush this process; otherwise you may lose your sense of direction.
- If you do feel lost, bring your full awareness to what you are experiencing and notice how it begins to shift as you give it enhanced nonjudgmental attention and immerse yourself within it. Pick a direction in which to proceed. If you find yourself back at the entrance, start over and maintain your focus on slowly and intentionally making your way to the center.
- When you arrive at the center, pause for a few minutes and open yourself to receive. You are now, with your question, at the center of your own being, in that place of tacit, inner knowing. Remember that while new knowledge may emerge in the form of thoughts, it may also appear in the form of emotions, images, or body sensations. All this information is valid!
- When you feel complete, begin your journey outward.
- Again, follow the path, opening yourself up to the experience of integrating all the many pieces of wisdom you received on your journey.
- How has your new knowledge transformed you? In what way(s) have you grown?

3

Philosophical and Theoretical Foundations of Heuristic Inquiry

Give up the notion that you must be sure of what you are doing. Instead, surrender to what is real within you, for that alone is sure.

~ Baruch Spinoza

Questions for Reflection

1. What is empiricism, and what is its value?
2. What biases do I hold about empiricism and its role in qualitative research?
3. Why do we learn about theory before conducting research?
4. What are my thoughts about how we gain knowledge? What personal experiences, values, attitudes, biases, and beliefs have informed my philosophy of knowledge acquisition? What are some ways by which I, personally, acquire knowledge?

This quote from Spinoza invites us to release our rigid grip on certainty and instead surrender to what resonates within us, implicitly. Yet how do we define reality? How do we begin to know what that looks like or what it means for each of us on an individual level? And how can we really know that this is what Spinoza is, in fact, talking about? After all, from a social constructivist perspective, I interpreted this quote based on my perception, and my perception is only *my* reality. What is *your* immediate response to this quote? Allow yourself to connect with your present-moment experience of it before finding a response that works for you. If your reaction is different from mine or is even a slight variation on mine, that is because we do, indeed, each have our own way of being in—and of knowing—the world. Thus, we also each have our unique way of interacting with various sources of information and with what Churchill (2005) refers to as "the very personal natural of what people call *knowledge*" (p. 324). In that sense, there is not any single way of knowing; there are many! Consequently, before we discuss the process of heuristic inquiry and how the data collection and analysis work, it is important to become familiar with some of the philosophical and theoretical structures that serve as a foundation for heuristic inquiry and infuse it with its singular identity.

In this chapter, I offer an overview of heuristic inquiry as a qualitative and social constructivist means for exploring questions and making sense of human experience and of the world. This begins with a discussion of the origins of empiricism in sensory experience and includes a review of some of the philosophical traditions of the social constructivist research paradigm, including ontological, epistemological, axiological, methodological, and rhetorical assumptions. The chapter also encompasses a review of some of the philosophers whose work inspired heuristic research:

- Edmund Husserl (1859–1938)
- Martin Buber (1878–1965)
- Carl Rogers (1902–1987)
- Abraham Maslow (1908–1970)
- Michael Polanyi (1891–1976)
- Eugene Gendlin (1926–2017)
- Maurice Merleau-Ponty (1908–1961)

Each of these creative thinkers identified unique ways of *being* and of *knowing* that transcend the superficiality and unidimensional nature of mere observation.

Why Do We Learn About Theory?

All research is guided by theoretical and philosophical foundations and assumptions. These assumptions are the bedrock on which research paradigms (e.g., post-positivist, pragmatic, social constructivist) are constructed. Likewise, whether or not you are aware of this, you do have certain beliefs and values, and your theoretical orientation as a researcher will influence each and every decision made throughout the research process. Thus, theory plays a number of key roles in every research endeavor. One of the primary roles of theory is to help us identify our personal assumptions and to create connections between them and our topic of inquiry. Conducting research from a place of knowledge and awareness is critical to ethical conduct. Other roles of theory include the provision of standard assumptions of our research framework (**paradigm**) with regard to ways of being (**ontology**), ways of knowing (**epistemology**), core beliefs and values (**axiology**), methods of research (**methodology**), and scholarship (**rhetoric**) and their placement within the direct context of the topic of inquiry. Table 3.1 contains brief, one-word descriptions of each of these philosophical assumptions (more on the roles of these assumptions later in the chapter).

To put it simply, theory proposes certain "givens" that influence and impact all stages of the research process, beginning with the researcher's budding awareness of a topic of interest and continuing on to publication of the final manuscript and beyond. Thus, it is important that you understand the core principles from which heuristic inquiry emerged so you have a grounded point of reference for your central research question, which you must keep in mind during every stage of your research journey. This is critical! As you begin your heuristic study, and throughout your research process, it will be essential for you to return—time and time again—to your central guiding question.

Whether you are consciously aware of it or not, your central question is inspired and informed by your theory, and the opposite is also true. In fact, we can say that your central guiding question and your theory have a dynamic, interactive relationship and that together they inform and guide your entire research process. To put it simply, the research question∞theory continuum both informs and is informed by each of the following: topic of inquiry, purpose of study, literature review, research methodology and design, and final manuscript (see Figure 3.1).

Without theory, your research study has no real foundation, and your research findings are questionable. Understanding the theoretical foundations

TABLE 3.1 • Philosophical Assumptions of Research

Philosophical Assumption	Expression
Ontology	Being
Epistemology	Knowing
Axiology	Values
Methodology	Approach/paradigm
Rhetoric	Language/narrative

FIGURE 3.1 • The Continuum of Research Question∞Theory and Research Process

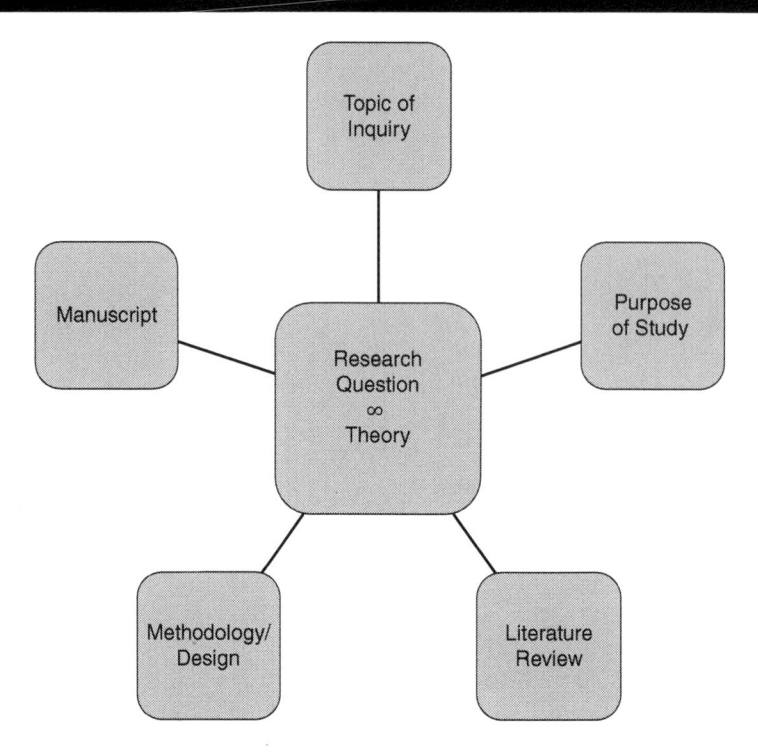

```
                    Topic of
                    Inquiry

  Manuscript                          Purpose
                                      of Study
                    Research
                    Question
                       ∞
                    Theory

              Methodology/    Literature
                Design         Review
```

of what we do (research question), why we do it (research rationale), how we do it (research methodology and methods), and with whom we do it (co-researcher sample) provides sources to which we may return if or when we feel our sense of direction is ambiguous. In a manner of speaking, theory infuses empiricism into any research endeavor, quantitative or qualitative, and prevents our research process from spiraling out of control.

Imagine this: In the midst of your data collection process, you ask one of your co-researchers a question that did not appear on the semi-structured interview protocol you sent him prior to the formal interview. Your co-researcher is curious about your motives for asking this particular question, especially as the question seems, to him, somewhat unrelated to the central topic of inquiry. He shares with you this curiosity. Here are a couple of potential scenarios:

1. You become flustered as you seek a suitable and satisfactory response to your research partner's inquiry. You realize that you really don't know why you asked this question; it just seemed like an okay question to ask. It also meant that the conversation would keep

flowing and you would meet the 60-minute minimum interview time. However, though imbued with practicality, this explanation would not necessarily pass muster with your research partner, would it? It would also potentially compromise your relationship with this co-researcher and other research partners, as well as your data collection and analysis and other phases of your research journey as it continues to pervade your process without being explored.

2. You immerse yourself in a reflexive process only to realize that you felt a personal connection with something your research partner stated and about which you wanted to know more. You share this with him. You then proceed to reflect on a variety of dynamics, including your personal involvement with the controversial follow-up question that was not on the interview protocol, how that question may potentially relate to your central guiding question, your research partner's reaction to that question, and the nature and meaning of the relational discourse between you as you work through this unexpected development in the data collection phase. As you do the above, you consider the theoretical foundations of your research methodology and recognize that they support your personal involvement and reflexive process. You also recognize that your personal values, interests, and attitudes are very much a part of the research approach you are using, as is reflexively engaging with those attributes. You share this information with your co-researcher as part of your ongoing discourse.

You get the picture?

Not only does theory bolster our research efforts and lend them rigor, it also supports the work we do outside and beyond research. It helps us conceptualize how we bring what we know into the workplace. Hence, theory helps us formulate and negotiate best practices. Truly, I believe that the supposed dichotomy between theory and practice is a false edifice and that theory and practice generate yet another colorful continuum (theory∞practice) within the spectrum of living experience. What follows is an example from my clinical practice.

Recently, one of my counseling clients (Pseudonym: Rick), after several weeks of working together, revealed to me a clinical concern that I had worked with only minimally in the past as it was not a concern in which I specialize. At that point, Rick and I had already established a warm and trusting rapport, and referring him to another mental health practitioner was not an option he was willing to consider. In fact, though I was quite transparent with Rick about my limited experience with his newly revealed concern, he insisted that I was still the therapist for him and he knew without a doubt that I could help him. Attempting to work with Rick's mental health concern without a solid knowledge and understanding of my clinical theoretical orientation would have been chaotic, at best. It would certainly have compromised my sense of assurance and confidence, placing Rick's mental wellness (and my license!) at risk. Instead, I explored cutting-edge research in the domain of Rick's concern and used my clinical theory as a framework for co-constructing (with Rick's collaboration) an understanding of this newly revealed experience and for creating and applying purposeful interventions. While this is an example of the practical use of theory in the workplace, it also demonstrates the relevance of relationship and collaboration as ways of being and of knowing. This is something to keep in mind as we work our way through this chapter and through understanding the core assumptions that underlie heuristic research.

Theory fosters competent practice, not only in psychotherapy but within a diversity of disciplines. It also promotes rigorous research as the researcher returns, again and again, to the theoretical foundations of the methodology to both assess findings and find inspiration for new perspectives from which to engage the topic of inquiry. Theory thus serves as a sort of lighthouse at the epicenter of the metaphorical labyrinth in that it provides, for the researcher, a reliable anchor while shedding light on the many twists and turns that lurk within the darkest corners of the research journey. If and when, as the researcher, you lack a sense of direction, you have but to return your gaze to center to recalibrate your compass.

Unfortunately, theory is also often used to oppress, marginalize, or impose. It may also be used as an excuse for maintaining an exclusive or deteriorating position of power or the status quo. As I write this, I am recalling the many decades of the so-called *paradigm wars*, charged with embittered battles between quantitative and qualitative researchers and thinkers as qualitative inquiry attempted to carve a niche for itself within the habitat of empirical research. I am also reminded of my personal experience of being counseled to justify, in objective, quantitative terminology not suited to qualitative research, my reasoning for adopting a heuristic approach for my dissertation research study and of having to become a fierce advocate for approval of my proposal to the institutional review board of my university. Although I risked receiving a denial of my proposed research because it was too personal and subjective, I refused to devalue heuristic inquiry simply because the majority believes that quantitative research approaches are superior. Instead, I presented a detailed, comprehensive background of heuristic inquiry, stressed the critical role of subjectivity in specific types of research, and drew countless parallels between the heuristic approach and my topic of inquiry. In short, I refused to be stripped of my voice or authenticity, and my proposal was approved. The point I am trying to make here is that ethical conduct dictates that theory not be used as a weapon of oppression or subjugation but as a tool to establish and maintain best practices in both practice- and research-oriented endeavors.

Heuristic Inquiry as an Empirical Process

Empirically supported rigorous research methods are part of the foundational basis for conducting any research. Yet empirical research takes many forms: not only those that attempt to operationalize, observe, and measure variables but also those that explore rich and complex phenomena. Historically speaking, empiricism is known as the acquisition of knowledge through sensory experience (Paley, 2008). One issue with applying this type of reasoning to researching first-person experiences, for example, is that subjective experience always includes introspection. The very idea of sensation that excludes perception and meaning-making is questionable (Churchill, 2005; Merleau-Ponty, 1945/2013) at best. Observation, in isolation, cannot describe or explain all experiences or phenomena. As Dilthey (1894/1977) famously stated, "We explain nature, we understand psychic life" (p. 27).

There is no doubt that one feature of sensory experience is observation. Yet to state that observation is *the* single feature of sensory experience is quite naïve as it implies that nature is but the sum of stimuli and qualities (Merleau-Ponty, 1945/2013) and that we are but eyes, ears, noses, and so forth that engage the world without consciousness. This is a restricted, restricting, and dehumanizing view of the vast human potential and results in what St. Pierre (2013) referred to as the collection of *brute* data—that is, data that exist independent of human meaning. Maslow (1966) asserted, "There is no substitute for experience, none at all. All the other paraphernalia of communication and of knowledge—words, labels, concepts, symbols, theories, formulas, sciences—all are useful only because people already knew them experientially" (pp. 45–46).

How about you? Do you believe in the possibility of interacting with stimuli within your environment without somehow becoming entangled in a personal narrative of thoughts, feelings, and sensations? How are you interacting on each of these various levels with the material you are reading right now? Above and beyond our ability to observe methodically is the inevitability of being with and reacting to what we are observing on a cognitive, emotional, sensory∞kinesthetic, perceptual, spiritual, and social∞relational basis, and from there drawing inferences and creating personal meaning. In our quest for integration, the instant we interact with an inner or outer stimulus is the very same instant our embodied meaning-making process begins, engaging our multiple ways of being and of knowing (see Figure 3.2). I invite you to explore some of these concepts in more depth in Exercise 3.1.

Consider this: On what basis is a hypothesis for a quantitative study formulated if not on the basis of the researcher's prior knowledge (or on the basis of theory, i.e., prior knowledge) and the researcher's understanding of it? Consider this, too: In a heuristic study, the inquiry begins with an autobiographical experience of a phenomenon that is so deeply felt it inspires in us researchers a question we are unable to ignore. This is a predominantly subjective process with elements of objectivity; that is, the researcher is wholly and holistically involved but is able to briefly detach and adopt an observant perspective. The researcher seeks further understanding for this question and embarks on a process of inquiry with others who have experienced this phenomenon. This is an objective process with elements of subjectivity; that is, the researcher approaches data collection with some detachment (bracketing) from her personal experience of the topic of inquiry to create a receiving space for the experiences of co-researchers. The research endeavor continues with

FIGURE 3.2 ● **Embodied/Integrative Ways of Being and of Knowing**

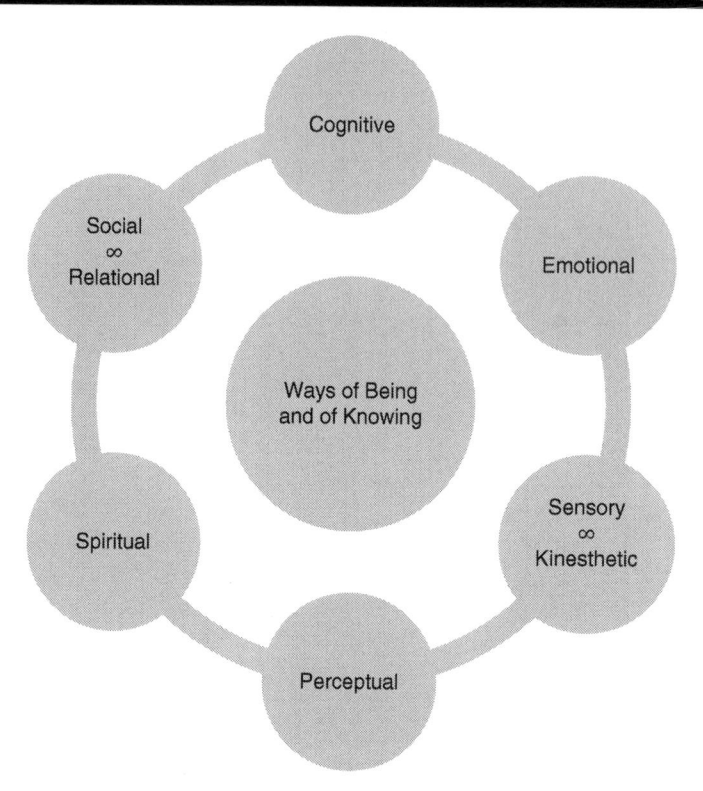

- Cognitive
- Emotional
- Sensory ∞ Kinesthetic
- Perceptual
- Spiritual
- Social ∞ Relational

Ways of Being and of Knowing

a back-and-forth between internal and external processes—subjective and objective—which involve the use of researcher reflexivity and include a synthesis in which the subjective and the objective blur into a cohesive gestalt. Thus, as with theory and practice, observation and experience *also* lie on a continuum that constitutes the very essence of empirical inquiry. Rather than being in opposition to qualitative research in general and heuristic research in particular, empiricism is in fact a principal feature of heuristic inquiry!

Mende (2005) makes an intriguing point of differentiating *empiricism* and *empirical*. He defines *empiricism* as "a restrictive methodological doctrine" (p. 189) and *empirical* as "a battery of very useful research methods" (p. 189). Ponterotto (2005), on the other hand, suggests that **empirical research** is that which involves the collection of raw data and its analysis and interpretation. Churchill (2005) argues, "With 'humanity' itself as the population of interest, there is an immediate problem with respect to the external validity of any research investigation" (p. 330). Finally, Abram (2000) emphasizes the primacy of carnal (based in the experience of the body) knowledge as the foundation for all knowledge. Although in-depth exploration of these well-intentioned and valuable assertions (and many others) surpasses the

EXERCISE 3.1
EXPLORING THE SUBJECTIVITY∞OBJECTIVITY CONTINUUM

One of the most prominent conflicts in scientific inquiry exists between those advocating a post-positivist approach to research and those promoting a social constructivist attitude. **Post-positivism** advocates an objective approach to research through which one truth or reality is sought and discovered, while social constructivism supports the co-construction of new knowledge in the form of multiple realities through subjective experience. These stances suggest that research may be either objective or subjective and that knowledge is attained either through discovery or through emergence. Yet heuristic inquiry is a demonstrably healthy fusion of both.

- Where do you find yourself on this subjectivity∞objectivity continuum?
- In your experience, is it possible to experience subjectively but not objectively? Objectively but not subjectively?
- How do you know that whatever answers you come up with are the only ones that are true?
- See if it's okay not only to examine your thoughts for answers to these questions but also to explore feelings and bodily sensations that may provide other answers.
- Now how about going out on a limb and asking a few people some of these questions?
- What was it like to create a shared experience with someone else?
- What was it like to explore the subjectivity∞objectivity continuum both with yourself and with others?
- How did you experience yourself while relating to the other? How did you experience the other as you interacted with her?

parameters of this book, these arguments clearly support the suggestion that not all empirical research is objective.

If we expand these ideas into the realm of heuristic inquiry, it is readily apparent that it is an empirical research approach grounded in sensory experience *and* inferential constructs. This takes us into the territory of what William James (1912/2009) called **radical empiricism**—a theory postulating that all experience occurs from an embodied perspective imbued with personal meaning and values. This theory was also prominent in the realm of earlier philosopher Emmanuel Kant (1781/1966), who stated that objective reality cannot be separated from the person who is experiencing it, processing it, and giving meaning to it (Ponterotto, 2005). Dewey (1925/2000) supported and expanded on these theories, suggesting that objective, observable data give rise to subjective, felt experience and that observation is undertaken through the interconnected lenses of self-interaction, interaction with others, and interaction with one's environment. Finally, it is critical that all researchers understand the incredible value of subjectivity to all who interact with both the research process and the findings. Subjectivity helps us identify our attitudes, values, beliefs, and biases and thus to interact with them and create sense of them. Additionally, subjective experience permits us to plunge to great depths with our research practices within communities and groups—and with topics—that may be inaccessible to most. This then helps us establish outreach and connection with others and situate personal experiences within broader contexts. Please keep this in mind as we discuss, later in this chapter, the influence of Husserl's (1900/2001) phenomenology and Merleau-Ponty's (1945/2013) embodied phenomenological philosophy—among others—on heuristic inquiry.

Heuristic Inquiry as Qualitative Research

What makes heuristic inquiry qualitative? The answer to that question lies within an understanding of the nature of **qualitative** (also known as **exploratory** or **inductive**) **research**. Denzin and Lincoln (2011) offer a generic definition for qualitative research as "a situated activity that locates the observer in the world" (p. 3), rendering the world visible and transformable. Qualitative research is unique in its capacity to provide us with rich, holistic, in-depth personal accounts of the subject matter (Braun & Clarke, 2013; Flick, von Kardorff, & Steinke, 2004; Krathwohl, 2009). In a qualitative study, the researcher usually focuses on a single concept inspired by personal curiosity, interests, beliefs, or values, and collects co-researcher meanings around this notion in an effort to understand a person, group, or situation (Berríos & Lucca, 2006; Creswell, 2009; Denzin & Lincoln, 2011; Erickson, 2011; Krathwohl, 2009). The research process is exploratory and emergent; the researcher does not usually enter the research journey with any presuppositions or expectations around findings, and remains open to whatever emerges. To put it simply, in qualitative research, there are no hypotheses to guide the research process. This is especially apparent in heuristic inquiry, as the researcher enters the research endeavor with openness and curiosity.

The researcher uses either interactive (such as interviews) or noninteractive (such as observation) forms of inquiry to collect data (Gehart, Ratliff, & Lyle, 2001), typically in the form of words (Braun & Clarke, 2013). Sources of data collection also include archival material, photos, artifacts (Krathwohl, 2009), memoirs, letters, and media sources (Sultan, 2015). Heuristic inquiry applies exceptionally purposeful and intentional use of researcher and co-researcher artifacts. In the interview format (predominantly used by heuristic researchers), the researcher asks research partners open-ended questions, and data collection proceeds in an unstructured or semi-structured manner. The researcher then reviews the data in an effort to identify recurring themes or patterns while also seeking divergences or unique features within the data (Braun & Clarke, 2013; Sultan, 2015). A study using qualitative methodology generally has a guiding question exploring the central concept being studied, followed by a maximum of five to seven subquestions. Questions delve into the *what* and *how* of the topic of inquiry (Creswell, 2009; Finlay, 2011; Krathwohl, 2009; Sultan, 2015), generating research that is process-oriented.

Qualitative methods are inductive. They emerge (Glesne, 2016; Maxwell, 2013) from personal assumptions and worldview (recall the autobiographical nature of the heuristic inquiry research question), stressing the following dimensions (Berríos & Lucca, 2006; Creswell, 2013; Sultan, 2015; Wertz, 2005), all of which are vital to heuristic research:

- Curiosity and openness in research dynamics
- Respect for researcher–research partner relationships
- Responsiveness to meaning-making
- Attention to process and content
- Emphasis on the richness of personal experience
- Comfort with ambiguity
- Non-attachment to outcome

There are many parallels between qualitative researchers and mental health practitioners in their perspectives on examining and exploring the dynamics of human nature (Berríos & Lucca, 2006; Finlay, 2011), which renders qualitative methodology an optimum approach to researching human experience for researchers practicing within a variety of helping disciplines such as psychotherapy, nursing, and conflict transformation. In fact, Denzin and Lincoln (2011) assert that qualitative research is used in many disciplines, including education, anthropology, sociology, communications, cultural studies, literary studies, and medicine. The heuristic approach is ideal for research in all the above disciplines, among others (more on this in Chapter 11).

Qualitative approaches honor the subjective experience of each individual in a research team (Minichiello & Kottler, 2010; Sultan, 2015) and are most useful in the following types of studies (Creswell, 2013; Krathwohl, 2009):

- Those designed to humanize and bring to life people, problems, contexts, settings, and situations

- Those that describe—in a nuanced and in-depth fashion—complex intra- and interpersonal phenomena that would be challenging to portray using the somewhat unidimensional scales used in quantitative approaches
- Those that emphasize knowledge in an area in which research is limited
- Those that focus on the internal dynamics of process versus on outcome or effect

Krathwohl (2009) remarked that qualitative inquiry is especially valuable in keeping researchers close to the data and accessing another's perceptions of a situation, which then allows us to understand that individual's behavior, adding that the primacy of perception has been corroborated by findings from functional magnetic resonance imaging (fMRI). He asserted that qualitative studies' real-life contexts are especially effective in communicating with practitioners, who can identify with the portrayed examples.

Exploratory research, in which the researcher is the key instrument of data collection and interpretation (Creswell, 2013; Denzin & Lincoln, 2011), is an empirical approach in that it involves the collection of raw data and their analysis and interpretation (Ponterotto, 2005). Qualitative researchers believe there are no fixed ways of being in or knowing the world. We aim to develop a holistic account of the phenomenon being explored through identification of its multiple facets within various contexts and situations and to report this account through the multiple perspectives encountered throughout the research process (Creswell, 2013; Minichiello & Kottler, 2010; Sultan, 2015). Qualitative research is capable of transforming both researcher and co-researchers by providing opportunities for the sharing and meaning-making of subjective experience (Cannella & Lincoln, 2012; Finlay, 2011); this is especially true of heuristic inquiry, which inspires the integration of highly autobiographical shared experiences.

Qualitative inquiry is also highly emancipatory in its recognition that those who are members of marginalized groups have perspectives that cannot possibly be encompassed within categories predetermined by those who are members of dominant groups (van den Hoonaard, 2008). In that sense, qualitative research provides researchers access to tools that transcend the parameters of rigid research approaches generated by individuals who are at the summit of social hierarchies. This characteristic is quite possibly a function of the long history qualitative research itself has had with being marginalized. One example of this marginalization is the many challenges qualitative researchers have consistently faced with their attempts to have the findings of their studies published in core research journals, as journal editors stress the need for manuscripts to use quantitative, objective, third-person language. Rather than being a reflection of any lack of rigor in qualitative inquiry and scholarship, this practice is a reflection of discrimination from a dominant group toward a nondominant group. Qualitative researchers have become advocates for the uniqueness of their approach and have responded to this type of oppression by creating journals committed to the dissemination of qualitative scholarship.

Exploratory methods (including heuristic inquiry) generally follow a social constructivist paradigm (Creswell, 2009), suggesting that all knowledge is based in personal and cultural contexts and meaning-making. Thus, qualitative research acknowledges and is influenced by the experiences and perceptions of the researcher as (in alignment with social constructivism) people are viewed as functioning within a subjectively experienced world in which relationships are reciprocal (Braun & Clarke, 2013; Merleau-Ponty, 1945/2013) and interactive.

Heuristic Inquiry as Social Constructivism

In the previous section, I demonstrated the exploratory and inductive essence of heuristic inquiry by describing and explaining the nature of qualitative research. To fully understand the spirit of heuristic inquiry, however, it is critical to also have some knowledge of the research paradigm that houses the heuristic approach. Different authors (Creswell, 2013; Denzin & Lincoln, 2011) propose different research paradigms and frameworks. The most widely known research paradigms are

- post-positivism,
- social constructivism,
- postmodernism,
- pragmatism, and
- critical/race theory.

Of the above, post-positivism and social constructivism are the dominant (and also the most highly contrasting) paradigms. See Table 3.2 for a side-by-side comparison of the post-positivist and social constructivist paradigms and the assumptions that underlie each framework.

As mentioned previously, most qualitative inquiry follows the social constructivist paradigm, and this is especially true of heuristic inquiry, which at its very core is a social constructivist research approach. Understanding the nature of the research paradigm within which a research methodology is housed provides a necessary structure for and informs the process of inquiry.

Social constructivism (also called **interpretivism**; Denzin & Lincoln, 2011) is both a philosophy of life and a research paradigm; that is, it is both a way of being and a way of knowing. It was heavily influenced by the developmental learning theory of Lev Vygotsky (1978), which stressed that thinking, processing, and learning all occur within a sociocultural context and, specifically, through collaborative, intersubjective (or relationally shared)

TABLE 3.2 ● **Dominant Research Paradigms and Their Philosophical Assumptions**

Philosophical Assumptions	Post-Positivism	Social Constructivism
Ontological (nature of being and reality)	Single, fixed reality that is observable and measurable	Multiple realities that are subjectively and socially constructed
Epistemological (knowledge acquisition)	Investigative, deductive approaches focused on objective and quantifiable data collection	Exploratory, inductive approaches focused on understanding meanings and essential natures of things
Axiological (role of beliefs and values)	Objective researcher; value- and bias-free	Reflexive researcher with subjective values, beliefs, attitudes, biases, and intuition that are made explicit
Methodological (research approach)	Experimental, quasi-experimental, non-experimental; noninteractive; outcome-oriented	Phenomenology, ethnography, case study, grounded theory, narrative research, heuristic inquiry, etc.; intersubjective and interactive; experiential; process-oriented
Rhetorical (manuscript)	Third-person, objective accounts; numbers	First-person, subjective accounts; words, photos, artwork, journal entries, memos, etc.

experiences. The social constructivist paradigm views the contexts within which all experiences occur as central to the experiences themselves; that is, the context of an experience shapes the essential nature of the experience. Another critical concept proposed by Vygotsky, and a crucial extension to intersubjective experience within the context of social constructivism, is what he termed private speech. Private speech is a way of guiding and regulating personal behavior. Inner speech, which evolves from private speech, is essentially internal deliberation, or simply thought. Thus, social constructivism is the interaction of communication and thought; learning is both internally and socially constructed. Along similar lines, reality exists only because we have created it. From a social constructivist perspective, there is no reality prior to our construction of it.

As a qualitative and social constructivist research methodology, heuristic inquiry relies on co-researchers' subjective experiences of the topic of inquiry and honors the various relationships between all members of the research team, including relationships between researcher and co-researchers. Thus, the central questions of a heuristic inquiry are generally open-ended, allowing for the diversity of each research partner's experience to shine. They are also grounded in the personal needs of the primary researcher and each member of the research team, as well as the needs of the greater community. All phases and aspects of the research process are collaborative, valuing and including both subjective and objective experiences toward a holistic cocreation of meaning. The researcher acts, primarily, as a facilitator for a colearning experience regarding the essential nature of the central topic of inquiry (Moustakas, 1990). Like all other research paradigms, social constructivist inquiry is guided by a number of philosophical assumptions that guide the research process, including ontological, epistemological, axiological, methodological, and rhetorical (Creswell, 2013; Denzin & Lincoln, 2011; Ponterotto, 2005), all of which apply to heuristic inquiry.

Ontological Assumptions

Ontology is concerned with the nature of being and reality (Creswell, 2013; Ponterotto, 2005). Social constructivists and heuristic researchers assume reality is relative and is constructed based on an individual's contextual and subjective meaning-making of personal and shared experience—that is, an individual's worldview (Lincoln, Lynham, & Guba, 2011). Thus, there is no single reality, but rather multiple realities exist. Essential meaning is believed to emerge through processes of deep introspection—or what Moustakas (1990) refers to as indwelling—stimulated by the dialogical and relational interaction between researcher and co-researchers. In this manner, reality and meaning are cocreated.

Let's suppose you and I are walking down a hall together. As you lug six hardback books in both hands, you describe the challenging weight you are carrying. Meanwhile, I am remarking about how heavy and exhausted I am feeling. We validate each other as we try to create some meaning of our intersubjectively shared experience of *heaviness*, and we make our way to an unoccupied room to take a needed break. Inside the room, there is one desk; nothing else is there. You walk to the desk and set down your heavy books, exhaling with relief. "There! Now my arms are free!" I walk to the desk and sit on it. "Ahhh . . . nice!" Our individual experiences just determined each of our realities. You saw the desk as an object that could relieve you of the burden of the heavy books you were carrying. I saw the desk as an object that could relieve my tired body. For you, the desk was a desk, while for me, it was a chair. Nevertheless, for each of us, it was a catalyst for physical relief. Such is the nature of reality, from the lens of the social constructivist paradigm.

Ontologically speaking, the purpose of a heuristic study is to allow for the emergence of the reality of the topic of inquiry from the perspective of each member of the research team, toward a representative synthesis of the essential nature of the phenomenon. Each research partner's contribution—as well as that of the primary researcher—is valuable and valid and highlights how the particular research partner's experience is both singular in some respects and shared (or potentially universal) in others. In this sense (and unlike the case with quantitative studies, which are generally housed within the postpositivist paradigm), there are no **outliers**—that is, individual findings that are considered to lie beyond the norm. All findings are viewed as normal and as reality, and all contributions are honored and represented using contributors' original voices and language so as to preserve their wholeness.

Epistemological Assumptions

Epistemology, on the other hand, is concerned with knowledge and with how we know what we know. A core facet of this is the relationship between *knower* (research partner) and *would-be knower* (primary researcher [Ponterotto, 2005], although it is important to understand that in heuristic inquiry, the primary researcher is also a *knower* and each research partner is also a *would-be knower*). Social constructivists advocate a subjectivist (Lincoln et al., 2011) and intersubjectivist position, maintaining that reality is a cocreated social construction. The relationship between researcher and co-researchers is critical to this cocreation process (Creswell, 2013) as, through this intersubjective relationship, the co-construction of knowledge will occur. Thus, instead of making efforts to maintain an objective and distant stance, social constructivist (and heuristic) researchers make efforts to minimize any gaps between themselves and members of their research teams to allow for multifaceted elaborations of knowledge.

Imagine that you are researching the experience of shyness, as it is a phenomenon that you experience with regularity and is highly personal to you. In your attempt to know and understand the essential nature of shyness, you have thought about, felt into, and journaled about shyness. Through these activities, you have acquired some knowledge of the essential nature of shyness. Yet you feel your knowledge is somehow incomplete, especially given your high degree of certainty that you are not alone in the world with this experience. You seek out other individuals and ask them about their experience of shyness, never once attempting to distance yourself from that experience or to disown it. Instead, you are quite transparent about the fact that you have an intimate relationship with being shy and that your personal experience with it is a primary motive behind your process of inquiry. Your self-disclosure resonates with your interviewees, and they feel comfortable sharing their experience of shyness with someone with whom they can exchange mutual empathy. Laura describes her experience to you by shaping her body in the form of shyness. "This is what it's like to be in my body when I'm feeling shy." As she shrinks her shoulders and back, you experience a sensation of tightness in those parts of your body. Matt, on the other hand, shows you a series of paintings he has created to better know and understand his shyness. The blues and purples in Matt's paintings touch a chord. Finally, Natalie shares with you a poem she has written about her lifetime experience with shyness, especially as a child. As you read Natalie's words, your eyes well up with empathic tears. Each of these contributions, though different and unique, is shared on some level. Each is a representation of shyness and contributes to the cocreation of our knowledge of that phenomenon holistically.

Epistemologically speaking, the purpose of a heuristic study is to cocreate knowledge and understanding of the essential nature of the phenomenon of inquiry. This process is facilitated through the intersubjective relationships maintained between the researcher and each research partner. Each research partner's contribution helps lay the foundation for the knowledge that is sought (Lincoln et al., 2011). Once again, knowledge is co-constructed with the understanding that it does not exist independent of its cocreation by researcher and research partners. The heuristic researcher and co-researchers each contribute their part toward the creation of the greater whole. Taking a bird's-eye view of heuristic inquiry, Moustakas (1990) declared that the methodology itself is a way of knowing. I concur!

Axiological Assumptions

Axiology is concerned with the role of the researcher's values within the research process (Creswell, 2013; Hiles, 2008a; Ponterotto, 2005) and potential ethical implications surrounding the inclusion of such values. Social constructivists maintain that there can be no separation between the researcher's experience and the research process, stressing the bracketing (recognizing and suspending) of researcher values without their elimination, with the understanding that the elimination of values and biases is a fallacy. Additionally, social constructivist researchers highlight the importance of maintaining close and protracted relational contact with co-researchers so as to facilitate the co-construction process (Ponterotto, 2005). With this in mind, it is challenging to imagine the possibility of separating one's personal values from the process of inquiry. In fact, any attempt on researchers' part to claim a separation from their beliefs and values or from their intimate knowledge of the topic of inquiry, may instill a sense of suspicion within co-researchers and compromise the relationship between researcher and research partners. There is also a possibility that research partners will feel shamed about their experience as the primary researcher makes claims of being dissociated from the phenomenon of inquiry. It is important for researchers to keep this in mind as we all make an effort to reduce marginalizing research practices and promote social justice.

Axiologically speaking, ethical practice dictates that heuristic researchers are transparent with regard to the role of their personal values in shaping the process of inquiry (Hiles, 2008a). The researcher does not assume or pretend distance from any facet of the research, including how choices were made regarding the central research question, the research paradigm and methodology, and presentation of the findings (Lincoln et al., 2011). Instead, the heuristic researcher openly acknowledges and identifies all values, attitudes, beliefs, and biases and their influence throughout the process of inquiry (Moustakas, 1990), in addition to what measures were taken to minimize marginalization, misrepresentation, manipulation, or exploitation of research partners and their narratives. From a social constructivist (and especially from a heuristic) perspective, rather than stripping a research study of its validity, this disclosure from the researcher serves as an "outing" mechanism (Finlay, 2002), thereby fortifying a study's trustworthiness and goodness.

Methodological Assumptions

Methodology is concerned with the procedures and process of research and is at least partially informed by the researcher's ontological, epistemological, and axiological positions (Ponterotto, 2005). Social constructivist researchers immerse themselves within the various contexts of their research partners and adopt an inductive, emergent approach to the data collection process (Creswell, 2013). Thus, data are collected "on-site" using such methods as interviewing and observation (Schensul, 2008), instead of within "neutral" settings predetermined by the researcher. There is attention to detail and particulars rather than to generalizations. Research questions are modified throughout the course of the study, based on the emergent data. This is designed to secure a collaborative construction of reality that emerges directly from within the research process (Angen, 2000; Lincoln et al., 2011).

Methodologically speaking, heuristic researchers collect data through extended interviews with their research partners and with themselves (Moustakas, 1990). These interviews are generally not restricted by the clock (more on this in Chapter 6) and are informed by a collaborative understanding between the researcher and research partner involved in the interview that the research partner has had an opportunity to fully express himself. While Moustakas (1990) advocated the informal conversational interview as most closely aligned with the general spirit of heuristic inquiry, the other approaches are also highly appropriate, especially as maintaining personal and ethical boundaries with co-researchers and keeping in mind time considerations become increasingly relevant.

Following data collection for each research partner, the heuristic researcher becomes immersed in the data to gain a comprehensive knowledge of the co-researcher's material. Once data have been collected from all co-researchers, the researcher then works to synthesize all the information and gain an understanding of co-researchers' collective living experience. The researcher goes back and forth between periods of intimate immersion with the data and distance and rest to allow for incubation. The final phase of data analysis in heuristic inquiry involves the elaboration of a creative synthesis that fuses the collective group experience of the research team. Thus, knowledge is co-constructed per the social constructivist paradigm.

Rhetorical Assumptions

Rhetoric is concerned with the language or narrative used to present the process and findings of the research to the intended audience (Ponterotto,

2005). Social constructivists adopt a first-person, personalized approach to presenting the findings, acknowledging the researcher's experience, values, biases, and expectations and the impact of these on the research. Also acknowledged are the philosophical assumptions underlying the research study and how they are represented within the study (Creswell, 2013). This is usually done in a similar fashion to this section, in which I am describing ontology, epistemology, axiology, methodology, and rhetoric and how they are exemplified in heuristic research.

Rhetorically speaking, heuristic researchers write their manuscripts with a mind to present information that holds both scientific and social meaning (Moustakas, 1990). As with most other qualitative research manuscripts, the heuristic manuscript (more in Chapter 9) includes the statement of the topic and research question; a literature review; a methodology section; a section in which the findings are presented (and usually citations from the first-person narratives of the research partners, as well as artifacts shared by research partners); and a summary that includes implications of the findings for future research, for the researcher, for the co-researcher population, for society, and for the researcher's profession, among others, in addition to directions for future research. The manuscript is written both structurally and texturally so as to resonate with readers. As the researcher, you are responsible for properly representing the research approach, theory, and philosophy while maintaining your connection with readers through creative and nuanced description of the topic of inquiry and the research findings that illuminate its essential nature.

Finally, and to connect any loose threads, social constructivist research relies on researcher and co-researcher views of the situation being explored, with questions being broad and open-ended, allowing for the emergence of findings that are co-constructed by the researcher and research partners through interactive discourse and meaning-making. Social constructivism takes the view that humans engage their world and make sense of it through a historical and social lens (Mertens, 2014). Social constructivist researchers recognize the mutual influence between themselves and what they are studying and the impact of their personal and cultural backgrounds on shaping the construction of knowledge. Merleau-Ponty (1945/2013) described this interactive process quite poetically:

> Here there is a being-shared-by-two, and the other person is no longer for me a simple behavior in my transcendental field, nor for that matter am I a simple behavior in his. We are, for each other, collaborators in perfect reciprocity: our perspectives slip into each other, we coexist through a single world. (p. 370)

Reflexivity, which occurs when researchers place under thoughtful scrutiny the research process, the intersubjective dynamics between researcher and research partners, and the extent to which their assumptions influenced the process of inquiry (Braun & Clarke, 2013; Finlay, 2011), is thus essential in helping researchers place into perspective their preconceived ideas and their personal attitudes, beliefs, values, and biases.

Justifiably, the social constructivist paradigm is the primary foundation for qualitative research methods (Creswell, 2009). Proponents of social constructivism emphasize lived (or living) experience, the primary experience being explored in phenomenology (Charmaz, 2006; Creswell, 2009; Krathwohl, 2009; Ponterotto, 2005) and in heuristic inquiry, both of which are social constructivist, qualitative approaches to research. As Denzin and Lincoln (2011) asserted, the qualitative (and indeed the social constructivist and heuristic) researcher "approaches the world with a set of ideas, a framework (theory, ontology) that specifies a set of questions (epistemology), which are then examined (methodology, analysis) in specific ways" (p. 11) and then written in manuscript form (rhetoric), all of which is informed by the perception of the researcher (axiology) and of every member of the research team.

Heuristic Inquiry as "Phenomenologically Aligned"

Now that we've covered some of the basics of the qualitative research approach and the social constructivist research paradigm, and how qualitative research and social constructivism help structure and inform heuristic inquiry, it makes sense to introduce the third and final side of the triangle that is heuristic inquiry—phenomenology. We sort of delved into that in Chapter 2, remember? I did not title that section "Heuristic Inquiry as Phenomenology," or anything similar. Instead, the section discussing the relationship between heuristic inquiry and phenomenology in Chapter 2 is titled, simply, "Relationship to Phenomenology." There's a reason for that. Clark Moustakas (1990) vehemently defended heuristic inquiry as a qualitative research methodology in its own right, and Douglass and Moustakas (1985) diligently outlined some of the core distinctions between heuristic inquiry and phenomenology (also discussed in Chapter 2). Yes, heuristic inquiry was inspired by many phenomenological concepts and ideas. And it unquestionably bears several quite striking similarities to phenomenology. Yet, while heuristic inquiry bears some relationship to phenomenological methodology, it is also a unique qualitative research approach. Still, some familiarity with the basic framework of phenomenology and its philosophical concepts that serve as a foundation for heuristic inquiry will help illuminate some of the nuanced similarities between heuristic research and phenomenology, as well as the divergences. It is important to understand how these methodologies were inspired and operate so you are better equipped to make an informed decision as you explore options.

Phenomenology is a social constructivist research approach that seeks to explore a complex human experience that has not been extensively researched in an attempt "to understand the world as individuals perceive it" (Krathwohl, 2009, p. 256). It is a qualitative, nonlinear method that allows for the illumination of deep meanings (Christensen & Brumfield, 2010; Creswell, 2009, 2013;

Sultan, 2015). Co-researchers are selected purposively (Creswell, 2013) based on their encounter with the phenomenon of inquiry and their willingness to share their perceived experience (Christensen & Brumfield, 2010) of that encounter. Such is also the domain of heuristic inquiry.

Phenomenology initially emerged as a study of philosophy, appearing in the writings of Edmund Husserl (1900/2001), whose aim was to develop a rigorous science based on philosophy, perceptions, ideas, and judgments. Husserl's goal arose from his growing discontent with a paradigm of science founded on the study of material things while ignoring human experience (Moustakas, 1994). Husserl proposed one of the first definitions of phenomenological research as a question that emerges from a perspective with no preconceptions or hypotheses and an answer that describes rather than explains (Christensen & Brumfield, 2010). Husserl advocated a return to things as they are (Moustakas, 1994). In phenomenology, perception is viewed as the primary source of knowledge.

Phenomenological researchers strive to understand the world of another as it is seen, felt, thought, and experienced by her (Moran, 2000). As we observe another and reflect, memory that is relevant to the phenomenon reawakens feelings and images, bringing past experience into the present (Moustakas, 1994). Merleau-Ponty (1945/2013), whose philosophy of embodiment and perception also influenced heuristic inquiry, offers an elegant description of this process:

> Perception's silent thesis is that experience, at each moment, can be coordinated with the experience of the preceding moment and with that of the following one, that my perspective can be coordinated with the perspectives of other consciousnesses—that all contradictions can be removed, that monadic and intersubjective experience is a single continuous text—and that what is indeterminate for me at this moment could become determinate of a more complete knowledge, which is seemingly realized in advance in the thing, or rather which is the thing itself. (p. 54)

Moustakas (1994) observed that phenomenology focuses on things as they appear and stressed the observation of entities from multiple angles toward a vision of the unified whole of the central phenomenon or experience (Sultan, 2015). The phenomenological researcher arrives at an understanding of the phenomenon through an embodied reflective, meditative, and intuitive process that generates ideas, concepts, judgments, and understandings. Phenomenology is concerned with describing experience, honoring "the original texture of things, their phenomenal qualities and material properties" (Moustakas, 1994, pp. 58–59). Descriptions of phenomena are presented in vivid language based on impressions, images, verbal elaborations, and sensory qualities such as sight, sound, touch, and taste. Max van Manen (1990) likened phenomenology to poetry in its aim to include "the voice in an original singing of the world" (p. 13).

The phenomenological researcher has a personal interest in what is being explored and is intimately connected with it (Moustakas, 1994). The researcher's curiosity is thus autobiographical, rendering history and memory critical facets of the discovery process both in the present and into the future (Sultan, 2015). What we see is interwoven with how we see it and with whom we see it, integrating subject and object. While intersubjectivity is a critical part of the process, the researcher's own thought, intuition, reflection, and judgment are the primary sources of evidence in the inquiry (Moustakas, 1994). Here, phenomenological attitude (Finlay, 2008, 2012) may be viewed as an ongoing dance between *reduction* (entering the research setting with no preconceptions) and *reflexivity* (engaging researcher self-awareness), toward creating a balance between bracketing preunderstandings and using them as sources of insight (Finlay, 2008). The research question is skillfully elaborated, with every word chosen with intentionality and designed to guide in the phenomenological process of observing, seeing, reflecting, and knowing. Every method employed in the process of inquiry relates back to the research question, portraying the phenomenon in a rich, textural, and layered manner (Moustakas, 1994). Merleau-Ponty (1945/2013) proposed that we are all embodied beings in an embodied world. Some phenomenological researchers embrace an idea of our bodies being inseparable from our cognitive, emotional, sensory∞kinesthetic, perceptual, spiritual, and social∞relational worlds. Yet unlike in heuristic inquiry, the body of the researcher is often absent in phenomenological research, with the focus being on narrative descriptions of participant experiences (Finlay, 2011). Phenomenological researchers may use their bodies to better understand participant experiences. Robert Romanyshyn (2007), in *The Wounded Researcher: Research With Soul in Mind,* stated:

> To linger and even loiter in the presence of what is present is to recover the animate flesh. It is the lived body that lingers in an erotic conspiracy with the world. . . . To begin with the ensouled body and its gestural fields is to acknowledge that between one's flesh and that of the work [research], like the relation in the transference field of therapy between the flesh of the therapist and that of the patient, a secret dialogue has already been in progress, a dialogue that now poses its questions to the researcher. The embodied witness is the one who interprets on the grounds that he or she has already been interpreted. He or she makes sense and derives meaning on the grounds of how he or she has already been made sense of. (p. 232)

As a function of its existential, holistic, humanistic, nondualist predilection, phenomenology invites researchers to slow down, direct their focus on the topic of inquiry, and dwell with it, bringing such values as empathy, acceptance, creativity, self-expression, and transcendence into play (Creswell, 2013; Finlay, 2011; Moustakas, 1990; Sultan, 2015; Wertz, 2005). Because a phenomenological approach to research in the social sciences and health services resonates with practitioners, it has the potential to offer valuable knowledge to those fields. Hence, phenomenological research has the capacity to bridge the gulf separating research from practice in the social and medical sciences.

Philosophers Whose Work Inspired Heuristic Inquiry

So far we've addressed the importance of learning about theories when engaging in scientific inquiry, identified what makes heuristic inquiry an empirical process, and highlighted the qualitative, social constructivist, and phenomenological origins of this unique methodology. Now we move on to learning about the philosophers whose wisdom has permeated the essence of the heuristic approach. In this section, I outline and describe how the philosophies of Edmund Husserl, Martin Buber, Carl Rogers, Abraham Maslow, Michael Polanyi, Eugene Gendlin, and Maurice Merleau-Ponty have given flesh to the ontological, epistemological, axiological, methodological, and rhetorical dimensions of heuristic inquiry. At the most basic level, we can break these great thinkers down into two groups: one that houses only Edmund Husserl and another that houses all the other philosophers. Husserl's work lays down the phenomenologically aligned foundation of heuristic inquiry, while the varied wisdoms of Buber, Rogers, Maslow, Polanyi, Gendlin, and Merleau-Ponty serve as its relational, creative, embodied building blocks. With the possible exception of Husserl, many of these philosophers were, in fact, contemporaries whose ideas deeply influenced and impacted one another.

Edmund Husserl

Discussing the thinkers whose philosophies were decisive to the formation of heuristic inquiry takes us back to our discussion of empiricism earlier in this chapter. As a reminder, traditional understandings of empiricism define it as a theory describing the acquisition of knowledge through sensory experience, with an emphasis on sensory perception of external stimuli. Additionally, while empiricism extols **a posteriori knowledge**—that is, knowledge based on experience—it discounts **a priori knowledge**—that is, knowledge that is innate.

In the early 20th century, the Austrian-German philosopher Edmund Husserl (1900/2001) recognized that to understand experience in a more complex, nuanced, and holistic manner, it would be necessary to adopt a novel view of reality as a first-person experience and to instill this view into scientific inquiry (Churchill & Wertz, 2015; Wertz, 2015). Recall that in the scientific method of research, objective observation is the primary means of understanding reality and collecting data. Through his new method of research, which he named *phenomenology*, Husserl proposed that human experience is qualitative and subjective and that one can truly understand reality only from a first-person perspective (Flick et al., 2004) that includes data collected from and processed through introspection and self-inquiry, as only first-person experience is truly evident. The primary purpose of Husserl's phenomenology is to reveal the essence of human consciousness (Soccio, 2013), with a focus on subjective experience. In fact, Husserl suggested that even objective judgments emerge from subjective experience as he contested Descartes' statement of *"Je pense, donc je suis"* (more commonly known as *"Cogito ergo sum"*), or "I am thinking, therefore I am," described in Descartes' *A Discourse on the Method* (1637/2006).

Central to any research exploring human experience is an understanding of consciousness, which Husserl (1913/1998) extended as **intentionality** (Churchill & Wertz, 2015). This concept describes the experience of unraveling the various layers of implicit meaning (Finlay, 2011) surrounding the encounter of a subject with an object. Essentially, intentionality asks the question, *What is my experience of . . . ?* which is the primary question asked within every phenomenological and heuristic study. Within such an encounter, the perceiver's interaction with the perceived is always informed by both first-person experience and context. Thus, Husserl challenged the Cartesian stance that internal mental representations constitute external reality, instead proposing that "the human and the experiential world are interactive" (Moss, 2015, p. 9). An example of intentionality is the one I used in the "Ontological Assumptions" section of this chapter; that is, the desk was for your tired arms a desk on which to set your heavy books, whereas it was for me a chair on which to rest my exhausted body.

The domain of scientific inquiry is aimed at gaining knowledge of the observable world through objective approaches independent of personal experience or awareness (Abram, 1996). Husserl (1900/2001), on the other hand, was primarily committed to returning to "the things themselves" (p. 10) and to researching the transcendental *épochè*, the essence underlying our understanding and acceptance of our perceived world (Finlay & Langdridge, 2007), by bracketing ourselves from experience to reflect on its essential nature (Carman, 1999). He formalized a scientific procedure (Moustakas, 1994) designed to lend rigor to his subjective process of inquiry, with an underlying understanding that research is a quest for knowledge that depends in large part on personal experience. Carman (1999) noted that Husserl's phenomenology underlined distinctions between inner and outer experience and between concrete and abstract concepts and entities. Thus, Husserl's phenomenology, though it acknowledged the role of the body in human experience, continued to view the body as a receiver and bearer of sensation, a *thing* inserted between subjective experience and the objective world (Carman, 1999; Sultan, 2015). One could say that, despite his refutation of Cartesian dualist thinking, Husserl extended a dichotomous reasoning of his own by viewing the self as separate from the phenomena it experiences. As you will later learn, Merleau-Ponty's philosophy, with its focus on intersubjectivity and embodiment, fills this gap and lends heuristic inquiry its highly relational edge. Nevertheless, Husserl's phenomenology proposed a number of subjective themes—including attunement to another (albeit with bracketing)—that were especially appealing to existential and humanistic thinkers and theorists who modified, built on, and/or expanded Husserl's philosophy and whose work was influential to heuristic inquiry.

Martin Buber

Relationship and dialogue are central features of any heuristic study. This is true not only because interviewing is the primary means of collecting data in heuristic research but also because the topics being explored are highly personal in nature and have been experienced by all members of the research team. One of the principal authorities on both relationality and dialogue is Martin Buber, a Vienna-born existential philosopher who proposed a form of existentialism that distinguished **I–Thou** (focused on the experience of being present with others and the world) from **I–It** (focused on the experience of the self) relationships (Moss, 2015). Buber (1923/1970) stated, "In the beginning is the relation" (p. 69) and "All actual life is encounter" (p. 62). Thus, the basis for existence or being, according to Buber, is encounter. Buber stressed I–Thou interaction as the foundation for gaining a true sense of oneself, as well as for developing authentic relationships through sharing our true selves with others (Greening, 2015) and attaining **intersubjectivity**. Fogel (2009) defined intersubjectivity as "the nonverbal sense of 'being with' another person, a direct result of the interpersonal resonance that occurs during coregulation of movements, sensations, and emotions" (p. 314). Essentially, intersubjectivity is mutual subjectivity—that is, a shared way of knowing and being.

Intersubjectivity is the foundation for the realm of encounter and relationship with the self, the other, and the world (Sultan, 2015). Thus, I–Thou relationships—that is, those engaged with presence and attunement—are central and essential to the very essence of being. The role of being in the present moment is vital to the functionality of any I–Thou interaction, as presence enhances authentic dialogue with and attunement to the other, free of the restraints of any egotistic vision of a predetermined end. In fact, Buber stressed that any attachment to a specified outcome in dialogue has the potential to transform the Thou into an It, as well as to divert relational engagement from honoring *what is* to *what should be* or *what could be* (Beisser, 1970; Smith, 1985; Yontef, 2005).

Within the context of heuristic research, an I–It approach places the primary researcher in a power role in which she may view co-researchers not as members of the research team or community but rather as objects or subjects whose presence can help the researcher attain her primary objective. In a sense, I–It engagement means that researchers can potentially dehumanize other members of their research team, as well as compromise their own authenticity, thereby jeopardizing inclusivity and equitability. Genuine I–Thou discourse, on the other hand, is a highly creative process that enables one to truly view events or experiences through the Thou perspective. "No purpose intervenes between I and You, no greed and no anticipation; and longing itself is changed as it plunges from the dream into appearance. Every means is an obstacle. Only where all means have disintegrated encounters occur" (Buber, 1923/1970, pp. 62–63). This creates the potential for fusing internal and external experience, for dissolving me-versus-you distinctions, and for both I and Thou to be transformed through our encounter. In this togetherness, the observer is also the observed (Krippner, 2015); that is, I–Thou actually begins to look more like I∞Thou. Then through our cocreated withness, we may cocreate social meanings of particular constructs and, thus, become integrated with them, as well as with one another. Within the context of research, all members of the research team are involved in benefiting the needs of the research study and in mutually benefiting one another within a cooperative and collaborative process. Thus, they are involved in a process of dialogical knowing, a togetherness within which new meaning is created between researcher and co-researcher (Polkinghorne, 1988), as well as between speaker and listener and reader and manuscript (Ricoeur, 1976).

Buber's (1923/1970) I–Thou philosophy, which engages self-searching and self-dialogic techniques and stresses intersubjectivity and betweenness (Buber, 1923/1970), is directly applicable to the heuristic approach, which honors all these experiences as necessary to the research process. In fact, Moustakas (1990) stated that the informal conversational interview, of three different basic interviewing approaches (all of which will be described in greater detail in Chapter 4), is the most consistent with the spirit of heuristic exploration. This is true as dialogue encourages expression and elucidation of the experience being explored. On the other hand, it is important to note that opening to the I–Thou (Buber, 1923/1970) (or I∞Thou) is done with the precaution of preserving a differentiated—though permeable—sense of self (Sultan, 2015). Thus, while there is a confluence of sorts, this confluence is maintained with the understanding that at some point I end and you begin, and vice versa. This is necessary to maintaining proper boundaries between members of the research team and to overall ethical research practices (more in Chapter 10), particularly in the case of heuristic inquiry, in which the topic of inquiry holds special personal meaning for all members of the research team.

Carl Rogers

Another key informant of both the relational and experiential dimensions of heuristic inquiry was American psychotherapist Carl Rogers, founder of the humanistic psychology movement and of person-centered psychotherapy. Rogers's (1961, 1980) work was influenced by the philosophical writings of Buber (1923/1970) on the nature of relationships, Maslow (1956, 1968) on the nature of the creative spirit and self-actualization (Polkinghorne, 2015), and Polanyi (1958, 1966, 1969) on the nature of tacit and personal knowing. Rogers (1980) was of the opinion that only when a realness in oneself encounters a realness in another can a true I–Thou encounter occur. From within the context of the person-centered therapy approach, Rogers (1980) suggested that the primary condition for a successful therapeutic experience is the relationship between therapist and client. Every therapist must possess three core characteristics:

- Congruence (genuineness or realness)
- Unconditional positive regard (acceptance of the other just as she is)
- Empathy (understanding the other from her point of view)

Rogers is one of the key figures associated with the idea of empathy in the field and practice of psychotherapy. However, as Rogers (1980) himself attested, his views and definitions of empathy evolved over time from being empirical to being experientially and subjectively based, and from being person-centered to being *we-centered* (Frankel & Sommerbeck, 2007). As a natural adjunct to this expansion of his philosophy, Rogers shifted his focus from an individual to a more universal approach (Pilisuk & Joy, 2015) to empathy and actualization, as evidenced through his global conflict transformation and peace work. The emphasis of Rogers's cross-cultural work was acknowledgment and openness (Arons & Richards, 2015), ongoing respectful discourse, and empathic understanding of the other. Rogers (1980) came to use the term *empathy* to describe the depth of one's presence within another's private world so as to clarify meanings within the awareness, but also below the awareness, of the other (Sultan, 2015). Rogers (1980) stated:

> An empathic way of being with another person has several facets. It means entering the private perceptual world of the other and becoming thoroughly at home in it. It involves being sensitive, moment by moment, to the changing felt meanings which flow in this other person, to the fear or rage or tenderness or confusion or whatever that he or she is experiencing. It means temporarily living in the other's life, moving about in it delicately without making judgments; it means sensing meanings of which he or she is scarcely aware, but not trying to uncover totally unconscious feelings, since this would be too threatening. It includes communicating your sensings of the person's world as you look with fresh and unfrightened eyes at elements of which he or she is fearful. It means frequently checking with the person as to the accuracy of your sensings, and being guided by the responses you receive. (p. 142)

Rogers added that, with this empathic engagement, a relationship transcends itself and becomes part of a greater whole. Rogers (1980) asserted this description of empathy was influenced by the concept of *experiencing* as formulated by Eugene Gendlin (1962), and especially the flow of the "felt meaning" (Rogers, 1980, p. 141) to which one can turn, again and again, to help the other carry the meaning further to "its full and uninhibited experiencing" (p. 141).

In the first chapter of his book *On Becoming a Person: A Therapist's View of Psychotherapy*, Rogers (1961) outlined a number of significant general pearls of wisdom he acquired by being in relationship with his psychotherapy clients and that address authentic relationships in general:

- It does not help to pretend one is something one is not—that is, to be fake.
- One is more effective when one can fully accept and be oneself.
- It holds enormous value to permit oneself to understand another person.
- It is enriching to open channels for others to communicate their perceptions and feelings.
- It is rewarding when one can accept another person as she is.
- One may feel less pressed to "fix" things when one remains open to the realities in the other and in oneself.
- The most personal experiences may also be the most general experiences.
- Experience is the highest authority.

As mentioned previously, later in his illustrious career, Rogers expanded these learnings and conditions and generalized them to all peoples and populations outside of clinical settings as a way of stating that we can all be better communicators, have more fulfilling relationships, and experience higher levels of communion and intimacy with other members of the human race by embracing some of these ways of being.

The characteristics suggested by Rogers are critical in tying together several threads of heuristic research, including the following. First, it is imperative to the success of any heuristic research endeavor for the researcher to be able to communicate effectively and relationally with all other members of the research team while creating space for difference. This is especially true if you will be using interviews as the primary source of data collection. Second, because you experience as much of an affinity for the topic of inquiry as any other member of the research team, a characteristic such as unconditional positive regard, or the ability to permit oneself to understand another and experience empathy, is helpful as you encounter other perspectives on a topic you hold extremely dear and about which you already possess strong opinions based on your personal experience with it. Moustakas (1990) provided a description of what this may look like:

> In heuristic interviewing, the data generated is dependent upon accurate, empathic listening; being open to oneself and to the co-researcher; being flexible and free to vary procedures to respond to what is required in the

flow of dialogue; and being skillful in creating a climate that encourages the co-researcher to respond comfortably, accurately, comprehensively, and honestly in elucidating the phenomenon. (p. 48)

Rogers began his research career as an experimental researcher (Krippner, 2015). However, he soon became aware of how some of the tenets of postpositivism seemed to clash with the subjectivist attitudes he often engaged as a humanistic psychologist. Rogers resolved this inner conflict by proposing a humanistic approach to research that integrated objective and subjective—experimental and experiential—ways of acquiring knowledge.

Abraham Maslow

Besides its distinctiveness as a relational research methodology, one of heuristic inquiry's many unique characteristics is its imaginative and creative nature. Other singular characteristics are heuristic inquiry's focus on process and content, its focus on the present moment, its nonlinear and fluid nature, and its humanistic spirit. While these features are in the domain of Rogers's (1961) work, they are predominantly in the province of Maslow (1966, 1968, 1971, 1976), an American psychologist who was influenced by existentialism and who influenced Rogers and helped create the humanistic psychology movement. Maslow is best known for formulating what is called Maslow's (1943) hierarchy of needs, a theory suggesting that all humans have similar needs ranging from the physiological (such as food, water, breathing, and sleep) to self-actualization (such as unconditional acceptance of self and others, spontaneity, creativity, and satisfaction). Maslow maintained that these needs "arrange themselves in hierarchies of prepotency" (p. 370). Thus, a typical method for representing Maslow's hierarchy of needs is a pyramid (see Figure 3.3).

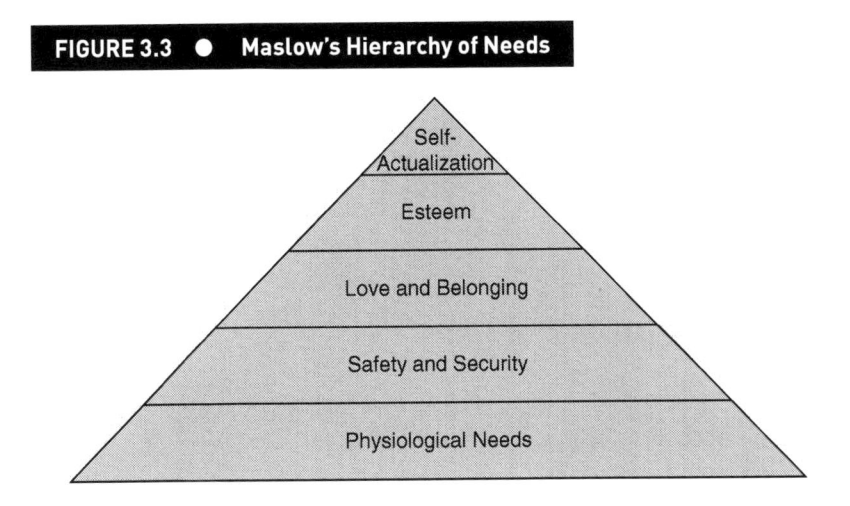

FIGURE 3.3 • Maslow's Hierarchy of Needs

- Self-Actualization
- Esteem
- Love and Belonging
- Safety and Security
- Physiological Needs

Maslow (1968) suggested that while most humans strive to fulfill the needs illustrated on this hierarchy, the processes by which such needs are attained and the relationships that are created within such processes are just as important as the attainment of the needs themselves. He argued that meaningful relationships are necessary to self-actualization, as only through connection with others and with the environment (Arons & Richards, 2015) is one able to open one's present-moment awareness to external reality, rather than remaining limited by and stagnating within internal experience, which in research may manifest as "navel-gazing." Additionally, Maslow suggested that, counter to the intuitive urge that such a hierarchy creates to view the human needs as following a sequential or linear progression, many of the needs may in fact coexist simultaneously. Alternately, humans may journey in a nonlinear fashion between various needs as they assess their present-moment experience in their effort to move toward self-actualization. Remember this symbol: ∞? And remember the labyrinth? So in what way is self-actualization even remotely related to heuristic inquiry?

Heuristic research demands a high tolerance for uncertainty and ambiguity, as well as non-attachment to specified outcomes. Such also are the defining traits of self-actualized individuals. Maslow (1976) described them as people who are "relatively unfrightened by the unknown, the mysterious, the puzzling, and often are positively attracted by it, i.e., selectively pick it out to puzzle over, to meditate on and to be absorbed with" (p. 88). He asserted that self-actualized people prefer not to linger with the familiar and, in their search for truth, are not attached to certainty or order. In fact, if called to do so, they are able to exist quite comfortably with chaos, doubt, and vagueness, all of which, adds Maslow, are desirable to science, art, and life in general. Additionally, self-actualized individuals have an acute ability to integrate what is happening within their internal landscape with whatever is going on in the outside world. This is facilitated by their high level of self-acceptance, which allows them to bravely perceive their outside world and to engage it holistically, facilitating their own wholeness and integration.

As mentioned earlier, relationship and collaboration are necessary to heuristic inquiry, especially as it attempts to balance subjectivity and objectivity. This balance is important so the researcher does not become self-absorbed. While heuristic inquiry may be conducted as self-research, a central idea of this approach is its ability to move from the very personal to the universal. Such also is the domain of Maslow's philosophy, which while it focuses on individual needs fulfillment also addresses widely universal patterns of human behavior.

Michael Polanyi

Douglass and Moustakas (1985) described heuristic research as "a unique, creative challenge aimed at revealing the intimate nature of reality and thus requiring methods that fit the particular investigation" (p. 42). One of the hard scientists most in touch with this idea and (in true humanistic fashion) with the need for humans to attain their highest potential was Michael Polanyi, a Hungarian–British chemist who challenged that the positivist approaches to research in which he was trained provide inaccurate knowledge and truth. Polanyi's largest contributions were not his scientific findings about physical science but rather his philosophical writings on the nature of tacit knowing (1966, 1969), an essential process of heuristic inquiry that Moustakas (1990) described as lingering "at the base of all heuristic discovery" (p. 20). Consider Polanyi's (1966) illustration of tacit knowing and the human process of developing knowledge:

> I shall reconsider human knowledge by starting from the fact that *we can know more than we can tell*. This fact seems obvious enough; but it is not easy to say exactly what it means. Take an example. We know a person's face, and can recognize it among a thousand, indeed a million. Yet we usually cannot tell how we recognize a face we know. So most of this knowledge cannot be put into words. (p. 4)

Thus, Polanyi described a human way of knowing that occurs beyond our ability to prove it or put it into words. This way of knowing occurs at a profoundly embodied and personal level that may not be measured or observed, and often prior to one's ability to conceptualize it. It occurs at the level of intuition, in the grip of cognitive ambiguity and the flow of embodied, contextual, experiential certainty. This level of knowledge is holistic in that, while the mind alone may be incapable of organizing its meaning into scientific chunks, its meaning is in fact held securely within the body∞mind∞spirit∞world continuum.

Serlin and Criswell (2015) suggested that the humanistic experience of tacit knowing shares some of the characteristics of intersubjectivity. Understanding intersubjectivity as a process that not only occurs between one person and another but also between one person and any entity within that person's environment sheds some light on the connections between tacit knowing, intersubjectivity, and the heuristic journey. Heuristic research is a series of processes that includes moments of meaning-making, understanding, and discovery that will forever transform and be meaningful to the researcher (Moustakas, 2015). This is also true for other members of the research team, all of whom have been involved in a process of discernment that has awakened feelings, thoughts, images, ideas, and sensations, all of which link directly to the emergence and/or discovery of new knowledge. Polanyi (1958) portrayed it thus:

> Having made a discovery, I shall never see the world again as before. My eyes have become different; I have made myself into a person seeing and thinking differently. I have crossed a gap, the heuristic gap, which lies between problem and discovery. (p. 143)

Eugene Gendlin

It is certainly not an exaggeration to state that heuristic inquiry was primarily inspired by a body psychotherapy modality and technique named **focusing**, developed by Gendlin (1981), a psychotherapist and philosopher, as well as by the ideas of Carl Rogers (1961, 1980, 1985), whose work significantly informed the field of psychotherapy because of its relational dimensions and with whom Gendlin worked. Thus, heuristic inquiry is dubbed an embodied and relational approach to qualitative research. Focusing is an inner-searching process (Heery, 2015) that stresses the inner **felt sense** experience that comprises what Gendlin (1981) referred to as "a body-sense of meaning" (p. 11) and what Westland (2015) described as residing within the domain of gut feelings and hunches. While the felt sense plays a significant role in a number of processes and phases of heuristic research, the impact of Gendlin's ideas does not end there. Gendlin proposed a philosophy that is fundamental to heuristic research—namely, that experience happens when a person and the world encounter one another (Polkinghorne, 2015) and that experiencing is essentially our interaction with life events and the bodily felt meanings these events have for us. According to Gendlin, experiencing is not a single event but rather an ongoing process that includes both thinking and feeling. In his book *Experiencing and the Creation of Meaning* (1962), Gendlin suggested that both conscious deliberation and language proceed directly from our bodily felt meanings. Gendlin described **felt meaning** as a "responsive interplay with the situated thickness" (Polkinghorne, 2015, p. 98) in which people live and used the sign ". . ." to refer to the experience of felt meaning as a way of emphasizing its ongoing, process-oriented nature. He expanded this philosophy to state that all knowledge of the self and the other transcends cognitive construction to include a bodily felt knowing informed by one's experiencing of interactions with oneself, with the other, and with the world. Thus, one's understanding of oneself, the other, or any situation or event emerges through one's embodied felt sense of the meaning of the interaction that occurs between one and the other. Each interaction acts as a vehicle for transformation and growth. These concepts are critical to several processes and phases of heuristic research, including indwelling, focusing, and explication, all of which will be explored in greater detail in Chapter 4.

Under the influence of Gendlin's ideas and practices highlighting the experiential dynamics of both being and knowing, one may view the interaction of the researcher (as informed by her own experiences) with members of the research team as a dimension of the intersubjective space within the researcher–research partner relationship, and the relationship itself as an existential or lived encounter of two phenomenal worlds (Moreira, 2012; Sultan, 2015). The intersubjective relationship created between the researcher and each of the co-researchers is also thus considered responsible for any transformation that occurs within either party. This transformation is magnified by the fact that each individual had the opportunity to gain knowledge and grow through his own felt sense rather than through any truth imposed by the other. Intersubjectivity and experiencing are, hence, pivotal facets of heuristic inquiry.

Maurice Merleau-Ponty

Whereas Buber (1923/1970) referred to the concept of intersubjectivity as *I–Thou,* Maurice Merleau-Ponty (1945/2013) referred to it as *intercorporeality.* Either way, intersubjectivity is the foundation for the realm of encounter and relationship with the self, the other, and the world. Regardless of the wording, all of the above-mentioned philosophers and theorists stressed the relational nature of being in the world and knowing. Likewise did Merleau-Ponty, a French philosopher whose work was inspired by the phenomenological movement and especially by the work of Edmund Husserl (1900/2001). Merleau-Ponty's philosophy was mainly a refutation of the dualist, rationalist philosophy separating body and mind extended by René Descartes.

The existential phenomenology (Churchill & Wertz, 2015) elaborated by Merleau-Ponty (1945/2013) locates and considers human beings within the context of their existence, both constituted with and inseparable from their lived world (Moreira, 2012; Sultan, 2015). Consequently, consciousness is not a measurable or intellectual phenomenon but a perceptual one (Moreira, 2012; Packer, 2011). Merleau-Ponty described perception as an elemental matrix for the everyday world, for science, and for philosophy. He argued that perception is a matter of perspective, is open, and is always transforming. As we move about in our world, objects emerge before us in new and different ways, and we encounter and engage with them in silent, reciprocal dialogue (Abram, 1996; Merleau-Ponty, 1945/2013; Sultan, 2015). Our understanding of our perceptual field is always constructed with reference to our perceiving body (Leder, 1990; Merleau-Ponty, 1945/2013). Thus, any truth gleaned through cognition necessarily depends on how the real is first experienced through perception; that is, first we perceive, and then we reflect on what we have perceived (Merleau-Ponty, 1945/2013; Packer, 2011; Sultan, 2015).

Merleau-Ponty's philosophy is established, in part, on the philosophy of Edmund Husserl (1900/2001), who founded phenomenology based on his acknowledgment of the subjective nature of experience. However, Husserl's phenomenology, as mentioned earlier, established distinctions between inner and outer experience, as well as between concrete and abstract concepts. Merleau-Ponty (1945/2013) rejected any assumptions of a disembodied or transcendental ego, dissolving distinctions between our perceived world and us (Sultan, 2015). His phenomenology viewed the body as the space within which consciousness and objectivity fuse into a horizon of full experience (Carman, 1999). From this perspective, the living body both holds and is held by experience as we become intertwined with the world that constitutes us. We are always in our world, creating it and in turn being created by it (Merleau-Ponty, 1945/2013; Moreira, 2012; Sultan, 2015). David Abram (1996), an American philosopher who has written extensively on the interweaving of ecology with phenomenology, observed that Merleau-Ponty rejected not only the body–mind duality but also other dualities such as subject–object, thought–feeling, and interior–exterior. Merleau-Ponty's philosophy is contemporary to 21st century thought and exploration in its ability to critique, surpass, and transcend the simplistic Cartesian view of human consciousness and the presupposition of absolute truths (Moreira, 2012; Sultan, 2015). Feminist philosopher Elizabeth Grosz (1994) used as a model the infinity symbol (∞) to represent the absence of distinction between dualities such as those rejected by Merleau-Ponty and to capture the interrelatedness of body and world (Sultan, 2015). (See Figure 3.4 for my rendition of the infinity symbol using charcoal on paper.) Once again, we find ourselves in the realm of nonlinear, fluid experience!

Merleau-Ponty (1945/2013) argued that everything we live or experience has multiple meanings but that we, as humans, tend to see reality from a single perspective rather than as a phenomenon in its entirety. Thus, as Polanyi (1966) also suggested, the truth of reality transcends our understanding of it. Merleau-Ponty's philosophy described a world of embodied meaning (Merleau-Ponty, 1945/2013; Morstyn, 2010). As he wrote:

> The body is the vehicle of being in the world and, for a living being, having a body means being united with a definite milieu, merging with certain projects, and being perpetually engaged therein. . . . I am conscious of the world by means of my body. (p. 84)

Hence, through the body, heuristic researchers may come into contact with their research partners.

Members of the research team will likely engage in "testing" the trustworthiness of the research relationship by studying their inner experience of each encounter within the research process. Within this context, all members of the research team have an opportunity to use their embodied, subjective experience of genuineness, empathy, insight, and trust to create meaning from within that embodied, intersubjective context. As Merleau-Ponty suggested,

FIGURE 3.4 ● The Infinity Symbol

our perspective shifts not as an intellectual act but when our experience shows us something meaningful and truthful. Each individual's perceptions are not independent of the other's but communicate within the same world.

This world, as Merleau-Ponty (1945/2013) described it, has no specific parameters or boundaries, as it is continually being re-created in the here and now through the interweaving of the many perspectives present. The idea of intercorporeality extended by Merleau-Ponty suggested that every individual inhabits and is inhabited by a multipersonal field (Diamond, 1996) and that intercorporeality bolsters our ability to engage with our environment and our world. This is generated first through intersubjectivity (Merleau-Ponty, 1945/2013; Morstyn, 2010), which includes various forms of empathy, in which the self extends beyond its own boundaries (Csordas, 2008; Rolef Ben-Shahar, 2010), sensing into the shared body that is the bond between the self and the other (Rolef Ben-Shahar, 2011) in a "mutual identification where self-understanding and Other-understanding is intertwined" (Finlay, 2005, p. 290).

Conducting research from this paradigm emphasizes the inter- and intrapersonal life of researcher and research partner, with each relationship created within the research process having the potential to evolve into an existential encounter (Moreira, 2012; Sultan, 2015). This view of the research relationship honors the living experience of every member of the research team, each of whom collaborates in the cocreation of new meanings from within the embodied space formed from two phenomenal worlds, rendering the responsibility of transformation through the process of research to the research relationship. Building on the philosophy of Merleau-Ponty, Abram (1996) suggested that meaning is created within the sensory world, "in the heat of meeting, encounter, participation" (p. 75).

Perception is viewed as the primary source of knowledge in heuristic inquiry. Heuristic researchers aim to understand the world of another as it is experienced by her. As we observe another and reflect, memory relevant to the phenomenon being observed reawakens feelings and images, bringing past meanings into the present (Moustakas, 1994). Thus, the heuristic process embraces an attitude of curiosity, wonder, and empathy as new perception inspires fresh perspectives, giving birth to knowledge that fuses past, present, and future, and expanding and deepening both meanings and essences (Moustakas, 1994; Sultan, 2015). As Merleau-Ponty (1945/2013) stated:

> The entire universe of science is constructed upon the lived world, and if we wish to think science rigorously, to appreciate precisely its sense and its scope, we must first awaken that experience of the world of which science is the second-order expression. Science neither has nor ever will have the same ontological sense as the perceived world for the simple reason that science is a determination or an explanation of that world. (p. xxii)

In his final text, *The Visible and the Invisible,* Merleau-Ponty (1964/1968) proposed the concept of perception as intuition.

Closing Reflections

Moustakas (1990) designed heuristic inquiry as an empirical, qualitative, social constructivist research methodology aimed at unraveling the essential nature of profoundly human experiences. Such, too, was the thinking of some of Moustakas's predecessors, including Maslow, Rogers, and Merleau-Ponty (Aanstoos, 2015; Taylor & Martin, 2015; Wertz, 2015). Thus, heuristic research occurs at the intersection of scientific methods with human interaction and relationship. Heuristic inquiry "offers a disciplined pursuit of essential meanings connected with everyday experience" (Douglass & Moustakas, 1985, p. 39). This creative fusion of science with the art of being human is what guides the direction of the research, informing every stage of the journey. Consequently, unlocking the essential nature of a human experience happens at the junction of subjective and objective experience. As Heron and Reason (1997) stated, "To experience anything is to participate in it, and to participate is both to mould and to encounter; hence, experiential reality is always subjective-objective" (p. 276). Rather than relying on predetermined hypotheses, the heuristic research team enters the labyrinth of the research journey with the intention of fully experiencing whatever the journey has to offer them, from there to gather information with which to channel the direction of the research and, eventually, to be transformed through the process of inquiry and the relationships formed throughout it. Moustakas (1990) suggested that the researcher must be "alert to signs or expressions of the phenomenon, willing to enter a moment of the experience timelessly and live the moment fully" (p. 44) to attain the knowledge being sought. In that sense, rather than being guided by a hypothesis that steers the research in one of two absolute directions, the researcher dives fully and fearlessly into an open search for the essence and meaning of the phenomenon of inquiry. See Exercise 3.2 to explore alternative dimensions of knowing and/or being.

Finally, Moustakas (1981) stated that in such a search, what is needed is discipline and commitment, a view of science as a process versus an outcome, and an understanding of knowledge as emerging from awareness rather than proof. He added that scientific inquiry is not an effort to measure or attain certainty but is, instead, a search for meaning. Do you dare to temporarily set aside the notion of certainty in your search for meaning?

EXERCISE 3.2
EXPLORING OTHER WAYS OF BEING AND OF KNOWING

You will need your journal and a writing tool.

- Take a deep, conscious breath. Exhale slowly and fully. Repeat this. Take your time.
- Find your center of gravity and connect with it. Take another deep, conscious breath.
- Ask yourself the following questions: *How do I view the nature of being/reality? What is my experience of being/reality? How do I define being/reality? How do I interact with myself, with others, and with the world?* Allow any thoughts, feelings, and body sensations to emerge as you sit with these questions. Write or doodle your experience. Connect with what is on your page. Ask yourself: *What other ways of being might I be censoring at the moment?* Open to receive new answers from yourself.
- Now ask yourself the following questions: *How do I believe that knowledge is acquired? How do I go about acquiring knowledge? How do I define knowledge and what constitutes it? How do I relate to and interact with what I know?* Again, allow any thoughts, feelings, and body sensations to be present, and bring to them your full awareness. Write or doodle your experience.
- Finally, explore any other forms of expression you might use to describe your experience of being and of knowing. Examples include collaging, dance/body movement, singing, and poetry. Immerse yourself fully within the flow of your experience. Do not censor yourself. What is it like to experience self-expression that is not controlled or predetermined? What is it like to encounter yourself and your experience fully and to be with it? What is it like to surrender to what is real?

As a collective exploration, you may expand this exercise to include others.

4

Heuristic Processes and Phases

You remember the old Roadrunner cartoons, where the coyote would run off a cliff and keep going, until he looked down and happened to notice that he was running on nothing more than air? I always used to wonder what would have happened if he'd never looked down. Would the air have stayed solid under his feet until he reached the other side? I think we're all like that. We start heading out across this canyon, looking straight ahead at the thing that matters, but something, some fear or insecurity, makes us look down. And we see we're walking on air, and we panic, and turn around and scramble like hell to get back to solid ground. And if we just wouldn't look down, we could make it to the other side. The place where things matter.

~ **Jonathan Tropper**

> **Questions for Reflection**
>
> 1. How do you envision initiating a heuristic study?
> 2. What are some good practices for navigating heuristic research?
> 3. How will you maintain a heuristic attitude over the course of the research journey?

Every qualitative researcher—in fact, every researcher—is on a mission to reach a final destination. For many researchers, the final destination is "the place where things matter." For heuristic researchers, our final destination is very much informed by our research question, as well as by our personal experience of the phenomenon of inquiry. The heuristic researcher has an intimate knowledge of the topic being explored, as well as a systematic research methodology that allows full engagement with the research question in both linear and nonlinear fashion. On the other hand, these tools must not interfere with the researcher's willingness to open to whatever may emerge, nor do they protect him from the reality of having to constantly negotiate absences and vacuums. Additionally, a heuristic researcher's final destination is often a segue into a new beginning. So as a novice heuristic researcher, what if you were to embrace this process of negotiating the unknown from a place of freedom instead of from a place of fear?

Imagine this: You have recently endured the unfortunate sudden loss of a loved one. Following the initial shock of the loss, you are plagued by questions, the most pertinent of which is, *What is this?* From a heuristic perspective, this question may be phrased as, *What is the essential nature of this experience that I am going through?* You have sat with this question unfalteringly and have explored the many facets of what it means to be enduring sudden loss through oscillating episodes of curiosity, intimacy, distance, indecision, disinclination, skepticism, aversion, and renewed curiosity. Thus, you have an idea of the essential nature of suffering sudden loss, however, only from your personal perspective. At this point, your only clear tangibles are your personal knowledge of the topic of inquiry and the question that inspired exploration of this knowledge in the first place. On the other hand, you are aware that, due to the relatively universal nature of human suffering and loss, you are not alone with your experience; others either have endured it before or are enduring it now. They may even be grappling with the same or similar questions. You decide that you would like to expand your knowledge base of what it means to suffer sudden loss by exploring the experience of that phenomenon among others who have shared it. Where do you go from here?

In this chapter, I provide you a step-by-step description of the seven processes and six phases of heuristic inquiry. I do this because, despite the fluid nature of heuristic inquiry, every research project must be guided by some structure. Without a specific methodology for conducting our research, we are flying by the seat of our pants! Nevertheless, while the description is highly structured to facilitate understanding of the heuristic methodology and mitigate some of the uncertainty that may come with running off of the proverbial cliff, it is important that you not constrain yourself within a predetermined linear path. Heuristic inquiry is unique in its high tolerance for the uncertain; it is, after all, a creative research approach that honors the power of imagination while challenging the very concept of absolute certainty. Creating room for flexibility within your heuristic study allows you to navigate freely among the phases and processes. You can then proceed with an attitude of conducting research "on behalf of the phenomenon" (Dahlberg, Dahlberg, & Nyström, 2008, p. 98) while trusting in the secure foundation of the heuristic design. In that sense, your research journey can look like this:

rather than like this:

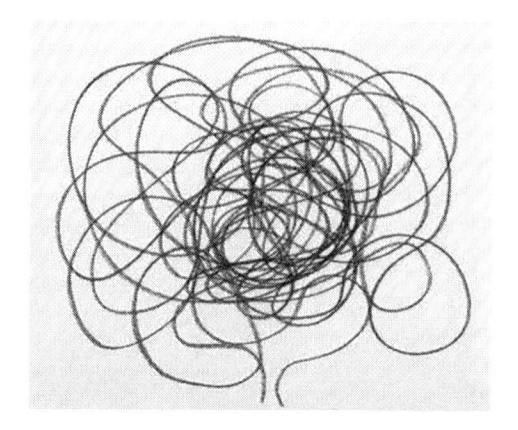

The heuristic processes and phases are designed to function mutually (∞); they do not operate independently of one another. Thus, you may experiment with some degree of chaos in that you may engage the following stages in whichever order makes the most sense to you, determining your direction based on the needs of your research while not straying from the actual processes and phases of heuristic inquiry. I liken this to my process of assigning papers to my graduate counseling students. In my instructions, I try to provide as much structure as possible to facilitate their understanding of my expectations for the assignment. This includes bullet points outlining various topics I expect students to address. Almost inevitably, a number of students ask if I want them to address the points in the order in which I listed them. My response is: "Not necessarily. Please address those points in whichever order they make the most sense to you, so long as you address every point." This often elicits anxiety and even cynicism. I assure students that I mean what I am saying. Those students who make the decision to go out on a limb and be inventive often produce the most creative, visionary, and genuine product. My experience with heuristic inquiry is quite similar: If you jump off the cliff and place your trust in the reliable foundation provided by the heuristic processes and phases without looking down and terrifying yourself to bits, you are almost guaranteed to make it safely to the other side. Ready?

The Seven Processes of Heuristic Inquiry

Heuristic research invites the researcher to comprehend the topic of inquiry more deeply by entering the research question, becoming one with it, and living it (Moustakas, 1990). The researcher arrives at this deep understanding of the phenomenon being explored by using the following seven processes: identifying with the focus of inquiry, self-dialogue, tacit knowing, intuition, indwelling, focusing, and the internal frame of reference. These seven processes may be used during any of the six phases of the heuristic research journey, depending on the needs of your study.

Identifying With the Focus of Inquiry

The focus of inquiry in heuristic research is what many other research approaches identify as the research topic, question, or problem. The focus of inquiry in a heuristic study is unique in that it is necessarily an autobiographical experience (Moustakas, 1990) for all members of the research team, including the primary researcher. Identifying with the focus of inquiry is, thus, about immersing yourself, in existential fashion, in the highly personal experience you are exploring to understand how you and others are orienting to and interacting with it. This may involve exploring questions such as the following:

- What do I know about this topic? How do I know what I know? What is my kinesthetic, cognitive, emotional, spiritual, and relational experience of this phenomenon?

- What might others know about the topic? How have they acquired their knowledge of it?

- What sources might I tap for further information (e.g., literature [professional or otherwise], individuals, groups, documents/artifacts)?

- Should I seek any of this information before I begin data collection, or should I include all processes of inquiry in my formal data collection procedure?

- What is my primary question about this phenomenon, and what are some best practices for finding the answers that will, eventually, constitute my raw data? Conducting interviews? Facilitating focus groups? Engaging in observation? Exploring the content of artifacts? Practicing reflection and reflexivity? Other ways?

- How might I go about interfacing multiple strategies of data collection to invite various perspectives and maximize my potential sources of knowledge and meaning?

Identifying with the focus of inquiry could also involve engaging in active perspective taking that may narrow down central research questions or help you gain a deeper understanding of how others are interacting with the topic. Moustakas (1990) cited Salk (1983), who prescribed taking an inverted perspective of an experience so as to fully understand it. As a heuristic researcher, your topic of inquiry lives within you, sometimes so deeply you may take for granted that you understand its essential nature and may therefore not probe for further understanding of it. However, remember that we are human beings with values, biases, beliefs, and attitudes, all of which color our perception and understanding of any phenomenon. So how do you go about acquiring a deeper understanding of your topic of inquiry that transcends your personal experience of it? You embody the phenomenon you are exploring! Let us build on the topic of suffering human loss as we explore the process of taking an inverted perspective.

Again you are caught in the midst of indescribable suffering following the loss of a loved one. Your suffering lives so deeply within you, you feel as though it has become a part of you. In many ways, it has. On some level, though, you recognize that this suffering is also its own entity. A necessary approach to knowing and understanding this entity more deeply is to explore it from its own perspective. To do this, you will need to imagine yourself as the very experience of suffering. You might consider role-playing suffering and exploring how suffering senses, thinks, feels, and behaves. One process that can facilitate this is the empty chair experiment. Empty chair is a gestalt therapy technique that invites you to greater understanding of an experience not by *thinking about* it or by *talking about* it but by *becoming* it. Let's try it (see Exercise 4.1)!

EXERCISE 4.1
AN EMPTY CHAIR EXPERIMENT TO FACILITATE IDENTIFYING WITH THE FOCUS OF INQUIRY

For this exercise, identify a phenomenon you have personally experienced that is highly meaningful to you and about which you wish to acquire a deeper understanding. For the purposes of demonstrating, I will use the example of suffering sudden loss.

- Place two chairs face-to-face (see Figure 4.1). Sit in one chair.
- Inhale deeply and exhale fully. Imagine the experience of *suffering sudden loss* sitting in the empty chair. If it is difficult to imagine such an amorphous experience sitting before you, it may help to give it a color and shape (e.g., black triangle), assign it a symbol (e.g., a claw), and/or give it a name (e.g., Suffering).
- See Suffering sitting in the chair facing you. Do not rush this process. Give yourself time to truly connect with being in the presence of Suffering in the here and now.
- Open yourself up to sense, perceive, feel, and think about what it is like to be with Suffering.
- Communicate to Suffering anything you need to say. Ask Suffering any questions you have. Share your perceptions, feelings, and thoughts. Suffering is listening!

FIGURE 4.1 ● **Chair Setup for Empty Chair Experiment**

(Continued)

(Continued)
- Do this until no further questions, thoughts, feelings, or the like are emerging.
- Stand up, take one deep breath, and as you exhale, shake yourself as though you are shaking yourself free, temporarily, of the experience of being you.
- Now sit in the other chair. Inhale, exhale fully, and open yourself up to sensing, perceiving, feeling, and thinking as though you were Suffering itself. Become Suffering!
- Communicate from this place with the person facing you (you!). Describe who and what you are. Do whatever it is that Suffering does, and be unequivocal about it. Be Suffering, abundantly and absolutely!
- Do this until no further questions, thoughts, feelings, or the like are emerging.
- Switch chairs, back and forth, until you attain a sense of integration or closure.
- It might add a new dimension of perspective taking to also try this empty chair exercise outdoors or in an altogether different location or with a supportive group of witnesses.

Processing the Exercise
- What was it like for you to *be* both yourself and Suffering?
- What new knowledge or understanding emerged for you about Suffering?
- What did you learn about yourself through the lens of Suffering?
- What else did you learn about both you and Suffering when you took the exercise to a different setting or did it with a group of supportive people as witnesses?
- How can you use this new collective information to focus your primary research question and/or other parts of your study?

Perspective taking can also take the form of observing an entity or taking a photo of it from different angles. Additionally, it can involve listening to an audio experience both with and without earphones or on different types of speakers.

Taking an inverted perspective challenges the somewhat passive and static nature of observing and exploring the phenomenon from a single viewpoint (yours alone or by engaging a single dimension of experience), allowing you to embody the phenomenon, thereby bringing it into the immediacy of dynamic here-and-now reality while remaining open to shifting perceptions. What is truly beneficial about using a perspective-taking experiment such as the empty chair is that it helps you connect with various facets of a single experience while engaging multiple dimensions of access, such as sensation, perception, affect, and cognition. Therefore, you no longer only think or feel *about* your topic of inquiry. You actively live it!

Self-Dialogue

As you may glean from its name, self-dialogue is all about communicating with yourself—and with your phenomenon—about your phenomenon. You may be asking, *Didn't we already do this in the previous process, identifying with the focus of inquiry?* Yes! Do you see where I'm coming from about the diffuse, nonsequential nature of heuristic inquiry?

Self-dialogue is about oscillating from concept to experience and back; from part to whole and back; from individual to general (or universal) and back (Moustakas, 1990; Sultan, 2015). This is a highly reflective and ongoing process as you engage and reengage your perceptual, emotional, cognitive, and sensory experience of all facets of the phenomenon. You do this with an attitude of wonder (Wertz, 2005), curiosity, attunement, trust, and receptivity to whatever might emerge, honoring the exploratory, serendipitous, and discovery-oriented spirit (Stebbins, 2008) of this heuristic process. While I mentioned the empty chair technique as a method of identifying with the focus of inquiry, it can also be used as a self-dialoguing tool. Additionally, you may choose to self-dialogue by simply engaging in discourse with your mind, with your body, or with your emotions. Talking to yourself aloud is especially helpful, as it facilitates awareness; sometimes we must hear what we are thinking to connect with it!

Self-dialoguing may also be done by way of a journal. Journals are very popular record-keeping devices that allow us to document such experiences as daily thoughts, dreams, travel memoirs, and future plans and aspirations. In heuristic inquiry, journals are necessary tools for depicting self-dialogue, engaging in self-reflection, and documenting other processes and phases. Journal excerpts are considered artifacts in heuristic research—that is, part and parcel of the raw data. When I mention journals, I do not mean only written journals. Art journals may also be used to document self-dialogue and other heuristic processes and phases, underscoring the imaginative facets (Maslow, 1976) of this unique research methodology. Art journaling is a creative way of documenting experience using words and illustrations. Essentially, a written journal becomes an art journal once drawings or illustrations are added. Box 4.1 includes a sample of self-dialogue excerpted from a written journal I kept for my embodiment study (Sultan, 2015). Figure 4.2 is a photo of a page from one of my art journals.

One core purpose of self-dialoguing is to attain a holistic understanding of the phenomenon being explored through self-exploration and self-disclosure. This is also one of the key objectives of identifying with the focus of inquiry.

BOX 4.1
EXAMPLE OF SELF-DIALOGUE IN A WRITTEN JOURNAL

This excerpt from a written journal depicts my process of dialoguing with myself about my dissonance with the phrase *lived experience* as I explored the essential nature of embodiment and my *living experience* of it.

N1: Something is not quite right. The word: *lived*. The phrase: *lived experience*.

N2: What about it isn't right for you?

N1: *Lived experience.* I say it out loud so I can feel it in my body, on my tongue. I say it so I can hear the sound of it as it rings inside my ears and falls over my eyes and shoulders. I say it with the hope of making some sort of meaning of it. But, meaning doesn't flow! How is embodiment—how is anything at all—a *lived experience* if I am actively *living* it?

N2: Say *lived experience* again. Say it louder.

N1: *LIVED EXPERIENCE.*

N2: Louder!

FIGURE 4.2 • Example of Self-Dialogue in an Art Journal

> **N1:** *LIVED EXPERIENCE!!!* Something about it feels stagnant. Stuck. To say that experience is *lived* is an oxymoron. Experience is always happening in the present. Even the past is *living* through the filter of the present.
>
> **N2:** *Living* what?
>
> **N1:** *Living experience?*
>
> **N2:** Is that a question, or a declaration?
>
> **N1:** It's a declaration masked within a question. It's a need to bring the past into the present. It's a need to make a change. Can we not move from *lived* to *living*?

Moustakas (1990) stated that self-dialogue brings us face-to-face with ourselves. Douglass and Moustakas (1985) highlighted the value of the self-disclosure that takes place through tools such as journaling: "At the heart of heuristics lies an emphasis on disclosing the self as a way of facilitating disclosure from others—a response to the tacit dimension within oneself sparks a similar call from others" (p. 50). As we connect with the essence of our experience and disclose it, we enhance our ability to attune to others empathically as we invite them to disclose, in the intimacy of I–Thou intersubjectivity (Buber, 1923/1970; Rogers, 1961), their experience. This summons the relational, authentic, and emancipatory dimensions of heuristic inquiry, enhancing our sensitivity to issues of inequity, oppression, power, and other systemic barriers (more on this in Chapter 7) and offering a more equitable foundation for the cocreation of new knowledge and authentic meaning. From this perspective, we are able to tap into both the vertical (personal) and horizontal (mutual) dimensions of experience.

Tacit Knowing

Tacit knowing serves as the very foundation for all heuristic discovery (Moustakas, 1990). It involves a revelatory process of meaning-making about the research question or topic of inquiry that allows for an implicit understanding of it and of the relationships between its various dimensions (Moustakas, 1990; Polanyi, 1969; Sultan, 2015). Here we are working with the realm of the *highly subliminally known,* or the *unknown known,* dimensions of experience. In essence, we are working with personal knowledge of phenomena we understand deeply (based on a variety of past experiences) without necessarily being consciously aware of the particular experiences that have constituted that knowledge or understanding. Because we have no direct sources from which to draw information about these phenomena, they are tacit, implicit. Yet we do not question our knowledge or understanding of them. We just know and trust that we understand them! Additionally, we may not have appropriate language to describe such phenomena. In that sense, these experiences are preverbal; that is, they are more likely to be understood by exploring body sensations (Westland, 2015) than they are to be understood by exploring thought. That is because many of these experiences were encoded kinesthetically before the mind was able to decipher a meaning for them using language. A concept that is closely linked to tacit knowing is **embodied knowing**, which highlights sensory experience (Ellingson, 2008) as a source of information. Embodied knowing views the researcher's body as an epistemological tool that has been shaped by its own living experience and that learns by immersing itself within the continua of certainty∞uncertainty, order∞disorder, objectivity∞subjectivity, and so on using the five senses.

To illustrate the nature of tacit knowing, I often use the example of recognizing a human being (as distinguished from other living beings). In this process of recognition, we may identify a face (or some part of it), an arm, a hand, a leg, or the like. We may also associate the sound emanating from that being as human, or we might use other sensory information such as smell, shape, color, texture, or size to assign it human characteristics. Additionally, we may use information from the environment to fill in some of the remaining gaps. We then combine all this partial information to conclude that what we are interacting with is, in fact, a human. Thus, we draw the conclusion (before ever seeing the rest of that person's being) that the flesh-toned hand extending to us for a welcoming handshake is part of a gestalt known to us as a human being.

Tacit knowing is a dynamic understanding of a phenomenon informed by both past and present experience of that phenomenon, with some degree of intentionality about future transformation. In the example of the hand, I might use my recognition of the human hand to make a decision about whether or not to engage with the handshake or to decide if maybe I need more information, for example, by looking for a face to confirm the humanness of the hand and to create some closure around my conclusion. Tacit knowing is essentially a process, rather than a static feature, that allows us to implicitly evaluate experience as new evidence presents itself, engaging in a dance between vagueness and sharpness of understanding (Polanyi, 1966) and between evaluation and intention for change. Thus, the wholeness—or gestalt—of a phenomenon emerges from deep understanding of its individual parts (Moustakas, 1990), with the whole being greater than the sum of its parts. Polanyi (1966) stated:

> Since we have no explicit knowledge of these unknown things, there can also be no explicit justification of a scientific truth. But as we can know a problem and feel sure that it is pointing to something hidden behind it, we can be aware also of the hidden implications of a scientific discovery, and feel confident that they will prove right. We feel sure of this, because in contemplating the discovery we are looking at it not only in itself but, more significantly, as a clue to a reality of which it is a manifestation. (pp. 23–24)

Moustakas (1990) added that curtailing tacit knowing in research restricts possibilities for knowledge. Heuristic and many other qualitative researchers use their personal experience (knowingly or unknowingly) to facilitate decision making with regard to selecting a topic of inquiry, identifying a research question, and collecting and interacting with the data. Thus, limiting tacit knowing restricts our ability to view things from different lenses and angles. Human experience is multidimensional and multifaceted; we are not independent objects living in an objective world. We are situated in a very intrinsic way within the perceptual, intersubjective, interpersonal world surrounding us, and it is likewise situated intrinsically within us (Merleau-Ponty, 1945/2013). Thus, tacit knowing is necessary to make sense of experiences whose complexity transcends what the objective domain can accommodate (Donmoyer, 2008). There must be room for both the explicit and the implicit in scientific inquiry, especially that inquiry which is concerned with human experience. Polanyi (1969) made this clear in his assertion that even explicit knowledge is, in the first place, tacitly understood and applied and that all knowledge is, therefore, either tacit or based in tacit knowledge. An interesting declaration from a chemist, wouldn't you say? So then, by which means can we link explicit with implicit understanding? I address this question in the next section, on intuition.

Intuition

Intuition is, as Moustakas (1990) described it, "the bridge between the explicit and the tacit" (p. 23) and "the realm of the between" (p. 23). Logic and reasoning are somewhat superfluous in the intuitive process. Both perception and observation provide the clues used to sense and then infer experience, honoring the experiential and embodied (Merleau-Ponty, 1945/2013; Sultan, 2015) dimensions of heuristic inquiry. While with tacit knowing we are often not using clear tangibles to understand a phenomenon, with intuition, there are clues that undergird our understanding. We use the clues we access through subjective (Douglass & Moustakas, 1985) and objective experience, observation, and perception to facilitate the formation of wholes, or gestalts, all of which emphasizes the existential-humanistic dimension of heuristic inquiry. The very act of integrating experience relies on the use of intuition, which connects us with both inner and outer experience in the here and now. Intuitive experience also guides the heuristic researcher's encounter with recurring patterns and themes, as well as the creation of new knowledge and meaning. But how does intuition actually work?

Intuition is that knowledge that allows me, for example, to make a decision with regard to whether or not to remain in a setting within which I am questioning my safety. While I may not have a clear recollection of being in a similar setting and experiencing danger, something within me *senses*, with a high degree of unequivocal certainty, that I am unsafe. Now let's play that forward using a couple of different courses of action and their potential consequences:

- I *trust* my intuition that this setting is unsafe, but I use that sense to explore my surroundings to gain more information. Once I have acquired that information (e.g., the place is well lit, there are no suspicious-looking people), I use it to make a decision to *stay*. Nothing harmful happens to me. I now have this experience to enhance earlier experiences that informed my understanding of the dangerousness of this location and to possibly inform future experiences.

- I *trust* my intuition that this setting is unsafe and I use that sense to explore my surroundings for more information. Once I have acquired that information (e.g., the place is dark, some people seem to be lurking about with no purpose), I use it to make a decision to *immediately leave,* without further exploration. Nothing harmful happens to me. I now have this new experience to add to my previously existing knowledge.

Of course, a number of other courses of action and their consequences are conceivable, such as questioning my sense, followed by further exploration or not, followed by leaving or staying, followed by eliciting harm or not, in each of these situations. The idea is to use my intuition (through active engagement of my tacit knowing [implicit experience], as well as my observation and judgment [explicit experience]) to determine my next move. As with all processes of heuristic inquiry, within any seeming dichotomy, we are actually working with the nonlinear flow of experience. In the case of intuition, we are working with the flow of implicit∞explicit experience.

Indwelling

This process directs your gaze inward (Moustakas, 1990) as you seek deeper understanding of a particular facet of human experience with the aim of comprehending it holistically. Indwelling involves tapping into the tacit and intuitive as well as the explicit dimensions of an experience by exploring every nuance of it. This is a highly reflexive and particular process that requires patience as you return to the phenomenon repeatedly to unravel its essential qualities. Indwelling is also a very embodied process in that it allows us to attend to the external facets of experience *through* the body (Polanyi, 1969). The body becomes the vehicle through which we relate to the subject of our observation. Thus, what or who we are observing is not an external object but a felt and experienced entity that is as much a part of our world as we are a part of hers/his/its. Let's return to the topic of suffering sudden loss to better understand how indwelling works.

I am guessing most of us don't necessarily look forward to interacting with or reliving an experience of suffering sudden loss. Nevertheless, to most accurately understand its essential nature, you must return to it again and again and identify

- how it manifests in your life (e.g., social distance or isolation, crying spells, feelings of loneliness, loss of meaning or purpose, attempts at social reengagement);
- within which social settings it emerges most powerfully (e.g., when you are at work, when you are with friends, when you are preparing for bed);
- how its expression is informed by social and cultural norms (e.g., how people are expected by society at large to behave when they and/ or others experience loss, cultural rituals/practices surrounding loss/ grieving); and
- how you interact with it on a cognitive, emotional, sensory∞kinesthetic, perceptual, spiritual, and social∞relational level (e.g., how you are thinking, feeling, sensing, perceiving, experiencing higher meaning and relating with others and yourself as you are in the throes of your suffering).

Going through this process repeatedly and tenaciously is critical, as it will eventually yield new knowledge to add to what you already know or understand of suffering, which may facilitate for you a process of transformation or growth. Again, we are doing the internal∞external, subjective∞objective dance as we turn inward to connect with how we live our phenomenon and then redirect our focus to outward modes to explicate the experience using words, the expressive arts, or other forms of description.

Focusing

As a process of heuristic inquiry, focusing has its roots in a body psychotherapy modality and a therapeutic technique initiated by Gendlin (1981) and carrying the same name. Within heuristic research, focusing invites the researcher to clear an inner space wherein thoughts and feelings needed to clarify a question or its constituents or to make contact with and illuminate core themes may arise (Moustakas, 1990). Moustakas described focusing as an act of pausing and clearing that allows facets of the experience the researcher may have missed (likely due to the presence of mental or emotional clutter) to come into awareness. Focusing allows heuristic researchers to separate the clutter that might be blurring their understanding, opening a space for hidden elements of an experience to surface (Moustakas, 1990). Oftentimes, researchers are too engrossed in the details of their study to devote time to sustained attention to their topic of inquiry. Much of the focus of a traditional researcher is directed toward managing the research process in such a manner that allows for a successful outcome. Due to the process-oriented and personal nature of heuristic inquiry, you must devote time to sitting with the questions and allowing experiences that are out of direct awareness to emerge. Focusing provides an avenue by which you can declutter your inner world and connect with multiple meanings of the topic of inquiry through conscious attunement using your senses, feelings, and thoughts. Thus, and maybe paradoxically, rather than acting as a challenge to time schedules, focusing may actually facilitate movement through the research process.

Focusing is an open-ended process that requires patience and persistence as you engage with various unknowns. It allows you to transcend the confines of traditional research designs that require the use of tangible variables or ideas and instead interact with experiences that exist within the realm of the ambiguous. I put focusing to extensive use during my embodiment study, especially as I directed my attention to identifying the themes held within the raw data. While returning repeatedly to the verbatim transcripts served as a means for verifying my findings, identifying each of the actual themes occurred through a series of focusing exercises through which I was able to clear a space to dwell with my research partners' narratives. Focusing was also helpful following the identification of all the themes as I sat with each theme and allowed its multiple layers of meaning to emerge.

Focusing invites active use of the felt sense to create and maintain openness and acceptance in the research process, with the idea that whatever develops holds the potential to inspire transformation within any member of the research team. Gendlin (1981) developed a six-step process for the focusing technique. Several adaptations of focusing have been put forth. Please see Exercise 4.2 for my adaptation.

The Internal Frame of Reference

The above-mentioned processes cannot take place successfully without researchers comprehending their experience deeply (Moustakas, 1990). The internal frame of reference serves as a catalyst for the various processes of heuristic inquiry as researchers return, again and again, to seek within themselves a deeper understanding of their perceptions, feelings, thoughts, decisions, and actions. "I must stay in touch with the unnumerable perceptions and awarenesses that are purely my own, without the interferences of restrictions or judgments, with total disregard for conformity or congruence" (Douglass & Moustakas, 1985, p. 47).

With this, I emphasize the importance of maintaining a balance between your attunement to your personal experience as the researcher and to the empathy, trust, and intersubjective experience unfolding between you and your co-researchers. What I am talking about here is the whole idea of I–Thou, though not quite that definitively, as I–Thou comes to look more like I∞Thou. This enhances the integrity of your study, as too much focus on your inner experience can undermine other processes and phases of the research and distract you from the *we-oriented* nature of this methodology. Recall that heuristic research is not necessarily self-research and is far more integrated when it

EXERCISE 4.2
SIX-STEP FOCUSING EXERCISE TO CLEAR AN INNER SPACE

This exercise provides a six-step sequential process; learning a multistep process is often best done sequentially. However, as you do the exercise more regularly and as you gain higher mastery of it, you may go back and forth between and among the steps.

Clearing a Space

- Become silent and draw your attention inward to a particular spot in your body (e.g., your stomach, your core) that might be feeling cluttered.
- Breathe deeply, slowly, and fully, and imagine that as you exhale you are clearing that part of your body of its "hoard."

Exploring the Felt Sense

- Identify a situation or question that has been at the center of your focus lately (this can be your research question or topic of inquiry).
- Set any thoughts about that situation to the side (you might imagine yourself standing back or stepping away from the thoughts).
- Explore your general sense of that situation or question. As you do this, focus on your overall experience of the situation rather than on a particular aspect of it.
- Allow yourself to connect with the vagueness of the situation.

Finding a Handle

- Now draw your attention to any words, phrases, symbols, or images that emerge from your felt sense of the situation.
- Be patient as you gently calm your mind so other dimensions of your experience (e.g., emotional, sensory) may also inform this process.

Resonating With the Flow of Felt Sense∞Handle

- Go back and forth between your felt sense and your handle (word, image, etc.).
- Ask yourself, *Do my felt sense and my handle "fit" together?*
- Allow your felt sense and/or your handle to shift if necessary; resonating is all about securing a goodness of fit between the felt sense and the handle.

Asking Questions

- Ask, *What is it about this situation or problem that is so intriguing, perplexing, etc.? What needs to happen for a shift to take place?*

(Continued)

(Continued)

- Sit with these questions patiently, asking them over and over.
- Experiment with exploring the questions from different angles. Allow all dimensions of your experience (cognitive, emotional, sensory∞kinesthetic, perceptual, spiritual, and social∞relational) to inform this process. Use your imagination!
- Do this until you experience a shift in your felt sense.

Receiving Answers

- Receive this shift in your experience with an open attitude.
- Allow yourself to be with this new felt sense of your situation for a while.

Source: Adapted from Gendlin, 1981

includes the exploration of others' experiences of the topic of inquiry. That is what allows heuristic research to flow between the realms of introspection and relationality, embracing both the personal and the universal seamlessly and with great versatility.

The Six Phases of Heuristic Inquiry

The seven processes of heuristic inquiry serve as a channel for the six phases of this research methodology in the sense that each of the six phases is facilitated through implementation of one or more of the seven processes. Thus, the processes and phases work in concert to support the exploratory, introspective, creative, experiential, and relational facets of heuristic research. Heuristic inquiry includes six prominent phases: initial engagement, immersion, incubation, illumination, explication, and creative synthesis (see Table 4.1). Again, these phases may or may not unfold in sequential fashion, depending on the needs of your study.

Initial Engagement

In this phase, the researcher embarks on an inner search and makes contact with a topic of intense and compelling interest that holds great personal meaning (Moustakas, 1990), as well as possible social and universal significance. This interest inspires self-dialogue, tacit awareness, and the use of intuition, all of which support the formation of a question that lingers with the researcher. Movement is generated as the researcher seeks more information from other sources.

On the surface, initial engagement may appear to address only that primary phase of a research study in which the researcher is contemplating a core

TABLE 4.1 ● The Six Phases of Heuristic Inquiry	
Initial engagement	Researcher's first contact with a topic of intense interest or a research question and/or with various other phases of the study
Immersion	Researcher's full commitment to living the question or topic, in all dimensions of life, as the question becomes the primary focus of the researcher's attention
Incubation	Researcher's temporary and deliberate withdrawal from the research question or topic to allow seeds of new knowledge to sprout
Illumination	Researcher's awareness (usually intuitive) of previously undisclosed information related to the research question, often coupled with altered perception of the topic
Explication	Researcher's exploration of emergent themes and fine-tuning of those themes in preparation for the creative synthesis
Creative synthesis	Researcher's integration of the multiple themes of the topic into a cohesive whole, usually using some form of creative interpretation

question. However, in heuristic inquiry, multiple opportunities exist for initial engagement. This is due to the exploratory nature of the methodology and its tolerance for ambiguity. Thus, initial engagement may occur throughout the course of your study, including such instances as the following:

- Formulating a core question and refining it
- Launching a literature review
- Locating and inviting co-researchers
- Collecting and organizing the data
- Synthesizing the data and generating themes
- Evaluating the findings/themes

Each of these processes informs and is informed by your research question. You will return repeatedly to your core question as you employ various processes and phases toward deciphering the essential nature of your phenomenon.

Immersion

Having identified and formulated a core question, you begin to live the question in every sleeping and waking moment (Moustakas, 1990), in every thought, feeling, and sensation. Everything in your life revolves around the question as you become intimate with it and remain open and receptive to possibilities of knowledge and integration (Moustakas, 1990). In effect, every moment of your life becomes centered on your topic.

As with other processes and phases of heuristic inquiry, immersion is not static or uniform. You will engage in immersion throughout your study, although the intensity with which you engage in it will vary depending on the study's emergent needs. For example, you might immerse yourself intensely and exclusively within your own experience of the phenomenon you are researching to generate your central guiding question. As you begin to do this, you might realize that your question is overly self-motivated and decide to redirect some of your attention outward. On the other hand, you might decide from the outset that you will immerse yourself moderately within your own as well as others' experiences of your topic as you formulate your question. Likewise, immersion may become a highly prominent phase as you work at transcribing your recorded interviews (I address this in more detail in Chapter 6). Either way, immersion has ambiguous boundaries and will more than likely saturate various parts of your study from beginning to end.

One of my go-to books is Stephen Levine's *Guided Meditations, Explorations, and Healings* (1991). In one of the brief (but golden!) chapters of the book, Levine describes how we interact with an itch that arises, unsolicited, somewhere on our body. We begin with unconscious occupation as we scratch the abominable irritant that is interrupting our equilibrium. As we return, over and over, to the spot that is becoming increasingly aggravated, we become increasingly aware of its actual existence. We might even begin to explore the origin of the itch and/or what in our environment may be supporting and maintaining it. Whereas earlier we were absentmindedly itching away for relief, we are now consciously attending to what we are doing and with what purpose; we are becoming actively engrossed in it. Thus, we transition from superficial and light immersion in our itching into a more intentional and deep immersion—one might say even an absorption. Levine masterfully describes our almost compulsive intention as we redeploy the intensity of our immersion from minor distraction into full-on emergency mode. Such is the capricious and mesmerizing nature of immersion!

Incubation

During this phase, the researcher withdraws from the intense and focused attention on the question and/or data to engage in activities unrelated to the research, allowing for the seeds of the process to germinate (Moustakas, 1990). Thus, even as you are deliberately disengaged from the question and contents of the study, the tacit dimension is at work, and understanding and growth are taking place beneath the level of your conscious awareness. To put it simply, incubation is the "sleeping-on-it" phase. Polanyi (1958) described what happens when we engage in heuristic activity as "a combination of active and passive stages" (p. 126). Incubation lies on the passive end of the spectrum. It is what is at play when we know we have misplaced our car keys. We recognize the keys are somewhere; we just cannot seem to locate them at the moment, despite a concerted effort to do that. In the heat of defeated agony, we give up the ghost and tell ourselves, *I don't have time to worry about the keys right now; they'll turn up,* diverting our attention elsewhere. Incubation is also what is at play when we experience the tip-of-the-tongue phenomenon (Brown, 1991), in which we are unable to retrieve a particular word or phrase from memory and strain ourselves mentally to locate the word to ease our tension. In both the case of the missing key and the tip-of-the-tongue experience, we are caught in a state of anguish in our struggle for contact with the "solution" and we have an absolute certainty of eventual success. We know we will eventually find the missing keys or will eventually retrieve the evasive word. Our certainty gives us room to leave the matter alone for a while, which also creates the space for the emergence of new knowledge and for its free movement as it relaxes into a new way of being.

Illumination

Whereas knowledge is being generated unconsciously in the incubation phase, it surfaces into conscious awareness in the illumination phase (Moustakas, 1990). Discovery takes place in moments of elucidation as the researcher awakens to new, previously unrevealed dimensions of the experience. "Illumination opens the door to a new awareness, a modification of an old understanding, a synthesis of fragmented knowledge, or an altogether new discovery of something that has been present for some time yet beyond immediate awareness" (p. 30). Here the internal frame of reference you previously held in place may be modified as those new facets of the experience are integrated. To continue with the example of the keys, just as you surrender to the reality of not being able to find your keys and direct your attention to other tasks, your keys show up or you remember exactly where you last placed them. Or in the example of the tip-of-the-tongue experience, just as you tell yourself, *I don't know; I can't find the words,* the words in fact find you.

Illumination is also at play when certain features of a situation, landscape, or environment that were previously distant from our perception suddenly emerge into awareness (Moustakas, 1990). For example, I listen to the audio recordings of each of the interviews I conduct with co-researchers repeatedly before transcribing the content and using the transcripts to identify themes. Following the illumination of what I think are all the core themes of the study, I listen to each recording one more time. At that point, I have not heard the audio recordings in a while. As I sit with each recording once again, a new theme may emerge. I liken this to what happens when we drive the same route to a specific location each time, noticing the same features and characteristics. Then one time, as we are driving that very same route, we discern something that has always been there, maybe even quite prominently, but that we have never before noticed: a commemorative plaque near a pedestrian crossing, a heart-shaped carving in the trunk of an old tree, or a walking path littered with flowers.

As with other processes and phases of heuristic inquiry, illumination will spark throughout the course of your research study. Yet nowhere will it twinkle more brightly than when the core themes of your study are emerging. Heuristic themes are not forced or made up; they are allowed to surface on their own once they are ripe. Thus, heuristic themes are illuminated through a process of immersion in the data followed by a period of incubation.

As I write this, I am recalling a *Garfield* comic strip (from way back!) that portrays just how seamlessly immersion, incubation, and illumination can unfold (see Figure 4.3). Note how Garfield goes from a state of extended, deep immersion into unintentional incubation (once he is distracted by Jon), then to instant illumination. Now, illumination may not happen quite as instantly as it did for Garfield, but it is almost certainly bound to happen if you give it some space.

Explication

Once the new dimensions and themes are illuminated, the researcher enters into a phase of exploring deeply what has come into awareness through indwelling, focusing, and self-disclosure (Moustakas, 1990). "The entire process of explication requires that researchers attend to their own awarenesses, feelings, thoughts, beliefs, and judgments as a prelude to the understanding that is derived from conversations and dialogues with others" (p. 31). The essences of the experience are refined in preparation for the creative synthesis phase. First the researcher prepares an **individual depiction** of the core themes illuminated from each co-researcher's raw data to construct a holistic **explication** that serves

FIGURE 4.3 ● **Garfield Comic Strip That Demonstrates Immersion, Incubation, and Illumination**

GARFIELD © 1979 Paws, Inc. Reprinted with permission of ANDREWS MCMEEL SYNDICATION. All rights reserved.

to present the findings of the study. From the collective wisdom of the individual depictions, a **composite depiction** is then created, representing a holistic rendition of the illuminated themes. Then two or more **exemplary portraits** are generated using the unique data of select co-researchers whose contributions, while they are singular, characterize the universal themes of the study.

Creative Synthesis

In the final phase of heuristic inquiry, the various strands of the experience and the understanding the researcher has gleaned from the research process are integrated into a whole using tacit knowing and intuition (Moustakas, 1990). While the **creative synthesis** is a personal undertaking of the researcher, it includes consideration of all the raw data as well as the final findings to generate an interpretation that accurately represents the experience as a whole. As the researcher, you will want to return to the various depictions you generated to seek inspiration for this phase. The creative synthesis may be expressed using any of a number of different forms, including the following:

- A drawing or painting
- A narrative story or tale
- A poem
- A photo, collage, or mandala
- A mosaic, sculpture, or tapestry
- An audio or video recording

The creative synthesis is a realization of the comprehensive essences of the topic of inquiry.

The Heuristic Phases in Action

Now that we have discussed each of the six heuristic phases, it might be helpful to see how they play out in an everyday situation. I will not directly identify which of the six phases is occurring at what moment but instead invite you to consider any phases and/or processes you perceive to be unfolding.

Imagine this: You are a fan of different forms of art produced during the Impressionist era. You learn that an installation of Impressionist paintings will be on exhibit at your local museum. You visit the museum website for more details and learn that the featured paintings include the work of a number of Impressionist artists you particularly admire. You decide you will purchase a ticket for the Impressionist exhibition.

As you enter the large exhibit room, you scan the vibrant and intriguing array of paintings decorating the walls beneath sensitively targeted lighting.

One painting captures your attention: Vincent van Gogh's *Starry Night Over the Rhône*. You walk closer to the painting to take in some of its fine details: the shimmering gold stars and the dance of their reflection on the rippling blue water, the two indistinct figures standing on the bank of the river closest to you, and the undulating array of buildings on the opposite bank. Captivated by the reflection of the gold stars, you move closer to get a better look. You stare at the bold yet still reflection in fascination, feeling as though you are entering the very scene. You allow yourself to fall into the dance of gold and blue.

Yes, you are there—immersed within the gentle glimmer of stars on water, surrounded by the splendor that you were observing just a few moments ago. As you fall deeper and deeper into this most intoxicating experience, you can almost feel the cool water and the flickering glow of gold on your skin. You shut your eyes and surrender completely to the illusion. After a few moments, you sense the urge to open your eyes, and you follow this impulse. Suddenly, you realize you can no longer see the other parts of the painting, but . . . it doesn't matter! You are *in* the painting—or are you?

In an instant, you become aware that you are *not* in fact in the painting. You just happen to be so close to it you have literally lost sight of not only the other dimensions of the work but of your entire surroundings. Something inside you clenches as you somewhat unconsciously attempt to make sense of your momentary interruption in flow and recalibrate. You find yourself turning away from the painting, directing your focus elsewhere. This is not necessarily a voluntary action; it is, rather, informed by some level of inner knowing. Something within you recognizes that you have reached a point of saturation with the details and identified the need for distance and space.

You walk around the exhibition hall and glance briefly at some of the other paintings on display. Your experience is a balance of interest and detachment; you are straddling the fence between engaged and disengaged. Not much later, you find that you have come full circle, back to *Starry Night*! The intimacy you shared with it not even 15 minutes ago washes over you. Your curiosity kicks in again and you bring your attention back to the painting, this time from a distance. New details emerge, seizing you in the delight of new encounter and new perception.

Maintaining a Heuristic Attitude During the Research Journey

There is never a dull moment in heuristic research. Conversely, as you go through the various processes and phases, you may have moments when things feel bumpy and unclear. With that, you may also experience moments of relief, followed by moments of questioning or illumination. Things do not unfold neatly in a heuristic study, not unlike in other forms of exploratory research. So how do you maintain a heuristic attitude through it all?

While I was deep inside the labyrinth of my dissertation research, I was also under clinical supervision since I was not yet fully licensed as a professional counselor. One of the topics my supervisor and I discussed frequently was the

EXERCISE 4.3
NEEDS SELF-ASSESSMENT EXERCISE

Take a few moments to be alone with your experience (it is not necessary that you physically withdraw or remove yourself from your setting).

- Get quiet inside, and allow your mind to take a brief break.
- Connect with whichever part of your body you consider to be the center or core of your being. Be in the *very present moment*.
- Ask, *What do I need right now?* You might find your mind drifting to next week's deadline or to a meeting you are scheduled to attend in an hour. Bring your awareness back to your *very present moment*. Ask the question again: *What do I need right now?*
- Receive the answers that come to you; do not censor yourself! The answer to your question may be as simple as: *I need a glass of water*. Or *I need to pull away from this and take a walk around the block*. Embrace the answer and act on it right away, if you can. The answer might also present as something a little more complex, like: *I need to stop dillydallying about my research questions and write them down*. If your answer looks like the latter, remind yourself that you are working at assessing your present moment's needs only, and make a mental note to carve out time to attend to bigger needs.

---

confusing, perplexing, and ambiguous nature of both the clinical work we do and my research process. My supervisor, who had completed her doctoral degree in the same program in which I was enrolled, was aware of the ups and downs of research. She was also highly attuned to my fluctuating levels of frustration with my own research journey and the moments when I was approaching my point of saturation. This was her wise counsel to me: "Keep your eyes on the prize." I listened!

Maintaining a heuristic attitude can also be done by way of what I call a needs self-assessment exercise (see Exercise 4.3). This process is inspired by the gestalt cycle of awareness (see Figure 4.4), which illustrates how we become aware of our experience and act on it to achieve integration and closure. The **needs self-assessment exercise** entails checking in with yourself about where you are (in the *very present moment*), identifying what is not working, and deciding what you might need to do for the situation to change.

FIGURE 4.4 ● Gestalt Cycle of Awareness

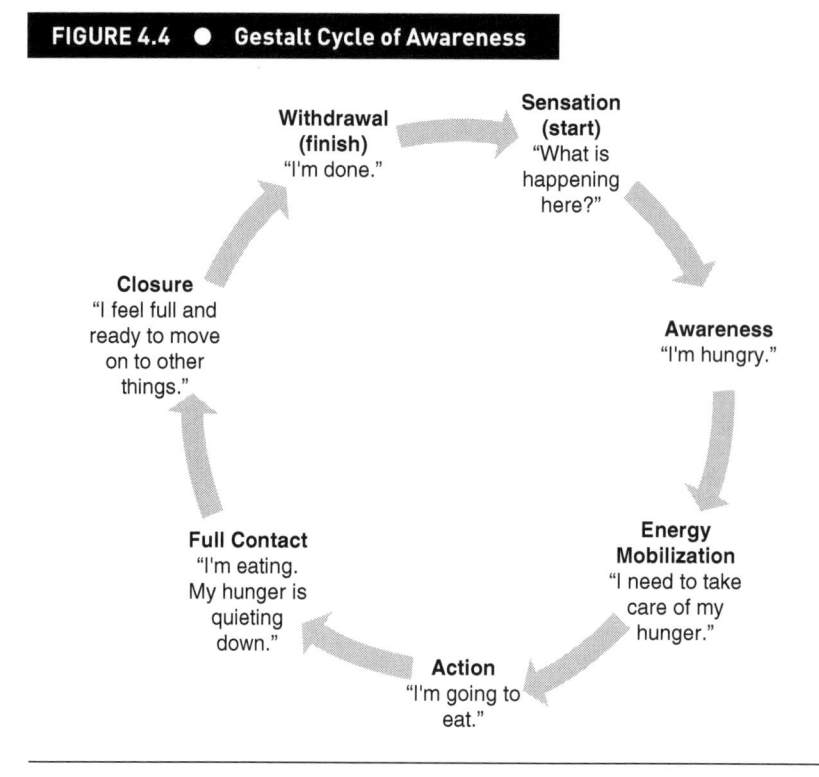

- **Sensation (start)** "What is happening here?"
- **Awareness** "I'm hungry."
- **Energy Mobilization** "I need to take care of my hunger."
- **Action** "I'm going to eat."
- **Full Contact** "I'm eating. My hunger is quieting down."
- **Closure** "I feel full and ready to move on to other things."
- **Withdrawal (finish)** "I'm done."

Source: Adapted from Woldt & Toman, 2005.

Closing Reflections

The heuristic journey is an intricate tapestry of the search to create or discover affinities and connections within the realms of internal∞external, subjective∞objective, and personal∞universal. It is an undertaking that should not be limited by confines of space or time. Nevertheless, we qualitative researchers often find ourselves dabbling with perplexity, and encounters with confusion may drive some of us to feel lost or at our wits' end. Heuristic researchers are invited to embrace the unknown with a spirit of curiosity and imagination while trusting that the process will unfold. After all, we never know what we might find, discover, or create. What I have learned is that the more I am open to discovering new knowledge, the more likely I am to find myself in a serendipitous encounter with it.

Give yourself permission to dwell with the uncertainty that may accompany you on your heuristic journey. In doing so, you are opening a portal to the discovery of worlds that transcend your most inspired fantasies. Remember that while you are on a labyrinthine journey, the labyrinth itself is already carved for you; the heuristic processes and phases are there to guide you.

You have but to hold your question close and trust your journey. As Johanson and Kurtz (1991) asserted, "The wise one stays in touch with both her roots and her direction while traveling through glorious vistas" (p. 71). Trust yourself, too, as you release the predictability of the known and launch into the winding labyrinth. Entertain doubt, by all means, but don't let it get hold of you! Look out, instead, into the openness and breadth of the labyrinth. Do you see those twists and curves, mysterious and abundant? They are your anchor! Draw them closer and closer until they grip you by the ribs and bring you face-to-face with worlds you never imagined possible, leaving you gasping, *More!*

5

Heuristic Research Design

To search means, first, I need Being, Truth; second, I do not know where to find it; and third, an action takes place that is not based on fantasies of certainty—while at the same time a waiting takes place that is rooted not in wishful thinking but in a deep sense of urgency.

~ Jacob Needleman

Questions for Reflection

1. What are the logistics of conducting a heuristic study?
2. How do I formulate a research question for heuristic inquiry?
3. How do I prepare for various aspects of the study?
4. How do I select and secure co-researchers?

Now that we have gone through a comprehensive overview of the seven processes and six phases of heuristic research, the next step is to tackle the logistics of a heuristic study. Heuristic research involves an exploratory journey that brings the words of great American philosopher Jacob Needleman to light. The heuristic endeavor is, indeed, a search for both Being and Truth that puts to use those selfsame concepts as catalysts for the search. Heuristic research magnetizes us into our very quest, embracing our urgent and pressing need for illumination, meaning-making, and transformation while asking us to pause, be patient, and trust the process, abandoning the need for certainty in the form of specified outcomes. Yet heuristic inquiry does not make such an invitation lightly! Indeed, it summons us to embrace this most captivating process in a disciplined and systematic manner (Moustakas, 1990). Thus, as a rigorous and empirical approach to qualitative research, heuristic inquiry entails attending to the following constituents, most of which are necessary to thorough data collection and analysis and successful completion of your research study:

- Becoming aware of a topic and formulating the research question(s)
- Conducting a literature review
- Preparing for the study (IRB proposal, form templates, etc.)
- Selecting and inviting co-researchers

Bear in mind that you will be using one or more of the seven processes and six phases of heuristic research as you work through each of these logistics; that is precisely the purpose for which those processes and phases were designed.

Becoming Aware of a Topic and Formulating the Research Question(s)

As the researcher, one of your primary tasks will be the identification of your topic of inquiry; without a topic, you have no study! The idea of conducting a study will usually emerge from your interest in a particular topic. On the other hand, you may be planning a study to fulfill educational or professional requirements (such as the completion of a doctoral degree), in which case the idea of conducting research may be in place before you have identified a topic. Once again, the topic of any heuristic study is autobiographical, personal, and subjective and emerges from the living experience of the primary researcher. So you will more than likely already be aware of a general topic, although the topic may be quite broad. If that is the case, you may want to consider narrowing your topic down so you are able to formulate a research question that does not take you on tangents. FOCUS. FOCUS. FOCUS. How? Through self-search, self-dialogue, self-reflection, and self-awareness. Essentially, to narrow down your topic to a meaningful question, you must enter your topic fully and reflexively, allowing yourself to be guided by purpose, inspired by curiosity, and informed by serendipity.

One of the most fascinating components of conducting a heuristic study is engaging in the playful back-and-forth of formulating the research question(s). It is critical that you not fall prey to rigid conceptualizations of what you *should* be exploring in your study. Instead, linger and visit with your topic, embracing the creative, serendipitous, and discovery-oriented nature of this task and allowing yourself to remain open to any and all of the possibilities that may emerge from your self-inquiry as you narrow things down to a meaningful query. Questions may materialize throughout your waking or your sleeping life (Moustakas, 1990), within daydreams, inner thoughts, or conversations. Here are some strategies for effectively capturing the ideas that will surface through some of these sources:

- In your reflexive journal, write every question that comes to you; do not censor yourself. While you may later decide not to use some of the questions, each question may hold information to guide you in the direction of your final research question(s).
- Doodle or draw any images or symbols that emerge around your topic. Explore what they mean in relation to your topic or what meanings of them you may be seeking.
- Create a word cloud, or brainstorm some words and phrases (Figure 5.1 depicts a brainstorm I created while lingering with the topic of my embodiment study).
- Read each question, word, or phrase, both silently and out loud. Are any of the concepts represented by the words or phrases similar? Are there any apparent themes? Are there any points of departure between certain words/phrases and others?
- Engage deeply with the images and/or symbols. Sense them. Touch them. Talk to them, and listen to what they have to say. See them. Feel them. Be with them. What are they telling you about the experience?
- Connect with any natural resonances between the words/phrases, the images/symbols, and your personal experience of the phenomenon.
- Do not fall into the struggle of trying to formulate your research question(s) before you have sat with each of the ideas you have identified.

Again, be playful and open with your process so nothing is forced or unnaturally identified. Once you have done this a number of times, you will be more prepared to compose a central research question that is informed by the richness and authenticity of your encounter with the topic. A well-formulated heuristic research question has the following characteristics:

- It focuses on a single concept.
- It is informed by theory and by the general purpose of your study.
- It is inspired by your autobiographical experience and is connected to your personal identity/self (Moustakas, 1990).
- It inspires you to seek out the narratives of others who have experienced the same (or a highly similar) phenomenon.

Chapter 5 • Heuristic Research Design 107

FIGURE 5.1 • A Brainstorm of the Phenomenon of Embodiment

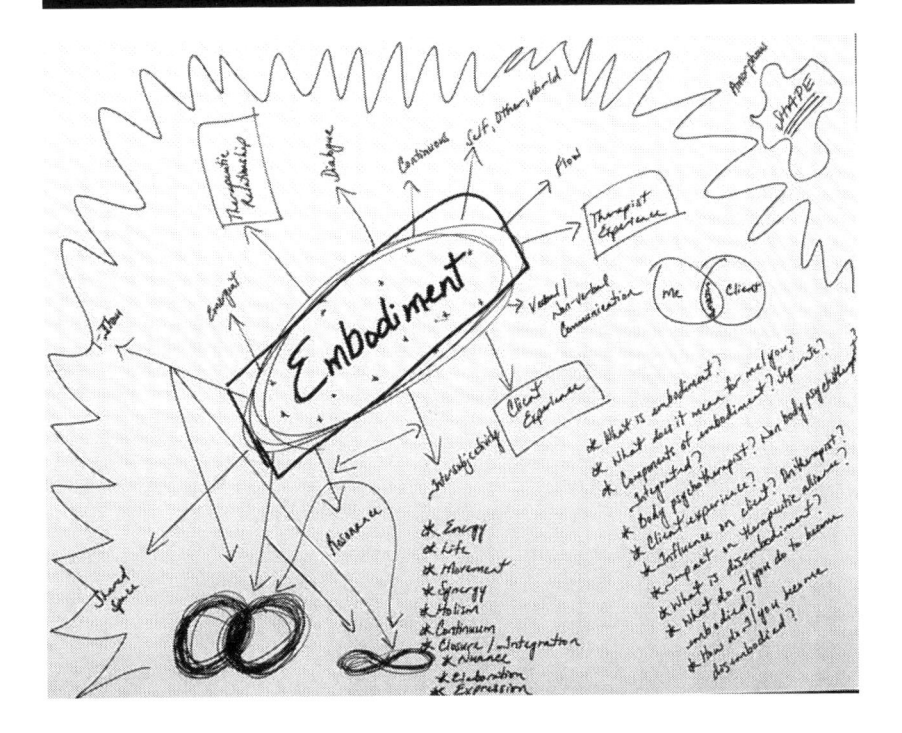

- It seeks to unravel the essential nature of the phenomenon being explored.
- It is relevant.
- It is clear and precise (Moustakas, 1990), formulated in such a way that any person who comes into contact with it is able to understand its meaning and purpose.
- It is open-ended and exploratory, inspiring further questions that may help focus and refine the process of inquiry.
- It is non-leading.
- It does not hypothesize specific findings or make assumptions about co-researchers.
- It is communicated in a relational, nonjudgmental, and empathic manner.
- It is informed by careful reflection on its implications for the researcher, research partners, and any others who come into contact with it.

Following are examples of neutral, clear, concrete research questions from heuristic studies:

- What is the experience of women engaging in a long-term yogic practice in terms of their overall emotional well-being (Alsobrook, 2015)?
- What is the lived experience of being spiritual for an atheist (Madden, 2015)?
- What does it mean for body psychotherapists to be embodied (Sultan, 2015)?

Each of the above questions focuses on experience and/or meaning; that is precisely the focus of a heuristic research question. Again, as mentioned earlier in the text, these very same questions may be asked within the context of other qualitative methodologies, such as grounded theory or phenomenology. On the other hand, asking these questions within other qualitative methodologies will yield a qualitatively different research process (one that does not include the processes and phases unique to heuristic inquiry), as well as findings that are not necessarily grounded in your autobiographical experience as the researcher and that may or may not illuminate the essential nature of the topic of inquiry within both personal and universal contexts. Additionally, your findings will not be represented using multiple forms of depiction such as individual, composite, exemplary, and creative (more on this later in the chapter), all of which are exclusive to the domain of heuristic research. Thus, as you consider your research question(s), consider, too, how you wish to approach the process of inquiry and to elaborate the findings. Again, in identifying a topic and formulating a research question, you will actively engage many dimensions of your personal experience, including dreaming, imagining, allowing, brainstorming, and defining. You will also want to consult the professional literature to gain some perspective on the history of questions and findings about the same or similar topics. This will give you an idea of how similar research questions were explored using other qualitative methodologies and clarify some of the gaps that may be filled through your heuristic study.

Conducting the Literature Review

Conducting a literature review is about digging deeper and probing the preexisting knowledge surrounding your topic of inquiry. It involves identifying sources of information that target the phenomenon you are exploring and perusing them. For a heuristic inquiry, these sources may include research studies, peer-reviewed articles, books, book chapters, transcripts of interviews with subject-area experts, and artifacts such as memos, photos, audio recordings, and works of art. Generally speaking, any source that provides you with reliable information about the phenomenon you are researching may qualify as professional literature.

Timing Your Literature Review

So when do I begin to look at the professional literature? you may be wondering. When it comes to heuristic research, you will want to look at the literature at different points throughout the course of your study:

- *Before formulating your research question.* As you identify a general topic, you will find that you are drawn to seeking out more information about it. As you scan the literature, you will have more questions; the more you read, the more you will want to know. Use the literature review to help you narrow the focus of your inquiry and formulate a clear question.

- *After identifying a research question, but before data collection begins.* You can wait until you have identified a central question and use that question to direct your attention to more specialized literature that focuses specifically on its content. After you have had a chance to peruse the literature, you can step away from it and allow some of the information you accessed to incubate before you begin data collection and analysis.

- *After analyzing your data and identifying themes.* I would caution engaging with the professional literature as you are navigating data analysis and identifying themes. I say this because you do not want to take the merest chance of "contaminating" your findings by reading, for example, the findings from another study (or ideas from an article) and walking away from that experience with an implanted suggestion. The power of suggestion is mighty! Err on the side of caution until you have taken a stab at analyzing your data and identifying a first round of themes. Then step back into the professional literature to see what it has to offer.

As an example, I conducted a literature review about body psychotherapist embodiment before I knew I was going to explore that topic for my study. My curiosity about the experience emerged from my personal encounter with it as I worked with my clients in therapy. I decided to review the literature because I wanted to know more, as well as to validate my experience and make sure I was not the only therapist in the world who was sensing things inside her body and using that information to guide the therapeutic process. I used the information I gleaned from my preliminary review to identify gaps in previous studies and narrow down my research questions. I then did a second round of literature review after I had some research questions in place. Reading more of the literature helped me laser my questions and imbue them with precision. Finally, after completion of my data analysis and identification of themes, I dove back into the literature to compare my findings with findings from previous studies.

Reviewing the Literature

The general purpose of a literature review for heuristic research is threefold: (a) to report your critical evaluation of the relevant literature; (b) to identify gaps in the literature (which may shape your research question) and help you make a case for your study; and (c) to locate your research study within the wider context of your topic, discipline, or field. Thus, your ability to peruse the professional literature and report key findings is critical to the success of your study. So how do you get started? Here are some ideas to get the ball rolling:

- *Identify some key words.* This is a highly intuitive and introspective process. Accordingly, a good starting place to locate key words is the reflexive journal you have been keeping. Look at words, phrases, and symbols you have documented, as well as reflections or focusing exercises you have tried.

- *Use databases.* Depending on your discipline or area of study, you can choose from among thousands of databases such as Academic Search Complete, Humanities International Complete, PsycINFO, MEDLINE, and JSTOR, to name a few. Heuristic inquiry is both imaginative and creative, so feel free to step outside the box of your discipline and search the databases of other disciplines. This will expand your access to perspectives and findings surrounding your topic of inquiry. Remember, too, that heuristic research is a social constructivist and autobiographical endeavor, so you get to personalize your search as you see fit, so long as you keep things relevant and cohesive.

- *Identify a date range.* Don't get lost in hundreds of articles, some of which may contain outdated information. Decide how old you want your oldest piece of professional literature to be. Then again, you may need to conduct a brief preliminary literature review to narrow things down to a time range appropriate to your study.

- *Evaluate the literature.* Solid critical evaluation involves identifying strengths, limitations, and most important, gaps in the literature. Be sure to also highlight the relevance of the literature to your study.

- *Immerse yourself in the literature.* Immersion in the literature allows you to sample the vast array of information available about your research topic. As you scan and read articles, book chapters, and other sources of information, take notes in the margins, on notecards, and most important, in your journal. Read your notes out loud and get a sense of how you are processing your experience of gaining new information. Your reflexive process and documentation of your encounter with the content will prove immeasurably helpful during data collection, organization, and analysis. Conversely, the balance for immersion is incubation. Be sure to take time to step away from the literature and allow the information you have received to brew.

Preparing for the Study

Identifying a research question and conducting a literature review are necessary components of most qualitative studies. A number of other processes are also involved in preparation for any type of study. Heuristic inquiry comes with its own methods of preparation, including the following:

- Writing a heuristic-friendly IRB proposal
- Creating a set of guidelines for the study
- Creating generic content and forms
- Selecting and inviting co-researchers

Writing a Heuristic-Friendly IRB Proposal

The IRB, or institutional review board as it is called in the United States, is a committee that reviews research studies for ethical and methodological soundness and approves them. In other countries, IRBs may be called ethics review boards, research ethics boards or committees, or other names with similar terminology. Generally speaking, I view the IRB proposal as your opportunity to solidify the purpose and justification of your research study and your choice of heuristic inquiry as the methodology. With regard to what to include in an IRB proposal that is specific to a heuristic study, I recommend the following:

- *A brief, concise description of your study and your research question(s).* Include information about the purpose of your study that highlights your research question(s), as well as your methodology and its unique contribution to the purpose of your study.

- *Identification of your research problem.* Explain your rationale for the study (Creswell, 2013), identifying some of the gaps found in the literature. Following is Pogge's (2013) rationale for a heuristic inquiry of the experience of living with chronic illness:

  > Chronic illness touches the lives of millions of individuals, and the issues among this group range in complexity. It is highly probable that members of the mental health field can expect to work with clients facing chronic illness and disability at some point and would be well served in gaining increased knowledge in this area (Bayliss et al., 2003). Taylor (2006) echoes that there is a growing need for the contributions made by the field of health psychology. (p. 147)

  It is also a good idea to explain how your intentionally phrased heuristic questions, with their focus on the essential nature of your phenomenon, may address gaps or provide novel and singular understandings about your topic.

- *A purpose statement.* Describe the primary objective of your study (Creswell, 2013) using words such as *explore, experiences, meanings,* and *essential nature.* Make sure your description is clear and to the point. Here is an example of a purpose statement from my heuristic inquiry of the embodied experiences of body psychotherapists (Sultan, 2015):

  > The purpose of this research study is to explore the meaning of embodiment and the embodied experiences of body psychotherapists within the therapeutic process. More specifically, this study examines how body psychotherapists use their somatic selves as an instrument in therapy and what they do with their somatic experiences. The focus is on the essential nature of embodiment—that is, the integrated body-mind-spirit experience—of the psychotherapist, within the context of the therapist-client relationship. Given that the therapeutic relationship remains, at the heart of all psychotherapies, the mechanism effecting change with the therapist being its central agent, this research study is essential to future research, theory, training, supervision, and clinical practice in the field.

- *Intended co-researchers.* Describe your ideal co-researcher sample, how you plan to recruit members, what makes those individuals ideal to respond to questions about the essential nature of your phenomenon, what your relationship is (if any) to those individuals, what compensation (if any) they will receive, and whether or not they constitute a vulnerable population. Vulnerable populations are those that may be harmed in the course of a research study and may include children, prisoners, immigrants/refugees/asylees, individuals with chronic illnesses, and pregnant women. If you are researching a vulnerable population, explain how you plan to address your co-researchers' needs to reduce risk. Highlight the strengths of heuristic inquiry in supporting some of the measures you take to prevent harm. Prepare to be an advocate for your population and for your research methodology; know your population and heuristic inquiry inside out!

- *Informed consent.* Prepare an open-ended informed consent form for approval (see Appendix C for a sample). Explain the ongoing nature of informed consent in heuristic inquiry and its basis in trust and rapport (Miller-Day, 2012), as evidenced by co-researchers' rights, for example, to ask questions throughout the course of the study and to withdraw from the study without incurring penalties.

- *Methods and procedures.* Go into more detail about your research questions and the heuristic approach. Provide an exhaustive description of heuristic inquiry that does *not* assume your proposal reviewers are knowledgeable about this approach. Explain why heuristic inquiry is the most suitable research methodology to explore your research topic.

- *Risks and benefits.* Outline potential risks to co-researchers, as well as potential benefits. Exploring the professional literature, your intended co-researcher sample, and the nuances of your particular study (e.g., central topic, central question, heuristic design) will help you identify co-researcher risks and benefits. Include a statement about strategies for addressing unanticipated issues (Miller-Day, 2012), such as a co-researcher revealing that she is contemplating suicide. Keep in mind the personal nature of your topic of inquiry as you assess for risks and benefits.

- *Rights of researcher and co-researchers.* Define your rights as a researcher, including the right to withdraw co-researchers due to unforeseen circumstances or predetermined conditions that are unmet. Identify the rights of co-researchers, including the right to (a) participate voluntarily and/or withdraw without penalty and (b) ask questions before and during the study. Again, your research topic and question will inform this content.

- *Limitations and delimitations.* Limitations may include anything from your research sample to time constraints. Identify potential limitations to your study (especially those influenced by or influencing your methodology) and explain how they may impact your findings. Delimitations describe parameters you have set in place or decisions you have made intentionally. They include things such as processes or phases you decide not to use or relevant studies you elect not to review. Explain and justify the reasoning behind your decisions as informed by the heuristic approach.

- *Research evaluation.* Evaluating heuristic research is designed to enhance the trustworthiness of your methodology and your findings. Describe how you will determine the quality, rigor, and trustworthiness of your data collection, data analysis, and findings.

- *Role of researcher.* Clarify your autobiographical experience with the topic of inquiry and your personal role as the primary researcher and instrument for data collection. Identify the personal beliefs, values, biases, and attitudes you are bringing to the research endeavor and their dynamics in your study. How might your personal experience, history, and identity influence critical aspects of the study, such as how you interact with co-researchers and with the data, and how might this influence your findings?

And here is a final bit of information and a recommendation based on my personal experience with the IRB that reviewed the proposal for my heuristic study: Because I was informed by two members of my dissertation committee that heuristic inquiry is not a widely known research methodology, I included an addendum with my IRB proposal. In the addendum, I provided a comprehensive description of heuristic inquiry based on an assumption that readers of my IRB proposal had no familiarity with the methodology. This allowed me to showcase heuristic inquiry's unique characteristics, as well as to highlight its applicability to my study and to the particular questions I was using to explore my phenomenon. Because the IRB reviewing my proposal was housed within an institution with a heavy focus on social justice, I felt it opportune to also highlight in the proposal the potential social justice implications of my study, especially with heuristic inquiry as an intrinsically culturally embedded and emancipatory methodology. I encourage you to learn as much as you can about the identities of the institution and the ethics review board with which your research is affiliated, ask questions about the feasibility of providing specific detailed information, and maximize the capacity of your proposal!

Creating a Set of Guidelines for the Study

Moustakas (1990) described a number of methods of preparing for a heuristic study, beginning with the creation of a set of instructions that serves to inform co-researchers about (a) the purpose of the study, (b) the research design, and (c) the role of co-researchers. This set of guidelines serves as a "contractual agreement" between the primary researcher and co-researchers and may also include the following information (Sultan, 2015):

- Inclusion and exclusion criteria for participation
- What to expect, as a co-researcher, before, during, and after data collection and analysis
- How data will be collected (interviews, artifacts) and used (data analysis, publication)
- How data will be stored and confidentiality maintained
- How findings will be evaluated (detailed descriptions of methodology)
- Information about the rights of co-researchers
- Primary researcher's contact information
- IRB contact information

Guidelines for the study are usually outlined in the invitation letter to potential co-researchers, as well as on the informed consent form. In addition to creating a set of guidelines to share with co-researchers, it is helpful to create some guidelines/instructions for yourself.

Creating Generic Content and Forms

Consistency is critical to any research endeavor as it promotes ethical conduct (more in Chapter 10) and enhances the trustworthiness of the findings (more in Chapter 8). One way you can maintain consistency in your heuristic study (especially when it comes to data-related processes) is to create generic forms. For my embodiment study, I created the following generic content:

- Cover/invitation letter (see Appendix A)
- Demographic information form (see Appendix B)
- Informed consent form (see Appendix C)
- Instructions for interview meeting (see Appendix D)
- Semi-Structured interview protocol (see Appendix E)
- Semi-Structured interview protocol with examples (see Appendix F)

These documents included the various guidelines for the study. I shared the content of Appendices B through E with each research partner. This helped me establish the overall purpose and direction of the study and provided opportunities for co-researchers to ask questions before data collection. Appendix F contains a reproduction of the Semi-Structured Interview Protocol in Appendix E, but with examples (in italics) illustrating the *how to* of the prominent sections. Finally, I created generic content for the preliminary e-mails I sent to potential co-researchers to inform them about the study and probe their interest. Naturally, the content of follow-up e-mails between co-researchers and me (including e-mails to address questions and thank-you e-mails) was personalized to address the unique needs of each correspondence.

Selecting, Inviting, and Securing Co-Researchers

Identifying potential co-researchers will, in many ways, shape the direction of your study. Be purposeful in your selection and invitation process. Be as specific as possible with regard to the demographic features of potential research partners and how those characteristics may or may not fill the gaps you are hoping to address through your study.

General Sampling Considerations

Moustakas (1990) identified age, gender, and education as important demographic characteristics. He also highlighted the importance of inviting co-researchers who are interested, cooperative, committed, willing, enthusiastic, and able to describe the experience you are researching. Depending on the needs of your study, other potentially important co-researcher demographic features include ethnicity, sexual orientation, religious/faith/spiritual orientation, marital/partner status, primary language, ability/disability status, geographic location, licenses/certifications, areas of specialization/concentration/focus, number of years of experience, primary occupation, and secondary occupation. Remember the importance of each of your co-researchers having an intimate relationship with your topic of inquiry (Wertz, 2005).

Your personal experience of the topic will also influence your identification and selection of co-researchers; as a heuristic researcher, your experience is just as important as that of any other member in the research team. As mentioned in Chapter 1, your sample will more than likely be purposive; that is, it will target a particular group of people based on the objectives of your study (Palys, 2008), on your personal knowledge of that group, and on potential co-researchers' experience of the phenomenon you are exploring (Creswell, 2013). It will also be decided based on the purpose of your study and on your personal judgment (Babbie, 2013) of the eligibility of potential co-researchers.

Thus, you will want to generate a set of **inclusion criteria** for your sample—that is, a set of conditions by which you determine co-researcher eligibility for participation in your study. Whatley (2015) for her heuristic inquiry of the lived experience of internalized racism of African American women created a four-question screening questionnaire to which affirmative responses for the first three questions, as well as confirmation of U.S.-born parents and grandparents, verified eligibility. The four questions included in the questionnaire were

1. Are you aware of negative stereotypes about African American women?
2. Do you think any of those stereotypes have affected your life in any way?
3. Are you willing to share some of your personal experiences?
4. Where were your parents and grandparents born? (p. 78)

Similarly, Holt-Waldo (2011) in her heuristic inquiry of being a holistic nurse educator specified the inclusion of co-researchers who were "willing to agree to an extended conversational interview, personal journaling, presentation of historical data, and publication of this study" (p. 96). Likewise, criteria for inclusion in my heuristic inquiry of the embodied experiences of body psychotherapists (Sultan, 2015) stipulated that co-researchers (a) self-identify as body psychotherapists and have received focused clinical training in somatic approaches in psychotherapy; (b) have at least 5 years of experience being a body psychotherapist; (c) have had personal embodied experiences in therapeutic work with clients; (d) be willing and able to describe their clinical embodied experiences; (e) speak English comfortably; and (f) be willing to have their interview with the researcher audio recorded.

A natural follow-up to determining inclusion criteria is deciding on **exclusion criteria**—that is, those conditions by which you conclude that potential co-researchers are *not* eligible for participation. For example, as a precaution, potential co-researchers confirming a history of trauma were excluded from my study due to the fact that discussing embodied experiences or past events may evoke intense affect (Adler & Adler, 2002) and/or traumatic memories (Fogel, 2009). Not determining this exclusion criterion may have influenced how I assessed risk to co-researchers in my IRB proposal. Interestingly, in my review of a number of heuristic studies conducted over the past few years, I found that many researchers did not define exclusion criteria for their studies. I would say it is good counsel to identify, before you begin data collection, any circumstances or conditions that may create ethical breaches or obfuscation of the raw data. For example, you may want to consider the ethical implications of including friends, family, clients, or colleagues as co-researchers in your study, or the legal implications of inadvertently becoming privy to classified information while interviewing government employees. You do not want to be thrown into the confusion of trying to handle an ill-timed episode as you are in the midst of navigating other complexities of your study.

Now that you have a dream list of potential research partners, you can officially invite their participation by sending out an invitation letter with detailed information about your study (see Appendix A). In alignment with the heuristic practice of collecting and analyzing data for one co-researcher at a time, you will build your research partner sample as you go, depending on your needs. Once you have received an affirmative response to your invitation, you can follow up with a second correspondence that includes potential interview dates and times, as well as an attached demographic information form (see Appendix B), informed consent form (see Appendix C), instructions for the interview (see Appendix D), and a semi-structured interview/focus group protocol (see Appendix E). You might also consider creating a spreadsheet or list documenting demographic and contact information about your co-researchers, as well as information about potential backup research partners in case one of your co-researchers withdraws from the study.

Sample Size

A final consideration for you will be the number of co-researchers to include in your study. In a heuristic study, deciding on a definitive number of research partners can be a challenge. Here is what Moustakas (1990) had to say about sample size:

> Although in theory it is possible to conduct heuristic research with only one participant, a study will achieve richer, deeper, more profound, and more varied meanings when it includes depictions of the experience of others—perhaps as many as 10 to 15 co-researchers. (pp. 46–47)

Sounds pretty straightforward, right? The fact is that although one can include "as many as" 10 to 15 co-researchers, it may not be necessary to include so many or it may prove necessary to include more. My experience is that, again, it will depend on your study. The nice thing is that in heuristic inquiry the raw data from each co-researcher are analyzed *before* data collection with other research partners continues. This means that borrowing an approach to determining sample size from another qualitative methodology is a logical choice.

For example, in my study of embodiment, I used saturation to determine my sample size. **Saturation** is a grounded theory concept that describes the point at which new data do not yield new insight (Creswell, 2013). Although saturation is not specific to heuristic inquiry, I felt that having a well-defined approach for determining sample size would enhance the overall trustworthiness of my study (recall, from Chapter 2, that bricolaging is a fairly common practice among qualitative research traditions [Denzin & Lincoln, 2011]). Saturation made sense, as I planned to complete the analysis of each co-researcher's raw data before proceeding with further data collection. As I collected and analyzed my data for each co-researcher, I checked my overall findings for saturation before making decisions to proceed with further interviews. I will note, however, that I used saturation with great caution. I was conscious of not restricting the flow of data collection just because it seemed I had attained saturation and of not overwhelming myself with unnecessary data just to promote trustworthiness. Balance is important!

Building Rapport and Trust

Selecting research partners and determining sample size facilitate the success of any research study. The more important facet of sample selection, however, is *securing* those co-researchers. It's no good inviting people to participate only to have them withdraw from your study at a later time. The researcher–research partner relationship is a key determinant of qualitative research success (Orb, Eisenhauer, & Wynaden, 2001). Take steps to build rapport and trust with each member of your research team (more on this in Chapter 7).

Building rapport and trust is not about going through the motions of forcing relationships through false shows of warmth and connection. It is about being transparent with regard to all aspects of the research study in which you have invited these individuals to participate. It is also demonstrating congruence between what you say and what you do. Thus, you can embrace genuineness and authenticity to enhance equitable opportunities and experiences for all members of the research team. Rapport and trust also encompass honoring the guidelines you have set for the study.

Researchers often create research study guidelines because they look good on IRB proposals, informed consent forms, and final manuscripts. Beware of this unprofessional practice! If you create guidelines for your study but fail to follow them, you are implicitly informing your co-researchers that your study is a sham and granting them permission to break the rules. More important, you are risking the loss of one or more research partners who may view your violation of your own guidelines as a violation of trust. Trust and rapport building are enhanced when we allow research partners to define their way of being in the world. In a heuristic study, an example is creating an open-ended demographic form in which co-researchers identify their own way of defining demographics. For example, rather than providing the usual choices of "male" and "female" for gender, provide a free space for co-researchers to identify their gender orientation as informed by their living experience of it. Or rather than selecting pseudonyms for research partners, allow them to create their own pseudonyms (see Appendix B for more examples). This is in keeping with the social constructivist, and culturally embedded and emancipatory, facets of heuristic inquiry, honoring the relative nature of reality. Simply speaking, building trust and rapport is about transparency, honor, authenticity, and social justice.

I recently participated in five qualitative research studies (none of which were heuristic inquiries). While I did not withdraw from any of these studies, I considered withdrawal from at least four of them, for the following reasons:

- The researcher informed us that our participation was confidential. She then thanked me, *in public, in a large gathering,* for my participation in her study. I bristled at this public violation of confidentiality.

- The researcher included within an e-mail a link to a qualitative questionnaire and assured us that the contents of the questionnaire would not be connected with us. A few days later, she spoke with me individually about some of my responses. My trust in the researcher was violated.

- The researcher informed us that the interview protocol would be sent prior to the interview and failed to send it. I felt the researcher was not taking his own study seriously.

- The researcher, in a face-to-face interview, appeared eager to present a rebuttal to my statements. I experienced her as nonpresent, non-attuned, and highly dismissive.

- The researcher assigned us pseudonyms. My pseudonym was a number, which led me to feel dehumanized and objectified.

- The researcher was abrupt about terminating the interview. He did not invite me to reflect on my experience of the interview and did not ask if I had anything else to share in relation to the topic. I felt a bit used.

While I experienced some ruptures in relating to the primary researcher of each of the studies in which I participated, I also experienced vibrant moments of connection and trust. Here are some of the moments when I felt most connected with the interviewer:

- The researcher self-disclosed appropriately (i.e., with relevance to the study and not in a leading manner designed to manipulate me into agreeing/disagreeing with his content).

- The researcher did not try to assume a stoic or detached attitude about the content of the study and was quite open about his personal connection with the topic of inquiry.

- The researcher allowed herself to be human (i.e., fallible, emotional, vulnerable).

- The researcher displayed a high level of awareness for power differentials.

- The researcher approached moments of difference and/or conflict with curiosity and interest, rather than with confusion and defensiveness.

Keep these things in mind as you work on establishing trust and rapport with your research team!

A final note: Whatever you decide to do in terms of your co-researcher sample, please recruit your own research partners. This is not a task you want to delegate. Your co-researcher sample is very specific to your topic, and your topic is very near and dear to you. No one can possibly understand your research questions or the purpose of your study as you do, so keep the task of selecting the partners who will accompany you on your heuristic journey for yourself.

Closing Reflections

Heuristic inquiry invites and embraces the inclusion of every researcher's sense of Being and Truth by highlighting the researcher's autobiographical living experience of the phenomenon of inquiry, as well as her perception of the meaning and reality of that experience. Likewise, heuristic inquiry honors the living experience of every research partner as a primary source of information. Yet what grants a heuristic study the capacity to capture the potentially transforming answers is first to ask the vital questions, some of which will be informed by the history of exploring the same or similar questions as identified through methodical review of the literature. However, your literature review does not end with the formulation of your research question but continues as you prepare for all other aspects of your study and beyond data collection and analysis. As you collect your raw data, I invite you to attend to the powerful role of relationships, boundaries, and ethical conduct while you work to maintain a healthy balance throughout your study. Having purposively selected potential co-researchers who have themselves experienced the phenomenon you are exploring, you are now prepared to collaborate in a shared process of inquiry geared toward attaining higher levels of Being and Truth!

6

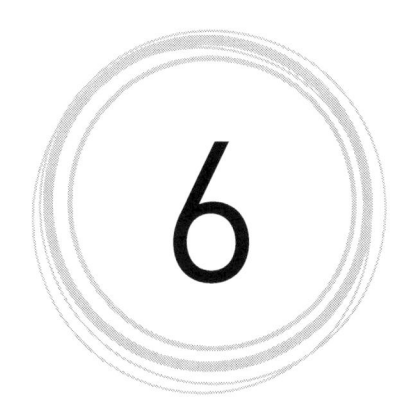

Heuristic Data Collection, Organization, and Analysis

You feed yourself. Make sure you have all the information, whether it's aesthetic, scientific, mathematical, I don't care what it is. Then you walk away from it and let it ferment. You ignore it and pretend you don't care. Next thing you know, the answer comes.

~ Ray Bradbury

Questions for Reflection

1. What are the most appropriate approaches for collecting data in heuristic research?
2. How do I organize the data and manage them in preparation for data analysis?
3. What is involved in heuristic data analysis?

So you have received institutional review board approval, generated a set of guidelines for your study (as well as the forms you will use to guide your process), and invited and secured agreement to participate from potential co-researchers. It is time to begin collecting your data. Again, you will use one

FIGURE 6.1 • Heuristic Data Collection, Organization, and Analysis

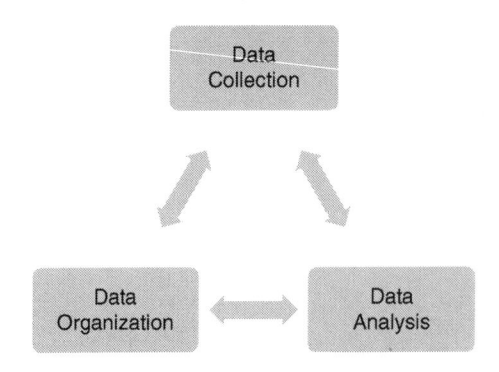

```
        Data
      Collection
       ↙    ↖
      ↙      ↖
 Data  ⟷  Data
Organization  Analysis
```

or more of the seven processes and six phases of heuristic research as you collect, organize, and analyze your data. In heuristic research, data collection, organization, and analysis are not discrete processes; data analysis begins as soon as you start collecting your data. You may or may not be aware that you are actively analyzing your data, especially if you are in incubation mode. But heuristic data analysis is not only about sifting through transcripts to identify recurring themes. It is a creative process that engages intuition, tacit knowing, self-dialogue (both conscious and unconscious), as well as the remainder of the seven processes. It is also about your capacity to observe and reason and to relate and be in relationship. As you and your research team unravel implicit meanings hidden within the data collection, organization, and analysis, the boundaries between the three processes blur (Finlay, 2011). Essentially, heuristic data collection, organization, and analysis operate collectively (see Figure 6.1).

Before we begin elaborating on these particular facets of heuristic research, I invite you, first, to linger with the words of science fiction and fantasy author Ray Bradbury, who encourages us to tap all the sources possible for various types of information that may answer our questions or satisfy our hunger for knowledge in some other way. This is what we call *immersion* in heuristic research. Bradbury then urges us, paradoxically, to walk away from the information and allow it to *ferment*. This is what we call *incubation* in heuristic research. With incubation comes the promise that answers to our questions will be *illuminated* just when we have shifted our attention from the search. Please keep Bradbury's wise words at the center of your awareness as we navigate heuristic data collection, organization, and analysis.

Data Collection

Data collection for heuristic research transcends the mere idea of gathering information. In heuristic inquiry, data collection is about immersing yourself within your topic through self-dialogue, as well as dialogue with individuals who share your interest. Heuristic data collection may be executed through a number of sources and/or processes such as interviews, focus groups, observation, and media sources (Internet, radio, television). However, due to the highly experiential nature of heuristic inquiry, the typical methods for collecting data are interviews, artifacts, and researcher journal entries/reflections. Let's take a closer look at what goes into each of these data collection methods and how they are applied in heuristic research.

Interviews

I have, thus far, focused rather consistently on interviewing when discussing data collection. In heuristic inquiry, interviewing is the most prevalent data collection method (Moustakas, 1990), partly due to the fact that it is challenging to comprehend the essential nature of a phenomenon without understanding those who have experienced it. It is also due to the relational nature of heuristic methodology and to the personal nature of the topic of inquiry. Social constructivists honor the centrality of researcher–research partner interaction and immersion in the research setting (Ponterotto, 2005) in generating genuine discourse and truthful findings. Thus, heuristic interviews are shaped by mutual interest, are highly relational, and are facilitated through the genuineness and presence of the researcher within an I∞Thou framework.

It will help both you and your research partners to enter each interview experience with an attitude of engaging in existential, humanistic, relational dialogue with a person with whom you share a compelling interest. While the interview should be structured and conducted formally, it should not "feel" like a formal interview. You and your co-researchers are coming together voluntarily (with your individual histories and identities in tow) to co-construct a novel way of understanding something you have each already embraced as a reality. Your joint venture holds the potential to transform how you each know and understand yourselves, how you know and understand others, and how you make sense of the world around you.

Preparing for the Interviews

Conducting heuristic interviews successfully requires a great deal of preparation and relational skill. Preparation will help you avoid being thrown off course by unanticipated details and can happen in a variety of ways, ranging from the mundane (making a list) to the unconventional (practicing a ritual). Appendix G ("Preparing for and Recording Interviews") shows as an example a set of instructions I created for my embodiment study in preparation for each interview. Having the documentation affiliated with the study in a neat stack, as well as the instructions for how to connect with co-researchers at the scheduled interview times, helped me maintain consistency and stay organized. It was also tremendously beneficial for fielding logistical questions from co-researchers.

I also had a 60-minute (or so) customary preinterview ritual that included about 30 minutes of focusing and 30 minutes of art journaling. The focusing exercise helped me clear a space for the shared experience in which I was about to participate and prepare to receive someone else's experience without having to abandon my own. Thus, I was able to leave behind the pretense of the detached observer and *be* with each of my research partners in a holistic manner. Additionally, I followed each interview with an authentic movement session. Authentic movement is a style of free-form, intuitive body movement performed with the intent to access and connect with personal awareness and presence. The movement sessions helped me integrate my interview experience and unwind and were also followed by some form of journaling.

Rituals are arguably universal (Legare & Watson-Jones, 2016) "formalized" acts designed to help us create meaning of life events and transitions (Sandstrom, Martin, & Fine, 2006) and can therefore have a therapeutic effect on participating individuals and groups. Collective and communal rituals include ceremonies such as weddings, memorial services, and religious rites. Rituals can also be performed individually and include practices such as completing a yoga sequence before going to bed. Due to their curious parallels with placebos (Benedetti, 2012) (e.g., ritualized ingestion of a "pill" to cure illness), rituals can help us shift perceptions of meaningful events and integrate experience and are thus popular in many cultures. Here are some ideas for pre- or post-interview rituals:

- Go for a walk (or a run or a swim).
- Take some fun photos (taking photos of the same subject from different angles is a cool perspective-taking exercise).
- Create a word map of assumptions and biases you *already* hold about the co-researcher you are about to interview (yes, you have assumptions and biases!).
- Take some sidewalk chalk outdoors and embrace your inner child.
- Identify an emotion or other experience that is getting in your way (e.g., fear, self-doubt). Write it down on a piece of paper and bury the paper in your backyard (or burn it or let it dissolve under running water).

A word of caution: Don't prepare too much, or you might wear yourself out. The idea behind preparing is to release stress, not to increase it. Too much of any activity can prove overwhelming, restricting, and dependence-inducing. Find one or two activities that resonate with your needs as a researcher and person, and do those in moderation.

Embodied Relational Interviewing

All prepped and ready to go? Good. This is the most fun part! I say this with caution. Interviews, like any other forms of dialogue, involve the relationship element. As you may know, some relationships seem to flow at first contact, while others . . . not so much. Yet relationships are key in heuristic research. Specifically, the quality of the data you collect will rely in large part on your ability to successfully facilitate the flow of relationship and conversation. Does this mean that you and your co-researcher have to agree about everything, avoid conflict, and like each other? Not really. Does it mean that you have to be "nice"? Not at all. Johanson and Kurtz (1991) suggested that preconceived ideas about "nice" and "not so nice" invite comparison and contests for power. While they extend this idea within the context of a therapeutic relationship, the process that unfolds between therapist and client is very much an interview process. Consequently, the ability of a therapist to successfully conduct an interview enhances the success of the therapeutic alliance. Likewise, being a successful heuristic interviewer means that you are responsible for modeling the conduct of respectful discord and civil relational engagement that will keep your process from derailing and enhance the trustworthiness of your findings. If you are a brashly opinionated and confrontational researcher, your research partners will almost undoubtedly follow your lead. You are responsible for setting the tone of the interviews!

Interview questions aimed at unraveling the essential nature of a profound human experience do not seek simple, single responses. In fact, the answers to such questions are often just as complex as the questions themselves. Likewise, some of the answers you receive may not align with answers you had in mind based on theory, the professional literature, or your personal experience. This can throw you into inner conflict as you attempt to make sense of a statement that may not be backed by theory or previous findings. As you struggle with your conflict, you may disengage from your research partner, who will undoubtedly experience some dissonance due to the break in connection that you shared just moments ago. This type of conflict may ensue if you rely exclusively on cognition (thinking) to process the content of your dialogue.

Your ability to maintain a balanced sense of engagement with your research partner will be informed by your capacity to maintain balance across multiple ways of being and of knowing—that is, by using your cognitive, emotional, sensory∞kinesthetic, perceptual, spiritual, and social∞relational dimensions. Engaging these various epistemological and ontological facets of yourself while interviewing, and allowing each to play a role in how you are processing your interview experience and engaging with your co-researcher is what I refer to as **embodied relational interviewing**. Here thought, emotion, sensation, intuition, memory, and perception each play a strategic role in data collection, laying the foundation for a holistic, relational experience that honors the experiences of all who are involved. Following are ideas for including different ways of being and of knowing as we engage in discourse with research partners:

- *Bring openness, interest, and curiosity to the encounter.* You already have some ideas about the "answers" to your central question(s). Come to the interview with an open spirit to receive a different way of interacting with ideas and concepts surrounding your topic.

- *Know your agenda, but see if it's okay to leave it at the door.* Imposing any type of agenda on your research study will almost invariably lead to skewed data collection, organization, and analysis as you strive to meet the predetermined outcomes it poses.

- *Begin with brief informal conversation.* The conversation does not have to be about issues related to your research. For example, I shared with one co-researcher that I had visited her home of origin. She then shared with me that she had visited mine. This brought us to a highly intersubjective conversation about our two nations of origin experiences with revolution and the thwarted quests for democracy, opening the door for empathic relational engagement, trust, and a highly efficient interview process.

- *Invite your co-researcher to participate in a brief relaxation-oriented exercise.* This can be something as simple as, "I wonder if it's okay to begin with a few moments of breathing and connecting with our bodies" or "Would you be interested in sharing a minute of quiet meditation?" Or you can facilitate a brief focusing exercise.

- *Be an active listener and receiver.* Active listening is what I call **embodied relational listening**. It engages, again, your various ways of being and of knowing. Be attentive and attuned to your own, as well as your research partners', experiences. Here is how:

    - *Listen with your mind.* What thoughts emerge as you listen to your co-researcher?

    - *Listen with your emotions.* What are you feeling as your co-researcher talks? Sadness, guilt, shame, fear, anger, and joy are core human emotions.

    - *Listen with your body.* What happens in your body as you interact? How does your bodily experience shift with the flow of the conversation?

    - *Engage your perception.* How does your perception shift as you shift your focus from your co-researcher's eyes to his hands? From his words to his vocal pitch?

    - *Attend to memory.* Keep in mind though that memory is an invariably malleable and fallible experience.

    - *Check in with yourself.* Are you feeling present, attuned, and connected? Are you feeling overly connected or perhaps enmeshed? How can you remain empathic while maintaining clear boundaries within the I∞Thou? If you are not feeling present, how might you return to connection and flow?

    - *Listen for underlying meanings.* What meanings might be present beneath the words? Ask questions and explore.

- *Attend to dissonances.* Listen for contradiction, repetition, exaggeration, and minimization. Be prepared to explore in a nonconfrontational manner.
- *Be alert to resistance and avoidance.* Do not try to force your research partner to go where she does not wish to go. Make a mental note to return to the topic later. If your co-researcher is still showing resistance, try a different communication strategy, rephrase a particular question, or use an example from your personal experience.
- *Practice intentional self-disclosure.* Don't be afraid to self-disclose appropriately—that is, in a relevant and nonmonopolizing way. Self-disclosure can be especially effective at facilitating discussion around challenging topics or questions.
- *Attend to the personhood of all involved.* Honor the experience of your co-researcher, as well as your own. You both have a personal stake in the study.
- *Immerse yourself inside your co-researcher's narrative.* Practice the self-discipline of not interrupting, not completing your co-researcher's sentences, and not imposing your own views. Listen to receive.
- *Identify the potential impact of context.* How might the setting(s) of your interviews be shaping the direction of your conversation?
- *Attend to sociocultural considerations.* What social norms may be informing your interaction? How impactful are they? Are you able to modify or transcend them? Or how can you include and honor them?

Bring awareness to these dynamics, using gentle, nonoffensive confrontation to address them as appropriate. This will require you to engage some probing and prompting skills.

Probing and prompting, when informed by active listening and when practiced with a relational and congruent attitude, can facilitate the flow of dialogue. Here are some examples: "I sense that our energy is shifting. Can we take a moment to attend to what that might be about?" "It seems that this is a challenging moment. Would you like to pause?" "I can relate to that. Would you like to share more?" See Appendix H ("Open-Ended Relational Probing and Prompting") for more examples.

- *Be alert to transference and countertransference.* These are concepts from the psychoanalytic therapy tradition that inform therapeutic as well as social encounters. **Transference** is a client's (research partner's) projection onto the therapist (researcher) of personality features of another person (usually a parent), along with reaction to the therapist as if he actually possesses those characteristics (Seligman & Reichenberg, 2014). Here is an example: "When you say my name, you remind me of my father. He pronounces my name like that." **Countertransference** is the therapist's (researcher's) projection onto the client (co-researcher). Some mental health professionals view countertransference as a potentially harmful experience to the client. From an embodied, relational perspective, however, countertransference can be transformed from something one experiences *against* the other into something one experiences *with* the other—that is, into a shared process.

Both transference and countertransference can manifest negatively, positively, or in both ways within an interview. Transference and countertransference are more likely to manifest negatively when either you or your research partner is being detached or objective. Paradoxically, the more appropriately present and self-disclosing you are, the less likely the person you are dialoguing with is to experience a transferential reaction to you. Transference and countertransference are highly relational experiences and hold the potential for both securing and rupturing a relationship. Be alert to how these experiences are manifesting to maintain intimacy without violating boundaries (more on this in Chapter 10). For example, as you are dialoguing with your research partner, should you have feelings of anger toward him accompanied by a haunting memory of a personal experience with a family member, it may be appropriate to ask yourself, *Is this anger directed at my research partner, or is it about my family member?* Processing experiences of transference and countertransference openly and respectfully is critical to healthy cocreation of new realities, informing growth and transformation for all members of the research team.

- *Use person-centered approaches and microskills.* Carl Rogers (1961, 1980) left the world a legacy of evocative dialoguing approaches such as active listening (see above), genuineness, empathy, congruence, unconditional positive regard, acceptance, focus on the here and now, appropriate self-disclosure, empowerment, paraphrasing, summarizing, mirroring (verbal and nonverbal), and reflection of feeling and meaning. While these approaches speak for themselves (see Chapter 3 for descriptions of congruence, unconditional positive regard, and empathy, and Appendix H for examples of the other skills), they are not intended to be used as *techniques* but rather as *ways of being* with research partners. Using relational approaches and characteristics as techniques makes your interaction gimmicky and false and compromises trust.

- *Attend to nonverbals.* **Nonverbal communication** is expressed through nonlinguistic means, usually through physical signals, messages, and cues (Eunson, 2015). Verbal and nonverbal behaviors are complementary and more often than not intersect. Here are some ways to attend to nonverbals:

  - *Remain alert to body language.* This includes body movements, postures, gestures, facial expressions, touch, and proxemics (i.e., personal space).
  - *Evaluate eye contact.* Is it invasive, inconsistent? Or does it seem about right?
  - *Evaluate levels of engagement and attunement.* Do you sense any disinterest, amplification, aloofness, or forced intimacy? Or is the presence just right?
  - *Attend to vocal processes.* This is especially important if not conducting a face-to-face interview. Does your research partner's voice (or yours) demonstrate fear, warmth, uncertainty? Are there pauses, silences, or changes in pitch and volume?
  - *Attend to incongruences between behaviors and words.* An example is when one smiles while speaking about a time when one struggled with physical pain.
  - *Evaluate touch.* Is there physical contact between you and any of your research partners? Is it relevant? Appropriate? What is your experience of it? What is your research partner's experience of it?
  - *Evaluate context.* Are you in a formal or informal setting? What other qualities of your setting may be informing your conversation?
  - *Ask questions.* Some individuals are more skilled at interpreting nonverbal behavior than others are. Be cautious not to make assumptions or jump to conclusions.
  - *Practice.* You can learn how to "read" nonverbals. Practice interpreting the nonverbals in your next communication with another or by yourself in front of a mirror.

- *Keep your research purpose and questions in mind.* Sometimes tangential conversation emerges, intentionally or unintentionally, as a distraction from the main topic. Bring your research purpose and questions back into focus when necessary.

- *Embrace the silences.* Think of silence as an open space that you and your co-researcher needed and thus cocreated using your authentic intersubjectivity. Don't rush to fill that space. Let whatever needs to fill the open space emerge on its own. I would suggest allowing your co-researcher to take the lead on this.

- *Practice cultural sensitivity.* Engage good judgment and use culturally sensitive approaches to navigate differences. Listen before speaking. Avoid making assumptions. Avoid making claims based on anecdotal evidence. Avoid making diffuse statements about another culture's truths or realities. Be humble. Remain open to accepting (even if you do not agree with) someone else's epistemological and ontological truths (more in Chapter 7).

- *Be attentive to what is not being said.* Your research partner may experience the need to talk around the issues. This may happen when feelings of discomfort, shame, or fear arise. Gauge the safety of taking the lead on introducing the topic. If it feels right to probe the unsaid, be as empathic and nonjudgmental as possible.

- *Attend to power differentials.* Power is a discernible presence in each and every interaction between one individual and another. With that, power is not stable or constant and will shift with the dynamics of your dialogue (more in Chapter 7).

- *Model honesty, transparency, and efficiency.* Modeling these characteristics encourages your co-researchers to also embrace them.

- *Know that I∞Thou interaction is not static.* The intersubjective space you share with each co-researcher will shift throughout the interview as shaped by power, culture, verbal and nonverbal exchanges, and other experiences (more in Chapter 7).

- *Highlight the shared moments and experiences.* You will share many moments of *withness* due to your shared interest. When those moments happen, name and celebrate them.

- *End with a question about co-researchers' experience participating in the research.* This is an integrating process; it allows you and research partners to debrief and attain closure.

- *Send your research partners thank-you messages.* Your co-researchers have volunteered their time, energy, and knowledge. Thank-you letters or e-mails are a great way to express your gratitude for their contribution to a collective scholarship venture.

- *Document your experience of each interview in your journal, as well as in the verbatim transcripts.* Your journal entries are part and parcel of the raw data. They are deeply meaningful and influential artifacts that carry meanings of their own.

- *Be yourself.* Don't fall victim to "phony researcher syndrome" (there's no such thing, of course, but you understand where I am coming from). As a heuristic researcher, you have a personal stake in this research study. Bring yourself to the table.

- *Enjoy the process!*

Disruptions in Flow

While heuristic interviewing can be a bonding experience for all persons involved, it can also be compromised by disturbances in flow. Here are some examples of disruptions that may occur or that may be happening in a peripheral manner:

- Technical failures (Internet connection, phone connection, time lag, etc.)
- Nerves (yours or a co-researcher's)
- Ruptures in trust (e.g., questioning of motives)
- Personal life events (surgery, illness, etc.)

I experienced a disruption in every interview I conducted for my embodiment study, with the exception of one. I did not foresee the disruptions. They happened because . . . well, life happens! Have a backup plan and embrace a constructive attitude. I have learned to view disruptions in research (as well as in other life experiences) as opportunities to pause and recalibrate.

Time and Structure Considerations

Heuristic interviewing includes tapping into multiple sources of information using a variety of data collection approaches such as observation, dialogue, listening, questioning, and attending to sensory experience and nonverbal communication, with a focus on the dynamics of I∞Thou interaction. The primary purpose of a heuristic interview is to explore and understand another person's in-depth living experience of the phenomenon you are researching. Patton (2002) proposed three interview approaches that may be suitable for heuristic data collection.

- *Informal conversational interview:* Discourse is generated spontaneously, and co-researchers engage in naturally emergent dialogue with the researcher.
- *General interview guide:* A set of issues or topics to be explored is shared with all co-researchers, and conversation remains within those common themes.
- *Standardized open-ended interview* (also commonly referred to as a *semi-structured interview*): A particular set of questions is predetermined for all co-researchers, with the understanding that other unique questions will emerge within individual interviews.

Moustakas (1990) identified the informal conversational interview as the one most closely aligned with the rhythm of heuristic inquiry. He underscored ensuring that each of your research partners has had an opportunity, through the interview process, to fully express herself, stressing that heuristic interviews are not restricted by time parameters. I concur—with caution!

In a perfect world in which time is not a pressing factor, that would be the ideal approach. An example of a situation in which you can use an open-ended approach to interviews is if you are conducting an informal inquiry. However, if you are conducting a formal study, you must set a schedule for completing different chunks of data collection (and other phases of research), as well as consider peripheral deadlines (e.g., completion of doctoral studies, time frame for a research grant) that may be impacted should you not complete your study in a timely manner. Additionally, given the potential for boundary and ethical breaches (more in Chapter 10) that may occur in the absence of time constraints, I would encourage the identification of some parameters, with room for flexibility. Defining a specific time range will help you and your co-researchers remain focused and ethical.

Being a psychotherapist in private practice, I am highly attentive to the necessity of establishing firm but flexible (50–60 minute) time limits on therapy sessions. At the same time, I am aware that the relationship between me and my clients (facilitated by my Rogerian characteristics of congruence, unconditional positive regard, and empathy [Rogers, 1980]) is pivotal to the success of our therapeutic process and that setting parameters may compromise my interactions with some clients. Inversely, I am cognizant of the fact that proper boundaries support a healthy therapeutic relationship and that without those parameters, the potential hazard of boundary violations looms. Within the contradictions lie the resolutions!

In my embodiment study, I set a 60- to 90-minute time limit on interviews with research partners. Setting a time range created a clear but malleable boundary that helped maintain consistency across all interviews while leaving designated room for movement. It also sent an implicit message to my research partners that, while we would be engaging in relational discourse about a highly personal topic to all of us, we would operate within a time frame designed to prevent sidetracking due to tangential subjects and friendly banter.

Along the same lines as setting fluid time limits is the idea of establishing a pliable structure for your interviews. Again, the informal conversational interview is ideal for ideal circumstances. However, many experienced researchers are aware of the imperfect nature of research projects. In the interest of maintaining consistency, timeliness, and ethical practice, I encourage you to consider the standardized open-ended/semi-structured interview. This invites you to create a uniform set of questions to use with all research partners while allowing space for the emergence of other questions that arise through your personal interaction with each co-researcher, with the resulting interview being a unique product. A word of caution: Do not fall into the trap of too much structure, which can place you in a position of power, undermining the social constructivist nature of the methodology and opening the door for potential ethical breaches. Once again, be creative and spontaneous in a manner that supports the flow of authentic and empathic dialogue while maintaining some level of consistency and fairness and ensuring proper boundaries. It's a balancing act that requires intention, attention, and plasticity.

If you are uncertain how to broach topics such as time and structure with your co-researchers, please put those insecurities to rest. You will have many opportunities to exchange with your research team information about time and content parameters, both before and during data collection. The information will be present in such documents as your invitation letter, your informed consent process, and your interview protocol, and your co-researchers will be able to ask questions. Also, since participation in your study is voluntary, each of your co-researchers can make the decision to withdraw at any time and for any reason (including their dislike for limitations you have set) without incurring a penalty.

Where and How

Two final interviewing issues are *where* (in a private setting, professional setting, etc.) and *how* (face-to-face, telephone, etc.) you plan to conduct the interviews and how you will document their content (video, audio, notes, combination of two or more approaches, etc.). There are strengths and limitations to every *where* and *how* of conducting interviews, although I do discourage note-taking during interviews as it tends to interrupt your ability to be fully present and attuned. With that, I suggest documenting the content of interviews through some type of recording. Allow the purpose, research question(s), research sample, and other facets of your study to inform your decision, making efforts to fill in the gaps and highlight the strengths of your approach. For example, although nonverbal communication is a well-documented and significant source of information for body psychotherapists, I made a deliberate decision to conduct virtual interviews with co-researchers (all of whom were seasoned body psychotherapists) for my heuristic study of psychotherapist embodiment (Sultan, 2015) rather than face-to-face interviews and to audio-record rather than video-record the interviews. My primary reasoning was that I sought to interview body psychotherapists in multiple geographic locations, with a focus on the nuances of voice and intonation (such as speech rapidity, volume, the use of the breath, pauses, and silence). Again, return to the purpose of your study, research questions, and other defining features to make a well-informed decision.

With that, the presence of any documenting device such as a camera, sound recorder, or notepad will influence your conversations with research partners. Again, we are all embodied beings in an embodied world (Merleau-Ponty, 1945/2013); we do not operate independently of our context. Thus, one of the issues I struggled with briefly as I deliberated among documenting options was how each form of documenting might influence relational interactions with co-researchers. I found that the more I focused on the potential negative impacts, the more I felt likely to carry inhibitions with me into the interview. I also recalled my hundreds of video-recorded and audio-recorded psychotherapy sessions with clients during my internship years. Most clients expressed initial distaste for the idea of having a camera in the session room.

Yet during a process of checking in with clients at the end of each session, the very same clients stated that once we got into the heart of our time together, they generally forgot that we were being recorded. Oh, the power of genuine interaction!

Researcher and Co-Researcher Artifacts

Besides interviews, other sources of rich information about your phenomenon of inquiry are researcher and co-researcher artifacts. The following may be considered artifacts:

- Stories, vignettes, and poems
- Artwork, photographs, and graffiti
- Letters and other forms of correspondence (including correspondence between you and co-researchers outside of time designated for data collection)
- Audio and video recordings
- Journal reflections and entries and other autobiographical logs

Essentially, any secondary documentation of the topic of inquiry that you or any member of your research team considers to be informative to your study is acceptable as an artifact.

Regrettably, artifacts are frequently disregarded as a source of data (Norum, 2008), as I came to discover while perusing dozens of heuristic research manuscripts. This is unfortunate, as artifacts often hold information not readily accessible through the usual data collection methods such as interviews (Norum, 2008). I firmly hold that certain types of artifacts have the ability to tell stories that words cannot possibly tell. Artifacts honor the process- and content-focused nature of heuristic research. I highly recommend the inclusion of any artifacts of relevance to your heuristic study. In the interest of maintaining the relational characteristics of heuristic inquiry, it may be helpful to collaborate with research partners on decision making about what is suitable for inclusion. Some co-researchers will want to contribute a variety of artifacts, while others will choose not to contribute any at all. Have a conversation with your co-researchers about artifacts and their particular meaning.

In my study of the embodied experiences of body psychotherapists (Sultan, 2015), research partners were invited to contribute artifacts with the understanding that the content of those contributions would hold comparable value to the content of our interviews. Four co-researchers contributed artifacts. Su contributed two photos of paintings she completed to help her make meaning of her embodied experiences as a therapist. The painting in Figure 6.2 depicts Su's experience of feeling trapped.

FIGURE 6.2 ● Artwork Su Created When She Was Feeling Trapped

Source: Su

The painting in Figure 6.3 depicts Su's experience of yearning for freedom.

Rainbow contributed excerpts of journal reflections documenting her experience as a body psychotherapist, the impact of her embodiment on clients, and the power of kinesthetic experience, shown in Rainbow's original formatting in Figure 6.4.

Additionally, I followed each interview I conducted with a time for deep reflexive practice and integration. I used a number of activities to process my interview experiences, including dance/body movement, journaling, taking mindful walks, and drawing/painting. Any artifacts produced during or after these activities were considered raw data. The artifact in Figure 6.5 is a drawing I created in my journal following my interview with Rainbow. It documents my experience of our well-boundaried yet intimate conversation about embodiment.

Artifacts should contribute meaningful information addressing your central guiding question. For example, each of the above artifacts included

FIGURE 6.3 ● Artwork Su Created When She Was Yearning for Freedom

Source: Su

information that addressed my central research question asking what it means for body psychotherapists to be embodied, as well as my subquestions asking how body psychotherapists use their embodiment within the therapeutic process, and the perceived impact on clients. Use artifacts (among other sources of information) as raw data as you conduct your data analysis.

Researcher Journals

While researcher journal entries are considered artifacts, journaling is in fact a key process for the primary researcher in heuristic inquiry. Although it is not explicitly identified as one of the seven processes of heuristic inquiry, it is implicitly understood that journaling is a primary method for documenting each of seven heuristic processes, as well as each of the six phases of heuristic research. Journaling honors the social constructivist, autobiographical, exploratory, process-focused, intuitive, introspective, creative, and humanistic facets of heuristic research, eliciting deeper knowing and multidimensional perception. Journaling involves both *reflective* (deep thought) and *reflexive* (self and other) processing of experience. Accordingly, it promotes novel ways of perceiving and understanding experience, as well as inspires new questions or processes of inquiry. Additionally, due to the transparency and clarity engendered by heuristic researcher journals (especially when excerpts of the journal

FIGURE 6.4 ● Rainbow's Journal Reflections of Her Journey in Body Psychotherapy

It's time for body psychotherapy to have its day. Enough hiding in the shadows. Everyone needs to know about it. This is bigger than me and I know it. I'm an instrument for something to manifest itself. I also know there is a connection to the divine feminine in this. As Riane Eisler puts it, it is gylanic. Mind and body reconnected once again. Partnership instead of patriarchy.

In the end it is not even about me. It changed my life and the universe set me on a course that I only needed to follow. How big is this? Where will it take me? There is a power in this I've never seen before. Nothing has come close to compare. Not just in my life, but I see it when I work with clients. I witness their transformation and can't believe my own eyes. The wisdom of the body. It is the portal into the divine.

I'm doing this because it is my calling. I'm good at it and I feel I have a unique contribution to make. I am drawn to this because every cell in my body becomes alive. I feel what I do is manifesting the divine. I have found my purpose and I am simply following that calling.

I see the coming back into the divine feminine. Where once we were in balance and saw the human body as the portal to the sacred mystery.

Oppression lives in the body. It shows up in energetic holding patterns, in how we limit our full expression of aliveness. Feminism speaks to how women's bodies are used as instruments of oppression. That energetic holding patterns are reinforced by social norms, gender norms. I guess addressing all this from a feminist perspective. Body psychotherapy does not get into gender. Feminism does not get into energy. But the body bridges both.

How do you incorporate the body in any study? It speaks a language of its own. Beyond words. Can images portray this? Maybe. We sure have a long way to go in incorporating the body into our human experience. We capture so little in the spoken language. Our physical form is our teacher on this plane. It records all that has happened to us, and wisdom of how to be in this world. The body never lies.

Source: Rainbow

FIGURE 6.5 ● Artwork I Created Following My Interview With Rainbow

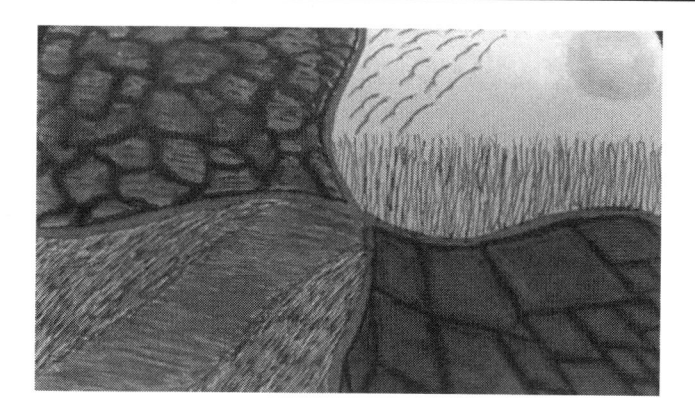

are included in the final manuscript for the study), engaging reflexively with your research experience using a journal is a potentially empowering and social justice–promoting activity.

There are few limits to what you can include in your research journal (see Chapter 7 for ideas). What you ultimately decide to share of that journal in your final manuscript or other ways of presenting the findings should serve the purpose of expanding an understanding of the findings. In that respect, your research journal is a further testament to your perspective on your role and that of each of your co-researchers, as well as on the general process and content of your study, lending your heuristic study rigor and trustworthiness.

Likewise, your journal reflections are not limited to narrative writing. They may include notes, drawings, diagrams, charts, phrases, words, word maps, brainstorms, poetry, symbols, unsent letters, imaginary dialogues, collages, or other meaningful representations of your experience. In fact, your journal may not be in the form of a traditional notebook; it may look more like a portfolio. You can use your reflections to supplement each co-researcher's experience (as elicited through the research interviews) as you prepare to generate individual depictions. Additionally, your reflections will help you process challenges that emerge throughout your study and attain insight about next steps. Most important, your journal will contain multiple sources of information about potential themes. Following are a few excerpts of narrative entries from heuristic researchers' journals.

Early in her heuristic research study of internalized racism, Whatley (2015) used her journal to address preliminary resistance she was feeling toward her study. Notice how she located her personal experience within the wider context of her topic of inquiry and society:

> The following early journal entries reveal the fear of exposure, fear of irrelevance, and sense of overwhelm that accompanied this inquiry. On 12/3/12, I wrote:
>
> A fear of exposure rises up in me. Is it a product of the unspoken culture of shame related to race? Or is it my own personal idealized self-image that does not want the flawed, immature, wounded parts of myself exposed, seen [?] Was it humiliation for being seen as less-than for having feelings—for not being sufficiently stoic, meeting all challenges with aplomb? Is it not enough that there is a Tiger Woods, the Williams sisters, etc. [?] Do I need to be perfect, too, to excel beyond imagination, to become the standard against which all else is measured? Is my personal best not good enough? Is it never enough? (pp. 91–92)

During her heuristic study of yoga and emotional well-being, Alsobrook (2015) journaled her decision to step away from the raw data of her study and take time to linger in a meditative place with the information. Take note of her attention to her thinking and emotional processes, as well as to her kinesthetic, social∞relational, spiritual, and perceptual experience. She wrote:

> I find myself overwhelmed by a deep sense of connectedness with these women, both in experiences and spiritually. We are all spiritual warriors on a path of universal connectedness with all things through the breath and positive energies. As they spoke of their physical experience while doing the asanas, I found my own body responding in kind, feeling their own feelings physically as they spoke and each time I managed their data. I realize this is likely due to muscle, mind, and cell memory, but the sensation adds to my own feeling of connectedness. It makes me think about the connectedness with all those who do yoga; can we all be or feel so connected? I believe so, and that concept is truly amazing and bigger than words can adequately express. Yoga is so much more than the label, more than the asanas, meditative states, and the breath, but the breath connects everyone as the same, no matter how they do the asanas. (pp. 63–64)

Finally, as I collected the data for my study of psychotherapist embodiment (Sultan, 2015), I documented my experience of each interview. The following is an excerpt from a reflection describing my experience with Stephen, who shared the disembodying and shattering loss of his brother and father to suicide, and his mother to a severe brain hemorrhage, all within a 7-year period. Note my attention to physical and emotional experience, thought processes, shifting perceptions, as well as the interrelationship of authenticity and embodiment (a theme in the study):

> I felt myself curling up for some sort of comfort as my own memories of loss and grief flooded me. I did not understand where this feeling was coming from. *You work with grieving clients all the time!* I reminded myself. Even then, I caught myself talking louder with Stephen and laughing very hard. With that came the awareness that I was trying to shield myself from the overwhelming desire to curl up completely. Or, was it Stephen I was trying to shield? Either way, I felt disembodied. Or, at least I *think* I did. Maybe I wasn't. As I live that moment yet again, now, I sense that maybe I was actually fully embodied. And maybe my spark of inauthenticity was but a jagged facet of my raw embodiment. (p. 186)

Note how each of us engaged in a process of reflection that included meaningful statements about our personal experience, as well as questions that emerged from our reflexive process. Note, too, that although journaling is a personal practice, each of these entries reflects a process of deliberation transcending the self of the researcher by reaching out into the world of her research partners and/or the world at large. This is how journaling serves to facilitate both an integration of personal experience and a bridge to connection with the experience of another!

Winding Down Data Collection

So you're well into collecting your data in the form of interview content, artifacts, and journal reflections. While you may have set fluid parameters for the length, breadth, and depth of your interviews, setting parameters around inclusion of artifacts, journal reflections, and documentation of nonverbal communication may prove a tad more complicated. It is plausible that one of your co-researchers will decide, following her interview, not to contribute an artifact only to change her mind later. Another research partner may request that you not include the content of an e-mail you exchanged. It is just as conceivable that you may wish to include your latest journal entry in your raw data although you are nearing the end of data analysis. And so on! The question to ask yourself, then, is: *How late is too late for data collection?*

When it comes to when to stop collecting data for a heuristic study, there are no absolute answers. You will need to make decisions as your research process unfolds and you have a firmer understanding of what is involved. As I mentioned earlier, whether or not to continue interviewing will be determined based on your assessment of further need—that is, you have reached saturation, or one of your research partners withdraws from the study. However, collecting raw data in other forms may not be as clean-cut. Your research topic is a living, breathing thing and an integral part of every aspect of your life; any sliver of information you encounter may constitute credible raw data. Therefore, I recommend creating some type of fluid parameter surrounding data collection and sticking with it. The last thing you need is to become overwhelmed with too much information. While heuristic inquiry is open-ended research, *open-ended* does not mean *without boundaries*, as this can lead to loss of focus. If it is emotionally challenging for you to even consider excluding late-arriving raw data, talk with the research partner(s) concerned and negotiate a compromise that is inclusive but reasonable. And remember (and remind your research partners) that the end of this study does not mean an end to further exploration of your phenomenon but is, possibly, a new beginning within new contexts.

Data Organization and Management

Upon completion of data collection for each co-researcher, it is time to organize the data in preparation for analysis. In heuristic inquiry, data organization includes becoming deeply familiar with the content through a number of immersion∞incubation∞reflexivity cycles and verbatim transcription of interviews.

Immersion∞Incubation∞Reflexivity

To acquire a deep and intimate relationship with the raw data, you will need to immerse yourself in it (Moustakas, 1990). This entails the following:

- Vertical and horizontal reading of notes, journal entries, and the content of correspondence between you and co-researchers
- Vertical and horizontal review of artifacts you have collected in their variety of forms
- Vertical and horizontal listening to audio recordings, and vertical and horizontal viewing of and listening to video recordings

I use the words *vertical* and *horizontal* because you are seeking both *deep* and *broad* understandings of the data. That is, you want to explore the deep, personal, individual meanings the experience holds for each research partner, as well as the broad, mutual, and potentially universal meanings the experience may hold for individuals outside of the research team (albeit as represented by your research sample). Again, in heuristic inquiry the phenomenon you are researching is highly meaningful for everyone involved in the study. In your quest to reveal the essential nature of the phenomenon, you will want to engage multidimensional processes that allow multiple iterations of understanding to emerge.

With that, any level of intimacy must be well boundaried and tempered. As you immerse yourself in the raw data, you must step away from it once in a while to allow the information you have received to incubate (Moustakas, 1990) and form into an integrated entity. By now, you know that immersion∞incubation is a complementary process that also involves deep reflexivity. Thus, you will engage in a dance of immersion∞incubation∞reflexivity with the raw data in an effort to make of it some preliminary sense. Going back and forth within this process will give you access to subjective and objective perspectives on the data. Additionally, you should engage with the data within different contexts. For example, if you organize your data and skim through it at your home on a Sunday morning, the next time you sit with it, do so in a different setting at a different time of day. Document your experience in your journal, as well as your perception of co-researcher experiences of participating in your study.

In my embodiment study, I listened to each audio recording repeatedly (numerous times per week over several weeks) and immersed myself in other content involving the co-researcher (artifacts, e-mail correspondence, etc.) to gain intimate familiarity with it, as well as with the uniqueness of the co-researcher. When I sensed organic disengagement from that co-researcher's raw data, I took a step back, and a natural process of incubation followed. Questions and ideas emerged as I came close to and/or distanced myself from the data. This was documented in my journal and, along with interview transcripts, used to support crystallization of an individual depiction for the co-researcher (more on this later).

Creating Verbatim Transcripts

The ideal way to represent heuristic audio and audiovisual data is by producing a verbatim textual depiction of it (i.e., a transcript). Braun and Clarke

(2013) define **transcription** as "the process of turning audio or audiovisual data into written text (a *Transcript*) by writing down what was said (and if audiovisual material, what was done), and in some instances how it was said" (p. 338). Transcribe verbatim the content of your interviews with co-researchers, and also note on the transcripts observations of your personal experience. For example, interviews for my embodiment study were conducted virtually and were audio-recorded. Verbatim transcripts included the exact dialogical exchange between co-researchers and me, plus notes and commentary about pauses, changes in voice tone, and interruptions, as well as how I processed those experiences in the following ways:

- *Kinesthetically* (sensory-based/somatic, e.g., sweating, increased heart rate)
- *Cognitively* (thought-based, e.g., *I wonder what invited her use of "authentic" rather than "genuine"*)
- *Emotionally* (feeling-based, e.g., sadness, fear, anger)
- *Socially∞relationally* (based on relational interactions and processes, e.g., empathy, intersubjectivity)
- *Perceptually* (based on my own objective∞subjective experience versus that of another)
- *Spiritually* (honoring vague, inexplicable experiences that may hold existential meaning)

Remember that you bring both your individual and your collective history, experience, perception, and identity to the interview encounter. Thus, as you translate the multidimensional living experience of that encounter into words, your depiction is influenced by your living experience, with implications for data analysis (Poland, 2008).

With this in mind, I highly discourage contracting transcription out to a service. Any individual other than you will have no familiarity with your topic or with the dynamics of your interview. The transcriber will not have experienced the live encounter with your co-researchers that rendered the interviews the unique relational artifacts they are. Furthermore, the very idea that someone other than you will transcribe the interviews will have an impact on your research partners. Co-researchers are real people with real narratives that hold deep meaning for them. How information they have shared with you is represented and shared elsewhere matters. Rather than bringing an outsider to your research team to transcribe the interviews, I highly recommend doing it yourself using a process I call **embodied relational transcription**. Following are the characteristics of my transcription approach (see Chapter 7 for an example of embodied relational transcription of a dialogical exchange with a student):

- *It is channeled by you, the primary researcher.* I use the word *channeled*, as your body acts as a medium—a receiver, holder, and transmitter of experience—and thus as a potential tool for new ways of being and of knowing.

- *It is deeply relational.* It involves profound engagement, attunement, and presence.

- *It is embodied.* This involves listening and depicting, as well as speaking and living, using the body∞mind∞spirit∞world to enter the experiences of your research partners. As you give voice to the narratives through your holistic experience, you will connect and resonate with certain words, phrases, or symbols, either cognitively or spiritually. Try a focusing exercise to laser those resonances, and make note of them in your journal or on the transcripts, as they may represent emerging themes. You will also connect and resonate with your co-researchers' living experience, especially as it relates to your living experience and to your topic of inquiry.

- *It is multidimensional.* It contains (beyond the verbatim documentation of words) the notation of a variety of elements, including pitch variation, pace, interruption, laughter, pausing, breathing, and silence. (There are many established notation systems. I encourage you to create your own, as you will acquire a deeper and broader grasp of it.)

- *It is holistic.* It transcends observation, listening, and cognition to include subjective experience of the body, emotions, relationships, and perception, and how these experiences are both impacting and impacted by the content.

- *It is reflexive.* It involves exploring how your personal experience and history may be impacting your perception of the interview. How are your biases, beliefs, values, and assumptions bleeding into the transcription? How may they be shaping its course?

- *It is member-checked.* That is, it is shared with the appropriate co-researcher with an opportunity for feedback and edits.

The importance of these features lies in their function as relational and dialogical facilitators or inhibitors and thus in their potential for augmenting or mitigating conflict and empowerment, their capacity for supporting or interrupting connection and communion, and their influence over the overall course of the study. For example, let's say you share a verbatim transcript with one of your co-researchers and he decides to change large chunks of a particular portion of the interview. The information he has chosen to delete is information you deem of high value, especially as you detect in it some themes that seem to align with themes you have identified in other interviews thus far. At the same time, technically speaking, the content of the data belongs to him, not to you. How you address this issue will depend in large part on the guidelines you set for the study (including researcher and co-researcher rights) and your ability to negotiate and communicate your perspective in an inclusive and empathic manner. Look at the various dynamics at play in your study (especially ethical dynamics), as well as at potential consequences for whichever courses of action you are considering, before making decisions.

Finally, be present, be real, and enjoy the process! To this day, I recall the first time I created a verbatim transcript of a video recording. The transcript was required for a mock therapy session assignment in Introduction to Counseling, one of my first courses as a graduate counseling student. The video recording was 20 minutes long, but I was required to transcribe only 10 minutes. I did not look forward to the task. In addition to the verbatim transcription, we were required to document any counselor microskills we used during our interaction (e.g., paraphrasing, open-ended question, summarizing, mirroring), as well as the intention behind our use of them. We were also asked to identify better alternative responses and reasons for these responses for select statements and actions we felt could have been made more intentionally based on information received from the client (not unlike your process of asking probing questions from a relational perspective). It took me no less than 18 hours to transcribe those 10 minutes of session. The reason for this time investment, as I am now certain, is that I was trying too hard to use my ears to listen, rather than using my body to *be* with my client, not only during transcription but even during the mock session itself. Essentially, I allowed my divided focus to sabotage my embodied presence and attunement to my mock client, who was a classmate with whom I happened to share a warm relationship. Additionally, I did not watch and listen to the video recording of the mock session before attempting to transcribe its content.

Conversely, it took me under 4 hours to transcribe each 60- to 90-minute interview I conducted for my embodiment study. The difference here was that I was present and attuned to each co-researcher as we dialogued. Likewise, I listened to each interview repeatedly, using full-body engagement and allowing high levels of presence and attunement. By the time I was ready to transcribe each interview, I felt as if I knew both the content and my co-researcher very intimately. From there, verbatim transcription flowed smoothly.

Once you have a finalized version of the transcript, sit with it, turn on the recording once again, and listen while you read. Listen deeply. Repeat out loud the words your co-researcher is saying. Repeat each sigh, each hum, each breath. Embrace the silences. Laugh with the laughter. Try this with earphones and also without them. Use your pause key when you need it. Listen. Speak. Embody. Feel. *This*, not the writing, is the most important part of the transcription: living the words and experiences of your research partners, breathing them, becoming them. Then step away from the whole experience and let it incubate.

Data Analysis: Theme Illumination and Identification

As I mentioned before, data analysis begins as soon as you make your first contact with co-researchers. The content of your communication becomes part of your raw data, and data analysis starts. However, formalized data analysis happens after you have collected and organized your data in the form of transcripts, journal reflections, and other artifacts. One note before we get into it: Just as in the case of interview transcription, data analysis using a qualitative data-crunching software program is not a good idea. Heuristic research is highly intuitive, imaginative, and creative. Thus, the optimal method for analyzing your raw data is to conduct the analysis yourself using the heuristic processes.

One thing to note here is that heuristic data analysis demands that you take a holistic approach when reviewing the data for themes. Unlike the process of coding used in grounded theory (which often involves careful line-by-line analysis of transcript content), data analysis in heuristic inquiry gives equal value to all co-researcher content. That is, co-researcher data is any content found not only in transcripts but also in artifacts and any other relevant media or communication. Essentially, you will review each set of data as a single unit of information about the co-researcher as you work to identify and generate themes. This helps maintain the wholeness of each co-researcher, even as you move from the realms of the personal into the universal domains of the topic of inquiry.

Following Clear Procedures

Moustakas (1990) provided us with a detailed outline for analyzing the data in a heuristic study. Here are the key recommendations he made:

1. Gather all the data (recordings, transcripts, artifacts, etc.) for one co-researcher at a time.

2. Immerse yourself fully in the data until you understand it clearly.

3. Set the data aside, and allow time for rest and incubation. Then reconnect with the data and identify preliminary qualities and themes. Begin to construct an individual depiction.

4. Return once again to the raw data to identify whether or not the individual depiction reflects the essential themes of that co-researcher's experience.

5. Begin data collection with your next co-researcher following the same process. Do this until you have created individual depictions for each of your research partners.

6. Gather all individual depictions and resume immersion and incubation (and reflexivity!) to generate a composite depiction representing the integrated experience of all.

7. Return yet again to the raw data and select two or three co-researchers whose data exemplifies the group as a whole, as well as highlights the uniqueness of each individually. From those co-researchers' data sets, formulate exemplary portraits.

8. Develop a creative synthesis that represents, in artistic form, your extended immersion in the phenomenon through your own as well as your co-researchers' experiences.

With these procedures, there are a number of other matters to consider when conducting heuristic data analysis.

Honoring Content and Context

In a heuristic study, we are working with words and meanings. Therefore, the higher focus in data analysis is on what is emerging within the dialogue versus how frequently it is emerging. That is not to say that frequency is not important. If several people are repeating similar ideas, you should not ignore that! However, frequency is not all. Remember that you are working to unravel the essential nature of a profound human experience, one that has special meaning for all members of your research team, including you. Thus, the primary purpose behind heuristic data analysis is to *understand*, with a vision to *cocreate new knowledge, make meaning,* and *foster individual and collective transformation*. With that, throughout data analysis, you will use one or more of the seven processes of heuristic inquiry as you bring your focus to two core constituents of your raw data:

- **Content**
    - Responses generated through exploration of your central research question(s)
    - Responses generated through exploration of other research-related question(s)
    - Responses generated through non-research-related discussion relevant to your study
    - Words, phrases, symbols, images, metaphors, analogies, examples, repetition, and the like

- **Context**
    - Intrapersonal dynamics (self∞self)
    - Interpersonal dynamics (self∞other)
    - Sociocultural/environmental dynamics (self∞world)

Maintaining your focus on content and context, as well as on their interrelationships, will help you efficiently unravel the meanings that are living within your raw data. It will also help you organize your themes and relate them back to the primary components of your study—that is, your central research question(s), your supporting theories, and the professional literature.

Deciphering Potential Themes

Begin by looking at the interview/transcript as a whole rather than as a series of precise words and phrases that contain the answers to all your interview questions. Deliberately fishing around for patterns may drive you to look for them where they do not exist, potentially privileging your biases over the actual content. On the other hand, taking a holistic view of the raw data keeps you out of the weeds, allowing you to see the big picture and easily identify emerging patterns within each of the content and context areas, as well as within the junction of content∞context. Here are some questions to consider as you unravel potential themes:

- What is my prior knowledge or understanding of the essential nature of the topic of inquiry?
- What are my overall impressions of this data?
- What was/were the research partner's response(s) to the central research question?
- What was/were the research partner's response(s) to other questions I asked or to subquestions of the study?
- What questions did I or the co-researcher intentionally or unintentionally avoid?
- What ideas did the research partner propose/discuss that seemed unrelated to the topic of the study? What relationship might they bear to the topic?
- What specific words, phrases, symbols, images, metaphors, analogies, or examples did the research partner use that seemed significant? What makes them significant?
- What similarities and/or differences are emerging within each research partner's data, as well as between the data sets of individual co-researchers?
- Did the research partner use repetition? What makes it significant?
- What nonverbals were present? What makes them significant?
- What was the role of context (intrapersonal, interpersonal, and sociocultural/environmental dynamics) within each of these interactions?
- How might context have informed my research partner's responses, as well as my understanding of those responses, and our ongoing dialogue?

- What unique, unexpected, or unanticipated (based on prior perusal of the professional literature and/or on personal experience, for example) features of the phenomenon presented themselves? What meanings do those features potentially hold?
- Based on what I know (or think I know) about my co-researcher, how does he engage with the phenomenon in contrast with how he speaks about it? How does he *live* it?
- How do I live the phenomenon, and how might my manner of living the phenomenon impact my understanding of how my research partner lives it?
- How might my understanding of the phenomenon shift if I were to try to live it from my research partner's perspective?
- What core features of the phenomenon are emerging based on my interaction with this set of raw data? How do they relate to previous findings in the professional literature?
- If I were to approach this research partner's raw data from another angle (e.g., drawing, collaging), what core themes might emerge?
- If I were to create a visual depiction (e.g., word map) of the core themes held within this research partner's raw data, what might be included?
- How does all this information help me better understand my research partner's living experience of the phenomenon? How does it help me view my own living experience of the phenomenon from a different perspective?
- Now that I have immersed myself in the data, what is my overall sense of it?

As you respond to each of these questions, make use of the following tools, as well as others you find helpful in representing your experience of the emerging themes:

- The seven processes and six phases of heuristic inquiry (especially immersion, self-dialogue, and incubation)
- Word maps and brainstorms
- Doodles, drawings, and sketches
- Charts, tables, and spreadsheets
- Notes and reflections

Be creative and do not limit yourself with categorical thinking (e.g., "Tables are for quantitative studies"). Use whatever platforms help you access the experience you are exploring. It is not necessary that any of the answers to your questions make sense, early in data analysis. In fact, in the beginning phases, the answers may not make much sense at all! The more you immerse yourself in the data, the more you will *see* and *live* the data. Living your research partner's experience is just as important as living your own as you lay the foundation for cocreating new meanings and understandings of the phenomenon.

Organizing Themes According to Research Questions

As you work to decipher themes from the data, remain open to specific words, phrases, or symbols that offer nuanced description of the topic of inquiry and encapsulate its essential nature in response to your research questions. Remember that in heuristic research there are no hierarchies within the various categories of data; all data are attributed equal value. See Table 6.1 for a sample of words, phrases, symbols, nonverbals, and implicit themes that seemed (based on tacit knowing and intuition) significant in the raw data of one of the co-researchers in my embodiment study (Sultan, 2015). Some of these later emerged in the data of other research partners, alerting me to their significance to the essential nature of the phenomenon. This preliminary theme identification was based on the following research questions:

1. What does it mean for you to be embodied?

2. How do you use your embodiment within the therapeutic process?

Note that while the words, phrases, symbols, and nonverbals were extracted directly from the raw data (transcripts and artifacts), the implicit meanings and themes, as well as the unanticipated themes, were inspired by my imagination and intuition. Once again, be creative!

Maintaining Discipline

I cannot stress enough the importance of maintaining disciplined (Douglass & Moustakas, 1985) attention to your data for data analysis and illumination of the themes to proceed smoothly. Theme illumination will *not* automatically unfold as you distance yourself entirely from your data and incubate without end. For theme illumination to occur, you should go about each immersion∞incubation∞reflexivity cycle within data analysis intentionally. Don't wallow in the shelter of incubation. Should you immerse yourself in a research partner's data for several days (or several hours) in a row and then realize you have hit a wall, withdraw and allow things to incubate . . . for a reasonable stretch of time and with a plan to return to the data soon and immerse yourself in it once again with a renewed sense of curiosity and perspective.

Unfortunately, some researchers allow incubation to extend indefinitely, placing their study at risk of losing momentum. Enter the immersion∞

TABLE 6.1 ● Preliminary Theme Identification

Words	Phrases	Symbols	Nonverbals	Implicit/Tacit Meanings/Themes	Unanticipated Themes
Accepting	Be with	Aura	Heavy breathing	Remaining aware and present	Social marginalization of somatic experiences
Allowing	Consensual reality	Bridge	Repeated coughing	Accepting and allowing	Pathologizing embodiment
Attuning	Empathic resonance	Mirror	Protracted silence	Listening with your body/attuning Mirroring	
Awareness	Felt connection	Third eye	Changes in pitch/volume/tone	Negotiating boundaries	
Between	Felt sense of self	Tuning fork		Resonating with another's experience	
Normalizing	Here and now			Creating a shared experience	
Present	Integrative process				
Refinding					
Shape	Normalize an aberration				
Shared	Sensory experience				
Space	Somatic resonance				

incubation∞reflexivity cycle of data analysis with an attitude of remaining as close as possible to your data, no matter which phase of the cycle you are working through. With that, staying close to your data does not mean forcing illumination but remaining present to what is emerging through your data analysis and attending or responding to it. Above all, stay focused, stay disciplined, and stay intentional.

Data Analysis: Theme Explication

Upon completion of preliminary theme illumination and identification, you are ready to explicate your findings. Heuristic theme explication involves four methods of representation:

- Individual depictions
- Composite depictions
- Exemplary portraits
- Creative synthesis

Including a variety of representation methods lends depth and rigor to your study. Let's take a look at what goes into each of these methods, with examples from heuristic studies.

Individual Depictions

The purpose of an individual depiction is to provide a holistic, detailed illustration of a co-researcher's personal living experience of the topic of inquiry. Individual depictions also serve to circumvent the potential loss of the individual's singular, unique experience within the unified gestalt/whole. An individual depiction is characterized by the following: (a) It contains a brief demographic profile detailing the identity of the research partner in keeping with his self-description (Sultan, 2015); (b) it is elicited from the raw data (usually in the form of verbal descriptions); (c) it includes verbatim excerpts of the interview (Moustakas, 1990, 2015); (d) it is enhanced by co-researcher artifacts relevant to the topic of inquiry; and (e) it highlights the core themes illuminated through numerous immersion∞incubation∞reflexivity cycles.

Once an individual depiction is completed, return to the original data to ensure the accuracy of your representation of the co-researcher's experience (Moustakas, 1990). You may share the individual depiction with the co-researcher as a way of checking accuracy and suggesting modifications. Moustakas (1990) suggested two questions to guide this process: "Does the individual depiction of the experience fit the data from which it was developed? Does it contain the qualities and themes essential to the experience?" (p. 51). If so, move on to the next collection∞organization∞analysis cycle.

If not, go through a process of revision to identify and remove nonessential facets of the phenomenon. Following is an excerpt of an individual depiction from Green's (2012) heuristic study of ecological writers' experience of nature:

> Ana is a feature writer, novelist, graphic designer, and photographer. She is the mother of four children and lives on an acre or so of land overlooking the city in which she lives. Although her family enjoyed camping when she was young, her first relationship to nature was through love of animals, particularly her, as yet unrealized, desire to own a horse.
>
> **Ana:** ... I had a sinking feeling one year on my birthday when I got a backpack. I didn't want a backpack; I wanted a horse. I loved animals and my head was always in the clouds. I liked animals in a dreamy way but going into nature wasn't part of it.
>
> She attended Prescott College as an undergraduate, and it was on her backcountry orientation and solo that she had her first undeniably intense experiences in nature.
>
> **Ana:** So we set out and I had no idea what was ahead of me, and what was ahead of me was a complete shedding of who I was.
>
> **Cinny:** So there was something in the first week that made you a totally different person? What was it? The effort? The landscape?
>
> **Ana:** ... One night we slept on the bank of this river called Clear Creek and I put my sleeping bag next to the water in a soft patch of sand. In the middle of the night, I popped awake, for no reason, wide awake, and heard something. It was the sound of water so I looked out of my sleeping bag and saw the river was trickling toward me. I jumped up and grabbed my sleeping bag. How did I know that the river was rising? My body knew something. (pp. 64–65)

Composite Depictions

Upon completion of an individual depiction for each co-researcher, bring all individual depictions together for more immersion∞incubation∞reflexivity work, this time using the collective body of findings to generate a composite depiction (Moustakas, 1990, 2015). Once you have gone through enough cycles of intimacy and distance with the data, a composite understanding of these data will emerge, representing the shared experience of the phenomenon among various research partners (Moustakas, 1990, 2015; Sultan, 2015). As with the individual depictions, the composite depiction includes verbatim excerpts and artifacts, and underscores the core themes "as experienced by the individual participants and by the group as a whole" (Moustakas, 1990, p. 52). Essentially, the composite depiction acts as an accurate, vivid

(Moustakas, 1990) unifying representation of the core themes illuminated through each of the individual portraits. Following is an excerpt from the composite depiction created by Leiby (2014) in her heuristic exploration of the use of the eyes as portals to innate presence:

> Mutual eye-gazing has the potential to facilitate a direct pathway to shared awareness between participating guide and guidee. Mutual eye-gazing is a gentle practice, with a radical result. It is attunement that brings forth the transformative experience of unitive consciousness. Described as an eye-to-eye and a soul-to-soul meditation, this experience opens an individual to a "very deeply dissolved dimension," accompanied by a sense of "great space and openness." In this openness a "feeling of availability" emerges. The participants of the current study expressed the ultimate satisfaction that this realization brings.
>
> Preparing the ground for awakening provides an open space for engagement. The guide first enters into his or her own dimension of inner stillness, and the guidee naturally attunes and aligns with this energy, entering into his or her own dimension of inner stillness. A felt sense of inner stillness involves quieting the mind. This is accomplished by bringing attention to the breath and to the body while holding focus through the eyes of another. At times, the guidee feels as if the guide is affecting or influencing the movement experienced within his or her body. However, it is the guidee's own energy movement that is matching the energy of the guide.

Exemplary Portraits

These portraits entail further development of two or three individual portraits to reflect the uniqueness of those co-researchers' experiences within the collective experience of the research team (Moustakas, 1990, 2015). What separates an exemplary from an individual portrait, or from a composite depiction, is that an exemplary portrait contains details about the co-researcher that were not present in the individual or composite depictions. For example, you might want to include detailed demographic information about the co-researcher (Moustakas, 1990) in the exemplary portrait as a way of showcasing that person's singular characteristics within the gestalt of the research team. Exemplary portraits bring into focus the topic of inquiry as experienced both individually and collectively, highlighting the potential of heuristic research to tap into both personal and universal characteristics of a phenomenon. The following excerpt is from Madden's (2015) heuristic exploration of the experience of being spiritual for an atheist:

> Portrait 2: P8. P8 was a 54-year-old white, divorced freelance editor/proofreader. His lived experience of being spiritual as an atheist came from an innate curiosity for the world around him and the scientific

method, as well as raising his daughter. His view of atheism was withholding his belief until there is evidence available. He viewed his lived experience of spirituality as similar to believers, but without the supernatural component. P8 grew up in a Catholic family, although he used the term "Cafeteria Catholic" to refer to his family because they chose what part of the religion to follow. He used the term agnostic since he was a teenager, mainly because he saw the term atheist as being so hated. He now uses the term atheist.

> I've called myself an agnostic as early as a teenager. I had to understand what those words mean because agnosticism was coined by I think Thomas Huxley just because the term atheist was so hated. Agnostic means without knowledge. A without a Gnostic, without knowledge. And to me, that's compatible with atheism.

His lived experience of being spiritual was tied to his emotional experience of joy. For him, joy was tied to gratitude. He has been able to experience joy in his daily life as he learns about science and the world around us, enjoys his favorite foods, and advances in medicine that allowed him to survive childhood asthma.

> The feeling of gratitude and my gratitude stems from just being alive against all odds of that happening. Knowing a little bit of biology and science, the possibility of me being here is slight and I think it's a great privilege to be able to be alive and enjoy life and to learn about the universe. (pp. 133–134)

Creative Synthesis

This process is personal and allows you to transform the data from its original format into a creative and aesthetic illumination of your sense of the essential nature of the phenomenon. Moustakas (1990) described the creative synthesis as encouraging a great range of freedom, as it involves many of the heuristic processes (tacit knowing, immersion, illumination) used throughout your study. The creative synthesis is a platform for explicating the *what* and *how* of the phenomenon following the analysis of all data sets and based on newly co-constructed understandings of it. It is an artistic and visionary synthesis of living experience with meaning-making. The creative synthesis can source any of a variety of creative outlets, including musical composition, story, artwork, metaphor, and poetry. Figure 6.6 shows my poetic rendering of embodiment as experienced by body psychotherapists (Sultan, 2015), illuminated through multiple immersion∞incubation∞reflexivity cycles and reflecting my co-researchers' and my collective experience of the phenomenon:

FIGURE 6.6 ● Poetic Creative Synthesis: The Experience of Body Psychotherapist Embodiment

Ubiquity, In Situ

What are you? You dodge me.
Or, am I the one who dodges you?

I search for you . . .
as if you will gift me
something I cannot gift myself.

I call to you . . .
as if you will answer
my labyrinth of questions.

On my shoulders hover words. I have yet to find.
And you? You skirt the perimeter of me.

I reach for you . . .
but you evade my touch,
as if you were a Jump of mercury.

I surrender to the ungraspableness of you.

But, now, how you rise inside and
around me—begging for completion!

And, you receive me with openness
and grace, extending your hands
to carry me home.

In unmeasured moments,
breath becomes flesh becomes essence.

You gift me the cadence of your presence.
My core bathes in iridescent flow.

Nothing will dam the tongues
of this surging flame!

Nothing . . . but
the deluge of your impermanence.

It collides with me timidly,
leaving me smoldering in fortressed quietude.

Undreamed,
I move slowly—
keeping vigil for your return.

Closing Reflections

Data collection, organization, and analysis are the flesh of your research study. As soon as you have collected your raw data, immersed yourself in them, and organized them, you can proceed with a smooth data analysis process. In fact, you will find that you have been analyzing the raw data all along, even during those quiet stretches of incubation. Nevertheless, it is important to keep the process moving, even when your path seems unclear. Don't doubt your process. Don't stall at the bends. Don't get lost in the weeds of overly examining and analyzing; analysis and outcome are not the essence of heuristic inquiry. Rather, heuristic research is a journey with process and content. So keep moving, slowly, carefully, embracing a sense of curiosity, awe, aspiration, and inspiration. Every once in a while, pause. Be still. Sit with your questions. Sink into that deeper place that exists beyond the parameters of thinking. Sense. Watch. Listen. Look within. And without. Trust the invisible process that is unfolding. Embrace your own creativity and imagination, giving permission to the interplay of serendipity, discovery, and emergence. Open up your potential for multidimensional perception. The answers you are searching for are there, waiting to emerge, most curiously, when you are not looking too carefully!

7

Relationality, Reflexivity, and Meaning-Making

The only true voyage of discovery, the only fountain of Eternal Youth, would be not to visit strange lands but to possess other eyes, to behold the universe through the eyes of another, of a hundred others, to behold the hundred universes that each of them beholds, that each of them is.

~ Marcel Proust

Questions for Reflection

1. What is the role of relationships in heuristic research?
2. How can relationships be used to negotiate conflict and connect with research partners?
3. In what ways does being a reflexive researcher contribute to the overall research process?
4. How do we explore with research partners personal and communal meanings toward cocreating new understandings of a universal human experience?

Discovery. Emergence. Serendipity. How do they happen? Proust cautions that visiting strange lands (exploring uncharted territory?) may not lead us to true discovery. He impresses upon us, instead, the importance of looking through the eyes of another that we may access the infinite possibilities that exist beyond the parameters of our own vision. In the above passage from Volume 5 of Proust's *Remembrance of Things Past,* the narrator is in fact speaking of the power of art to transport us, the observers, into the inner world of the artist. Another person's art lends us her eyes, from which we may view a certain experience or landscape with which we may be deeply familiar, rendering visible novel perspectives and understandings of the landscape, as well as of the personhood of the artist herself. Thus, we attain the *fountain of Eternal Youth,* the recognition of the existence of other worlds, and the infinitely rekindling universe of shared socially constructed meanings and understandings.

In this chapter, I discuss the roles of relationships, researcher reflexivity, and meaning-making toward the illumination of new discovery. Here, the word *discovery* also encompasses the experiences of serendipity and emergence, allowing for both intentional and unintentional advents into the essential nature of a human experience. As we navigate relationships and their role in heuristic research, I present some of Carl Rogers's ideas on experiential learning and its inherently shared quality. I reflect on the influence of relational contact and intersubjectivity. I discuss the importance of negotiating power differentials and conflict and of exploring personal and collective empowerment and agency. I address the value of researcher reflexivity, locating the self of the researcher within the research process and demystifying the role of the researcher. Finally, I delve into the process of exploring personal and collective meanings toward the co-construction of new narratives and understandings, as well as the impact of this on the researcher, research partners, and readers of the findings. This chapter offers us new eyes from which to view qualitative and heuristic research with the ethos of the 21st century in mind.

Relationality

Distinguished Brazilian educational philosopher Paulo Freire (1970) argued:

> Some may think it inadvisable to include the people as investigators in the search for their own meaningful thematics: that their intrusive . . . influence will "adulterate" the findings and thereby sacrifice the objectivity of the investigation. This view mistakenly presupposes that themes exist, in their original objective purity, outside people—as if themes were *things.* Actually, themes exist in people in their relations with the world. (p. 106)

Heuristic inquiry is a humanistic research approach, bringing to the fore the personhood and wholeness of human beings and highlighting the relational processes between individuals as they collaborate to better understand a shared human experience. As Gendlin (1996) stated, "The essence of work with another person is to be present as a living being" (p. 297). It is with this humanistic spirit and with the knowledge that the topic of a heuristic study is deeply meaningful for all individuals involved, that heuristic researchers refer to research partners as, indeed, *research partners* or *co-researchers*. Besides being holders and deliverers of information, our co-researchers are our companions and collaborators on a journey that will ultimately transform each of us: researcher, co-researchers, and readers of the findings. It is our shared journey that renders the process of discovery possible.

Shared Experiential Learning

Rogers gave the world of psychotherapy the client-centered model, a humanistic approach that honors the relationship between therapist and client as the most powerful mechanism effecting transformation and growth (with the therapist being the central agent of that alliance) and that views the client as the expert on her own life. In Rogers's psychotherapy model, which serves as one of the theories on which heuristic inquiry was based, we find many parallels to heuristic inquiry. For example, the therapist may be viewed as the researcher and central agent for the relationships with all research partners. The research partners may be viewed as clients, although including them in the study does not place them in a position of receiving interventions. Instead, co-researchers' participation is fueled by their own intense interest in the topic of inquiry and by an innate desire to understand its essential nature.

In addition to client-centered theory, Rogers (1969) put forth an experiential theory of learning in which he proposed that significant adult learning is cultivated when

- it is motivated by personal interest in the subject matter and a search for meaning;
- it is based on direct contact with personal and/or social issues;
- it involves the participation of the learner in determining its course and progression;
- it is nonthreatening to the person of the learner; and
- it is self-initiated, involves the whole person of the learner, and is thus enduring and pervasive.

He described the task of the educator as follows:

- To create an open and positive learning environment
- To clarify the purpose of the learner or learning group
- To make available a wide range of learning resources
- To facilitate processing of both intellectual and emotional content

- To eventually become an active member in the learning process and to share her experience without imposition
- To remain alert to the dynamics of the learning environment and address them using empathy and understanding
- To accept her own limitations

Can you discern the connecting lines between educator-researcher and learner-research partner? Do you notice how the educator-researcher is a leader, facilitator, and mediator, as well as a learner-research partner? Freire (1970) presented a similar argument for dialogue as an epistemological relationship and education as social change in his classic text *Pedagogy of the Oppressed*. In such a learning model, individuals are not passive recipients of new information but are motivated to make choices surrounding the knowledge that is most meaningful in relation to their personal and professional lives. Such is the process of shared learning and growth in which we participate with co-researchers in a heuristic study.

Connecting, Disconnecting, and Reconnecting

As the research team navigates the heuristic journey, we create powerful relationships nurtured by our shared experience of the phenomenon we are exploring. As with relationships, however, our communication is not static but is shaped by

- our ability to resonate with the meanings held within one another's experiences;
- our willingness to honor uniqueness, difference, and conflict and use them as rays of light that illuminate our path;
- our capacity to negotiate multifaceted and often complex issues surrounding power and privilege; and
- our commitment to advocating personal and collective empowerment and agency.

Empathy, Resonance, and Intersubjectivity

In Chapter 3, we defined intersubjectivity as the nonverbal experience of *withness* between two—that is, a shared way of being and of knowing between I and Thou. Intersubjectivity is cultivated through **resonance**, which emerges when we attain such a high state of empathic presence with another that we may unconsciously mirror that person's body postures, tones of voice, and facial expressions (Cozolino, 2014). Anderson (2008) suggested, "Intersubjectivity implies that knowing or understanding is not an individual endeavor but rather is socially situated; knowing cannot exist in a vacuum or a cognitive abstract system" (p. 469). She added that in qualitative research, intersubjectivity highlights the many ways we share understanding with others, as well as underscores "that meaning and understanding lie along a continuum of mutual intelligibility" (p. 469). This allows us to merge internal with external experience, laying a foundation for the cocreation of new meanings, as well as for personal and collective transformation. As mentioned before, relationships are dynamic entities filled with adjustment and movement—shaping and reshaping—all mediated through our interactions with one another and with our context. Thus, we may view intersubjectivity as a liminal space that expands and contracts depending on our empathic engagement with another (see Figure 7.1).

American physicist David Bohm (2004), in his highly insightful book *On Dialogue*, maintained that true dialogue between individuals is motivated by an interest in truth and meaning. It transcends the mere cognitive exchange of words or ideas, entering into the realm of intuition and deep mutual trust. Genuine discourse also invites high levels of presence and attunement. As you interact (both verbally and nonverbally) with co-researchers, remain alert to the shifting dynamics of empathy, resonance, and intersubjectivity. When you notice that a research partner is behaving in a manner that challenges your ability to relate and inhibits your resonating capacity, give yourself (and your co-researcher) permission to pause and allow the dust to settle. Empathy offers us rare insights into the worlds of others, as well as the world around us. It also helps us resonate with the similarities, of which we share far more than we do differences. Try to embrace any ruptures in empathic resonance as momentary disconnections that provide you the necessary opportunity to get back in touch with your inner experience and compare notes. Ask yourself, *What might this disturbance have to teach me?* Use the essence of what created the temporary disconnection and scan your history for a moment when you may have experienced something similar. For example, if at the heart of your disruption is a dynamic of anger, try to recall a time when you felt angry and how that emotion shaped your way of being with yourself and with others.

A student (pseudonym: Genna) once shared with me that she experienced great difficulty interacting with the husband in a couple she was seeing for therapy. Below is an excerpt of our relational exchange. Note how I (a) helped

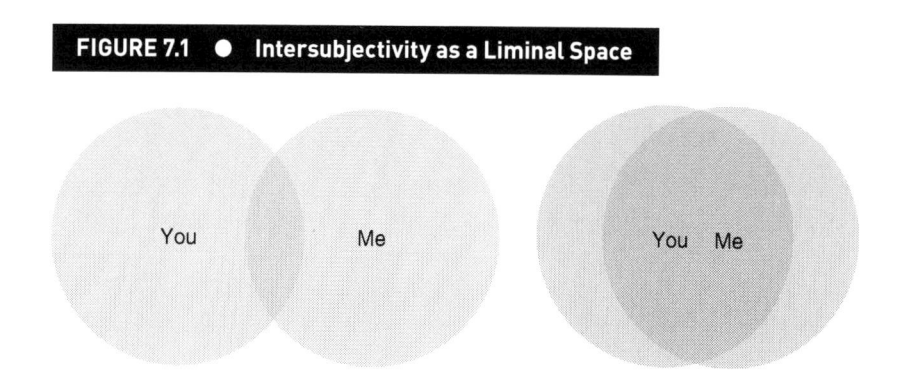

FIGURE 7.1 • Intersubjectivity as a Liminal Space

Genna explore her experience, (b) affirmed her experience, (c) used appropriate self-disclosure, and (d) redirected her attention to reconnecting with her empathy:

Genna: He talks about her [his wife] in the third person when she's right there. He won't even let her go to the bathroom without standing outside the door. It's outrageous *(higher pitch and louder voice)*!

Me: *(pause)* What is it like for you to be with him?

Genna: I don't know. *(pause)* I always feel a bit rattled, like someone is about to take away from me something very precious *(making a fist)*.

Me: Mmm . . . That's a difficult experience, feeling like someone wants to take away something we value. What does this *(replicating Genna's fist)* bring up in you? What thoughts? Emotions? Sensations?

Genna: I feel protective and hyperalert, and my body goes numb.

Me: For whom do you feel protective, and towards whom do you go numb?

Genna: *(pause)* I feel protective of me . . . and of her. I [feel] numb towards him.

Me: So, it sounds like you're connecting with what she may be going through, but you're having some difficulty relating to him. Does that seem accurate?

Genna: Yes. I mean, it's not that I don't want to relate to him. It's just hard *(tearing up)*.

Me: Yes, it's especially difficult when we're coming from entirely different places but still trying to understand and connect with one another. *(pause)*

Genna: *(sobbing and sniffling gently)*

Me: *(tightness in chest)* You seem to be taking quite a bit of responsibility for this situation.

Genna: *(nodding)* I feel like I'm being unempathic, but I don't mean to do that.

Me: Mmm . . . I can relate to that confusion. Sometimes we shut someone out not because we lack empathy, but because they say or do something that seems so diametrically opposed to our own values, we find it difficult to be in their shoes. *(pause)* Would it be all right with you if we turned to him for a moment?

Genna:	*(nodding and wiping away tears)*
Me:	Can you identify what may be triggering his behavior towards his wife?
Genna:	Mmm-hmm. I think . . . culture. Family. Gender roles, for sure.
Me:	Mmm . . . And, what do you think is going on inside him when he's standing outside the bathroom door?
Genna:	Oh, I don't know. . . . Maybe . . . insecurity? Or, well . . . probably more like fear. *(pause, eyes darting around)* Yeah, fear. Like he might lose her, or something.

I then encouraged Genna to reflect on, connect with, and sense into a time when she felt fearful, as if she were going to lose something or someone, and how that sense of fear impacted her holistically, influencing her inner world as well as her interactions with others. Essentially, I invited her to disengage from the threat of difference and connect, from an embodied place, with the promise of likeness. Genna had a light bulb moment, drawing an immediate connection between her male client's fear and her own feelings of dread when in his presence, coupled with her high sense of protectiveness toward her female client and herself. The moral of the story is to release judgment, check in with *I*, explore your own assumptions, and recalibrate your empathic compass. This will better prepare you to expand back into the *withness* of I∞Thou.

Honoring Difference and Conflict

Given that we are all unique individuals with distinctive histories, backgrounds, and ways of being and of knowing, it is essential to recognize that conflict will happen during our heuristic journey. This is true because, although our research team may have come together to unravel the essential nature of a phenomenon we have each experienced, it is more than likely true that our perception of the phenomenon will vary from one person to another. This throws a monkey wrench into the whole concept of *shared reality*, begging the question, *Is shared reality even real?* It depends on whom you ask!

In 1950, Akiro Kurosawa directed a Japanese film titled *Rashomon*, in which he depicted four different individuals describing a single criminal act. While each of the narrative descriptions of the criminal event contradicted the others, the film afforded us four visual perspectives, each supporting one version of the story. In fact, *Rashomon* "commits itself to, and convinces us of, the truth of each version in turn" (Heider, 1988, p. 74), without sugarcoating the ending for viewers. *Rashomon* served as the inspiration for the phenomenon we know today as the **Rashomon effect**, a situation in which different individuals provide contradictory interpretations of a single event based on individual perception, with no evidence to disqualify any of the interpretations (Anderson, 2016). I see the Rashomon effect at play almost unswervingly in couples and family therapy sessions. The couple or family as a unit agrees that a specific event took place. I ask all the members of the family to describe the event from their own perspectives. I never hear the same story! Not only that, but I sit in awe of the eye rolling and jaw dropping in response to other members' narratives of the event, together with the vehement verbal argument, "That is *not* how that happened, and you know it!" What absolutely grips me is the flawlessly evident sense of inner anguish and conflict that capture all members as they try to sort through their version versus another's version of reality. The Rashomon effect speaks to the power of subjective∞objective experience in informing human perception, memory, and interpretation.

Conflict occurs when we encounter dissonance (such as the Rashomon effect) at the junction of our inner experience with something that is taking place in our environment. Because of the circular relationship between self and environment (Merleau-Ponty, 1945/2013), when we experience dissonance, it is likely that whoever (or whatever) triggered it is having a similar reaction. Therefore, conflict, too, is a shared encounter! Conflict happens because we experience what is different (as informed by social and cultural contexts) as potentially threatening. However, different need not be scary.

Imagine that you value a person's choice to take her own life. This value is held deeply within you based on your personal journey with a friend who struggled with chronic pain and the knowledge that her illness was terminal before she made the decision to end her life. It is also informed by your cultural beliefs and attitudes surrounding the concept of autonomy and freedom of choice for individuals. On the other hand, your co-researcher sees ending one's life as an escape from one's responsibility, as well as a selfish act that will impact not only the person committing it but also that person's community. Additionally, your research partner views life not as a choice but as an experience one endures regardless of the circumstances. His values are informed by his collectivist culture as well as his personal beliefs about one's life journey. Conflict takes place when your deeply meaningful value becomes challenged (and maybe even compromised, at least in your perception) by your co-researcher's value that is deeply meaningful to him. As you begin to perceive his value as a potential threat, you cling with tenacity to your value. You may unintentionally express this clinging through a defensive statement. Your co-researcher may then perceive your statement as a potential threat to his value, leading him to cling, as well. In response, your co-researcher might make a defensive statement. And, well . . . you sort of know where it goes from there, right?

Should conflict occur between you and a research partner, first address openly that there is some type of interruption or discontinuity in your interaction. Again, this can sound something like, "I sense that our energy has shifted. May I suggest pausing for a few moments to process things?" Reframing the conflict as an occasion for breaking briefly from each of your ontological and epistemological realities so you are better able to interact with and learn from each other's will help set things back on track. Reflect on the social constructivist nature of reality and on the fact that each of you has brought to your encounter both your individual and your collective histories and perceptions, all of which are inevitably (and fiercely!) shaping your interaction. Remember, too, that you are here together because of your profoundly compelling interest in the phenomenon you are exploring. Use the temporary rift as an opportunity for exploring viewpoints you may have previously overlooked or denied. Then see if it's okay to open, listen, and receive a point of view that, though it may not necessarily speak to who you are, places you in a position of engaging in that educator-researcher∞learner-research partner dance that promotes more equitable cocreation of new knowledge. This is done with the understanding that accepting another person's perspective or values does not mean having to give up your own.

One of the most powerful interventions I use when the Rashomon effect emerges in a couples or family therapy session is to invite each member of the family to retell the story as another member told it. This places the person retelling the story in the shoes of another family member who experienced the same event, lending her the sense of *what it is like to be the other person*, enhancing empathy, and facilitating acceptance of other perspectives as relevant. My counseling students often ask, "Does becoming a counselor and accepting another person's values mean that I have to give up my own values?" My answer is, invariably, "Absolutely not!" Accepting another person's truth or reality does not equate to embracing that way of being as my own. It means only that I am giving that person the space to be who she is without judgment.

Negotiating Power and Privilege

Ruptures in communication and conflict are often triggered by issues surrounding power (Braun & Clarke, 2013) and privilege, marginalization and oppression. This can lead to what Sandstrom, Martin, and Fine (2006) and Kvale (2002) refer to as **asymmetrical relationships**—that is, relationships in which one person attempts to impose dominance over another. Both privilege and oppression are deeply embodied experiences (Johnson, 2015). We may not even realize we are living through either until we come face-to-face with the perfect trigger! Power differentials exist and are constantly negotiated within any and all relationships, often at an unconscious level. As a psychotherapist, I am keenly aware of the power differentials present between a client and me and how shifts in power inform our various interactions, often within the same session and with the same client. As counselors, we are encouraged to develop awareness of our own power and privilege. However, the idea of the consistently powerful or privileged therapist is challenged as counselors also take initiative to tap into client experiences of power and privilege (Ratts, Singh, Nassar-McMillan, Butler, & McCullough, 2016). The same applies to research. There is a conventional idea that the researcher always has the upper hand. However, social issues and demographic characteristics such as gender, ethnicity, race, sexual orientation, age, and socioeconomic status play a substantial role.

In my heuristic study of body psychotherapist embodiment (Sultan, 2015), the co-researcher sample included experts in the field of body psychotherapy with far more training and experience than I had. Additionally, the majority of my co-researchers were older, and two of my six co-researchers were male. Negotiating power dynamics was challenging but provided multiple opportunities to process the role of empathy and genuineness in human interaction.

To start, I had a keen awareness of needing each of my research partners to complete my study successfully. With that, I often found myself trying to journey with a co-researcher through the labyrinth (as guided by the central questions and purpose of the study) only to find my co-researcher grabbing me by the hand and saying, "No! We're not going that way!" This metaphor emerged in reality as one co-researcher, for example, attempted (perhaps unconsciously) to turn the study into a narrative about professional achievements. My attempts to bring the co-researcher's attention back to the purpose and questions of our study were met with, "We're getting there." My internal responses to these exchanges were shaped by self-narratives informed by my age, gender, professional experience, and cultural background, all of which in turn informed how I was interacting with that co-researcher. While our interaction was initially pebbly, I was able to connect with that co-researcher at a more authentic level using my relational skills.

I often found myself in the awkward situation of trying to meet my co-researchers' needs using a variety of relational approaches (e.g., change in vocal tone, inviting a brief pause to take a deep breath and rechannel energy) while struggling with my own feelings of vulnerability and confusion. This was followed by a sense of resolve to keep the study on course, leading me back to a space where we could gently uncover the shift using appropriate self-disclosure, allow for individual and shared reflexivity, and hopefully reconnect. Using relational skills moderated by warmth and genuineness facilitated working through issues with decorum.

On the opposite end of this spectrum are research partners who are vulnerable, persecuted, and marginalized, and/or a researcher who is an instrument of power and oppression or one who implicitly or unconsciously shames or marginalizes a co-researcher. Implicitly shaming messages can be exchanged as early as the invitation to participate is extended to potential research partners but may emerge throughout the research process—especially during interviews. The researcher may implicitly adopt a domineering approach while resting within the comfort of convincing herself that she is in fact engaging relationally. The danger here lies within the power of self-deception; that is, if you tell yourself what you are doing is virtuous and fair, you will believe it is so! Reflexivity and self-dialogue may mitigate this. Remaining attuned (Cook, 2012) to the unfolding verbal and nonverbal narratives between you and co-researchers supports early identification of marginalization within the research team and allows you to actively attend to what is emerging, using relational skills, and to take preventive measures.

As you balance multiple iterations of marginalization and privilege across the spectrum of the research team, you will want to exercise reflexivity and revisit your role as the researcher (Moustakas, 1990) and what it entails (more on this later). You will also need to take a look at some of the systemic or social dynamics (e.g., setting, gender, ethnicity, race, ability/disability, age) surrounding the emergence of any power struggles. Wallowing too long within a power imbalance may result in researcher (or research partner) manipulation and undermine the genuineness of your interaction, as well as your overall relationships with co-researchers, potentially compromising your entire study. In some cases, this requires initiative on briefly addressing power issues openly but nonconfrontationally, especially if you and a research partner hit an impasse, holding up the process of inquiry. It is helpful to revisit the guidelines of your study, exchange perspectives about the roles of researcher and research partners, exchange appropriate self-disclosure (Braun & Clarke, 2013), and review once again informed consent and the primary purpose of the study. Shifting the spotlight back to the purpose facilitates movement from personal agendas to a point of shared interest and connection.

Advancing Empowerment, Agency, and Social Justice

Let us return briefly to Rogers's (1961) legacy of client-centered psychotherapy, in which he considered human agency, motivation, and self-actualization. McGettigan (2008a) argued that "human agency is very similar to the notion of free will in that agency may be understood as the capacity to exercise creative control over individual-level thoughts and actions" (p. 15). Individuals exercise agency when they perceive evidence that conflicts with their perception of reality and reconstitute their understanding to better comprehend the conflicting evidence.

Heuristic inquiry offers research teams opportunities to explore highly personal experiences that are potentially universal but may not have been explored empirically, or that may have been implicitly or explicitly marginalized due to their personal nature. In many ways, heuristic research is empowering and emancipatory in that it gives voice to those who may have kept their personal experience to themselves, inspiring them to highlight their expert knowledge about the topic of inquiry. Such an opportunity, while affirming on a personal level, is also collectively empowering as all members of the research team collaborate to create new understandings of the phenomenon they are exploring. Likewise, heuristic research is intrinsically amenable to advocacy efforts through its inclusion of often marginalized experiences and voices and its openness to reorganizing traditional power structures. As an example, my embodiment study gave voice to expert body psychotherapists whose practice is often criticized within traditional psychotherapy circles as being non-evidence-based. It also highlighted the essential nature of embodiment as a human experience that, although often misrepresented, misunderstood, marginalized, and pathologized by social (and even professional) power structures, involves high levels of relational attunement and empathic presence. Through my study, I was able to demonstrate an evidence base for body psychotherapy and embodiment in alignment with Rogers's (1969) highly evidence-based core therapeutic factors that act as a baseline for a *way of being* with clients. Heuristic inquiry both includes co-researchers' voices and allows for exploration of relational dynamics and the role of each member of the research team (Davis, 2008), including the primary researcher. As the researcher, you are no longer an invisible examiner operating behind the scenes but are fully outed (Finlay, 2002) by revealing your own role in the research process.

Not unlike other qualitative approaches, heuristic research lends to researchers tools that enable them to transcend the parameters of methodologies generated by members of majority groups (van den Hoonaard, 2008), supporting individual and collective agency and the identification of unconventional findings. The phenomenon being explored is no longer marginalized as researcher and co-researchers work to give it more adequate meaning aligned with *their* version of the Truth (McGettigan, 2008b), rendering them creators of their own reality. The ability to redefine reality supports individuals in emancipating themselves from rigid social contexts, and acting in a self-defining and self-actualizing manner (McGettigan, 2008a; Sandstrom et al., 2006). It also fosters equity across social contexts, offering individuals freedom to pursue their aspirations and promoting social justice (Miller, 2008a).

Reflexivity

Denzin and Lincoln (2011) asserted that "all research is interpretive: guided by a set of beliefs and feelings about the world and how it should be understood and studied" (p. 13). Heuristic research is especially interpretive as it is inspired by the researcher's autobiographical experience. Fully bracketing your experience and separating yourself from your topic of inquiry may prove impractical, unviable, and arguably, unethical. Critically but nonjudgmentally evaluating and addressing your personal values, beliefs, biases, and attitudes with regard to your topic and process of inquiry and locating yourself within the research study are essential tasks for the heuristic researcher. Your personal involvement in your study begins from the moment you take an active interest in a potential topic of inquiry (Moustakas, 1990) and continues beyond the completion of the formal process (Lumsden, 2013). Therefore, openly locating yourself within the broad configuration of your research study and defining your role are necessary. Using a journal to document your reflexive practice is especially helpful in that it supports access to and connection with your holistic experience of the study. In reality, this level of transparency lends rigor and trustworthiness to your heuristic study.

Approaching Reflexivity Holistically

As mentioned in Chapter 6, journaling involves both reflection and reflexivity. While reflection tends to operate specifically within the cognitive domain, I view reflexivity as an embodied venture that includes our multidimensional ways of being and of knowing, as well as our multifaceted ways of making sense of the contextual dynamics. In a manner of speaking, what I like to call **embodied reflexivity** lies within our ability to engage our cognitive, emotional, sensory∞kinesthetic, perceptual, spiritual, and social∞relational selves to process the intersection of intrapersonal, interpersonal, and sociocultural/environmental dynamics unfolding throughout the course of the study and its impact on the process of research (see Figure 7.2).

From this perspective, reflexivity honors the idea that how we know is essentially an embodied and relational process informed by our social interactions with ourselves and our environment (Merleau-Ponty, 1945/2013). Reflexivity lies on the internal∞external continuum of experience, inviting us to participate in the dance of ongoing communication, both verbal and nonverbal.

Evaluating Values, Beliefs, Biases, and Attitudes

We are all part of a greater whole. Our values and beliefs are informed by social contexts that, though they are greater than the sum of their parts, cannot exist without the parts of which they are constituted. Likewise, our social and cultural contexts inform our biases and attitudes toward others, especially

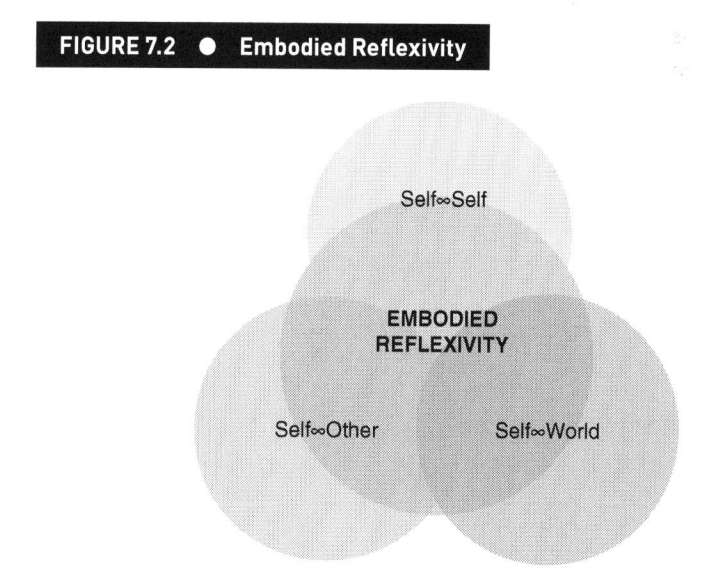

FIGURE 7.2 • Embodied Reflexivity

Self∞Self

EMBODIED REFLEXIVITY

Self∞Other   Self∞World

those in whom we perceive difference. In a manner of speaking, values, beliefs, biases, assumptions, and attitudes are collective experiences that speak to our being a part of a greater gestalt. On the other hand, these ways of being and of knowing are also informed by our inner landscapes and our ability to individually process experience and create meaning out of it. Once again, we are talking about the internal∞external continuum.

Our values and beliefs, attitudes and biases constitute some of our most prized epistemological and ontological realities, act as normative and moral compasses for our experience, and give true meaning to who we are. Yet these social constructs also have the ability to minimize and reduce others. It would be easy enough to tell ourselves to identify which of these constructs have the potential for creating social disorder and excise them. Then again, how do we excise what is most dear to us? Additionally, while our values and beliefs may be readily apparent to us and simple to evaluate, our biases, assumptions, and attitudes are often implicit and not so readily accessible. This is true because we engage in **confirmation bias**; that is, we protect our biases by deliberately interpreting new information as confirmation of their validity. Because heuristic inquiry is autobiographically informed across all members of the research team, the potential for confirmation bias is especially high. As we interact with other individuals who have shared the same or a similar experience, in our collective effort to better understand the phenomenon, we encounter interpretations of the phenomenon that may conflict or collide with our own perspectives. When this happens, we experience a threat to everything from our social construction of the phenomenon to our very beliefs and values.

But not all hope is lost. It is possible to evaluate our values, beliefs, assumptions, and attitudes and develop a high degree of self-awareness by engaging in ongoing intentional self-inquiry. Some of the following questions may help you get started:

- How does this situation relate to the purpose of the study and the research questions?
- Besides being the primary researcher, what are my other roles?
- What role are demographic factors (gender, ethnicity, age, etc.) playing?
- What other stories and/or meanings are implicit to what is emerging between us?
- Are we being genuine with each other? Empathic?
- What are we each bringing to the table? What are we cocreating?
- What do I think I know about the phenomenon? About my co-researchers' experience? About my own experience?

- What emerges inside me when a co-researcher and I see things differently?
- How do I define the terms *personal* and *communal/collaborative*? How does each of my research partners define those terms?
- What am I hoping to get out of this shared journey? What is each of my co-researchers hoping to achieve? Can we find some points of connection?
- How is participating in this project impacting me physically? Emotionally? Spiritually? Perceptually? Relationally? Cognitively? How is it impacting my research partners?

Not only can we evaluate our values and attitudes, but we can also be playful with exploring what it might be like to assume alternative values, with the understanding that we are not actually required to assume them. Give Exercise 7.1 a try.

If you find this exercise challenging, try exploring your own and others' values using focusing or empty chair. Or ask someone you know to take the position of Other and debate together from that perspective before switching places. Then see if it's okay to give Exercise 7.1 another try.

EXERCISE 7.1
EXPLORING OUR OWN AND OTHERS' VALUES

- Draw a dotted line down the middle of a blank sheet of paper. On one side, list some personal values you are absolutely not willing to compromise. On the other side, list some values you are not willing to embrace. Don't censor yourself!
- Enact a debate between both sides (do this out loud).
- Just for kicks, allow the side with the values you are not willing to embrace to win. Alternately, allow some of the values from that side to shift to yours.
- Be playful. Engage this exercise with the knowledge that you are not giving up your values but experimenting with varying degrees of intimacy with and distance from them.

Locating Oneself Within the Research Process

Many qualitative research methodologies promote locating the self of the researcher without resorting to excessive self-disclosure and self-magnification (Lillrank, 2012). Locating yourself involves exploring and describing your personal connection with the topic of inquiry and your personal journey to explore it. Heuristic research is highly grounded in the researcher's personal experience due to the fact that both the process and content of inquiry are inspired by the researcher's autobiographical experience of the phenomenon. This includes everything from identifying a topic of interest to the explication of themes and creative synthesis. Consequently, your research partners will likely have their own assumptions about how your personal experience is manifesting throughout the process of inquiry. Inherent in locating yourself is exploring which dimensions of yourself or your experience you deem to be the richest filters through which you perceive your topic (Lillrank, 2012). In my embodiment study, I disclosed my personal interest and role as informed by my cultural background, family background, education, social∞relational experience, experience with artistic expression, and personal and professional experience of embodiment, as those lenses were the most relevant to the phenomenon I was researching. Being transparent about the nature of my *self of the researcher* elucidated my personal involvement with the process and content of the study, enhancing its rigor and trustworthiness.

Demystifying the Role of the Researcher

Due to the autobiographical nature of heuristic research, one of the implicit roles you have as the researcher is that of research partner; that is, you are participating in your own study. That is what makes heuristic inquiry a collaborative qualitative methodology. On the other hand, while heuristic inquiry is empowering and emancipatory, it is necessary that the primary researcher lead the research process. In heuristic inquiry, you are the research instrument (Moustakas, 1990); that is, you are responsible for guiding and facilitating the research endeavor from its very beginning phases to its final destination.

Moustakas (1990) advised that the heuristic researcher take leadership of the study, not with the intent of becoming autocratic or unfair but with the purpose of maintaining equilibrium during the research process. He stated that the researcher is "the only person in the investigation who has undergone the heuristic inquiry from the beginning formulation of the question through phases of incubation, illumination, explication, and creative synthesis not only with himself or herself, but with each and every co-researcher" (p. 32). Therefore, even as we are on a joint mission with research partners, it is our duty to guide the trek through the labyrinth. In many cases, our co-researchers expect us to keep things in order. After all, in a heuristic study, we design and initiate the study, create the protocols for conducting it, and then invite co-researchers to collaborate and share their expertise. Supporting a free-form and purely organic study, while it seems equitable, may result in disruptions, fostering potentially inequitable circumstances. Your study is approved by an institutional review board to be carried out according to a proposal outlining your study's purpose, its central questions, and your role as the researcher. Deviations from the approved proposal may place your study at risk.

Again, you are not the autocratic leader but the group facilitator and person responsible for making sure the research process supports the integrity of the study without compromising your research partners. You are charged with building and maintaining trust, rapport, professional demeanor, and relational boundaries with research partners without succumbing to habitual power dynamics. You are also there to support a potentially transforming experience for each member of your research team (including yourself). Embrace this role both empathically and unapologetically. Should you fall short of maintaining collaborative leadership, issues of power and privilege may prove especially thorny and demanding, diverting your attention away from your purpose and compromising your research team and your shared mission.

Using the Journal as a Reflexive Tool

As mentioned earlier, journaling is an essential process for any heuristic researcher (Moustakas, 1990). You can use the research journal to document your experience of the study, including how you are using the various heuristic processes and their impact on data collection, organization, and analysis. You may also use it to engage in reflexive practice, which is especially important given some of the previously considered social∞relational issues that will emerge as you interact with research partners and with various events throughout the research process. Awareness of relational ruptures that may occur due to assumptions or misconceptions about members of different groups is facilitated through ongoing embodied reflexivity.

So how do we maximize our use of the journal as a heuristic tool? What do we include in our reflexive journal? Essentially, you can document any of the following experiences in your research journal, using words or other forms of expression (art, doodles, etc.):

- Interest in the research topic/phenomenon
- Research-related events, processes, and procedures
- Thoughts/self-dialogue, feelings, and kinesthetic sensations
- Your role and roles of co-researchers
- Observations and reactions/responses
- Methodological/research design considerations and ideas
- Relational dynamics (e.g., issues of transference, countertransference, conflict)
- Contradictory narratives
- Analytic processes, emerging themes/meanings, gaps, and alternative options

- Unanticipated findings/events
- Beliefs, values, biases, and assumptions (especially concerning your topic of inquiry) and impact on the study
- Dreams (or daydreams) in relation to your study or similar/peripheral topics
- Day-by-day interaction with professional literature, raw data, and various research processes and phases (tacit knowing, immersion, incubation, focusing, etc.)
- Challenges to cocreating new meanings with research partners
- Insights generated through conversations with nonmembers of your research team
- Ethical dilemmas/concerns, potential courses of action, and consequences (more on this in Chapter 10)
- Explanations for phenomena and alternative explanations
- Evaluation of research process and progress
- Locating your study within the grander scheme of your inner and outer worlds
- Information that is difficult to document elsewhere
- Insights and future directions for action and change

Don't limit yourself to these options; feel free to include whatever seems relevant. You never know how impactful one journal entry may be to the direction of your entire study!

Revisit your entries regularly. Journaling offers unique access to the interplay of past and present experience with future directions, action, and change. Reviewing earlier documentation of an experience offers us an opportunity to reengage with it from a different perspective (Rainer, 2004), advancing insight into the dynamics of our research process and ideas for next steps. It also affords us a rare glimpse into *what I know* and *how I know it*, illuminating the potential for exploring *other ways of knowing*. Your reflexive journal acts as a transparent and/or visible (Lamb, 2013; Ortlipp, 2008) holding space for information about the research process, some of which may clarify and enhance meaning- and decision making. If you are interested in learning more about journaling reflexively in a manner aligned with heuristic research, I highly recommend a classic by Rainer (2004) titled *The New Diary*. In the meantime, Exercise 7.2 provides a method for exploring a personal dilemma using your reflexive journal.

Meaning-Making

As previously discussed, heuristic inquiry, being a social constructivist, embodied, nonlinear, and culturally embedded approach to qualitative research, is deeply grounded in the context in which it is taking place. Likewise, the

EXERCISE 7.2
EXPLORING A PERSONAL DILEMMA USING THE REFLEXIVE JOURNAL

- Consider a personal issue in your life. Ask yourself, *Who is involved in this dilemma? What is happening?*
- Use your imagination to visualize your dilemma. Take your time.
- Connect with any symbols or images that emerge. Do not censor your experience.
- Make a rough sketch of the images and symbols. Do not allow your inner critic to say things like, *I don't know how to draw.* A basic rendition is all you need.
- Sit with your drawing. Ask, *If I could place a frame around a specific part of this drawing, where would I place it?*
- Sketch a frame around that part of your drawing. Ask, *If this framed part had a voice and could speak, what would it say?*
- Allow the framed part to dialogue with you, as well as with other parts of the drawing.
- Document the various interactions.
- Draw lines identifying relationships between and among interactions.
- Underline or highlight specific words or phrases that evoke thoughts, feelings, or bodily sensations. How might those words or phrases be *potential themes* for a phenomenon that is especially figural or consequential in your life at the moment?

experience of each member of the research team with the topic of inquiry is both content- and context-specific; that is, it is informed by both meaningful exploration of narratives and the intrapersonal, interpersonal, and sociocultural dynamics within which it is unraveling. Consequently, unpacking the meanings lying within an experience does not happen in a vacuum but in relation to individuals' values, interactions, and active exchange of ideas within the specific social scenes in which meaning-making takes place (Manning & Kunkel, 2014). Meaning-making becomes a process of reflexive immersion in one's own experience to attain higher self-awareness and, thereby, empathy for and understanding of the experiences of others. In that sense, meaning-making is not a one-time action but an ongoing reflexive process that is unremittingly shaped by the environment surrounding it and the relationships unraveling within it.

Heuristic inquiry provides a secure arena within which personal narratives of intimate encounters with specific human experiences may be shared. This type of verbal and nonverbal discourse invites exploration of a spectrum of potential responses with regard to the ways of being and of knowing that are most actively engaged when we are in contact with our phenomenon, and how those ontological and epistemological realities inform our personal understanding of its essential nature. Thus, we have an opportunity to grapple with the big questions surrounding *what* the essential nature of the phenomenon is and *how* it manifests for each of us. Through the exchange of personal narratives, dissonances rooted in unique personal experience may emerge and undergo a shared exploratory process of renegotiation and reconstruction. Our original perspective is significantly enhanced through comparison and discussion with others (Pontecorvo, 2007). Dropping expectations informed by convention, remaining open to novel ideas and perspectives, and attuning to what is being communicated implicitly bridges seemingly contrasting ways of knowing, fostering the emergence of new understandings. Encountering novel understandings of holistically meaningful experiences holds transformative power at the individual and communal levels. Not only are you and your research partners transformed, but you are also inspired toward new questions and avenues of inquiry. Likewise, readers of your findings are granted access to each of your personal narratives, your collective renegotiation and reconstitution process, as well as your newly cocreated meanings and understandings. Through such access, your readers are launched into their own journey of potential self-discovery and self-transformation.

Closing Reflections

Human relationships allow us to enter the infinitely fascinating worlds of others, granting us access to their perspective of experiences with which we have had intimate encounters. On such a relational journey, we are all educator-researchers, as well as learner-research partners. Therefore, give yourself permission to remain open to everything you come across. Experiencing empathy and resonance finds us in the realm of intersubjectivity. Experiencing dissonance and confusion means that we are on the cusp of encountering something new. What new discoveries might we miss should we close that window of opportunity? Be playful with the idea of looking through the eyes of others that you might gain some awareness of how they make meaning of a phenomenon that brings you together on a mission of exploration, emergence, discovery, and transformation. Do not get lost in power struggles and discord. Embrace conflict as an opportunity for deeper learning and growth. Identify and acknowledge your own role and presence within the process of inquiry. And always keep a reflexive awareness about your entire research process. Finally, keep in mind that you are interacting with fellow human beings. Honoring those persons' dignity and worth overrides whatever nuggets of data you deem meaningful and conclusive. In the intimacy of genuine human interaction emerges true collective meaning!

8

Evaluating the Research
A Collaborative Process

Reality is what we take to be true. What we take to be true is what we believe. What we believe is based upon our perceptions. What we perceive depends on what we look for. What we look for depends on what we think. What we think depends on what we perceive. What we perceive determines what we believe. What we believe determines what we take to be true. What we take to be true is our reality.

~ **David Bohm**

Questions for Reflection

1. What criteria should be considered in evaluating heuristic research?
2. What strategies are involved in evaluating heuristic research?
3. How does evaluating heuristic inquiry diverge from evaluating other qualitative methodologies?
4. How does collaboration contribute to the heuristic inquiry evaluation process?

There is no such thing as absolute reality, according to American physicist David Bohm, whom I mentioned in the previous chapter in reference to his thoughts on genuine dialogue. That's a pretty controversial proposition, coming from a physicist! Yet the quote above, from a 1977 lecture given at the University of California, Berkeley, highlights Bohm's perception of perception as the foundation of reality. This brings into the spotlight the question of evaluation and some of the traditional methods of evaluating both quantitative and qualitative research, including those that imply that by using certain instruments, software, formulas, or objective observation, we will arrive at some type of confirmation of a single reality or truth as represented through our findings. Bohm argues that our perception serves as a filter for every implicit and explicit process of evaluation we undertake, which is the very same argument Merleau-Ponty (1945/2013) extended decades ago and which social constructivist research approaches continue to espouse (Patton, 2008, 2015). In this chapter, we briefly define the concepts *rigor* and *trustworthiness/goodness*, and we look at traditional evaluation criteria and strategies and how they may be implemented in evaluating a heuristic study. We also explore criteria specific to heuristic inquiry with the intent of evaluating the integrity of the study. Additionally, we discuss the collaborative nature of the evaluation process, as well as the leadership role of the primary researcher, keeping in mind how the researcher's role is influenced by subjective experience.

A Primer on Heuristic Evaluation

As mentioned previously, when evaluating a heuristic study, you are evaluating both process and outcome. While this may seem fairly standard across a number of other qualitative research approaches, it is not necessarily good counsel to use standardized evaluation methods for all qualitative studies. Schwandt (1996) is credited with launching the discussion around setting aside some of the traditional ideas of qualitative evaluation criteria. Miller (2008b) suggested that "it is overly simplistic—indeed inaccurate—to describe global qualitative criteria" (p. 910) for any and all qualitative studies, clarifying that the purpose and methods of each study will inform the selection of relevant criteria. Similarly, Patton (2008) affirmed, "People conducting qualitative studies or reviewing findings through different paradigmatic lenses will render different judgments because they use different criteria of quality" (p. 302). I agree! With that, we will be reviewing the characteristics of heuristic inquiry later in the chapter and looking at questions that may facilitate evaluation of the integrity of your heuristic study. We will also explore relevant evaluation criteria and specific evaluation strategies for guiding the collaborative evaluation process, which is designed to showcase your study's rigor and trustworthiness/goodness, with the understanding that these evaluation approaches are not discrete but quite interactive (see Figure 8.1). Certain evaluation practices will evoke, mirror, or support others, which may lend the appearance of redundancy. In fact, you are promoting transparency, rigor, and trustworthiness. Before moving into the details of that process, let's first clarify what we mean by *rigor* and *trustworthiness/goodness* within the context of heuristic research.

FIGURE 8.1 ● The Interactive Process of Evaluating Heuristic Research

- Evaluation Criteria
- Evaluation Strategies
- Strategies for Evaluating Integrity of Heuristic Methodology

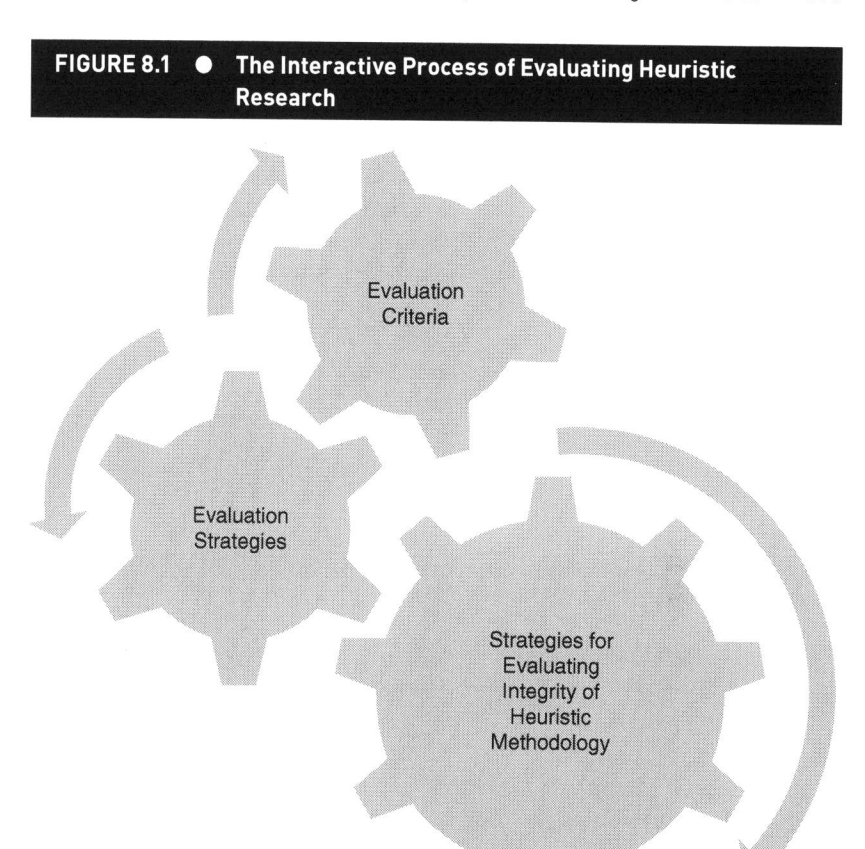

Defining Rigor and Trustworthiness/Goodness

Moustakas (1990) outlined an evaluation process for heuristic inquiry that he called "The Validation of Heuristic Research" (p. 32), which is primarily concerned with whether or not the findings represent the meanings and essences of the topic of inquiry. Because the word *validation* is generally associated with quantitative research evaluation (and in the interest of minimizing confusion), I elect to use the words *rigor* and *trustworthiness/goodness* when discussing heuristic evaluation, as these terms tend to be more aligned with the qualitative research tradition, and especially with social constructivist methodologies (Patton, 2008, 2015) such as heuristic inquiry. I also encourage the idea of evaluation being not only a post-hoc method for justifying the findings of your study but an ongoing process that begins with your identification of a focus of inquiry and continues beyond the termination of your study. In fact, it is quite feasible to use feedback from readers of your findings as evaluation material. Likewise, in the context of heuristic inquiry, one might consider evaluation as a tool for enhancing rigor and trustworthiness rather than a way of decreeing an absolute existence of validity.

Saumure and Given (2008) proposed the following understanding of **rigor** in qualitative research: "As a concept, rigor is perhaps best thought of in terms of the quality of the research process. In essence, a more rigorous research process will result in more trustworthy findings" (p. 796). On the other hand, Given and Saumure (2008) (same authors, different source) described **trustworthiness** as the ways qualitative researchers ensure that the rigor of the qualitative research is evident. In other words, rigor promotes trustworthiness, and trustworthiness demonstrates rigor. Do you note the circular relationship? Lincoln and Guba (1985) identified four features of trustworthy qualitative research (all of which are described in more detail in the next section of this chapter). Jones, Torres, and Arminio (2006) used the word **goodness** in tandem with trustworthiness as a way of asserting that a study's findings can be used to inform and justify action and change. One can also say that a study's trustworthiness is a reflection of its inherent goodness (Lincoln, 1995), or vice versa, or both. Either way, within the context of heuristic research, rigor∞trustworthiness are interrelated concepts that also demonstrate the interrelationship of process∞outcome. That is, a rigorous process promotes a trustworthy outcome, and a trustworthy outcome demonstrates that a rigorous process took place. In heuristic research, trustworthiness is established through rigorous self-reflection and self-inquiry involving inner processes such as intuition and tacit knowing, and by returning to the data repeatedly (Moustakas, 1990). Keeping in mind the nature of heuristic inquiry, I would suggest using specific traditional qualitative criteria and strategies to evaluate the trustworthiness of the study's findings, as well as criteria informed by heuristic characteristics to evaluate the integrity of the study. This offers a diversity of evaluation approaches that address both process and outcome.

Evaluation Criteria

Lincoln and Guba (1985) broke down evaluation for rigor and trustworthiness in qualitative research into four criteria: credibility, transferability, dependability, and confirmability. Let's take a look at how each of these concepts is defined and how it can be applied to the evaluation of heuristic inquiry.

Credibility

Although we will be looking at the question of the integrity of a heuristic study in more depth later in this chapter, **credibility** is primarily concerned with the concepts of confidence and believability, especially with regard to the research design—that is, the methods and approaches used to collect and analyze the data (Lincoln & Guba, 1985) and represent the findings (Patton, 2015). When evaluating your heuristic study's credibility, you should determine how comprehensively you described the design of your study, including the purpose, guiding questions, sample, and theoretical framework. You should also evaluate the degree to which your findings (a) align with your research process, (b) accurately and truthfully interpret and represent your data, and (c) reveal the essential nature of the topic of inquiry beyond your (the primary researcher's) personal experience of it. Strategies for enhancing a study's credibility include triangulation, member checking, peer debriefing, and external audit/review, as well as prolonged engagement with study content and process, the use of negative/alternative explanations, the use of thick description (Lincoln & Guba, 1985; Patton, 2015; Toma, 2011), and researcher reflexivity. Each of these strategies will be contextualized with reference to heuristic inquiry in the section of this chapter titled "Evaluation Strategies."

Transferability

Context is critical in heuristic research. The concept of **transferability** speaks to the importance of the context, setting, and/or situatedness of the study. Helpful information to clarify these points can be elicited from descriptions of the sampling procedure and the application of the theoretical framework to the study. Guba (1981) stated that transferability is not about indiscriminately *generalizing* the findings of your study but about the potential for *applying* aspects of those findings to other populations or contexts. This is a vital distinction, as generalizability tends to lend credence to the idea of a single reality or truth, whereas transferability does not assume any single truth. In heuristic inquiry, transferability allows consumers of the research to assess for similarity (Guba, 1981; Patton, 2015) and to conceptualize the applicability of the findings to other contexts without breaching fidelity to co-researchers' original descriptions of their living experience of the topic of inquiry. Strategies for enriching opportunities for transferability include prolonged engagement, triangulation, and the use of thick description (see Table 8.1).

Dependability

Consistency is a hallmark of **dependability**, a criterion of trustworthiness that speaks to how you are justifying your choice of research methodology and data collection process, as well as how your findings align and harmonize with that methodology (Lincoln & Guba, 1985). Again, this is a circular relationship by which your research methodology may explain and substantiate your findings, and your findings may support your choice of methodology. The dependability of your study will rely in large part on your ability to construct a solid rationale for selecting heuristic inquiry as a methodology as informed by the nature of your study and, primarily, by your central research question(s). Lincoln and Guba (1985) described dependability as an indicator of whether the process of inquiry was logical and well documented. Evaluation strategies for enriching dependability include thick description, triangulation, researcher reflexivity, and external audit/review.

Confirmability

Lest there be any confusion about the trustworthiness of the findings in relation to the data, **confirmability** calls for clear identification of links between findings and interpretations (Lincoln & Guba, 1985; Patton, 2015) as a way of verifying that the researcher is not making random assertions. As we have discussed previously, heuristic (and most other qualitative) inquiry is quite subjective and therefore has the potential to be highly influenced by the researcher's personal biases, attitudes, values, and experiences. One critical strategy for enhancing confirmability is researcher reflexivity—that is, exploration of the researcher's perspective and/or role and its potential influence on data analysis and interpretation. This might call for the inclusion of excerpts from the researcher's reflexive journal or other documentation of the researcher's interaction with and meaning-making of the research process and content. Triangulation, external audits, thick description, member checking, peer debriefing, and negative/alternative explanations are also relevant strategies for confirmability.

Evaluation Strategies

In the previous section, we discussed four criteria you can use to evaluate your heuristic study and identified specific strategies for each criterion. Your selection of strategies is an intentional process informed by your assessment of the specific needs of your study. Table 8.1 includes a breakdown of a number of traditional evaluation strategies of relevance to heuristic research, a brief description of each strategy with links to the heuristic perspective, and the evaluation criteria they support. The content (not including links to the heuristic perspective) was consolidated from Creswell (2009, 2013), Denzin (2009), Lincoln and Guba (1985), and Patton (2015).

Evaluating the Integrity of Your Heuristic Study

Traditional evaluation criteria and strategies lend structure and consistency to the evaluation process. At the same time, they are not sufficient in that they may not address, in a holistic manner, the integrity of your heuristic research study. For that, it is necessary to use an evaluation approach that is customized to your research methodology. Evaluating a heuristic study is best executed by exploring whether the study has addressed the various characteristics of heuristic inquiry (see Table 1.1), as this helps you answer the critical question, *Is this study truly a heuristic inquiry?* It is not uncommon for a researcher to embark on a journey of unraveling the essential nature of a particular phenomenon through the heuristic lens only to wind up using approaches and methods that are more aligned with, say, grounded theory. If you are planning to identify your study as a heuristic inquiry, your study should represent and demonstrate that particular methodology. Table 8.2 provides a structure for evaluating the integrity of your study using questions informed by the characteristics of heuristic inquiry. Please note that all questions are asked in the present tense with the understanding that heuristic inquiry is a highly here-and-now approach to qualitative research and that the evaluation of your heuristic study begins as soon as you identify a topic of interest.

TABLE 8.1 ● Evaluation Strategies Relevant to Heuristic Inquiry

Evaluation Strategy	Description and Links to the Heuristic Perspective	Related Evaluation Criteria
Prolonged engagement	Extensive immersion in and dwelling with the phenomenon and with relevant individuals and sites (content and context), allowing for humanistic and exploratory unfolding of the research process and development of a detailed, credible, and multifaceted manuscript describing the process and findings	Credibility, transferability
Thick description	Clear articulation and communication of the research process and findings, including multiple perspectives on process and content, to enhance transparency	Credibility, transferability, dependability, confirmability
Negative/alternative explanations	Presentation of alternative or contradictory perspectives on identified themes in alignment with the social constructivist concept of multiple realities	Credibility, confirmability
Member checking	Ongoing relational collaboration with co-researchers to enhance authenticity and equity, mitigate power differentials, and determine accuracy of findings, including theme interpretation and articulation, and meaning-making	Credibility, confirmability
Peer debriefing	Inclusion of an impartial outsider to enrich dialogical interaction, explore implicit aspects of the study the researcher may be overlooking (or over- or underemphasizing), facilitate awareness of biases and assumptions, and assess emergent themes from broader perspectives (including other disciplines and universal foci)	Credibility, confirmability
External audit/review	Inclusion of a researcher unfamiliar with the study charged with examining and vetting the research process, evaluating accurate portrayal of the findings, and promoting movement from the personal to the universal	Credibility, dependability, confirmability
Triangulation	The use of multiple sources of information or perspectives (e.g., data collection methods, data sources, theories) to enhance credibility, justify findings, and affirm multiple realities	Credibility, transferability, dependability, confirmability
Reflexivity	Introspection, and clarification and acknowledgment, of researcher's biases, values, beliefs, attitudes, perspectives, and role, as informed by personal experience	Credibility, dependability, confirmability

TABLE 8.2 ● Strategies for Evaluating the Integrity of Your Heuristic Study

Characteristic of Heuristic Inquiry	Evaluation Questions
Qualitative	• Do the central guiding questions of your study focus on the *what* and *how* aspects of the topic of inquiry, with the aim being to achieve an in-depth understanding of its essential nature? • Does the study follow a design that allows you to determine next steps based on what is emerging in the study?
Social constructivist	• Are your research questions and process based on the assumption that reality is relative and subjective? • Do you acknowledge your role, including biases, values, and attitudes and their potential impact on the research? • Do you use the first person when discussing the research or presenting the findings? • Do the findings of your study reflect multiple iterations of reality?
Phenomenologically aligned	• Do your guiding questions explore a real-life human experience? • Does your process of inquiry follow the assumption of perception as the primary source of knowledge? • Does your research process highlight the importance of immersion in the topic of inquiry? • Does your study focus on illuminating deep understanding and uncovering the essential nature of the topic of inquiry? • Does your study follow and use the seven processes and six phases of heuristic inquiry?
Autobiographical	• Do the guiding questions of the study originate within you? • Do the guiding questions and subquestions make room for the integration of past, present, and future personal experience in the here and now?
Exploratory, serendipitous, and discovery-oriented	• Does your research design indicate the use of multiple strategies to collect, organize, and analyze the data? • Do you bring curiosity, openness, and wonder into your process of inquiry? • Is there room for an emergent process and for spontaneous response to that process, including the refinement of research questions based on information gathered? • Is there room for both prearranged and accidental discovery?

Process- and content-focused	• Is your study primarily informed by process and the emergent findings? • Do your processes of inquiry and data collection highlight dialogue, both verbal and nonverbal? • Does your research content include collected artifacts (yours and co-researchers') such as writing samples, poetry, journal entries, photos, and artwork?
Intuitive, introspective, and reflexive	• Does your research process acknowledge the implicit dimensions of experience as informed by intuition and felt sense? • Do you allow a variety of representations, including words, images, symbols, phrases, and memories, of your process and topic to emerge? • Do you attend to your personal experience and to that of your co-researchers, as well as to how both experiences are interfacing?
Experiential, embodied, and holistic	• Are your central research questions and approach to the study informed by subjectivity and the role of the body as an information receiver that can be used to guide and make meaning of the process of research? • Does your approach to the study acknowledge and include the various facets of human experience (e.g., cognitive, emotional, somatic, spiritual, and relational) and their integration? • Does your study honor both verbal and nonverbal experience? • Does your study allow for the intersection of *being* and *knowing*?
Existential and humanistic	• Does your study focus on questions of how humans know and/or make meaning of their world and on their approaches to attaining their highest potential? • Is your study characterized by personal involvement and full engagement with the topic of inquiry?
Culturally embedded and emancipatory	• Do you maintain a focus on and sensitivity to the social and cultural context of your study and on diversity-related issues (e.g., gender, age, ethnicity, religion, social class, ability, and sexuality)? • Does your study inspire members of the research team and readers of the findings to reconsider or reconstitute their understanding of reality to embrace novel perceptions without conflicting with personal views? • Does your study promote change and social justice, either directly or indirectly?

(Continued)

TABLE 8.2 ● (Continued)

Relational, authentic, and participatory	• Is your research process informed by relational dynamics and discourse, including intense personal contact, trust, presence, self- and other-awareness, empathy, and intersubjectivity? • Does your study support self-disclosure and meaning-making of shared subjective experience? • Do you remain true to the phenomenon you are exploring? • Do you take an inclusive, equitable, awareness-enhancing approach that promotes empowerment, action, and change?
Imaginative and creative	• Does your study highlight the intersection of persons' uniqueness with people, events, and circumstances in their lives? • Does your research design support freedom, spontaneity, boldness, self-acceptance, and integration? • Does your study design demonstrate nontraditional approaches to data collection, organization, and analysis? • Does your study allow for nonliteral representations of perceived reality (i.e., representation of findings through poetry, artwork, photography, musical composition, etc.)?
Nonlinear, fluid, and flexible	• Does your study support the idea of multiple experiences and perceptions? • Does your study design (and do you) tolerate ambiguity for the unknown? • Are you able to remain detached from a specified outcome or goal and focus on acquiring an understanding of the essential nature of the phenomenon? • Do you find the research design adaptable to the needs of researchers within diverse disciplines? • Do you find the research design adaptable to working with phenomena that may be challenging to observe, measure, or document?
Living versus lived	• Does your research approach honor the interconnectedness of human experience and view it as one continuing cycle, rather than as a series of discrete, disconnected historical events? • Does your study explore the topic of inquiry as a present-moment, ongoing, *living* human experience, even when exploring its manifestation in the past? • Do you include rich, textured descriptions of the phenomenon through the voices of those who have experienced it?

Heuristic Evaluation as a Shared Experience

As demonstrated in the numerous evaluation strategies above (both traditional and heuristic inquiry oriented), the evaluation process is highly subjective. With that in mind, taking a collaborative and communal approach to evaluation enriches transparency, boosting rigor and trustworthiness. In that manner, the purpose behind heuristic evaluation is foundationally similar to the purpose behind evaluation in other qualitative research methodologies. Heuristic evaluation is not performed to *confirm* the rigor or trustworthiness of a research study but to shed light on the various and diverse avenues through which the perceptions of the primary researcher, as well as those of the research partners, were explored, honored, and included, thereby supporting the findings of the study and advancing their applicability and utility.

Evaluating heuristic inquiry is, once again, a highly subjective enterprise informed by personal experiences and perceptions. Consequently, this type of research evaluation, by its very nature, should involve a collaborative process that includes all members of the research team but also invites outsiders to share their perspectives on the process of inquiry and findings. Such a communal approach to evaluation fosters integration of the research experience, as well as of the variety of personal experiences that originally inspired the central research question(s). Heuristic evaluation creates opportunities for all members of the research team to make further sense of their experience of the phenomenon, as well as of the research process itself. One can say that in heuristic research, the evaluation process serves as a ceremonial closure of sorts, one that invites reflection from each member of the research team on the following:

- The integrity of the study (both process and content) as a heuristic inquiry

- One's personal contribution to the study (especially through the rich, textured narrative of one's living experience of the topic of inquiry)

- The confluence of the personal dimension with the holistic, universal vision of the essential nature of the phenomenon that unfolded during the research process and emerged through the many voices of members of the research team

- The capacity of the findings to inspire transformation within each member of the research team, as well as within readers of the findings

While evaluation is of great value to all members of the research team, involving outsiders allows for the inclusion of multiple perspectives. Indeed, Lincoln, Lynham, and Guba (2011) asserted that evaluating qualitative research involves exploring the rigor with which a research methodology was applied, as well as seeking "community consent" (p. 120) for the salience of the findings and interpretations. Agreed!

As an individual researcher, you bring your personal experiences, thoughts, beliefs, attitudes, biases, and ways of being and of knowing to the research table. However, you are already aware that your ways of being and of knowing are not exclusive and that others' perspectives also matter. That is one of the reasons you are conducting a study with a research team! Indeed, collaborating on evaluation may, for example, invite novel perspectives on the creation and refinement of future research. Including a variety of worldviews in the evaluation process creates opportunities for defining and refining questions for new heuristic studies and allows your co-researchers to identify ways they may be involved. It is very possible one of your co-researchers may decide he would like to explore a specific aspect of the current study more comprehensively in a new study and may even invite you to be a co-researcher. This creates interesting opportunities for the reversal of roles and for exploring new interactions with power differentials. Keeping heuristic inquiry's social constructivist identity in mind, collaboration creates opportunities for the emergence of multiple realities and interpretations, which supports our ability to draw threads between the personal and the universal.

Likewise, taking a collaborative approach to the evaluation process creates opportunities for empowerment, promoting action and change. Extensive contact with co-researchers and with outsiders allows for open and ongoing dialogue, embodied relational listening, and the refinement of I∞Thou engagement. It also opens up rich opportunities for shared learning and for expanded thinking and being. Ongoing respectful and affirming discourse supports the construction of community, even as every individual's journey and experience is honored. Pausing in the reflexive space of the evaluation process invites questions such as the following:

- *Who are you? Who am I? Who are we, in our shared experience?*

- *What is the essential nature of this experience that we share? How do we each live it and make meaning of it?*

- *How has being in this shared space with you reshaped my way of being with this phenomenon? My way of being with myself? My way of being with others? My way of being in the world?*

- *How has our shared experience reshaped my way(s) of knowing?*

- *What might I like to take away from this shared experience? What do I wish to leave behind, in this shared space?*

Creating knowledge and understanding is an experience we share with ourselves, with others, and with the world; it involves *inner* and *outer* dimensions, as well as dimensions of *with* and *between*. In that respect, collaborating on the evaluation of a heuristic study is a highly embodied communal practice that allows for multiple rehearsals of meaning-making, as well as for integration and closure of the research process, even as we work together to critically assess the soundness of our shared research experience.

The Importance of Reflexive Leadership in Evaluation

Although heuristic evaluation is collaborative, I reiterate that it is essential to the cohesiveness of your study that you maintain your leadership role within the process of evaluation. I concur with Moustakas's (1990) and Polanyi's (1969) assertions that the primary researcher is charged with leadership of the research process and with making final decisions about both process and findings. Again, this is not to empower co-researchers and outside collaborators only to turn around and dismiss their contributions but rather to mitigate confusion and conflict. The idea behind the collaborative approach is to attempt to hear and include the experience and voice of every person involved as a way of promoting equity. With that, human interaction is a highly complex art that requires great patience and relational aptitude, and discussing and researching topics that are of personal meaning lends further complexity to such interaction. Again, you are the one person who has been involved in the study from its earliest phases and the only one likely to remain involved well past its termination. You are the only person intimately familiar with every detail of the study, every twist and turn of the labyrinth. Therefore, embrace your leadership role unapologetically as you make decisions about both process- and outcome-related issues.

For example, you may want to collaborate with co-researchers on generating specific questions or requests for peer reviewers or external auditors regarding parts of the study to evaluate and specific criteria and/or strategies to implement. You might then take responsibility for relaying this consolidated information to the outside reviewers and making sure they comply with the instructions as a way of enhancing consistency throughout the evaluation process. Or on the opposite end of the spectrum, you might decide as a research team that you do not wish to standardize your requests of outside reviewers, instead allowing reviewers to provide you the feedback they deemed most relevant. Once you've received the reviewer feedback, you can work together with your research team to appraise the significance of its various facets, with the understanding that you will make the ultimate decisions about what stays, what goes, and what is modified and how, based on all input received. Again, this is not to disempower (even as you are attempting to collaborate) but to maintain consistency as you manage the many moving pieces of the project, including working with the data, supporting the wholeness and vitality of the process, and maintaining genuine and respectful relationships with and between co-researchers, peer debriefers, and external auditors.

As a way of enhancing the diversity of feedback (and ultimately, of the study), you might consider inviting evaluation from individuals from other disciplines as well as your own. Similarly, you may wish to elicit feedback from researchers who use other qualitative methodologies or from quantitative researchers. Diversifying your evaluator pool will challenge disciplinary and methodological boundaries and, ultimately, enrich the quality of your feedback. Conversely, managing the exchange of such a wide variety of inputs and viewpoints is challenging. Therefore, as you work with multiple sources of feedback, including co-researchers, peer reviewers, and external auditors, one question that might help keep things on track is, *How does this viewpoint illuminate the topic of inquiry?* With that, I must close this section with a word of caution: Guard against using your leadership role to impose any predetermined processes, decisions, or outcomes with which you have become comfortable. Heuristic research is about going beyond our personal worldviews and inviting others into a meaningful discussion to illuminate the universal through the personal, without diminishing any person's unique contribution. This is where reflexivity is, again, helpful.

To truly transcend your own experience (without necessarily giving it up!), engage in a reflexive process on what might happen should your paradigm coexist with other paradigms. You will more than likely experience some discomfort with this. Again, the topic of inquiry is quite personal to you. But it is also personal to all other members of your research team. Trying to remain within your comfort zone is your way of maintaining a grip on the rightness or worthiness of your paradigm because others' ways of being and of knowing may seem threatening. Remember, however, that in heuristic inquiry, multiple realities are welcome. Therefore, challenge yourself to engage with alternative viewpoints, return repeatedly to the data, and be open to sharing with your collaborators your decision-making process to increase transparency and to receive feedback about your decisions and engage in reevaluation. Know why you are deciding what you decide, and be open about it. Maintaining a reflexive attitude about how your subjective experience is informing the evaluation, and communicating about your role in both initial and ongoing informed consent are critical.

Closing Reflections

Heuristic evaluation is designed to enhance the rigor and trustworthiness of a study's process and outcome and includes implementing traditional qualitative research evaluation criteria and strategies, as well as identifying distinguishing characteristics of heuristic research that are present and therefore serve to identify the study as heuristic inquiry. Yet the evaluation process is not about ascertaining ultimate truths or realities. Heuristic evaluation is about bringing our collective perceptions, thoughts, and beliefs into a shared space as we work to unravel multiple understandings of the essential nature of a specific human experience while exploring its personal and universal dimensions and meanings. It is as subjective and circular a process as all other aspects of a heuristic study, in which, after all is said and done, our reality is what we take to be true, and what we take to be true is our reality.

9

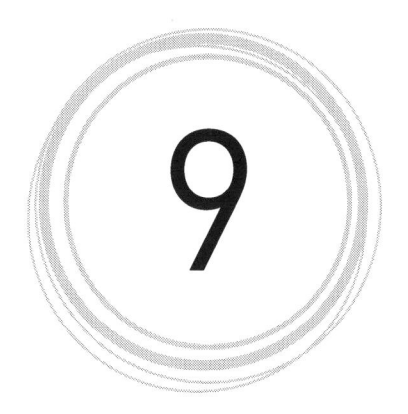

Writing a Living Manuscript
An Embodied Relational Approach

Learning is discovering that something is possible.

~ Friedrich (Fritz) Perls

> **Questions for Reflection**
>
> 1. What goes into a heuristic inquiry manuscript?
> 2. What makes writing from an embodied relational perspective important?
> 3. How might you balance rigor with an intriguing voice?
> 4. How can you create a manuscript that promotes social justice?
> 5. What might support the publication of your heuristic manuscript?

Language is both a way of being and a way of knowing. It is a gateway to awareness, emergence, and discovery. Let's pause for a moment with Perls's words. As you read these words, written by the well-known and controversial German-born pioneer behind the holistic and awareness-oriented gestalt psychotherapy approach, do you find yourself probing your thoughts about what they might mean? Or do you sense your body∞mind∞spirit∞world connecting with (or disconnecting from) some aspect of them and resonating with a familiar felt sense, although you may not necessarily understand which specific aspect or why? I ask you to sense into this question, as both reading and writing can be embodied (as well as embodying) activities. That is, they can involve and engage multiple epistemological and ontological frameworks (with the understanding that the body is the point of encounter between inner and outer experience), rather than connecting exclusively with and through cognition. As Ellingson (2006) asserted, "Writing is done with fingers and arms and eyes: It is an embodied act, not mental conjuring, and we should reflect on the experience of writing our research just as we reflect on our experience of being at a research site" (p. 304). This is not to minimize thinking; thinking is critical! However, as we have discussed throughout this book, it is not the only way of being or of knowing; this is especially true within the realm of heuristic inquiry.

Writing a heuristic manuscript engages multiple ontological and epistemological perspectives as a way of honoring the indivisibility and wholeness of human experience and representing social constructivist views of the multiplicity of truth and reality. The success of your manuscript lies in its ability to relay critical information to readers while inviting them to establish and maintain a relationship with the material that transcends the parameters of their reading session. I think of a heuristic manuscript as an opportunity for a dialogical encounter among the writer/primary researcher, co-researchers, and readers on a path to self- and other-awareness and, ultimately, to transformation. Indeed, Moustakas (1990) described the heuristic manuscript as one that brings together "an experience that has profoundly affected the investigator and which holds possibilities for scientific knowledge and social impact and meaning" (p. 53). Similarly, Polanyi (1958) stressed the duty of researchers to make personal knowledge public. Each of these thinkers recognized the importance of not only disseminating new knowledge but also making contact with readers in a manner that enables shifts from stagnation to movement, from inaction to agency, and from the personal to the universal. In short, they emphasized the realm of possibility!

In this chapter, I describe various components and features of a comprehensive heuristic manuscript and how to elaborate them as a way of representing the heuristic methodology. I also elucidate the value of writing from an embodied relational perspective, honoring the holistic and communal nature of heuristic inquiry. The written word holds far more power and meaning than any of us can possibly imagine. With that understanding, I outline means of balancing rigor with an intriguing writing voice that resonates with meaning, energizing and empowering your readers toward learning that inspires action and change.

Components of a Heuristic Manuscript

A solid research manuscript begins with proper and diligent organization and should include a set of general features that allow you to share with readers the findings of your heuristic study comprehensively and holistically. Most of the features listed below can be found in any respectable qualitative research textbook. But let's look at how you can customize these components so your manuscript accurately and comprehensively embodies and exemplifies the heuristic methodology from beginning to end.

Title

Potential readers will check the title of a manuscript to assess its relevance to them. Your title should include the topic of inquiry in a manner that reflects its human nature. Additionally, you may want to give a nod to your discipline, name your sample, or include information about the philosophical/theoretical foundations of your study. Most important, be sure the phrase *heuristic inquiry* is present. As you work some of these pieces in, keep in mind the general disposition of the publication to which you are hoping to submit. For example, the title of my unpublished dissertation manuscript is *A Heuristic Inquiry of the Embodied Experiences of Body Psychotherapists in the Therapeutic Process* (Sultan, 2015), while the title of the manuscript I submitted for publication in a peer-reviewed journal is "Embodiment and the Therapeutic Relationship: Findings From a Heuristic Inquiry" (Sultan, 2017b). The title of my unpublished dissertation demonstrates the discipline, research methodology, topic of inquiry, and sample. On the other hand, the title for the peer-reviewed manuscript identifies my discipline and the study as a heuristic inquiry and names the phenomenon explored, with a demonstrable focus on humanistic theory (via the therapeutic relationship), as I planned to submit it to the *Journal of Humanistic Counseling*. Here are a couple of other titles of heuristic manuscripts, both unpublished dissertations: *Disenfranchised Grief in Postpartum Women: A Heuristic Inquiry Into Women's Lived Experience of Loss of the Dreamed-of Birth* (Kudeva, 2015) and *The Experience of Parental Suicide: A Heuristic Inquiry* (Emerson, 2002).

Abstract

The abstract is a narrative paragraph of about 50 to 200 words that highlights key points of your study. A heuristic abstract might include brief information about the background of the study, main topic, research design, sample, and general findings. Use heuristic terminology to prepare potential readers with a general sense of the methods used to explore the topic of inquiry. For example, the abstract for the peer-reviewed article (Sultan, 2017b) based on my dissertation included terms such as *illuminate, creative, relational, embodied, perceived*, and *reflexive*.

Keywords

Keywords are the terms researchers and readers will use when searching for manuscripts using databases or search engines. Select three to five words or phrases, one of which should be *heuristic inquiry*. Other keywords can represent discipline, sample, theory, or other features highlighted in your manuscript. I used the following keywords for my peer-reviewed article (Sultan, 2017b): *heuristic inquiry, embodiment, somatic experience, mind-body therapies,* and *therapeutic relationship.*

Introduction and Clear Articulation of Topic and Research Questions

The topic of inquiry is what your research study is all about. Clearly state in a few sentences early in your manuscript your topic and key concepts associated with it, and briefly describe your research question in narrative form. A sharp focus on a core issue serves to unify your manuscript. In addition, share with readers (and future researchers) the exact questions you used in your study. Because the central questions in a heuristic study are autobiographical and directly related to a distinctly human experience, it is possible that others have asked the same or similar questions, though perhaps informally. Listing the central questions explored through your study may be a primary point of connection between readers and the topic and between readers and your research team.

Theoretical Framework

As mentioned earlier, the theoretical framework is the lens (or perspective) used to guide the movement and advancement of your research. Include at least one brief informative paragraph about the theoretical framework that guided your study. In most cases, the theoretical framework will bear a connection to the heuristic methodology. Find that point of connection and articulate it clearly. For example, I elected to use Merleau-Ponty's (1945/2013) philosophy of perception to guide my exploration of body psychotherapist embodiment and included a brief description of that philosophy in my manuscript. I then delineated for readers the connection between this philosophy and my topic of inquiry by underscoring the perceptual, relational, and kinesthetic ethos of body psychotherapy.

Rationale for the Study

Every researcher has reasons, both personal and professional, for conducting specific studies and for exploring particular topics. One reason you decided to explore your topic of inquiry formally in a heuristic study was your personal experience of the phenomenon, one that made such a profound impact on you, you were curious how others experienced it and how it may have impacted them. Briefly mention your autobiographical connection with the topic of inquiry, and identify any gaps in the previous research. How did the findings that emerged from your specific exploration fill those gaps, validating your rationale?

Comprehensive but Concise Literature Review

The literature review section highlights key research studies and literature that have probed topics of relevance to your study. In this section of your heuristic manuscript, review those bodies of knowledge, clearly identify the strengths and limitations of each, state how your study filled some of the gaps in each, and describe how application of the heuristic approach facilitated that process. As an example, I closed out the literature review section of my peer-reviewed manuscript (Sultan, 2017b) by identifying strengths and limitations for each source reviewed, delineating how my study addressed limitations and filled gaps, and stating that my study's heuristic lens lent it a previously unexplored creative, reflexive, and relational perspective that was a necessary and unique complement to the topic of inquiry (i.e., embodiment).

Method

This section opens with a brief recap of your topic and purpose, as well as identification of the heuristic methodology and what made it suitable for exploring your research question(s). Contrast your choice of methodology with alternative choices, and lay out your research design. Follow this with a short listing of the heuristic processes and phases and a concise description of each, as well as tie-ins between particular heuristic methods and certain aspects of your study, clarifying your disciplined application of the methodology. Finally, provide an overview of your role by identifying your personal involvement with the topic and how you included yourself without compromising the integrity of the study.

Co-Researchers

Discuss the principal features of your sample and sampling procedure, underlining the demographic variations of relevance to the guiding questions of the study. What inclusion and exclusion criteria did you set for your sample? How did you pinpoint specific demographics for a sample based on the needs of the study? What made this sample ideal for responding to the guiding questions, and how did you evaluate germaneness of the sample in comparison with alternative choices? How did you locate co-researchers who had had a personal experience with the topic of inquiry? How did your co-researchers interact with both the topic of inquiry and the heuristic methodology? How did they interact with you? How did you know it was time to stop collecting more data? Most important, describe *who* your research partners are by portraying each of them using excerpts from their rich narratives, thereby giving each a voice, in alignment with the deeply personal, relational, and emancipatory heuristic spirit. Co-researcher artifacts are a great way to bring every member of your research team, and your topic, to life.

Materials and Procedure

In this section, share with readers a synopsis of how you reached out to potential co-researchers (e.g., personal e-mail, group e-mail) and, after securing their approval to join your research team, what documents were included in your correspondence (e.g., informed consent form, demographic information form). How did you schedule time for interviews and for sharing instructions and addressing questions about upcoming procedures? It is important to highlight, in this part, how your materials and general research procedure tied in with the *developing a set of instructions, developing a contract*, and *creating an atmosphere of trust* (Moustakas, 1990) components of heuristic research.

Data Collection and Analysis

Discuss your data collection method (e.g., interviews, focus groups) in some detail. For example, if you conducted interviews, what type of interviews were they (e.g., one-time semi-structured 60-minute video interviews)? Explain your choice of data collection, organization, and analysis methods and how these methods complemented your topic of inquiry and sample. In alignment with heuristic research, bring some attention to the relational dynamics of the interviews. Also, mention artifacts contributed by co-researchers, as well as reflexive excerpts from your research journal. Address any efforts you made to minimize deception throughout the course of the study, as well as to enhance co-researchers' experience of being members of a heuristic research team. Describe your documentation approach (e.g., embodied relational transcription), your reflexive process as you sat with the data, and how you engaged the various heuristic processes and phases (e.g., indwelling, focusing) to illuminate themes representing co-researchers' perception of the essential nature of the topic of inquiry. Finally, describe the methods you used to evaluate your study for trustworthiness and rigor.

Findings

Although you have relatively free license when it comes to sharing the findings of your study, consider breaking down this section of your manuscript into subsections to make for a clearer, more organized reading experience. One of the simplest ways to do this is to categorize your findings by research question, as this demonstrates how your findings actually answer those questions. Identify each theme by name, and include excerpts from co-researcher narratives supporting it. Also identify any unanticipated findings, showcasing your ability as a researcher to step away from preconceptions and assumptions informed by your personal experience and explore other perspectives of the topic of inquiry. Make it clear to readers which parts of this section are direct excerpts of co-researcher narratives of their living experience and which parts are your elucidation. Finally, explore alternative perspectives on the data (Moustakas, 1990, 1994) to inspire readers into their own exploration during and beyond the reading experience.

Discussion

When I scan a manuscript, I go to the introduction and discussion sections first. By reading those two parts, I am better able to assess whether reading the entire manuscript will be worth my time investment. The discussion section is essentially where you describe the findings in a manner that brings the many moving parts of the study together into a cohesive whole, offering a collective, living understanding of the topic of inquiry in context and answering the question, *So what?* Briefly reiterate the central premise of the study and how the findings contribute to the general knowledge base, with a focus on areas of knowledge relevant to your particular topic and to the heuristic methodology. Focus on why conducting a formal study was important, and address any ethical issues that arose and how you attended to them. State how the findings may contribute to future research, as well as to theory, training, and practice (or to other key facets of your discipline). Touch on the themes (including any that were unanticipated), and draw connections between them and (a) the theoretical framework for the study and (b) the knowledge base summarized in the literature review. Finally, identify implications based on the emergence of this new knowledge. For example, consider discussing how your findings may be of worth to a specific research community or broader community, such as a particular culture or subgroup. Or include reflections on how your findings might be relevant to understanding topics similar to the phenomenon you researched and how they may be transferred to other individuals, groups, situations, or settings. How might they inspire movement toward action and change?

Limitations

This part of the manuscript offers yet another opportunity to be transparent with readers about the process of research and some of the roadblocks you encountered. Every study has limitations, to be certain, but a great deal rests on how we enumerate those limitations. I have come across countless qualitative research manuscripts that apologetically state that the study they describe was flawed simply because it was qualitative and, therefore, subjective (i.e., not empirical or not good enough). Please don't go there! Researcher subjectivity is a virtue and not a vice of heuristic inquiry; it is one of your tasks as a heuristic researcher to highlight that throughout your manuscript. On the other hand, do share with readers some of the limitations that may have emerged around your research design. As an example, I addressed in my peer-reviewed manuscript (Sultan, 2017b) the primary limitation of my study, which was the use of technology, as it created unpredictable interruptions in the study's progression when it failed. On the other hand, in my dissertation manuscript (Sultan, 2015), because I had more freedom with word count, I elaborated on how even this limitation served as an opportunity for relational bonding and for reflecting on the vulnerability and imperfection of the human experience, thereby addressing issues of relevance to the topic of inquiry and to my co-researchers.

Conclusions and Future Directions

This is the final part of your manuscript. Outline some conclusions that may be drawn based on the new knowledge offered by the unique findings of your heuristic study and their applicability to your discipline, as well as to wider epistemological and ontological contexts. Highlight heuristic methodology by drawing threads between (a) the unique knowledge that emerged through your exploration using the heuristic approach and (b) future research efforts.

Embodied Relational Writing: Balancing Rigor With Intriguing Writing Style

Now that you have some suggestions to help you create an organized structure for your manuscript, let's look at how to use what I call **embodied relational writing** to imbue it with authentic voice, language, style, and connection. Why embodied relational writing? As I mentioned earlier, writing can be both an embodied and an embodying act. It can also be highly disembodying. Have you ever raced through a writing project only to read over it later and wonder when in the world you wrote one part or the other of it? This approach to writing can come off as robotic, creating distance between your content and readers and compromising opportunities for connection. Additionally, writing is in many ways both a solitary activity and an act of empathy. Embodied relational writing emanates not only from your bodily felt sense but from all dimensions of your being, embracing your embodied reflexivity and multiple perspectives and inviting your audience directly into the shared journey you initiated with your research team. The idea is to find a fluid balance between rigor and intersubjectivity. Below are some ways of practicing embodied relational writing, many of which follow a similar approach to that used in embodied relational interviewing and embodied relational transcription.

- *Be relational, reflexive, and authentic.* One of the biggest challenges you will face when writing the manuscript for your heuristic study is to remain authentic, relational, and fascinating while upholding academic standards. With that, heuristic inquiry is not designed to showcase the academic or intellectual prowess of an omniscient researcher. Its purpose is to apply academic and rigorous standards to bring to light the human encounter with life's most perplexing and inspiring experiences. Allow your manuscript to reflect this fusion of science and art by keeping your narrative professional but also inclusive, personable, forthcoming, and humble. Write as the curious explorer you are—not as an authoritative informer of facts but as a human engaged in warm I∞Thou conversation with other humans. Instead of stating and reporting, invite through the elucidation of possibilities. Engage readers' curiosity. Draw them into your shared experience. The tone of your manuscript should inspire confidence while steering clear of proposing definitive truths. As Krathwohl (2009) attested, "Trust is absolutely essential to accepting the findings of a study" (p. 341). Confidence and trust may inspire provocative thoughts, questions, ideas, images, feelings, and sensations, taking readers on a deeply embodied journey. Keep in mind: Only when you tap into and connect with your own genuineness will you gain readers' confidence and leave them resonating with the multiple possible truths represented in your manuscript. This takes us back into the space of embodied reflexivity, through which we engage with self∞self, self∞other, and self∞world. Thus, engage a reflexive attitude as you work to keep your writing voice genuine, unassuming, purposeful, and intentional. Steer clear of phony, inappropriate, incendiary language. Keep your writing—and yourself—human and real.

- *Be present.* Write from a place of holistic engagement and immediacy. Write from a here-and-now (even if you are writing about past events) perspective, one that includes your cognitive, emotional, sensory∞kinesthetic, perceptual, spiritual, and social∞relational experience.

- *Write from the body∞mind∞spirit∞world.* Reading and writing may at first blush seem like purely cognitive acts. However, what we read and write is not only deeply conceptualized but also deeply sensed and felt (Gendlin, 1962) in the body—the site at which inner and outer experience interact (Merleau-Ponty, 1945/2013), giving rise to resonance on the emotional, cognitive, and meaning-making levels. Use multiple ways of being and of knowing to depict the richness of the research experience holistically and cohesively, giving voice to the narratives of your research partners by engaging heuristic processes such as focusing, indwelling, tacit knowing, and incubation. Include multiple aspects of your sensory experience of the content as you go about the writing process, and trust what emerges. What body sensations did you experience as you interacted with a particular co-researcher? How might those sensations have impacted your interaction? For example, while one of my co-researchers and I discussed his embodied experience of loss and grief, my stomach curled inward and I felt a cold adrenaline rush in my body as I recalled some of my own encounters with grief. I also tuned out of my co-researcher's narrative briefly, possibly in self-protection or denial and possibly to recalibrate. I wrote about this in my research journal and then included an excerpt in my dissertation manuscript (Sultan, 2015) to bring to readers the shared experience of grief between my co-researcher and me. This is how we honor multiple epistemological and ontological perspectives, inviting readers also to connect with our narratives holistically, to process how the reading experience is impacting their meaning-making of the findings, and to reflect on potential avenues for further exploration based on what is of relevance to them (Lawler, 2002). Thus, you create what I call a **living manuscript** (or **living narrative**) of a *living experience*—a creative, embodied, transformative narrative that transcends the single sitting required to complete it, carving pathways for emergence and discovery within readers, co-researchers, and you.

- *Communicate your findings holistically.* This is closely connected to writing from the body∞mind∞spirit∞world, with the added recommendation to communicate the findings using diverse approaches, including artifacts such as artwork and poetry, in keeping with the heuristic methodology.

- *Use first-person, active voice.* Patton (2015) suggested that the reflexive voice and the first-person active voice (which uses *I*) are one. Refrain from calling yourself "the researcher." It dehumanizes you and flies in the face of everything heuristic methodology is about. Use *I* when referring to yourself and *we* when referring to your research team. This lends immediacy, gives voice to multiple perspectives, and as Gough (2008) suggested, promotes responsibility-taking. It also affirms the autobiographical nature of the topic of inquiry and study, as well as the importance of inclusion and the collaborative spirit of the heuristic journey. Along similar lines, because heuristic inquiry is a highly active and person-oriented approach to research, use active versus passive narrative. Passive sentences merely state that something was done; active sentences clearly identify *who did what*. For example, instead of writing "Data was collected, organized, and analyzed," write, "I collected, organized, and analyzed the data." Own it!

- *Represent and affirm multiple perspectives.* Underscoring a variety of perspectives helps readers understand that your findings are not definitive, which may inspire further questions to explore or other realities to perceive. Providing evidence of collaboration enriches transparency, rigor, and trustworthiness, as it allows readers of the findings to form their own thoughts of your representation of the study and to consider ways those findings may or may not apply to their personal experience of the topic of inquiry. An optimal method for representing other perspectives is to include verbatim excerpts of your research partners' living narratives, especially when presenting the themes. Having these samples of your co-researchers' accounts gives readers an opportunity to elaborate their own themes or to generate other questions of relevance to the study that they might wish to explore. Also, include alternate methods of communicating the findings (e.g., artifacts, tables, figures, and charts). Some believe that there is no place for tables and diagrams in qualitative research. I disagree. Because tables can provide a clear visual representation of multiple pieces of information that would be quite challenging to both describe and understand, I used tables in my dissertation manuscript (Sultan, 2015) and in my peer-reviewed article (Sultan, 2017b)— one demonstrating the demographics of my co-researchers (see Table 9.1) and the other presenting the themes that emerged from the data analysis (see Table 9.2). Additionally, a clearly articulated way of communicating multiple perspectives is to use language such as *may, might, possibly, seems,* and other words that indicate provisional or possible realities. While such language is generally frowned upon in many research traditions, it is highly relevant to heuristic methodology.

- *Keep your writing clear, organized, and relevant.* Use professional and accessible language with sound grammar and word choice that clearly conveys your key points, and include examples to support your narrative. Demonstrate how your findings are relevant to your theoretical framework, the existing body of knowledge you addressed in your literature review, your guiding research questions, and the various processes and phases of heuristic inquiry. Use transitions appropriately and accurately to maintain momentum

TABLE 9.1 ● Co-Researcher Demographics

Name	Age	Gender	Years in BP Practice	Country of Residence/Origin	Primary Theoretical Orientation	Body Psychotherapy Modality
Su	61	F	8	Hong Kong/Hong Kong	Satir family therapy	Hakomi/Somatic Experiencing
Rainbow	42	F	12	Canada/Canada	Critical/postmodern feminism	Integrative Body Psychotherapy
Courtenay	66	M	31	UK/UK	Eclectic/integrative	Biodynamic Psychotherapy
Verena	58	F	22	USA/Italy	Object relations	Dance/Movement Therapy
Leo	66	F	33	Australia/Australia	Psychodynamic/humanistic	Radix
Stephen	55	M	10	USA/USA	Multiple	Therapeutic Massage/Somatic Experiencing

TABLE 9.2 ● Emergent Themes

Themes	Su	Rainbow	Courtenay	Verena	Leo	Stephen
Somatic experience and bodily awareness	X	X	X	X	X	X
Presence and attunement	X	X	X	X	X	X
Allowing and accepting		X	X	X	X	X
Creating a shared experience	X	X	X	X		X
Therapist embodiment practices	X	X	X	X	X	X
Trust, safety, and support	X			X	X	X
Connection, energy, and flow		X	X		X	
Authenticity	X		X		X	

and flow. Clarify any obscure terminology, especially words or phrases that describe heuristic processes and phases (e.g., *tacit knowing, indwelling*). Avoid generalizations, as heuristic studies tend to explore specific (albeit ambiguous!) experiences.

- *Be transparent, truthful, and accurate.* There are no so-called failed studies in heuristic inquiry and, consequently, no need to embellish. Encourage confidence in what you are reporting by disclosing key information from your study design and process and avoiding misrepresentation of processes or outcomes. If you and your research partners get anything at all out of the experience itself, then your study has served a higher purpose and change is in the works. With that in mind, be attentive to how you word your narrative, and present the research experience as you perceived it, as accurately and truthfully as possible. Support your narrative with co-researcher accounts and accurate citations, allowing readers to evaluate the authenticity of your content (Fossey, Harvey, McDermott, Davidson, 2002). Document any divergences from heuristic methodology, and identify the gaps these were designed to fill. Eschew deliberate omissions. As with all other aspects of heuristic inquiry, this is subjective terrain. Again, be transparent about your subjectivity and motivation and how they may be influencing the writing of your manuscript and your choice of what to include and/or exclude, anchoring your study in the social and cultural context. The more transparent and open you are, the more trustworthy your account will be.

- *Use creative, evocative, and accessible expression.* Recall that heuristic inquiry embraces both verbal and nonverbal, conscious and unconscious communication. Allow yourself maximum access to your own creativity as a vehicle for connecting with the ever-changing research experience and for sharing the exceptional findings with the world. Arons and Richards (2015) stated, "Creativity involves both *originality* and *meaningfulness*" (p. 161). Take risks and push boundaries! Your manuscript should inspire a shift in perspective and creative insight within readers, inspiring them to nontraditional ways of interacting with your topic of inquiry, which, due to its potentially universal themes, may have a history of being explored in a limited manner. In addition to your verbal narrative, include any artwork, poetry, musical compositions, journal entries, vignettes, or other forms of creative expression depicting cognitive, emotional, social, intuitive, somatic, and spiritual facets of your and co-researchers' experience of the topic of inquiry. This expands your manuscript, allowing it to tap into both the implicit and unambiguous dimensions of the emergent knowledge while unifying your co-researchers' contributions with your reflexive perception to create cohesive and inclusive content. It also permits your readers to deepen their relationship with the phenomenon by accessing what is present and living within each co-researcher's narrative (and your living experience of the entire process) and to thereby take a more nuanced, resonant, and memorable approach to connecting with it, both personally and professionally. Finally, accessibility is key! To that end, keep your narrative focused on the humanness of the topic of inquiry, include examples and details that demonstrate what you are attempting to articulate, and once again, maintain a conversational tone. Remember that heuristic inquiry is research that allows us to access the junction of the personal and the universal.

- *Revise.* Your manuscript is your line of communication with others regarding your study. Reread each draft both silently and aloud. Listen for the sound of your narrative. Hear it in your ears, and sense it in your body. Is it clear and modest, or is it stuffy? Does it flow smoothly inside you, or does it get stuck somewhere as you attempt to decipher what it means? Listen, with every aspect of your being, for resonances and dissonances. Exercise 9.1 is designed to jump-start you in the practice of embodied relational writing and to facilitate your revision process.

- *Get outsider feedback.* In the spirit of affirming multiple perspectives, creativity, and relationality, seek feedback on your manuscript. Ask an academic peer and/or each of your research partners to read the manuscript

EXERCISE 9.1
EXPERIMENTING WITH EMBODIED RELATIONAL WRITING

- Select a random piece of writing (not yours), and take time to read it. Imagine you are in the scene of that manuscript. Once you have completed the reading, step away from it.

- In your reflexive journal, scribble any words, phrases, images, or symbols that stand out, as well as any meanings that emerged for you.

- Close your eyes and take a deep breath. Without focusing on the reading sample, allow words, phrases, images, or symbols to come into your consciousness, and then let them go. Do this for a few minutes, letting words in and out, in and out. Repeat with your eyes open.

- Engage your sense of smell. Again, allow words, phrases, images, and symbols to emerge and disappear. Repeat with each of your other senses: taste, touch, and hearing.

- Allow time for each sense, and document any new meanings of the reading sample that emerge with each. Let your intuition determine when to transition to the next sense. What words, phrases, images, or symbols are at the edge of your awareness, in the here and now? Select one that is especially resonant.

- Imagine being physically and psychologically embedded in this word, phrase, image, or symbol. What sensations arise in your body as you linger there? What emotions arise? What thoughts? With what behaviors do you feel inspired to engage?

- Allow one other event happening in your life at present to emerge in your awareness. Identify the key people involved. What are their characteristics and traits? Their values, beliefs, and attitudes? Their overall worldviews? What is your role in this event?

- Return your attention to the reading sample. What connections can you draw between it and the event in your life, and between it and the people involved in your event?

- Take 15 to 20 minutes to freewrite your experience of interacting with a variety of inner and outer stimuli. Return your attention to the reading sample. What new meanings arise?

- Share the reading sample with a few friends and acquaintances, and do the exercise as a group. Document and exchange your experiences with one another.

- Alternatively, draw connections between the reading sample and a dream or daydream.

- Once you have completed your freewriting, set it aside for some time, and then return to it and read it aloud. Listen for verbosity, idealism, exaggeration, or deceit. Listen for terseness, skepticism, understatement, or coarse morality. Listen for and sense into the tone. Mold and shape this freewriting into a formal piece of writing.
- Share the revised writing sample with a friend/colleague. Invite her feedback on any resonance and/or dissonance she experienced while reading your account.

carefully and offer insights you may have overlooked. Once you are embedded in a manuscript, it can be challenging to create distance from it, and a single-handed attempt at revision may not be sufficient. The more feedback you elicit and receive, the higher the benefit. You are not required to agree with or accept all the feedback (especially if one reviewer's comments contradict another's), but you can strengthen your manuscript exponentially if you embrace the review process and strive to respond to feedback regarding your explication of methodology, data analysis and interpretation, implications, and even technicalities such as language use.

Promoting Social Justice, Action, and Transformation

When we write, we write for an audience (Creswell, 2013). Due to the deeply personal though potentially universal nature of heuristic findings, you want to reach as wide a relevant readership as possible. To that end, keep your focus on the topic of inquiry and on the individuals whose accounts highlight how this phenomenon is a living, present-moment, real-life human experience. In the interest of inclusion, I suggest the use of nonacademic language to connect with a diversity of individuals and populations, engaging them with the phenomenon and granting them an opportunity to live it, as well. I use the words "granting them an opportunity," as it is not our responsibility to coerce readers into thinking about or responding to our narrative as we would prefer. I do believe, however, that it is one of our responsibilities to encourage our audience to reflect. A heuristic manuscript is a shared experience, just as all other aspects of heuristic inquiry are shared. Readers are not passive receivers of information (Freire, 1970). Therefore, our job as creators of heuristic manuscripts is to describe our personal and professional account of a felt human experience in a manner that expands readers' understanding of the phenomenon while allowing them to participate in the creation of new meanings and iterations of that phenomenon. To put it simply, we write the account, and readers get to decide what they wish to do with it. We researchers are not by any means experts on the topic (despite having conducted a detailed study!), nor are we its owners.

As researchers and documenters of human experience, we should always keep power dynamics in mind, even with our invisible audience. When we speak of social justice, many imagine that this involves guiding a process of transformation by leading others toward change. This form of social justice stems from a limited awareness of how heavily our personal experience influences our own process of growth and change, but more so how our perception might impact another's process of transformation. While this may be helpful in some instances, it may also prove harmful or at the very least uneventful. Even when helpful, such an approach is more concerned with doing for others rather than teaching them how to navigate for themselves, promoting charity rather than change (Miller, 2008a). Although charity is not in and of itself reprehensible, it is an act of *fixing* that may disqualify and/or marginalize, even when that is not the intention behind it. It also speaks volumes about how our personal need to feel important and necessary can lead us (or our egos) to behave in ways that limit others rather than help them grow. Consider this: Providing temporary financial assistance to a person while facilitating her discernment of feasible avenues toward financial freedom is rather different from continuing to provide for her. Providing without end may lead her to financial dependence on me, stalling her agency and her capacity to grow through her own creativity and potential. So how do we work with this part of ourselves that wishes to be inclusive and supportive while minimizing marginalization?

Especially with the most empirical parts of your manuscript (i.e., methodology, findings), write in a tone that encourages reflection in readers rather than one that promotes singular perspectives on knowledge and action. Make an effort to keep your audience engaged by establishing connections between the empirical/methodological parts of the manuscript and the social embeddedness of the phenomenon, transcending the potential limitations imposed by maintaining exclusive focus on the study. Due to the rich and detailed narrative quality of heuristic findings, there is the risk that readers will lose sight of the proverbial forest while attending too closely to the trees. Be sure to invite reflection on and meaning-making of the textured detail of each co-researcher's narrative in relation to the greater whole (outside the study) as you facilitate movement and expansion from the personal to the universal. This enables readers to use their access to novel conceptions of the topic of inquiry to reshape their perspective in a manner that connects them with new meaning and with motivation toward action and change, in alignment with heuristic inquiry's social constructivist, exploratory, humanistic, participatory, and emancipatory spirit. As McGettigan (2008a) asserted,

Acquiring knowledge that might conflict with views that are already present in the minds of agents can be accomplished by participation in communication environments, through solitary reflection, or through various encounters with the empirical world. . . . The impetus (communication, reflection, or encounters with the physical universe) that impels actors to redefine reality is not as critical to the process of generating agency as is the ability of actors to perceive phenomena of which they had no prior conception and then to reconstruct their view of reality to accommodate their newly realized perceptions. (p. 16)

Take note: I attest that I often experience the need to protect my readers from having their understanding of reality and/or identity perturbed. It's a truly human feeling to know one is protecting others from harm, isn't it? There is a certain heroism about it, at least for me. It speaks to the altruist in each of us. And, well, it's an ethical principle in many socially oriented disciplines. If you have a leaning toward heuristic inquiry, you more than likely have a profound interest in human experience, coupled with a spirit of thoughtfulness and sensitivity to all things human. With that, be cautious of shielding your audience members from their own harsh realities (whether self-conceived or socially informed), which may impede their journey of growth and transformation. While having one's foundation of reality disturbed is rarely pleasant, it may be rattling enough to lead one to the exploration of broader perspectives and motivation to change. Recalling McGettigan's (2008a) wise words, we provide optimal support and the promotion of agency, social justice, and transformation when we summon actors to reformulate preconceptions and act on their emergent awareness of the need for change. And not unlike heuristic inquiry, transformation is a holistic and embodied experience, too! Rather than providing your readers easy escapes from their challenging realities, allow your own (and your research partners') subjective, vulnerable, spiritual, and nonomniscient ways of being and of knowing to be guiding lights through the research labyrinth. So suppose your manuscript were to generate conflict within readers. Well, I say that would not be an entirely negative thing! Conflict often arouses within us seeking capacities that lead us in the direction of inner and outer awareness and, ultimately, growth and transformation. Then again, suppose your account were to generate other experiences altogether: affirmation, validation, crystallization, encouragement, reinforcement, or integration. Again, there are no failures or losses, only gains. The moment readers connect—with no uncertainty—with a single flutter of recognition (whether it be harmonious or perturbed) is the moment they begin a process of emerging from stagnation and thriving toward Maslowian self-actualization. Imagine the possibilities!

Writing a Publishable Heuristic Manuscript

In the first part of this chapter, we discussed the various elements that go into a heuristic manuscript. But what factors might you need to consider to enhance the chances that your manuscript will actually be accepted and published, whether in journal article or book format? Well, to begin with, you will want to ensure that all those elements we discussed are included, in addition to the intriguing and embodied writing style we addressed. Furthermore, I suggest that you justify and/or demonstrate two things:

- Need/demand for your publication
- The quality of your manuscript

My personal premise is that outlining the importance of your publication is best done in your cover letter. The cover letter is a brief narrative "proposal" that offers you multiple opportunities, including the following:

- To present yourself and your co-researchers
- To highlight the uniqueness of your methodology and topic of inquiry
- To represent, verbatim, your central research question(s)
- To outline the theoretical and philosophical foundations that guided your study
- To highlight some of the core findings of the study
- To suggest how your article aligns with the general subject matter of the journal and/or publisher

Likewise, highlighting the quality of your manuscript may be achieved by a number of means, one of the most auspicious of which may be to demonstrate that some of the evaluation criteria we addressed in Chapter 8 have been met and given generous coverage:

- Credibility
  - Do you adequately describe the research design, especially the methods and approaches used to collect and analyze the data and represent the findings?
  - Do you accurately outline the purpose, the guiding questions, the sample, and the theoretical framework for the study?

- Transferability
  - Do you devote attention to how the findings of your study may be applied to various populations or contexts?

- Dependability
  - Do you present a justification of your choice of research methodology and data collection process?

- Do you expand on how your findings align and harmonize with that methodology?

- Confirmability

  - Do you openly describe your role as the primary researcher and how it may have influenced data analysis and interpretation?
  - Do you include excerpts from your reflexive journal or other documentation of your interaction with co-researchers, or with the process or content of the study?

In addition to underlining the need for your manuscript and highlighting its quality, I would recommend reading a number of articles published in the journals (or perusing some of the books put out by the publishing companies) to which you are considering making submissions. Finally, as qualitative research manuscripts in general continue to strive toward visibility and recognition, please keep in mind that heuristic inquiry is a more obscure qualitative methodology than other inductive approaches (such as grounded theory or narrative research) and may, therefore, demand more attention and advocacy.

Closing Reflections

Documenting the heuristic journey may prove a solitary and challenging feat, but it can also be an abundantly creative, relational, and communal undertaking. Releasing your grip on the commitment to promote a singular iteration of reality is a positive first step. While one of your primary missions as a heuristic writer is to relay essential information to readers, strive to do so without any presumption of omniscience. Using a clear and professional structure to organize your writing and present your findings promotes transparency about the research methodology and design, enhancing confidence in the study and accessibility for readers. Embracing an embodied relational approach invites audiences into the world of the study, promoting connections between each reader and you, your co-researchers, and the humanness of the topic of inquiry. Write from your body and your core. Identify your role in the research journey unapologetically. Be human and be real. Don't propose answers and solutions. Instead, propose curiosity, wonder, possibility, inspiration, and motivation. Let your manuscript be a guide to readers into the labyrinth, but allow them to decipher their way out using their own processes of immersion, inquiry, intuition, and illumination. Extend your narrative of shared reality as an invitation to growth, one that documents others' personal experiences of the topic of inquiry within a universal framework honoring uniqueness while celebrating shared experience, uncovering pathways to knowledge never before encountered and to action never before dared.

10

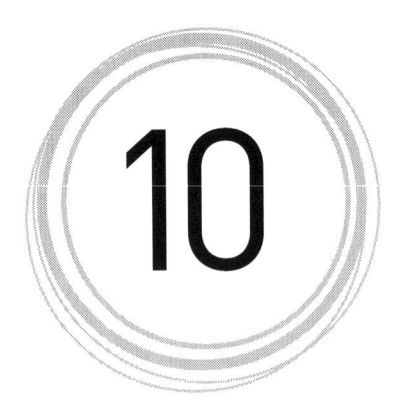

Ethics of Heuristic Research

Unless someone like you cares a whole awful lot, nothing is going to get better. It's not.

~ **Dr. Seuss**

> **Questions for Reflection**
>
> 1. What is the value of ethics in heuristic inquiry?
> 2. How might you address a research-related ethical dilemma?
> 3. What measures can you take to protect your well-being during a heuristic study, and what makes self-care important?

Heuristic inquiry is the exploratory study of the essential nature of a personal human phenomenon that is potentially universal. In that respect, it is rife with personal human experience. Therein lies its beauty. Therein, too, lies its challenge! Every heuristic study emerges from the primary researcher's autobiographical experience with the topic of inquiry. Unlike in other research traditions, a high level of personal interest, familiarity, and involvement on the part of the researcher is not only desirable but expected. You care, and that is an inherently good thing, as your caring has the potential to transform you and any other person who comes into contact with your study. On the other hand, you are human, and your personal experience may impact both the process and outcome of your study—positively, negatively, or anywhere on that continuum. How do you balance the personal nature of the research content and process with the need to maintain high ethical standards that protect you, your co-researchers, the integrity of your study, as well as any person who gains access to it? In this chapter, we define ethics briefly (especially as it relates to heuristic research), we discuss ethical issues that may arise while planning or conducting—or in the aftermath of—a heuristic study, and we outline ethical courses of action. In addition, we look at some of the potential hazards of conducting research of a deeply personal nature and the importance of maintaining researcher well-being using a self-care regimen. Let's begin by defining ethics from a heuristic perspective.

Understanding Ethics

Ethics is a vast philosophical dimension of human experience that has been applied to countless disciplines ranging across medicine, mental health, social science, education, business, political science, research, and beyond. Oancea (2014) defined ethics thus:

> The study of what are good, right, or virtuous courses of action; applied ethics focuses this study on particular and complex issues and contexts. Research ethics is a branch of applied ethics focused on the specific contexts of planning, conducting, communicating, and following up research. (p. 36)

As heuristic researchers, we are most concerned with the research-related branch of applied ethics, as we explore complex socially and culturally situated human experiences of deep value to all persons involved, and potentially to others. Thus, in heuristic inquiry, ethics is applicable to a variety of issues surrounding a study, including but not limited to becoming aware of a topic, proposing the study and gaining approval for it, designing the study and executing it, managing relationships during the research process, communicating the findings, and beyond. So how do we even begin to identify what is good, right, or virtuous as we work to manage all the moving pieces of a study, as well as the complex interpersonal and intrapersonal relationship dynamics involved? Because heuristic inquiry is so personally oriented—and because it is not a matter of *if* ethical issues emerge but *when* they do—it is important to have some type of plan for working with emergent challenges. While it is unrealistic to attempt to predict every potential ethical dilemma, it is certainly helpful to anticipate possible ethical issues (Creswell, 2009; Hesse-Biber & Leavey, 2006; Oancea, 2014). It is especially helpful to have tools that facilitate deliberation and decision making, both of which have ethical implications and consequences.

Core Ethical Principles and Codes

The rights, dignity, worth, and well-being of research partners should be every researcher's primary consideration. Coupled with that is the researcher's social responsibility to benefit society, maintain professional standards and integrity, respect national and international laws and regulations, and affirm demographic differences (Dench, Iphofen, & Huws, 2004). So why should we researchers be concerned with these issues? Well, research has an illustrious history of not caring for the well-being of human subjects and research partners. Consider the unethical experiments conducted by German doctors on Jews during World War II, Stanley Milgram's obedience study, the Tuskeegee Syphilis Study, the Willowbrook study, the tearoom sex study, and the Stanford Prison Experiment. We humans are quite capable of conducting ourselves unethically in the name of science and knowledge!

A number of disciplines have published standards of ethical conduct that may apply to practice or research (Krathwohl, 2009). These standards are fairly uniform across disciplines, with some variations among disciplines. In a manner of speaking, one can say that codes of ethics offer information that is fairly intuitive to most human beings. Given that heuristic inquiry was pioneered by a humanistic psychotherapist to help him explore his deeply personal experience of loneliness, let's take a look, as an example, at the core ethical principles of the American Counseling Association (ACA), the largest international organization for counseling practitioners. The following core ethical principles are included in the *ACA Code of Ethics* (2014), along with a comprehensive code of conduct for everything related to professional counseling, with guidelines for topics such as confidentiality and privacy, professional responsibility, relationships with other professionals, research and publication, and how to resolve ethical issues.

- *Autonomy:* The right to self-determination and self-direction
- *Nonmaleficence:* Nonharm, or the avoidance of actions that may cause harm
- *Beneficence:* Working for the good or benefit of individuals and of society
- *Justice:* Equitable treatment that fosters fairness and equality
- *Fidelity:* Honoring promises and commitments, including responsibilities of trust in professional relationships
- *Veracity:* Truthful interaction and communication

While these ethical principles are particular to ACA, they are fairly standard across a number of other disciplines and professions. The codes of ethical conduct for a number of other disciplines that may be of relevance to heuristic research are easily accessible online, including the following:

- Ethical Principles of Psychologists and Code of Conduct of the American Psychological Association, approved in 2016, available at www.apa.org

- Code of Ethics of the American Anthropological Association, approved in 2009, available at www.aaanet.org
- Code of Ethics of the Canadian Nurses Association, approved in 2017, available at www.cna-aiic.ca
- Ethical Framework for Good Practice in Counselling and Psychotherapy of the British Association for Counselling and Psychotherapy, approved in 2012, available at www.bacp.co.uk
- Code of Ethics of the National Education Association, approved in 1975, available at www.nea.org
- Code of Ethics of the American Sociological Association, approved in 1997, available at www.asanet.org
- Code of Ethics of the Australian Community Workers Association, approved in 2017, available at www.acwa.org.au

In addition, some organizations have designed specific codes for conducting ethical research. Here are some examples:

- Ethical Guidelines and Regulations of the National Institutes of Health, approved in 1979, available at https://humansubjects.nih.gov
- Ethical Principles for Medical Research Involving Human Subjects of the World Medical Association Declaration of Helsinki, approved in 2013, available at www.wma.net
- Code of Human Research Ethics of the British Psychological Society, approved in 2010, available at www.bps.org.uk
- An EU Code of Ethics for Socio-Economic Research, approved in 2004, available at www.respectproject.org

Ethical principles and guidelines help us make sense of ethical dilemmas using frameworks and guides that facilitate fair and equitable processes of discernment. I highly recommend you keep a couple of ethical codes handy throughout your heuristic journey. With that, please note that as some codes of ethical conduct are not socially situated (Hewitt, 2007), you may need to take further measures to lend them social relevance. For example, consider consulting with peers.

Facets of a Heuristic Study That May Prompt Ethical Concerns

As mentioned earlier, while we may do everything possible to design what seems like ethically sound heuristic research, we cannot predict every ethical dilemma. Identifying facets of heuristic research that may rouse ethical concerns is helpful as it brings focused attention to specific issues you can target early on and throughout the course of your study.

Informed Consent

Informed consent is grounded in the ethical principles of autonomy and beneficence (Marzano, 2012; Oeye, Bjelland, & Skorpen, 2007). While autonomy may not be highly valued within certain collectivist cultures, potential co-researchers who have participated in other studies expect to be informed of the details of the study in which they have been invited to participate, and rightfully so. It is ultimately their choice to participate or not, to continue participating or not, and to determine the parameters of their participation, such as what to share and what to withhold. On the other hand, not all co-researchers in your sample pool will have had the experience of participating in research studies. You are responsible for communicating clearly, to all potential co-researchers, any information affiliated with the study and with their participation, and for continuing to do so throughout the course of the study. Lack of clear communication may be perceived as omission of information, which does not accurately represent the relational and participatory nature of heuristic research.

Consent implies that those giving it have both the right and the capacity to understand what they are consenting to do so that they will be able to make informed decisions. It also means that individuals are not placed under duress to consent or participate, in alignment with the emancipatory and participatory nature of heuristic research. With that, it is fairly common knowledge that failure to consent to any aspect of a study precludes participation, not as punishment or as a display of power but for the safety and protection of all persons involved.

Each time I teach Ethical, Legal, and Professional Issues in Counseling to graduate counselors-in-training, the question emerges of whether or not informed consent is true consent if the person being asked to provide it will not be accommodated should he withhold consent. For example, a student might ask, "If I tell a potential client I will break confidentiality if she reveals an intent to harm herself and she refuses to consent to that, I have the right to deny her counseling services, but then she won't get the therapy she needs. And if I coerce her to consent, I'm violating her autonomy." My response to that is that individuals *almost invariably* have a choice, with the understanding that every choice or decision comes with consequences that should be fully explored. For example, when I provided counseling services to mandated clients, they were required to consent to receive those services but were also mandated to be in counseling to meet legal requirements overseen by their probation/parole officers. When going through the informed consent process with these clients, I made the following clear: (a) While they were required to consent to be in counseling, they reserved the right to share what they wished during counseling, and (b) they retained the right not to consent and face the legal consequences. On the surface, it may seem these mandated clients had no choice except to consent, even if they did not wish to attend counseling. However, they did have the choice of neither consenting nor attending, although with the consequence of being reported for violating the terms of their parole/probation. Situations such as this may have led to what van den Hoonaard (2008) termed the *pet factor*, meaning clients viewed me as taking sides with law enforcement. Co-researchers in similar "captive" or vulnerable situations may view you that way, too—which in and of itself raises a whole set of ethical concerns. In the case of my mandated clients, a couple of them chose not to attend their counseling sessions and to face, instead, what they termed the *revolving door* of entering and being released from prison repeatedly. It may not seem like an ideal choice, but it was nevertheless a choice. While this is a seemingly hyperbolic example, keep in mind that you may face similar situations in a heuristic study, depending on your topic of inquiry and your co-researcher sample.

In the case of a heuristic study, you must provide comprehensive information to co-researchers about the study—throughout the study—with the understanding that they may participate only if they consent. Below are some aspects of informed consent to which you may wish to pay extra attention in a heuristic study. When addressing these issues, keep in mind your role as the primary researcher and the importance of maintaining your leadership responsibilities.

Confidentiality. De-identification is critical in most types of research. Confidentiality and privacy are hallmarks of ethical research. But what do you do if one of your research partners reveals, during the study, that he is contemplating taking his life and has come up with a suicide plan? Or what if your co-researcher tells you she physically abused her elderly and disabled mother repeatedly while her mother was in her care? Or what if, after consenting to using a pseudonym, your co-researcher decides he would like to be identified using his real name? While conducting my dissertation study (Sultan, 2015), I faced an ethical dilemma when one of my co-researchers expressed a desire to forgo confidentiality. Why was this an ethical dilemma? Because the study included questions about clients and specifically about the impact of therapist embodiment on clients, which meant detailed discussion of client cases. The study was also a heuristic inquiry, characterized by an existential, humanistic, emancipatory, and participatory spirit. The dilemma emerged as I attempted to balance confidentiality with support for human agency. This is how I initially processed potential decisions and their consequences:

- By accepting my research partner's choice to forgo the pseudonym, I would be supporting agency and promoting self-direction (Giordano, O'Reilly, Taylor, & Dogra, 2007), which aligns with the nature of heuristic research on multiple levels. On the other hand, accepting might jeopardize the confidentiality of my co-researcher's clients; three of the research questions were client-related.

- By denying my research partner's choice, I would minimize confidentiality breaches of my co-researcher's identity and, thereby, of any clients that co-researcher discussed. On the other hand, by denying this co-researcher's choice, I would be making the assumption of knowing what was best for both co-researcher and clients, which is pompous and patronizing, and I would be marginalizing that co-researcher's voice (van den Hoonaard, 2008), which is disempowering.

The big questions with which I found myself struggling were, *Who is responsible for whom and for what? Am I responsible for protecting the confidentiality of co-researchers and their psychotherapy clients, of co-researchers only, of clients only, or of myself only? Who is responsible for the process and outcome of the study? In the case of this study, am I only a researcher, or am I also a licensed mental health practitioner, or both? Which code of ethics governs me? Do I get to make a choice, or am I responsible for upholding multiple codes of ethics? Who is held accountable if confidentiality of any parties named or referenced (e.g., psychotherapy clients) is breached? What should I do?* These and other questions emerged as I found myself mired in a perplexing ethical dilemma with far-reaching influence and consequences. My process of deliberation involved consideration of a number of factors, including the topic of inquiry, my co-researchers and their roles and responsibilities, and the purpose of my study (Guenther, 2009). In your ongoing informed consent process, be clear about how you plan to address emergent confidentiality-related issues. It may also be helpful to assess shifts in preferences around confidentiality during different stages of the study (Kaiser, 2012).

Compensation. Will your research partners be compensated for their efforts? Some forms of compensation (money, gift cards) may be viewed questionably by research review boards (Cook, 2012) as they imply bribery or coercion, especially if your co-researchers are in need of such compensation. Conversely, non-compensation may be viewed as self-serving versus promoting a mutual good. In the interest of upholding heuristic inquiry's social constructivist spirit, consider various definitions of *compensation* (perhaps in concert with co-researchers). Bring some awareness to what is informing your decisions about compensation of research partners. If you decide in favor of compensation, engage in some reflexive processing. Here are some example questions: *Who is funding the study? What is the role of the funder, and what are the parameters of that role? Does the funder have the right to make judgments about the study? If so, how does this impact research partners? How does it potentially influence the course of the study?*

Benefits. What unique value will your co-researchers get out of their participation in the study? For example, a potential benefit of participating in a heuristic study is existential movement toward self-actualization and integration through individual and communal reflection and meaning-making. But what if a co-researcher does not value the concept of self-actualization or finds it inconsequential? Explain your perspective of benefits clearly so your research partners are aware of any discrepancies with their own worldview. What you perceive as a benefit may not be similarly perceived by one or more research partners.

Risks. What potential harm or danger are your research partners facing through their participation? For example, one risk I mentioned in the informed consent form for my dissertation study (Sultan, 2015) was the potential triggering of intense affect (Adler & Adler, 2002) and traumatic memories (Fogel, 2009) due to discussion of embodied experience or past events. This was an evidence-based communication (based on knowledge from previous research and clinical experience) to potential co-researchers (all of whom were experienced psychotherapists), coupled with my personal belief that many therapists are led to the mental health professions via their personal wounding. As with the explanation of benefits, discuss definitions and perceptions of risk.

Participation and Withdrawal. Be very clear about policies regarding co-researcher participation (i.e., voluntary vs. involuntary). Likewise, openly articulate the process of withdrawal. In keeping with heuristic inquiry's humanistic and participatory nature, it is less likely you will have involuntary co-researchers. Allow research partners to withdraw from the study at any time, with no penalty—no questions asked. Prohibiting voluntary participation and withdrawal compromises the integrity of heuristic inquiry, especially in its focus on agency and empowerment.

Beyond these standard concerns—and with an eye on the ethics of care—informed consent is also about having a genuine concern for the well-being of your research partners, not only in their role as members of your research team but beyond the study (Marzano, 2012). This raises the issue of whether informed consent is valid forever or is open for negotiation, placing on us the responsibility of maintaining ongoing interest in the well-being of research partners and sharing ownership of their responses and reactions to matters related to informed consent.

Research Methodology and Design

It is fairly common for ethical dilemmas to arise during the course of any type of formal study. Because we are in the realm of exploratory research, issues may emerge around specific aspects of the research method and/or research design, including the topic, research questions, data collection∞organization∞analysis, evaluation, or writing/publication. Specifically, heuristic inquiry applies both scientific and person-centered methods in alignment with its existential, humanistic nature, which may generate questions about fidelity to science versus art, as well as about overall consistency and trustworthiness. As for research design, suppose you are in the midst of the data collection∞organization∞analysis process when you realize one of your research questions has the potential to expose not only the identities of co-researchers but also those of other individuals whose accounts are being shared by co-researchers, unbeknownst to those individuals? Or suppose while going through the member checking process, a co-researcher refuses to validate the thematic findings of the overall study (Sandelowski, 2008)? While it is our desire as researchers to maintain balance and equity, we heuristic researchers are also humans exploring extremely human and personal topics. Thus, should you have the vaguest suspicion of an ethical concern, do not avoid the issue. Bring awareness and reflexivity to the table, and allow yourself, your research partners (and any others involved), and your study the benefit of addressing the dilemma comprehensively.

Relational Boundaries With Co-Researchers

Heuristic inquiry is a fundamentally relational and personally motivated research methodology and is, therefore, inclined toward empathy, intersubjectivity, inclusion, and reflexivity. Additionally, we've established that heuristic researchers do not separate their subjective experience from the process of research; as social constructivists, our biases, attitudes, and values (Lincoln, Lynham, & Guba, 2011) are inextricably linked to the process and outcome of research. On the other hand, as the primary researcher, you are responsible for maintaining formal interaction with each and every research partner. I say *formal*, as communication about certain topics (e.g., informed consent) is formalized within the heuristic design and must be executed in a well-boundaried—though relational—manner. This places us in somewhat of a quandary as we navigate I∞Thou relationships with co-researchers and attempt to balance reflexive subjectivity with scientific inquiry, all while trying to keep the process as nonintrusive as possible and relevant enough to prompt some level of transformation. Again, who you are as a person and how you are socioculturally situated directly impacts each and every interaction, deliberation, and decision you make, and the same holds true for each of your co-researchers. So how do you reconcile?

In the face of an ethical dilemma and the potentially mounting tension that emerges within the research team, I remind myself that heuristic inquiry is as much an educational and personal growth process as it is a cocreated process of inquiry. This very much flows with Lincoln and colleagues' (2011) perspective on qualitative research processes being awareness-enhancing and action-oriented as researchers work to gain knowledge in response to co-researchers' needs while engaging the idea of transformation as a long-term collaborative and reflexive process. Simply stated, each of us is involved in the heuristic study in question to learn more about a specific phenomenon we each personally experienced.

You may have strong reactions to certain information your co-researchers share. Human narratives can stir up emotions, thoughts, bodily responses, and other reactions to which you may or may not be alert. Engaging reflexivity and remaining attuned to how you respond to interactions (especially with research partners) and how you process those responses based on your personal values and assumptions is foundational to ethical research. As I mentioned in Chapter 6, countertransference and transference are present in many social encounters and may occur especially frequently in heuristic inquiry due to the personal nature of the topic of inquiry to all members of the research team. Should you experience a countertransferential reaction, or should you become aware that a co-researcher is potentially experiencing transference toward you, bring some attention to the temporary shift in your encounter (see Chapter 6 for more). Assess the utility—to the co-researcher, to the study, and to yourself—of disclosing your countertransference. Also, have predetermined support systems in place, for yourself and for co-researchers, so there is minimal blurring of roles during the study.

For example, suppose you are a therapist-researcher and during a study interview a co-researcher experiences distress. You may feel the urge to embrace your therapist role and provide therapeutic care for this co-researcher. In fact, not doing so may cause you extreme discomfort (Orb, Eisenhauer, & Wynaden, 2001). However, doing so presents an ethical conflict in separating your dual roles of therapist and researcher and can result in serious boundary breaches should you lose your grasp on facilitating the study and, later, struggle to redefine your role. To minimize this type of issue, one support that is regularly offered in psychotherapy-related studies is a referral for low-cost or free therapeutic services provided by an outsider to research partners who experience distress. For research in other disciplines, it may be helpful to suggest or secure the services of a supervisor, consultant, or mentor. Should a seemingly irreconcilable interruption in interaction take place with a research partner, become aware of any discrepancy between your behavior toward that particular research partner compared with your behavior toward others, as well as any conflicts of interest that arise. Review relevant ethical guidelines and codes, engage an ethical decision-making model, consult with an external auditor or peer reviewer, and consider consulting your review board and, if you are a student, consulting your research advisor.

Being both a psychotherapist and heuristic researcher, I truly believe the success of the heuristic research process lies within warm and supportive researcher–research partner relationships. As researchers, it is our task to maintain proper boundaries that serve to protect both co-researchers and ourselves, and to remain alert to fluctuating patterns of the power differential (see Chapter 7 for more information). It is simply a matter of maintaining the balance on the subjectivity∞objectivity continuum, although maintaining that balance is hardly a simple matter, as it demands constant attention. Maintaining I∞Thou interaction within the framework of professional conduct is critical while being mindful not to impose unwanted relationship dynamics on research partners and to respectfully and nonjudgmentally explore any seemingly boundary-breaching exchanges. You will publicly share some of the intimate accounts co-researchers freely shared with you, which may lead some of them to feel deceived (McGinn, 2008) or exploited. Again, reflexive, self-aware engagement with all aspects of your study, review of ethical codes and standards, and consistent, authentic dialogue with co-researchers will help you bring interpersonal dynamics back to balance.

Transparency

We discussed the matter of transparency in heuristic research in Chapters 8 and 9 within the context of evaluating the study and writing the research manuscript. However, transparency is a far more complex issue that transcends the parameters of evaluation and writing. From an ethical perspective, transparency encompasses sharing information about the goals and expectations of the study with co-researchers, as well as exploring and exchanging information about the role of each member of the research team. It also involves revealing your personal agenda and inviting (but not coercing) your co-researchers to explore and disclose the same; this includes information about funding or conflicts of interest. From a structural standpoint, being transparent means including details about the research methodology and design, as well as relating and reporting the research process and findings accurately (Braun & Clarke, 2013) and discussing the strengths and limitations of your study (Preissle, 2008).

Researcher Competence

Heuristic inquiry is a fairly obscure qualitative research methodology (I'm selfishly hoping this will soon change!). It's very possible you've never conducted a formal heuristic study, although it's quite possible you have conducted many informally. If you are contemplating conducting a formal heuristic study (I imagine you might be, if you are reading this book), please allow yourself an opportunity to apply the heuristic methodology in an informal exploration first. Find a topic that is near to you—a phenomenon that you have experienced and that has haunted you since time immemorial and just won't let you be—and spend some time exploring it through the heuristic lens. Pretend you are conducting a formal study and go through the various processes and phases, documenting your experience in a journal. Get a feel for the terrain and vibe of this very unique research approach before plunging into a formal study.

Addressing Emergent Ethical Dilemmas

I use the word *emergent* intentionally; anything can come up in a heuristic study! Earlier in the chapter, we discussed decision making and consequences.

You may have noticed that when I mentioned the ethical dilemma that emerged surrounding the request from one of my research partners not to remain confidential, I did not offer a resolution. In fact, I deliberately refrained from mentioning my course of action. When an ethical dilemma arises, there are usually no clear answers, which is why you have an ethical dilemma. Instead of telling you what I decided, let's review some actions you can take to facilitate your deliberation and decision-making processes, including consulting discipline-related ethical codes, using ethical decision-making models, and engaging reflexivity.

Consulting Discipline-Related Ethical Codes

Earlier in this chapter, we went over the ethical principles of ACA as documented in the *ACA Code of Ethics*, and I provided a list of a few other discipline-related ethical codes. Upon your first encounter with an ethical dilemma, seek out an ethical code from your discipline or from a similar discipline if your profession does not have its own code. Reading through discipline-related ethical codes clarifies a profession's stance and will help you decipher discrepancies between that profession's standards and your own attitudes. Ethical codes provide us with a standardized set of ethical considerations that help us maintain consistency in deliberation and decision making.

Using an Ethical Decision-Making Model

Making moral judgments is a fairly common human experience fueled by our desire to make sense of issues that are challenging for us to comprehend. Because morals are usually informed by social norms, it may seem appropriate to make a moral judgment surrounding an emergent ethical dilemma. However, making moral judgments brings personal biases, values, and attitudes center stage in the decision-making process, minimizing and marginalizing other perspectives. As heuristic researchers, we already have high stakes in the research study we are facilitating and guiding. To create some balance between our personal interests and the interests of others involved in the study, and with the study itself, it's helpful to have a guiding structure for ethical decision making. Ethical decision-making models exist for a number of socially oriented disciplines. For example, in the counseling profession, we have a variety of ethical decision-making models from which to select, including the social constructivist model (Cottone, 2001) and the transcultural integrative model (Garcia, Cartwright, Winston, & Borzuchowska, 2003). Since I used the *ACA Code of Ethics* earlier in the chapter as an example of a discipline-related ethical code, I'd also like to offer you an at-a-glance breakdown of an ethical decision-making model from the counseling profession (Forester-Miller & Davis, 2016) to demonstrate the general structure of such models and their utility in working through ethical dilemmas you may encounter in a heuristic study:

1. Identify the problem.
2. Apply the *ACA Code of Ethics* (or a code of ethics of relevance to the topic or discipline of your study).
3. Determine the nature and dimensions of the dilemma.
4. Generate potential courses of action.
5. Consider the potential consequences of all options, and determine a course of action.
6. Evaluate the selected course of action.
7. Implement the course of action.

To this and any other ethical decision-making model from any other discipline or profession, I would add the following:

- Apply any relevant legal codes (e.g., national, federal, state, provincial).
- Seek consultation from peers, experts, or ethics task forces.
- Document every phase and action of your ethical decision-making process.

Using an ethical decision-making model lends structure and accountability to your ethical decision-making approach, enhancing the overall transparency and rigor of your study.

Engaging Researcher Reflexivity

I recognize that I've mentioned reflexivity numerous times in this chapter and repeatedly throughout this book. However, I cannot stress enough the importance of this process to ethical heuristic research. As you work with reflexivity during your study, I strongly recommend using such heuristic processes as self-dialogue, tacit knowing, intuition, and focusing. To facilitate reflexivity while pondering an emergent ethical issue, below are some questions with which you can begin your work:

- What do I *think* is the central ethical issue? What do I *sense* is the central ethical issue? How do I make sense of any disparity?
- If/when I present this concern to another person, what does he view as the central issue?
- Who are the individuals involved in this dilemma, and what are their roles?

- What is my general understanding and/or sense of how this dilemma is impacting them?
- Are all those involved allowed to voice their perspective? Why or why not?
- If there is a potential for harm, who is at risk of being harmed, how, and to what identifiable degree?
- Have I done everything possible to minimize risk?
- What is the social/cultural backdrop of this dilemma?
- What decision-making process do I plan to use? How did I go about selecting this particular process in lieu of other approaches for decision making? Am I taking a purely cognitive approach, or am I engaging other ways?
- What do I need, both personally and professionally, from this study, and what role might my need be playing in this dilemma?
- How am I constructing and co-constructing new knowledge through this ethical dilemma?
- Have I done everything I can to support my own and others' ethical conduct?
- Are the rights, dignity, and worth of all individuals involved being considered?
- Will any decisions I make promote justice and empowerment? What other benefits might each member of the research team, including myself, reap?
- Did my co-researchers have opportunities to ask questions and participate in decision making?
- How am I assessing the rightness or goodness of my choices? Am I thinking those choices through? Am I allowing space for emotions and felt sense?
- From a *cognitive* perspective, is this methodology still appropriate for my topic? What about from a *felt sense* perspective?

Now let's take this reflexive exploration one step further in an exercise that offers you an opportunity to experiment with ethical dilemma scenarios using some of the methods discussed above, including referring to an ethical code, applying an ethical decision-making model, and engaging reflexivity (see Exercise 10.1). Although the dilemma scenarios are categorized by topic, the foci of the ethical issues and concerns may overlap.

EXERCISE 10.1
EXPLORING AND ADDRESSING EMERGENT ETHICAL DILEMMAS IN HEURISTIC RESEARCH

- *Confidentiality.* In your study of the experience of resentment toward one's siblings, a co-researcher reveals that her experience of resentment is so consuming, she has considered poisoning her brother. You explore the issue further and realize she has not only considered sibling homicide but has a plan for carrying it out.

- *Participation and withdrawal.* In your study of the experience of sexual harassment in occupational settings, you have collected and analyzed data for your study when a co-researcher decides he is uneasy about what he has shared during the interview process. He informs you that he is considering withdrawing but doesn't want to compromise the study. He seeks your opinion, stating that it is an important part of his decision making, as he feels torn. You are aware that this co-researcher's data provided support for an unanticipated theme that emerged in one other co-researcher's data.

- *Relational boundaries.* In your study of the experience of poverty in early childhood, a co-researcher first affirms your autobiographical experience of childhood poverty, then challenges you to prove that your poverty, or the poverty of any of the other research partners, was more desperate than hers. To amplify the challenge, she provides additional information about factors that complicated her poverty, including sexual and emotional abuse, homelessness, substance addiction, and a pregnancy at the age of 14. In the midst of your dialogue, this co-researcher breaks down into inconsolable sobbing.

- *Compensation.* You are considering conducting a study to explore the experience of living with chronic back pain and for which you require outside funding. A potential funder offers two methods of sponsorship: (a) a cash grant to support your research expenses and (b) participation of all members of the research team (including you) in a 6-month clinical trial of a new pain medication. This funder lays down the condition that you must accept both methods of support simultaneously; that is, you cannot accept only the cash grant and decline the clinical trial. No other funders have come forward, and without external funding, you cannot proceed with your study.

The Perils of Researching Sensitive Topics: Maintaining Researcher Well-Being

Qualitative research suffers a questionable reputation among other research methods due primarily to its subjective, personal approach. Unfortunately, select forms of qualitative research that include the personal experience of the researcher (such as autoethnography and heuristic inquiry) suffer such a reputation even among some qualitative research traditions, with accusations such as *self-centered, narcissistic,* and *self-indulgent* leveled against researchers who embrace such methodologies. Despite this, and despite the history of risk assessment in research being focused on the experience of co-researchers (Liamputtong, 2007), there is rising interest in the emotional demands of qualitative research and the impact on researchers (Dickson-Swift, James, Kippen, & Liamputtong, 2008, 2009; Lee & Lee, 2012). One reason behind this is that the researcher's state of being reflects on co-researchers, other individuals participating in the study (such as peer reviewers), and the study itself.

While researchers stand to gain from conducting studies about personal and emotional topics, adverse reactions inevitably emerge within the shared space between researcher and co-researchers—within the I∞Thou of intersubjectivity. Some of the many emotions researchers may experience include fear, anger, disgust, helplessness, vulnerability, and grief. Yet those emotions are as much a part of the research as any other elements. Denzin (2007) encouraged the use of both cognitive and emotional information to attain understanding. On the other hand, heuristic inquiry demands engaging the multidimensional self, transcending the cognitive and emotional, and including the sensory∞kinesthetic, the perceptual, the spiritual, and the social∞relational in the pursuit of new knowledge. With that in mind, heuristic researchers may, in addition to cognitive and emotional symptoms, experience physical symptoms, sensory and perceptual incongruities, and spiritual and relational disconnection. This exerts taxing pressure on researchers, especially as they are tasked with carrying out most duties associated with the study, including data collection∞organization∞analysis and transcription (which demands that we relive our co-researchers' narratives over and over).

As a psychotherapist who specializes in trauma and grief, I am all too familiar with terms such as *vicarious trauma, compassion fatigue,* and *burnout*. Vicarious trauma is a transformation in therapists' inner experience resulting from empathic reaction to clients' traumatic experiences (Adams & Riggs, 2008; Sultan, 2017a). It places therapists in the situation of living the clients' experiences as if they were the therapists' own. Compassion fatigue is a similar condition but is caused by preoccupation with client concerns (Sultan, 2017a). Symptoms of compassion fatigue include apathy, desensitization, repressed emotions, and isolation (Figley, 2002). Burnout is a condition instigated by a combination of numerous physical and emotional concerns that may jeopardize therapist efficacy and well-being (Lee, Cho, Kissinger, & Ogle, 2010).

As a mental health practitioner and human ready to embark on a heuristic research endeavor, I had researched, written about, and personally experienced vicarious trauma, compassion fatigue, and burnout. Tasked with exploring poignant and often distressing human experiences, I guessed that one or more of these phenomena might make an appearance during my dissertation study (Sultan, 2015). I substituted *researcher* for *therapist* and *co-researcher* for *client*, and thought I had things in the box. This was especially true because I *am* a therapist and planned to research other therapists' experiences of embodiment, a phenomenon that is fairly acknowledged among body psychotherapists (i.e., my study population). So what could possibly go wrong? I discounted the countless informal explorations of human phenomena I had carried out heuristically throughout my lifetime (as poignant and consuming as they were) as insignificant and irrelevant, assuring myself that because I was conducting a formal study, I would manage to hold things together. *This will be different*, I told myself. I should say, I deceived myself!

As my co-researchers and I embarked on our co-exploration of the experience of embodiment in body psychotherapists and impact on clients, a number of topics emerged immediately and repeatedly, including accounts of divorce, chronic physical illness, mental illness, immigration, isolation, loss of a sense of identity, dissociation, social marginalization, and the suicide of family members. Many of these accounts told of the shared experience between therapists and clients as mediated by therapist embodiment. My triggering began with the first interview. Thankfully, I had a lengthy break between my first and second interviews. However, following the second interview, I got into a frenzy of transcribing, organizing, and analyzing in an effort to remain on task (or maybe I was distracting myself?). By the third interview, I was reeling from emotional exhaustion, and I recognized I was experiencing symptoms similar to those I had suffered during my counseling training as I worked with parents who had lost children—and with children who had lost parents, siblings, grandparents, and family friends—to suicide, homicide, chronic illness, or sudden death. My symptoms included crippling pain in my neck, shoulders, and upper back and incessant ringing in my ears, coupled with leaps between emotional numbing, crying spells, and feelings of social isolation. By the fourth interview, I felt insecure in myself and my ability, both as a researcher and as a therapist. I questioned the purpose of my research, of my doctoral studies, of wanting to be a counselor educator, and of being a therapist.

Because our profession is highly supervision- and consultation-friendly, I sought support from each member of my dissertation committee (all of whom are licensed mental health practitioners). Each of them provided me a unique support approach, which helped me get fully back on track. I also created some space for incubation by distancing myself briefly from further data collection, immersed myself in journaling, took lengthy walks in nature, and amped up my meditation and body movement practice. It didn't take long for me to recover, and I plunged back into the study, telling myself that

I now knew what to expect and how to address whatever came up. During my second-to-last interview, I hit another wall with an especially heartrending account that rekindled memories of loss, inconsolable grief, and feelings of guilt and shame. This was when I recognized just how vulnerable heuristic research can leave us. It wasn't until then that I realized that due to the time constraints imposed by the research and other professional and personal commitments, I had not visited my therapist in several months. I knew it was time for me to take that next step.

As you can see, despite being a therapist with the supposed know-how of handling human suffering, my heuristic research journey was laden with challenges. What helped keep me in check was consultation, personal counseling, journaling, and other strategies for minimizing risk and attending to self-care. Regardless of your discipline and due to the highly subjective nature of topics undertaken through heuristic studies, you may experience similar challenges. Formal strategies for minimizing risk usually involve others and may include the following:

- Enhanced heuristic research training with a seasoned qualitative researcher or proficient heuristic researcher
- For nonclinical researchers, training in basic counseling skills and concepts (with the caution that retaining such skills may also present an opposite effect)
- Peer debriefing and mentoring (minimal level of structure)
- Supervision and consultation (higher level of structure)
- Allowing space between interviews

Strategies for attending to self-care tend to be more individually oriented and may include the following:

- Personal counseling
- Journaling or art journaling (some experiences may be too challenging to process verbally)
- Mindfulness
- Mindfulness-oriented journaling (Sultan, 2017a)
- Meditation
- Spiritual practices (e.g., chanting, prayer, fasting, gratitude)
- Body movement
- Social and informal support networking
- Maintaining a healthy work–life balance

Finally, I'd like to invite you to become an advocate for researcher risk awareness. Perhaps your upcoming heuristic study is an opportunity to begin a conversation with your review board about the perils of researching human experience using the whole self as an instrument. It may also be an occasion for members of such boards to realize that though the path of a heuristic journey is labyrinthine and murky, it embraces and affirms the blemished magnificence of being human.

Closing Reflections

When ethical issues emerge during the course of a heuristic study, you may struggle with the threat of losing your direction. Do not abandon the process. Explore and gain a clear understanding of your ethical dilemma. Follow the ethical guidelines of your discipline or profession to gain clarity on where to direct your focus. Engage an ethical decision-making model as well as various processes of heuristic inquiry reflexively. Also, remain in dialogue with research partners and other individuals, such as peer reviewers or mentors. Consultation is key to conducting ethical research, is a collaborative approach that aligns with the relational nature of heuristic inquiry, and should be part of exploring any ethical decision-making process. Keep in mind, however, that you are tasked with making the final decisions.

Decision making will hardly ever be a straightforward or clean-cut process and will depend in large part on the nature of the dilemma. To avoid frustration, keep in mind that there are no straight or right answers. Simply put, there are no elegant endings or resolutions to ethical dilemmas. With that, as with all other aspects of heuristic inquiry, working through ethical dilemmas demands attention, rigor, collaboration, and open and authentic dialogue. Mutual consideration of ethical concerns invites the possibility of mutual tolerance and understanding. Additionally, conducting ethical research demands your keen awareness of how you are interacting with the various phases of the study and especially of any triggers you may experience while engaging with potentially traumatic co-researcher narratives. Researcher well-being impacts the overall health and success of a heuristic study and can be maintained through self-awareness and proactive measures that minimize potentially damaging emergent content- and interaction-related issues. Again, mutual dialogue and self-care practices open doors for self- and other-understanding, clarity, and integration. Nestled within the challenge of conflict lies the gift of imperfection, offering the opportunity for growth and transformation!

11

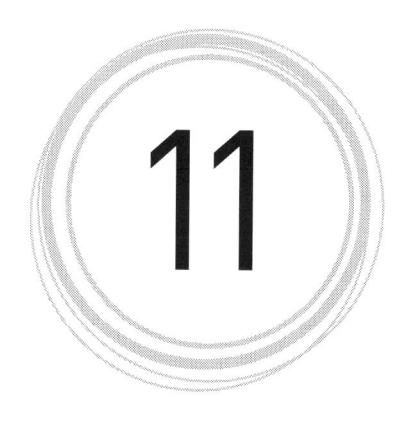

Universal Applications of Heuristic Inquiry

Bridging Research and Living Experience

One must—as in a swimming pool—dare to dive from the quivering springboard of trivial everyday experience and sink into the depths, in order to later rise again—laughing and fighting for breath—to the now doubly illuminated surface of things.

~ **Franz Kafka**

Questions for Reflection

1. To which disciplines and professional settings is heuristic inquiry most applicable as a formal research methodology?
2. How can heuristic inquiry be applied as an informal approach for researching the essential nature of human phenomena?

Oh, Kafka! He speaks of the exploration of human experience as though he knew of heuristic inquiry prior to its nascence. Then again, many of us *tacitly know* how to explore heuristically—how to immerse ourselves within the depths of our living experience and linger there, with the understanding that when we rise back to the surface to encounter the world, we return with more elevated knowledge and understanding of both experience and self. Truly, while Clark Moustakas (1990) pioneered the formalized process for heuristic exploration, heuristic inquiry has (I daresay) been around since the dawn of mankind as an informal process for understanding the essential nature of a variety of human phenomena. Therein lies its versatility!

The complexity and effervescence of human experience demand that we probe both more broadly and more deeply than many traditional qualitative research approaches permit. How humans internalize and express their living experience is fundamental to recognizing the expanse of human potential and identifying options for transformation and growth. Heuristic inquiry can be used by researchers, practitioners, and the general public alike—both formally and informally—as a vehicle for exploring the essential nature of innumerable human phenomena across various disciplines, including education, political science and government, health care, conflict transformation, and counseling and psychotherapy.

In this final full chapter, I profile a number of disciplines and professional settings in which heuristic inquiry may be engaged as a formal approach for exploring human experience. I highlight a number of heuristic studies of topics explored by researchers affiliated with those disciplines, as well as sample topics for which heuristic inquiry may be adopted within disciplines for which I was not able to locate any heuristic studies. Please note that the heuristic study examples cited do not necessarily represent the heuristic approach seamlessly; no study is perfect. Thus, given what you know about heuristic inquiry now, I invite you to explore the strengths and limitations of each study and to engage in creative play with novel ideas and approaches. I also provide a description of how heuristic research can be applied informally (including with colleagues, friends, and/or family members) to explore various human experiences or to study deeply personal heuristic research processes and phases such as tacit knowing, focusing, and incubation. Given the versatility of the heuristic approach, topics that are explored formally may also be researched informally and vice versa.

Using Heuristic Inquiry Formally in Various Disciplines

In beginning our discussion of the applicability of the heuristic methodology to formal research within specific disciplines, I would like to underscore, once again, the holistic nature of heuristic inquiry and the unique edge the heuristic approach offers through its multidimensionality. Recall that all humans (including researchers and co-researchers) engage life using multiple ontological and epistemological contexts, rendering heuristic inquiry an ideal methodology for exploring a wide range of human experiences and phenomena. With that, I have selected a number of disciplines to which heuristic research may be applied to gain an understanding of the essential nature of specific human phenomena of relevance to those disciplines while affirming the interconnectedness of the body∞mind∞spirit∞world of all persons, experiences, and contexts. Heuristic inquiry invites researchers and practitioners in a variety of disciplines, settings, and practices—as well as members of the general public—to explore human phenomena holistically, minimizing the body∞mind∞spirit∞world split that has been a mainstay of most formal research for time immemorial. This is by no means an exhaustive discussion of disciplines or topics but a mere sampling of possibilities in the exploration of various dimensions of human living experience. Please feel free to flow with the creative spirit of heuristic inquiry and reflect outside the box!

Education

Education is a rapidly evolving discipline for instructors, students, administrators, and of course researchers. Understanding some of the underlying features and dynamics of multiple educational stages demands the exploration of the essential nature of everyday education-related phenomena. However, prior to the 1960s, the field of education did not benefit from the nuances of qualitative research (Erickson, 1985, 2011). Given that not all human experience is directly observable and that educational experiences may be especially negligible due to the redundancy of day-to-day operations and the restrictions of time for educators and students, qualitative approaches in educational research may create opportunities to establish the following: (a) the visibility of everyday life, (b) detailed understanding about various practices of education (e.g., teaching, administration), (c) insight into the specifics of local settings, (d) understanding of differences between local and wider social settings, and (e) understanding of patterns and dynamics beyond the parameters of social settings (Erickson, Florio, & Buschman, 1980; Erickson, 1985). As a counselor-educator and former student, I attest that education should not be viewed from a standardized perspective, nor should it be seen as a *deliver-and-receive* endeavor, in alignment with Freire's (1970) pedagogical philosophy, which celebrates perception and meaning-making of personal experience as the most elevated pathways to knowledge and self-transcendence.

We learn based on our perception of how our socially situated identity interacts with the meaningfulness of individual events. Exploring the experience of education using standardized approaches may minimize individual living experience, presuming universality without first gaining insight into nuanced individual differences, as well as similarities that transcend variations in situatedness. Heuristic inquiry opens doorways to the application of nonstandard research processes in the exploration of education-related phenomena, challenging assumptions and offering deep insight into highly sensitive everyday education-related events. Thus, we gain access to rich accounts of phenomena that may otherwise be overlooked, providing students and instructors with opportunities for reflection, awareness, and growth.

In a heuristic inquiry of the social and academic experiences of graduate students with visual disabilities, Perez (2013) explored the phenomenon of living within the *liminality of blindness and sightedness* as a graduate student. The findings of the study reveal some of the challenges of living with a visual disability, as well as sources of empowerment to achieve success in graduate school. Perez highlighted that co-researchers' reframing of their disability into a positive context empowered them toward self-advocacy during their studies, which aligns seamlessly with heuristic inquiry's spirit of inspiring growth and transformation. See Box 11.1 for details of this study.

Political Science and Government

Political science, as a discipline, has both enjoyed and suffered from the strengths and weaknesses of quantitative and qualitative approaches to research, according to Gschwend and Schimmelfennig (2007). Yet these authors also stated, "At the end of the day, we are interested in why stuff happens in order to provide explanations and improve our understanding of cause-effect relations in the social world" (p. 12). I concur that cause–effect relationships are crucial to understanding the dynamics of political science and government. But how do we begin to understand, for example, the living

---

BOX 11.1
EXAMPLE OF HEURISTIC INQUIRY IN EDUCATION

Citation: Perez, L. (2013). *The perspectives of graduate students with visual disabilities: A heuristic case study.* Unpublished doctoral dissertation, College of Education, University of South Florida, Tampa.
Research questions: How do I as a student with a visual disability perceive and describe my social and academic experiences in graduate school? How do other graduate students who have visual disabilities perceive and describe their social and academic experiences in graduate school? What barriers and challenges do we as graduate students with visual disabilities encounter in graduate school? What factors empower us as students with visual disabilities to achieve success in graduate school?
Theoretical framework: No clear theoretical framework identified besides heuristic inquiry
Co-researchers: Graduate students with visual disability
Data collection: Personal exploration, semi-structured interviews, journals, artifacts
Themes: Empowering factors: personal characteristics of students, supportive relationships; barriers and challenges: access to instructional materials, social isolation
Data representation: Individual depiction, composite depiction, exemplary portrait, creative synthesis
Creative synthesis: Self-portrait and poetry

experience of being a 36-year-old African American female member of a political think tank with a majority membership of white males over the age of 50? And how, for example, do we make sense of the living experience of on-the-spot political decision making? How do we probe the nuances of such human experiences beyond the tidiness of cause and effect?

In an intriguing discussion of the application of cognitive approaches in foreign policy analysis, Rapport (2017) discussed cognitive theory and the various approaches humans may apply in decision making, including belief systems, cognitive biases, and heuristics (as distinct from heuristic inquiry)—as informed by context and perception. He also outlined some of the limitations of applying cognitive theories to foreign policy analysis, as such theories tend to be biased toward Western, rich, industrialized, and democratic systems. This leads me to envision the use of heuristic inquiry, which transcends clear-cut unidimensional methods, so that we may gain a clearer sense of the living experience of the whole person. By the way, I was not able to locate any heuristic studies in the discipline of political science and government. That's not to say such studies don't exist; they may. However, I think we can safely say that the possibilities for heuristic exploration in this field are virtually boundless! See Box 11.2 for details of a proposed heuristic study in political science and government, inspired by Rapport's (2017) compelling discussion.

Now, just for fun, imagine substituting the word *intuition* in the proposed heuristic study with the word *ego* and then applying, maybe, a Jungian psychology approach within the theoretical framework. Of course, that would mean that the primary researcher would have to have sat with the question

BOX 11.2

SAMPLE OF A PROPOSED HEURISTIC INQUIRY IN POLITICAL SCIENCE AND GOVERNMENT

Proposed title: The living experience of using intuition to engage in political decision making: A heuristic inquiry

Research questions: What is the meaning of intuition for you as a politician? What is your experience of using your intuition to make political decisions? What is your perception of similarities and differences between making personal and political decisions using your intuition? What is your perception of the impact of using your intuition to make political decisions?

Theoretical framework: Social constructivism/interpretivism, political psychology

Co-researchers: Individuals who have used intuition to engage in political decision making

Data collection: Personal exploration, semi-structured interviews, journals, artifacts

Data representation: Individual depiction, composite depiction, exemplary portrait, creative synthesis

of her own ego in political and personal decision making before taking on the formal heuristic inquiry and inviting co-researchers on board. Wouldn't that be something?

Health Care

Today's health care professionals are having to navigate increasingly complex issues as they work in a field that requires maintaining an intricate balance between validity and humanity. To that end, a primary focus of health care has been on medical research and evidence-based decision making, with evidence being informed by standardized knowledge pertaining to general populations rather than individuals (van Wijngaarden, van der Meide, & Dahlberg, 2017). Additionally, Ellingson (2006) stated that health care research "has focused on three main areas of research: doctor-patient (or patient-provider) communication, health information dissemination, and social support" (p. 301). Such approaches to researching the human experience of health care, in addition to being potentially dehumanizing, are unidimensional and flat, rendering both researcher and co-researchers (or patient and provider) invisible and inaccessible. This impacts all members of the research team, as well as readers of the findings and future researchers. While verbal communication and information dissemination are highly relevant to successful health care, might it not also be fascinating to explore the experience of nonverbal communication between patient and provider, or nonverbal methods of disseminating health information to the public? And might it not add to the lexicon of social support in health care to explore the living experience of *social support* or to explore the essential nature of a holistic social support experience within a health care setting? And might it not add even more layers of humanness to health care to highlight the potentially messy nature of the living experience of, say, being an oncologist or oncology nurse while suffering from cancer? How might this type of health care research—as subjective as it is—promote mutual trust, unraveling the holistic experience of suffering for both patient and provider while highlighting the similarities between them, bringing richness and complexity to the process and findings of a study, and revealing multiple layers of experience and reality?

In a heuristic study of the experience of living and working in Australian nursing homes, Kingsley (1998) explored the source and nature of *meaning* as experienced by both residents and staff members in relation to their lives within those homes, as well as the question of how these individuals live and work within this setting with a sense of *wellness*. The findings of the study offered insight into the daily experience of living and working in nursing homes. Kingsley stated that the study was initially a grounded theory, but upon realizing the deeply personal nature of the topic and the focus of grounded theory on coding, it became clear that heuristic inquiry would allow more space to capture the uniqueness of individual experiences while highlighting the shared and/or universal facets. See Box 11.3 for details of the study.

> **BOX 11.3**
> **EXAMPLE OF HEURISTIC INQUIRY IN HEALTH CARE**
>
> ***Citation:*** Kingsley, A. E. (1998). *Meaning, identity, and wellness: The experience of living and working in Australian nursing homes.* Unpublished doctoral dissertation, School of Occupational Therapy, Curtin University of Technology, Bentley, Perth, Western Australia.
> ***Research questions:*** What is the source and nature of meaning experienced by residents in relation to their lives within Australian nursing homes? What is the source and nature of meaning experienced by staff in relation to their work within Australian nursing homes? How can residents and staff of Australian nursing homes live and work with a sense of wellness?
> ***Theoretical framework:*** Social constructivism/interpretivism, occupational science, existentialism
> ***Co-researchers:*** Residents and staff of Australian nursing homes
> ***Data collection:*** Personal exploration, informal interviews, semi-structured interviews, journals, discussion
> ***Themes:*** Residents: maintaining a sense of connection (personal, social, and environmental) with one's identity; staff: maintaining balance between personal and professional facets of identity
> ***Data representation:*** Individual depiction, composite depiction, exemplary portrait, creative synthesis
> ***Creative synthesis:*** Poetry

Conflict Transformation

Conflict is a daily experience for virtually all humans across all societies and cultures, whether or not we are consciously aware of its presence. Galtung (2004, 2010) described conflict as incompatibility between the goals of two entities, adding that conflict is both relational and systemic. Thus, when conflict occurs in a relationship, the homeostatic states of both the relationship and the system are disturbed. Humans have developed formal and informal mechanisms to "manage" the instability that accompanies conflict situations (Galtung, 1996; Levinger, 2013). *Conflict management* and *conflict resolution* are terms once used to identify professional methods for addressing conflict. In the 1980s, Lederach (2003) coined the term *conflict transformation* in an effort to re-language, motivated by his experience working in Central American countries and by his personal views of conflict work as a quest for justice-oriented "constructive change" (p. 4).

Lederach's (2003) approach invites a focus on understanding the roots of conflict, not with a mind to eradicate conflict but, rather, to harvest the necessary resources to respond to and transform it. From an intervention standpoint, Lederach outlined four areas of focus: (a) *personal*, to address the conflict as an individual, using physical, emotional, intellectual, and spiritual ways of being; (b) *relational*, to minimize poor communication and enhance interpersonal understanding while acknowledging fears and hopes toward interdependence; (c) *structural*, to understand the social causes of conflict, minimize combative confrontation, and enhance human agency; and (d) *cultural*, to pinpoint cultural patterns that promote violence and identify resources for constructively responding to conflict. Foundationally, conflict transformation, per Lederach (2003), "directs us towards change, to how things move from one shape to a different one" (p. 29). In a manner of speaking, then, conflict transformation is about mutual learning in an effort to *reconstitute* or *reshape* conflict.

In a thought-provoking paper about field research in conflict environments, Cohen and Arieli (2011) stated that "in conflict environments, the entire population is marginalized to some degree, making it 'hidden' from and 'hard to reach' for the outsider researcher" (p. 423). I propose that this holds true in any conflict environment, whether that environment is a geographic location or a relationship between two individuals. Heuristic inquiry addresses this issue of marginalized populations implicitly by virtue of the role of the primary researcher, for whom the topic of inquiry is both personal and autobiographical. Naturally, potential co-researchers may initially be unaware of your personal involvement with the topic of the study. However, the informed consent process of heuristic inquiry necessitates communication about the study with potential co-researchers. Additionally, with words such as *change, transformation, personal, relational,* and *cultural* being so intricately woven into the fabric of the conflict transformation discipline, exploring human experience within this field from a heuristic approach may serve to magnify one's understanding of the essential nature of various conflict-related phenomena.

Again, I was not able to locate a heuristic inquiry in the discipline of conflict transformation. Please see Box 11.4 for details of a proposed heuristic study in this discipline, inspired by Cohen and Arieli's (2011) further discussion of conflict and its complexities, including the often resulting mistrust and suspicion that pervade conflict-ridden situations.

Now, how about you experiment with substituting the word *mistrust* with other words, perhaps as informed by one of your personal experiences with a conflict situation? Keep in mind that you may have to modify each of the guiding research questions slightly or considerably, depending on the focus you wish to take. You may also need to alter your theoretical framework, data collection methods, data representation methods, and co-researcher sample. Or you might even want to try on an entirely different conflict-related topic. Have fun with your imagination!

Counseling and Psychotherapy

Clark Moustakas, a humanistic psychologist, pioneered heuristic inquiry as a research approach focused on exploring questions of the essential nature of various facets of the human condition. Therefore, it should come as no surprise that heuristic research is ideal for conducting qualitative studies in the general

> **BOX 11.4**
>
> **SAMPLE OF A PROPOSED HEURISTIC INQUIRY IN CONFLICT TRANSFORMATION**
>
> ***Proposed title:*** A heuristic inquiry of the living experience of mistrust in a conflict situation
>
> ***Research questions:*** What is your experience of mistrust in conflict? What is your perception of threat in conflict? What would you identify as your basic needs for satisfying constructive novel understandings of trust/mistrust in conflict situations? What methods of interaction do you perceive as potentially beneficial in creating pathways for transforming conflict situations within which mistrust is conspicuous?
>
> ***Theoretical framework:*** Social constructivism/interpretivism, conflict theory, systems theory
>
> ***Co-researchers:*** Individuals who have experienced mistrust within conflict situations
>
> ***Data collection:*** Personal exploration, semi-structured interviews, journals, artifacts
>
> ***Data representation:*** Individual depiction, composite depiction, exemplary portrait, creative synthesis

discipline of counseling and psychotherapy, including professions such as psychiatry, clinical psychology, counseling psychology, professional counseling, social work, and marriage and family therapy. Unfortunately, biases remain, even within the field of counseling and psychotherapy, surrounding the use of qualitative research in general, as indicated in a 10-year review of research in counseling in which qualitative research represented less than 20 percent of all research-related article publications in counseling division journals from 1988 to 2007 (Ray et al., 2011). Despite this statistic, I am noticing a rise in the number of qualitative research publications (at least in counseling) over the past 10 years. Morrow (2007) stressed the key role of qualitative research in adequately exploring "the depth and complexity of the human experience" (p. 209) and making meaning of it. Hays and Wood (2011) also stated that the need for enhanced focus on qualitative research is increasing across various disciplines (including counseling and psychotherapy), as findings from positivist methodologies are often not applicable to marginalized groups. The authors outlined various qualitative approaches that allow researchers to bridge this gap.

In addition, exploring human experience qualitatively within this field provides opportunities for clinical practitioners to identify interventions that support growth and transformation. Heuristic inquiry, with its deeply collaborative spirit, provides an exemplary framework within which researcher-practitioners may infuse their personal experience and knowledge of the phenomena they are exploring with the experience of co-researchers to distinguish and cocreate specific change efforts. In perusing volumes of heuristic inquiries, I perceived that the greatest number of studies conducted explored questions of highest relevance to the discipline of counseling and psychotherapy, although in some instances the topics of inquiry appeared to link two or more disciplines. This speaks to the versatility of heuristic inquiry, as well as its tolerance for ambiguity and mutuality.

In a heuristic study of the phenomena of shared trauma and resiliency, Miller (2015) explored the experience of military mental health providers who have deployed to combat environments to treat soldiers on deployment. The study focused on traumatic and acute stress as a shared experience between mental health providers and their clients. Miller defined *shared trauma* as the experience providers face while delivering clinical services even as they struggle with the same issues their clients are going through and defined *resiliency* as a process of interpreting a stressful situation in relation to overall life experiences. See Box 11.5 for details of the study.

BOX 11.5

EXAMPLE OF HEURISTIC INQUIRY IN COUNSELING AND PSYCHOTHERAPY

Citation: Miller, T. (2015). *Shared trauma and resiliency among military mental health veterans: A heuristic inquiry.* Unpublished doctoral dissertation, College of Social and Behavioral Sciences, Walden University.

Research questions: How do military mental health providers describe difficulties they faced as they attempted to navigate the personal aspects of trauma? How do military mental health providers describe difficulties they faced as they attempted to navigate the professional aspects of shared trauma? What meanings do military mental health providers choose to assign to their shared trauma experiences? What were the most difficult psychological aspects of deployment for military mental health clinicians? How did the clinicians attempt to care for themselves while simultaneously caring for others during deployment and the 6 months following return from deployment?

Theoretical framework: Social constructivism/interpretivism, theories of shared trauma and resiliency, existentialism

Co-researchers: Deployed military veterans providing mental health services in a combat zone

Data collection: Personal exploration, semi-structured interviews (Skype and telephone), reflection notes

Themes: Environmental hazards, mission purpose, posttraumatic growth, shared trauma

Data representation: Codes (this is an example of bricolage, as coding is not a heuristic method), themes, discrepant data; no individual or composite depictions, exemplary portrait, or clearly identified creative synthesis

Creative synthesis: The researcher described a process of creative synthesis but did not use a specific artifact to represent this process.

Engaging Heuristic Inquiry Informally

As you may have discerned from the variety of disciplines and heuristic studies sampled above, heuristic inquiry is a fairly versatile methodology with room for creativity and exploration. With that, and as I mentioned in Chapter 10, it may be a good idea to try out a heuristic inquiry or two informally before plunging headfirst into a formal study. This gives you an opportunity to play with the heuristic methodology to become better acquainted with its colorful processes and phases and to experiment with the infinite variety of topics you may explore through that lens. With heuristic inquiry's autobiographical bent, any phenomenon you have experienced is fair game for exploration (with a mind on ethics, of course—especially when conducting informal studies). As you work to become knowledgeable about heuristic inquiry, exploring one of its personally oriented processes (e.g., tacit knowing, intuition, focusing) or phases (e.g., immersion, incubation, illumination) might be a good idea. For example, some guiding research questions on the topic of *tacit knowing* might be as follows:

- *What is your experience of tacit knowing?*
- *What is your perception of the impact of tacit knowing in your daily life?*
- *How do you create meaning of the experience of tacit knowing?*

You can always start the study on your own (naturally, you will do this as a process of identifying with the focus of inquiry and self-dialogue), and once you have gone through the various processes and phases, you can invite a friend or colleague who has experienced tacit knowing to share her account. As with a formalized and approved study, be sure to practice proper informed consent. You are always obligated, whether conducting formal or informal heuristic inquiry, to inform your collaborators of your intentions and to secure their consent.

In addition to researching various processes and phases of heuristic inquiry, you may want to informally explore other personal human phenomena with universal potential. Some ideas that are not necessarily connected to particular disciplines but are more concerned with the human condition and with existence include the creative process, free will, autonomy, gratitude, compassion, change, self-transformation, absence, fear, awe, and wisdom. The list goes on. Recall that heuristic inquiry emerged as a process of inquiry as Moustakas (1961) grappled with his challenging yet compelling experience of loneliness. What in life has challenged you? What has given meaning to your existence? What has twisted you and churned you? What has pulled you out of your slumber and into acute alertness and awareness? Dig deep and find those experiences that have dared you completely! When you do, pick one to follow into the labyrinth. Go slowly and willfully. Most important, go trustfully, allowing yourself to be guided by the well-laid-out path, knowing that if you immerse yourself fully in your exploratory experience, you will emerge with new understandings not only of the phenomenon but also of yourself, of others, and of the world.

Closing Reflections

In this final full chapter, I reviewed a sampling of disciplines (in no way exhaustive) that may gain from applying heuristic inquiry as a qualitative methodology for exploring questions of relevance to them. Within each discipline, I either outlined the details of an actual formal heuristic inquiry or proposed a potential formal heuristic study as a way of illuminating possibilities and/or highlighting findings. Additionally, I explored the utility of applying heuristic methods to explore questions of the human condition informally. Thus, formalized inquiry is no longer an intimidating entity with indecipherable features and shadowy dynamics. Instead, we dare to plunge into the shadowy depths of our existence and explore the hidden recesses of what makes us who we are. In weaving fluid threads of communication and points of connection between the formal and the informal and between the personal and the universal, we create new habitats within which research and living experience may coexist.

12

An Ending∞Beginning

Well, here we are, dear colleagues—at the end of our shared journey! We've wound our way through the dark, coiled pathway of the labyrinth, immersed ourselves in curious exploration, scuffled through the ebb and flow of imagination and experiential learning, skirmished quite fearlessly with uncertainty and ambiguity, and taken one leap of faith after another. All done then, are we? My hope is that this book has energized you toward conducting your own heuristic study, be it formal or informal. Perhaps you are already at the threshold of doing so. Or maybe you are engaging briefly with the dynamics of heuristic inquiry as you explore it and other qualitative research methodologies prior to making a decision about the best fit for your study. May I share with you where I am at this moment?

As I am writing this, it has been about 2 weeks since Hurricane Harvey made its inelegant departure from southeast Texas. Although my home and subdivision were spared Harvey's brutality, the suburb in which I live took a massive beating. Many of our Kingwood (just northeast of Houston) neighbors less than half a mile away lost their vehicles, homes, and family businesses to the destructive flooding. They have nowhere to go, and they don't know where to begin with rebuilding their lives. The green, lush landscape of Kingwood that surrounded us just a few days ago endured an unforgiving purgatory of fire and water and is now smeared with broken glass, gutted insulation, cracked concrete, and demolished wood frames. Downtown Houston, where I both teach and maintain my psychotherapy practice office, faced similar challenges.

As the sky fell ceaselessly for several days, Houston's intricate web of rivers, bayous, and reservoirs flooded, and many of the major highways that connect one end of the greater Houston area with another became completely immersed in water. Inevitably, the university at which I teach announced closure for several days to allow students, staff, and faculty members to attend to their basic needs. I decided to close my therapy practice, as well, a decision that was unavoidable given that all the major highways in the greater Houston area were underwater. Over the following few days, my husband and I faced grave uncertainty as we confronted numerous flood and tornado threats, sprinkled with persistent power outages. It wasn't long before our phone and Internet networks dropped, as well, rendering us unable to make or receive calls, or send or receive e-mail. *What will we do if we have an emergency?* we pondered both to ourselves and out loud as we tucked our IDs into plastic bags and secured them in the pockets of our windbreakers in case we had to evacuate our home. As we sat on the floor of our utility room and contemplated what we were up against, I was overwhelmed by a feeling of *What is this?* I asked myself: *Hopelessness? Not exactly. Uselessness? Temporarily, yes. Helplessness? Yes, that's it. Well, I think. Helplessness. Yes. Maybe. I don't know.*

Thankfully, we did not need to evacuate. However, once Harvey passed and some of our services were restored (i.e., power, phone network), I was immediately called to check in with my students and clients. In an effort to catch up on the events of the previous few days and become informed about my surroundings, I turned on the news. I watched and listened in disbelief as reporters held their microphones up to receive the story of one survivor after another: people of every race, religion, gender, and age. I shrank with grief as I witnessed people from other states who had driven to Kingwood and the greater Houston area to help with rescue efforts. *There's our favorite grocery store—less than one year old and completely inundated. There's the family-owned pizza place we order from every other Friday night—what will they do for income? The gas station. The massage parlor. The tutoring center. The family medical practice. That house . . . those houses! How many houses? Hundreds of houses. Hundreds of thousands of cars. All completely demolished! How will this ever be restored?* The widespread devastation was etched on every person's face and body, in gestures and expressions. I experienced an overwhelming sense of incapacitation and guilt as one of my clients recounted a terrorizing account of being stuck on the top floor of her rapidly flooding home and toying with the idea of jumping out of a window to save her life. In each of the stories I witnessed or heard, one word echoed: *helplessness*. As my own sense of helplessness hit home without mercy, I noticed myself shrinking into denial. *I am not a helpless person! We are not helpless people!* I told myself repeatedly. Before long, another word dared throughout the greater Houston area: *resilience*. *I am a resilient person,* I affirmed. *We are resilient people. We have options; we always do! But what are those options? How do we come back?*

Now that the worst of Harvey is behind us, I am able to take a step back and let things incubate. I am allowing the words *helplessness* and *resilience* to have their time within my being. A couple of questions have been circulating: *What is my/your/our experience of helplessness? What do I/you/we do to emerge from my/your/our helplessness?* These questions are emerging from my personal experience of *helplessness* and *resilience* during Hurricane Harvey, as well as from what I internalized as a potentially universal experience of each during the hurricane. I sense an indelible connection between the personal and the universal and would like to know more about this. I feel that exploring these phenomena can transcend the gifts of discovery and knowledge, offering hope, healing, integration, and transformation. It seems a worthy endeavor!

And so to you I say: Wherever you are in your professional or personal journey, please do take a moment to check in with your intuition and listen, to grant yourself the opportunity to be with your felt sense and to be present—in the most open, most embodied way—to your own personhood and to the personhoods of those around you. I invite you, as a researcher and as a person, to always keep your living experience close and your humanness closer. With that, I wish you and your future co-researchers the humblest, wildest, most human, most creative, and most transforming adventures with heuristic research. Let the journeys begin!

Kingwood, Texas
September 2017

• Appendix A •
Sample Cover/Invitation Letter

Dear Colleague,

My name is Nevine Sultan, and I am a doctoral candidate in the Counselor Education and Supervision Program at St. Mary's University, with a master's degree in clinical mental health counseling. For my doctoral dissertation, I am conducting a research study titled *A Heuristic Inquiry of the Embodied Experiences of Body Psychotherapists in the Therapeutic Process*. The purpose of this study is to capture, in a one-time web-based interview, body psychotherapists' descriptions of their lived experience of embodiment in the therapeutic process. I am seeking research partners who would allow me to interview them regarding this experience. I invite you to consider participating in this important and timely research study.

Those who participate in this study will: (a) describe what it means for them, as body psychotherapists, to be embodied; (b) describe how they use their embodiment within the therapeutic process; (c) provide clinical examples of how they used their embodiment in therapeutic encounters; and (d) describe the perceived impact of this on clients.

The interview is expected to last from 60 to 90 minutes and will be digitally audio-recorded using technology that safeguards confidentiality, transcribed verbatim, and verified (and modified if needed) by the respondent. The content of the interview will constitute the raw data for the study. Co-researchers will also be invited to include any relevant poetry, artwork, stories, music, journal entries, or other forms of creative expression that have contributed to the meaning-making of their embodied experiences in clinical practice.

Relevant themes and patterns will be identified from this information, culminating in a creative synthesis of the essence of research partners' collective experience. To preserve confidentiality and anonymity, co-researchers will indicate a pseudonym of their choice. Using pseudonyms will allow me to determine themes without identifying co-researchers and will be the only means of identifying co-researchers in the writing of the findings.

There is minimal to no risk anticipated in participating in this study. Benefits of participation include contributing to the existing body of empirical research on body psychotherapy and embodiment and having an opportunity to assimilate and integrate lived experience. You will not be compensated for your participation.

The criteria for inclusion in this study are as follows:

1. Co-researchers self-identify as body psychotherapists and have received focused clinical training in somatic approaches in psychotherapy.
2. Co-researchers have at least 5 years of experience being a body psychotherapist.
3. Co-researchers have had personal embodied experiences in therapeutic work with clients.
4. Co-researchers are willing and able to describe their clinical embodied experiences.
5. Co-researchers speak English comfortably.
6. Co-researchers are willing to have their interview with the researcher audio-recorded.

As a precaution, practitioners confirming a history of trauma will be excluded from the study, as discussing embodied experiences or past events may evoke traumatic memories.

If you meet the above criteria or feel confident nominating a colleague who does, or if you have any questions about this research study, please e-mail me at *(insert e-mail address)*. Once you have expressed interest in participating in the study, I will e-mail you the informed consent form, the demographic information form, the interview protocol, and a few possible times for the interview, along with instructions on how to connect with me for the interview. Please know that you may ask questions about the study at any time.

The data collected from this inquiry will be used for education and publication purposes. Reported findings will not be identified with you personally. Your participation in this study is voluntary, and you may withdraw from the study at any time without penalty. Likewise, I may withdraw you from the study at any time for reasons such as communication or language difficulties.

Any questions about this study or any related concerns may be directed to the principal researcher, Nevine Sultan, MA, LPC, NCC, at *(insert phone number)* or at *(insert e-mail address)*.

Any questions about your rights as a research partner or concerns about this research study may be directed to the chair of the Institutional Review Board, St. Mary's University, at *(insert phone number)* or at *(insert e-mail address)*. All research projects carried out by investigators at St. Mary's University are governed by requirements of the university and the federal government.

Thank you for considering participation in this research. I value the unique contribution you can make to this study, to the understanding and evidence base of body psychotherapy and embodiment, and to the overall knowledge base of mental health care. I am excited about the possibility of your participation and look forward to hearing from you.

Sincerely,
Nevine Sultan, MA, LPC, NCC
*** INSERT IRB APPROVAL STAMP HERE ***

• Appendix B •
Sample Demographic Information Form

Pseudonym: _____ Country of residence: _____

Age: _____ Country of origin: _____

Phone number: _____

Highest degree earned: _____

Licenses/certifications: _____

Additional training: _____

Approximate # of years in practice as a body psychotherapist: _____

Primary theoretical orientation: _____

Body psychotherapy modality/approach: _____

Type of practice (check all that apply):

___Private practice ___Group practice ___Institution/hospital ___Agency

___Other (please specify): _____

Gender: _____ Ethnicity: _____

Marital/partner status: _____

Any other relevant demographic information:

• Appendix C •
Sample Informed Consent Form

A Heuristic Inquiry of the Embodied Experiences of Body Psychotherapists in the Therapeutic Process
Informed Consent

Please consider this information carefully before deciding whether you wish to participate in this research study.

Purpose of the research: To explore, in a one-time digitally audio-recorded telephone interview, body psychotherapists' descriptions of their experience of embodiment in the therapeutic encounter and how these experiences have informed the therapeutic process and potentially impacted clients.

What you will do in this research: This study will involve your participation in a one-time digitally audio-recorded telephone interview.

Time required: Interview: 60 to 90 minutes. Transcript and emergent theme verification: Will vary depending on your schedule.

Risks: There is minimal to no risk anticipated in participation in this study. If you have a history of trauma and have chosen not to disclose this during the screening process, please consider carefully whether you wish to continue your participation in the study. Discussing embodied experiences or past events may evoke traumatic memories. Please note that I have elected, as a precaution, to exclude from the study potential co-researchers who have confirmed a history of trauma.

Benefits: Benefits of participation include contributing to the existing body of empirical research on body psychotherapy and embodiment; informing training and field supervision, practice, and theory; and having an opportunity to assimilate and integrate lived experience.

Compensation: You will not be compensated for participating in this study.

Confidentiality: Your participation in this study is entirely confidential, and your identity will not be stored with your data. All responses will be assigned a pseudonym of your choice. If you do not select a pseudonym, I will select one for you. The list of research partners connecting your name with your pseudonym will remain confidential, under three locks (desk, office, and building).

Participation and withdrawal: Your participation in this study is entirely voluntary; you may withdraw at any time without penalty. If you wish to withdraw, please inform the researcher (no questions asked).

How to contact the researcher: Any questions about this study or any related concerns may be directed to the primary investigator, Nevine Sultan, MA, LPC, NCC, at *(insert phone number)* or at *(insert e-mail address)*.

Whom to contact about your rights in this research: Any questions about your rights as a research partner or concerns about this research study may be directed to the chair of the Institutional Review Board, St. Mary's University, at *(insert phone number)* or at *(insert e-mail address)*. All research projects carried out by investigators at St. Mary's University are governed by requirements of the university and the federal government.

Oral informed consent: The nature and purpose of this research have been sufficiently explained. I agree to participate in this study and to allow the researcher to digitally audio-record the interview. I understand that I am free to ask the researcher questions about this research study at any time and that I may withdraw from the study at any time without incurring any penalty. I also understand that the researcher may withdraw me from the study at any time for reasons such as communication or language difficulties.

*** INSERT IRB APPROVAL STAMP HERE ***

• Appendix D •
Sample Instructions for Interview Meeting

Dear XXXXX,

Following is information on when and how to connect with me online for our web-based audio interview. All you have to do is type or copy and paste the link below into the address bar of your Internet browser at the time of the meeting. You won't need to download any software. Here is your link:

(LINK)

When you enter the meeting room, please enter as a GUEST.

Interview date: XXXX XX, XXXX

Interview time: XX:XX (XXXXXX Time; your time)

XX:XX (Central Time USA; my time)

Interview length: 60 to 90 minutes

Please let me know if you have any questions. Again, thank you for your willingness to participate in this study. I am deeply grateful.

Warmly,
Nevine

• Appendix E •
Sample Semi-Structured Interview Protocol

1. Start recording devices.
2. Verify researcher receipt of completed Demographic Information Form.
3. Review Informed Consent Form, and obtain oral informed consent for participation.
4. Thank co-researcher for volunteering participation.
5. Engage in dialogue, answer questions, and so forth to "break the ice" and create relational flow.
6. Do brief embodiment exercise (connect with the breath, the body, and the present moment).
7. Introduce interview with a review of central purpose of study.
8. Orient co-researcher to interview questions.
9. Begin interview.
10. Conduct interview using the following guiding questions:
    - What does it mean for you to be embodied?
    - How do you use your embodiment within the therapeutic process?
    - Can you provide clinical examples of how you have used your embodiment in therapeutic encounters?
    - How do you think your embodiment may have impacted clients?
11. Listen to co-researcher, engaging researcher embodiment, empathy, and relational attitude.
12. Respond, prompt, and clarify when necessary, engaging researcher embodiment, empathy, and relational attitude.
13. Thank co-researcher again for volunteering participation and taking the time.

14. Remind co-researcher that interview transcript and findings will be sent to her/him for verification (and suggested modifications if needed).
15. Ask if co-researcher has any final thoughts to share.
16. End telephone interview; stop recording devices.

• Appendix F •
Sample Semi-Structured Interview Protocol With Examples

1. Start recording devices.

2. Verify researcher receipt of completed Demographic Information Form.

3. Review Informed Consent Form, and obtain oral informed consent for participation.

   We're going to begin with a formality, informed consent, which is required by institutional review boards and is standard practice. I'm aware that you've read the form and know its contents. I would like to emphasize that I'm committed to safeguarding your confidentiality, and to stress that it's important to me that you know you have the right to withdraw from the study at any time with no questions asked. Besides that, do you have questions about the informed consent? Do I have your consent to participate in this study?

4. Thank co-researcher for volunteering participation.

5. Engage in dialogue, answer questions, and so forth to "break the ice" and create relational flow.

6. Do brief embodiment exercise (connect with the breath, the body, and the present moment).

   I'd like to invite you to take a moment to just drop inside yourself, clear your mind of any concerns you might be having, connect with your breath and your body, and come into the present moment with me. (Pause) Do you feel ready to begin?

7. Introduce interview with a review of central purpose of study.

   The purpose of this research study is to explore in depth the meaning of embodiment and how body psychotherapists use it to inform the process of therapy. This research project is a heuristic inquiry, which is a qualitative approach. Do you have any questions about the purpose of this study or about the research design or methodology?

8. Orient co-researcher to interview questions.

    I'm interested in your personal experience of embodiment. I would like for us to explore

    - *what it means for you to be embodied,*
    - *how you use your embodiment to inform the process of therapy,*
    - *a specific experience in session with a specific client during which you felt embodied, and*
    - *how you think your embodiment may have impacted your client.*

9. Begin interview.

    I understand that you practice (MODALITY OF BP) from a (THEORETICAL PERSPECTIVE) approach. Based on your experience of (number of YEARS) doing this work and as a body psychotherapist . . .

10. Conduct interview using the following guiding questions:

    - *What does it mean for you to be embodied?*
    - *How do you use your embodiment within the therapeutic process?*
    - *Can you provide clinical examples of how you have used your embodiment in therapeutic encounters?*
        - *Can you recall a specific experience, in session with a particular client, during which you felt embodied?*
        - *What did you do with that?*
    - *How do you think your embodiment may have impacted your client?*

11. Listen to co-researcher, engaging researcher embodiment, empathy, and relational attitude.

12. Respond, prompt, and clarify when necessary, engaging researcher embodiment, empathy, and relational attitude.

13. Thank co-researcher again for volunteering participation and taking the time.

    I appreciate your openness and willingness to share your experiences with me. I've learned a lot from you that will contribute to this study, to the professional literature about embodiment and body psychotherapy, and to our work as mental health practitioners.

14. Remind co-researcher that interview transcript and findings will be sent to her/him for verification (and suggested modifications if needed).

    I'd like to remind you that I will be sending you the interview transcript to review and either approve as is or suggest modifications. Please know that the interview content is a reflection of your personal experience and that you are free to modify it as you see fit.

15. Ask if co-researcher has any final thoughts to share.

    - *Were there any topics regarding embodiment or body psychotherapy that you wanted to discuss but that we did not get around to today?*
    - *Let's take a moment to see if it feels right to end our conversation here or if there is something else you would like to add.*
    - *Do you have any questions for me as we end our time together?*
    - *Do you have any artwork, journal entries, photos, or other forms of creative expression that you would like to include with your data? Would you mind e-mailing copies to me?*
    - *What was it like for you to speak with me about your embodied experiences in psychotherapy?*
    - *Do you have a colleague who meets the criteria for this research study and whom you are willing to speak with about volunteering participation in the study?*

16. End telephone interview; stop recording devices.

    Document thoughts, feelings, sensations, and impressions in journal promptly following the interview.

• Appendix G •

Preparing for and Recording Interviews (Sample)

Preparing for Interviews

- Print out the following documents:
    - This document
    - Interview Protocol
    - Cover Letter
    - Informed Consent Form
    - Demographic Information Form
    - Open-Ended Relational Probing and Prompting

Recording Interviews

- Use Adobe Connect to create a web-based meeting for each interviewee.
- Extend duration of meeting to 4 hours (to ensure ample time and full recording).
- Allow registered users and guests.
- Finish and receive link; send link by e-mail to each participant.
- Activate only microphone (no video/camera) on Adobe Connect.
- Activate volume; disable video/camera on Adobe Connect; cover webcam on laptop with sticky note.
- Pull down **Meeting** button and select **Record Meeting**.
- Use **PAUSE** (not **STOP!**) button to place co-researchers on hold.

- Save recording.
- Download recording to a flash drive that will be kept in a secure location under three locks.
- Sign out of Adobe Connect.

• Appendix H •
Open-Ended Relational Probing and Prompting

- I'd like to go back to something you mentioned earlier. Could you please tell me more about . . . ? What stands out for you about that?
- I'd like to hear your thoughts on . . .
- I'm not quite sure I understood. Could you tell me more about that?
- I'm not certain what you mean by . . . Could you give me some examples?
- You talked about . . . Could you tell me more about that?
- You mentioned . . . What is your sense of that?
- How did that come about?
- What does _____ mean for you?
- I think what I heard you say is . . . Did I understand you correctly?
- What I hear you saying is . . .
- What was that like for you?
- What are some of your reasons for . . . ?
- Can you give me an example of . . . ?
- Tell me what it was like when . . .
- Tell me about the first/last time that you remember this happening.
- You just told me about . . . I'd also be interested in knowing about . . .
- What other examples of this have you experienced?
- What comes up for you as we discuss this? Thoughts? Feelings? Sensations?
- It seems that was perhaps a challenging moment?
- I can certainly relate to that. Could you say more about your experience?

- I'm sensing an energy shift between us. I wonder if it would be okay to return to this question a bit later. Would that be all right with you?
- I can appreciate the difficulty of discussing this. Would you like to pause for a few minutes?
- I sense your joy and exhilaration as you speak! Would you like to say more about this?
- Let's take a moment to see whether it feels right to end our time together here or if there is something else you might wish to add.
- Do you have any questions for me as we end our time together?
- Is there anything that you would like to say about _____ that we didn't get around to?
- What was it like for you to speak with me about _____?
- Do you have a colleague who meets the criteria for this research study and whom you are willing to speak with about volunteering participation in the study?
- I appreciate your openness and willingness to share your experiences with me.
- I'd like to remind you that I will be sending you the interview transcript to review and either approve as is or suggest modifications. Do you have any questions about that process?
- Do you mind if I reach out to you with any questions or need for clarification?

• Glossary •

a posteriori knowledge: knowledge based on experience

a priori knowledge: knowledge that is innate

asymmetrical relationships: relationships in which one member attempts to impose dominance over another

axiology: the study of core beliefs and values

bracketing: the process of assessing, recognizing, and suspending or setting aside one's personal motives and values, with the objective being to minimize the imposition of such values on the research process

bricolage: a qualitative research approach in which researchers piece together techniques, perspectives, practices, or tools from a variety of qualitative methodologies

coding: a popular method for categorizing data in grounded theory studies

composite depiction: a heuristic inquiry data representation method that illustrates a composite understanding of the data, representing the shared experience of the phenomenon among various research partners

confirmability: a process that calls for clear identification of links between research findings and interpretations

confirmation bias: a process whereby one protects one's biases by deliberately interpreting new information as confirmation of their validity

countertransference: a psychotherapist's (or researcher's) projection onto the client (or the co-researcher) of personality features of another person, along with reaction to the client (or co-researcher) as if she or he actually possessed those characteristics

creative synthesis: a heuristic inquiry data representation method that represents a researcher's integration of the multiple themes of the topic into a cohesive whole, usually using some form of creative interpretation

credibility: primarily concerned with the concepts of confidence and believability, especially with regard to the research design (i.e., the methods and approaches used to collect and analyze the data and represent the findings)

dependability: a criterion of trustworthiness that speaks to how one is justifying one's choice of research methodology and data collection process, as well as how one's findings align and harmonize with that methodology

embodied knowing: a way of knowing that highlights sensory experience; see also *tacit knowing*

embodied reflexivity: a researcher's process of engaging her/his cognitive, emotional, sensory∞kinesthetic, perceptual, spiritual, and social∞relational self to process intrapersonal, interpersonal, and sociocultural/environmental dynamics unfolding throughout the course of a study

embodied relational interviewing: an interviewing approach in which thought, emotion, sensation, intuition, memory, and perception each play a strategic role in data collection, laying the foundation for a holistic, relational experience that honors the experiences of all persons involved

embodied relational listening: a dialoguing approach that engages various ways of being and of knowing, as described in *embodied relational interviewing*

embodied relational transcription: a data-transcribing approach that engages various ways of being and of knowing, as described in *embodied relational interviewing*

embodied relational writing: a manuscript writing approach that engages various ways of being and of knowing, as described in *embodied relational interviewing*

empirical research: research that involves the collection of raw data and its analysis and interpretation

epistemology: the study of ways of knowing

exclusion criteria: conditions by which potential co-researchers are determined *not* to be eligible for participation in a study

exemplary portrait: a heuristic inquiry data representation method that contains details about the co-researcher that were not present in the individual or composite depictions, bringing into focus the topic of inquiry as experienced both individually and collectively

explication: a researcher's exploration of emergent themes and fine-tuning of those themes in preparation for the creative synthesis

exploratory research: See *qualitative research*

felt meaning: understanding of oneself, the other, or any situation or event that emerges through one's embodied felt sense of the meaning of the interaction that occurs between one and the other

felt sense: a body-sense of a certain event

focusing: a process of inner searching developed by Eugene Gendlin as a method of self-inquiry and self-awareness

goodness: a way of asserting that a study's findings can be used to inform and justify action and change

heuristic inquiry: a qualitative, social constructivist, and phenomenologically aligned research methodology inspired by the primary researcher's autobiographical experience

I–It: a way of relating focused on the experience of the self

I–Thou: a way of relating focused on the experience of being present with others and the world

illumination: a researcher's awareness (usually intuitive) of previously undisclosed information related to the research question, often coupled with altered perception of the topic

immersion: a researcher's full commitment to living a question or topic, in all dimensions of life, as the question becomes the primary focus of the researcher's attention

inclusion criteria: a set of conditions by which you determine co-researcher eligibility for participation in a study

incubation: a researcher's temporary and deliberate withdrawal from the research question or topic to allow seeds of new knowledge to sprout

individual depiction: a heuristic inquiry data representation method that provides a holistic, detailed illustration of a co-researcher's personal living experience of the topic of inquiry without compromising the individual's singular experience

inductive research: See *qualitative research*

indwelling: a process of turning inward or deep introspection to arrive at insight into a central phenomenon

infinity symbol: an inverted figure-eight symbol (∞) used to represent nondual, fluid relationships

initial engagement: a researcher's first encounter with a topic of extreme interest through an autobiographical experience that, though it is internal and personal to the researcher, is of potentially social and universal significance

intentionality: the experience of unraveling the various layers of implicit meaning surrounding the encounter of a subject with an object

interpretivism: See *social constructivism*

intersubjectivity: a nonverbal sense of *withness* with another person

labyrinth: an ancient, archetypal symbol constituted of a series of winding spirals that form a circle representing a whole that is greater than the sum of its parts

lived experience: a term used in phenomenological research to describe firsthand involvement in human experience

living experience: a term that describes firsthand involvement in human experience while honoring its interrelated, interconnected, and continuing nature

living manuscript: a creative, embodied, transformative manuscript, narrative, or report that transcends the single sitting required to complete its reading, carving pathways for emergence and discovery within readers, co-researchers, and oneself

living narrative: See *living manuscript*

methodology: the study of the methods, procedures, or processes of research

needs self-assessment exercise: a process of checking in with oneself about where one is in the present moment, identifying what is not working, and determining what one might need to do for the situation to change

nonverbal communication: communication that is expressed through nonlinguistic means, usually through physical signals, messages, and cues

ontology: the study of ways of being and of reality

outliers: individual research findings that lie outside the norm

paradigm: a framework for conducting research

phenomenology: a qualitative, social constructivist research approach that seeks to explore a complex human experience as individuals perceive it

post-positivism: a research paradigm that supports deductive, objective approaches in research with a focus on single reality

purposive sample: one that targets a particular group of people based on their experience of the phenomenon being explored

qualitative research: exploratory, inductive research conducted in an effort to understand a person, group, or situation and in which the focus is usually on a single concept, topic, or phenomenon

radical empiricism: a theory postulating that all experience occurs from an embodied perspective imbued with personal meaning and values

Rashomon effect: a situation in which different individuals provide contradictory interpretations of a single event based on individual perception, with no evidence to disqualify any of the interpretations

reflexivity: the process by which researchers place under scrutiny the research process, the intersubjective dynamics between researcher and participants, and the extent to which their assumptions influenced the process of inquiry

research team: the collective group of researcher and research partners/co-researchers

resonance: a high state of empathic presence and responsiveness to another that may result in unconscious mirroring of that person's body posture, tone of voice, and facial expressions

rhetoric: the language or narrative used to present the process and findings of research to the intended audience

rigor: a term used to describe the quality of a research process

saturation: a grounded theory concept that describes the point at which new data do not yield new insight

social constructivism: a philosophy of life and research paradigm that stipulates that reality is both internally and socially constructed and that there are no single truths or realities; also called *interpretivism*

tacit knowing: implicit knowing or knowing that lies beyond what may be readily observed or articulated; see also *embodied knowing*

transcription: the process of converting audio or audiovisual data into written text by writing what was said and done and how it was said and done

transferability: a term used to highlight or describe the importance of the context, setting, and/or situatedness of the study

transference: a psychotherapy client's (or a research partner's) projection onto the therapist (or the researcher) of personality features of another person, along with reaction to the therapist (or researcher) as if she or he actually possessed those characteristics

trustworthiness: a term used to describe the ways qualitative researchers ensure that the rigor of the qualitative research is evident

• References •

Aanstoos, C. M. (2015). Humanistic psychology in dialogue with cognitive science and technological culture. In K. J. Schneider, J. Fraser Pierson, & J. F. T. Bugental (Eds.), *The handbook of humanistic psychology: Theory, research, and practice* (2nd ed., pp. 243–254). Thousand Oaks, CA: Sage.

Abram, D. (1996). *The spell of the sensuous: Perception and language in a more-than-human world.* New York, NY: Vintage Books.

Abram, D. (2000). All knowledge is carnal knowledge: A correspondence. *Canadian Journal of Environmental Education, 5,* 167–177.

Adams, S. A., & Riggs, S. A. (2008). An exploratory study of vicarious trauma among therapist trainees. *Training and Education in Professional Psychology, 2,* 26–34.

Adler, P. A., & Adler, P. (2002). The reluctant respondent. In J. F. Gubrium & J. A. Holstein (Eds.), *Handbook of interview research: Context and method* (pp. 515–536). Thousand Oaks, CA: Sage.

Alsobrook, R. F. (2015). *Yoga and emotional well-being: A heuristic inquiry into the experience of women with a yoga practice.* Unpublished doctoral dissertation, Harold Abel School of Social and Behavioral Sciences, Capella University.

American Counseling Association. (2014). *ACA Code of Ethics.* Alexandria, VA: Author.

Anderson, K. T. (2008). Intersubjectivity. In L. M. Given (Ed.), *The SAGE encyclopedia of qualitative research methods* (pp. 468–469). Thousand Oaks, CA: Sage.

Anderson, R. (2016). The Rashomon effect and communication. *Canadian Journal of Communication, 41,* 250–265.

Angen, M. J. (2000). Evaluating interpretive inquiry: Reviewing the validity debate and opening the dialogue. *Qualitative Health Research, 10,* 378–395.

Archive for Research in Archetypal Symbolism. (2010). *The book of symbols: Reflections on archetypal images.* Cologne, Germany: Taschen.

Arons, M., & Richards, R. (2015). Two noble insurgencies: Creativity and humanistic psychology. In K. J. Schneider, J. Fraser Pierson, & J. F. T. Bugental (Eds.), *The handbook of humanistic psychology: Theory, research, and practice* (2nd ed., pp. 161–175). Thousand Oaks, CA: Sage.

Ashworth, P. (2003). An approach to phenomenological psychology: The contingencies of the lifeworld. *Journal of Phenomenological Psychology, 34,* 145–156.

Babbie, E. (2013). *The practice of social research* (13th ed.). Belmont, CA: Wadsworth.

Beisser, A. (1970). The paradoxical theory of change. In J. Fagan & I. L. Shepherd (Eds.), *Gestalt therapy now* (pp. 77–80). New York, NY: Harper & Row.

Benedetti, F. (2012). Placebo-induced improvements: How therapeutic rituals affect the patient's brain. *Journal of Acupuncture and Meridian Studies, 5,* 97–103.

Berríos, R., & Lucca, N. (2006). Qualitative methodology in counseling research: Recent contributions and challenges for a new century. *Journal of Counseling & Development, 84,* 174–186.

Bohm, D. (2004). *On dialogue.* New York, NY: Routledge.

Braun, V., & Clarke, V. (2013). *Successful qualitative research: A practical guide for beginners.* Thousand Oaks, CA: Sage.

Brown, A. S. (1991). A review of the tip-of-the-tongue experience. *Psychological Bulletin, 109,* 204–223.

Buber, M. (1970). *I and thou* (W. Kaufmann, Trans.). New York, NY: Simon & Schuster. (Original work published 1923)

Butler-Kisber, L. (2010). *Qualitative inquiry: Thematic, narrative, and arts-informed perspectives.* Thousand Oaks, CA: Sage.

Cannella, G. S., & Lincoln, Y. S. (2012). Deploying qualitative methods for critical social purposes. In S. R. Steinberg & G. S. Cannella (Eds.), *Critical qualitative research reader* (pp. 104–114). New York, NY: Peter Lang.

Carman, T. (1999). The body in Husserl and Merleau-Ponty. *Philosophical Topics, 27,* 205–226.

Charmaz, K. (2006). *Constructing grounded theory.* Thousand Oaks, CA: Sage.

Charmaz, K. (2007). Constructionism and grounded theory. In J. A. Holstein & J. F. Gubrium (Eds.), *Handbook of constructionist research* (pp. 319–412). New York, NY: Guilford Press.

Charmaz, K. (2011). Grounded theory methods in social justice research. In N. K. Denzin & Y. S. Lincoln (Eds.), *The SAGE handbook of qualitative research* (4th ed., pp. 359–380). Thousand Oaks, CA: Sage.

Charmaz, K. (2014). *Constructing grounded theory* (2nd ed.). Thousand Oaks, CA: Sage.

Charmaz, K., & Bryant, A. (2008). Grounded theory. In L. M. Given (Ed.), *The SAGE encyclopedia of qualitative research methods* (pp. 375–378). Thousand Oaks, CA: Sage.

Chase, S. E. (2011). Narrative inquiry: Still a field in the making. In N. K. Denzin & Y. S. Lincoln (Eds.), *The SAGE handbook of qualitative research* (4th ed., pp. 421–434). Thousand Oaks, CA: Sage.

Christensen, T. M., & Brumfield, K. A. (2010). Phenomenological designs: The philosophy of phenomenological research. In C. J. Sheperis, J. S. Young, & M. H. Daniels (Eds.), *Counseling research: Quantitative, qualitative, and mixed methods* (pp. 135–150). Upper Saddle River, NJ: Pearson.

Churchill, S. D. (2005). Humanistic research in the wake of postmodernism. *The Humanistic Psychologist, 33,* 321–334.

Churchill, S. D., & Wertz, F. J. (2015). An introduction to phenomenological research in psychology: Historical, conceptual, and methodological foundations. In K. J. Schneider, J. Fraser Pierson, & J. F. T. Bugental (Eds.), *The handbook of humanistic psychology: Theory, research, and practice* (2nd ed., pp. 275–295). Thousand Oaks, CA: Sage.

Clarke, A. E. (2005). *Situational analysis: Grounded theory after the postmodern turn.* Thousand Oaks, CA: Sage.

Cohen, N., & Arieli, T. (2011). Field research in conflict environments: Methodological challenges and snowball sampling. *Journal of Peace Research, 48,* 423–435.

Cook, K. E. (2012). Stigma and the interview encounter. In J. F. Gubrium, J. A. Holstein, A. B. Marvasti, & K. D. McKinney (Eds.), *The SAGE handbook of interview research: The complexity of the craft* (pp. 333–346). Thousand Oaks, CA: Sage.

Corbin, J., & Strauss, A. (2015). *Basics of qualitative research: Techniques and procedures for developing grounded theory.* Thousand Oaks, CA: Sage.

Cottone, R. R. (2001). A social constructivism model of ethical decision making in counseling. *Journal of Counseling and Development, 79,* 39–45.

Cozolino, L. (2014). *The neuroscience of human relationships: Attachment and the developing social brain* (2nd ed.). New York, NY: W. W. Norton.

Creswell, J. W. (2009). *Research design: Qualitative, quantitative, and mixed methods approaches* (3rd ed.). Thousand Oaks, CA: Sage.

Creswell, J. W. (2013). *Qualitative inquiry and research design: Choosing among five approaches* (3rd ed.). Thousand Oaks, CA: Sage.

Csordas, T. J. (2008). Intersubjectivity and intercorporeality. *Subjectivity, 22,* 110–121.

Dahlberg, K., Dahlberg, H., & Nyström, M. (2008). *Reflective lifeworld research* (2nd ed.). Lund, Sweden: Studentlitteratur AB.

Davis, C. S. (2008). Empowerment. In L. M. Given (Ed.), *The SAGE encyclopedia of qualitative research methods* (pp. 261–262). Thousand Oaks, CA: Sage.

Dench, S., Iphofen, R., & Huws, U. (2004). *An EU code of ethics for socio-economic research*. Brighton, UK: Institute for Employment Studies.

Denzin, N. K. (2007). *On understanding emotion*. London, UK: Routledge.

Denzin, N. K. (2009). *The research act: A theoretical orientation to sociological methods*. Piscataway, NJ: Transaction.

Denzin, N. K., & Lincoln, Y. S. (2011). Introduction: The discipline and practice of qualitative research. In N. K. Denzin & Y. S. Lincoln (Eds.), *The SAGE handbook of qualitative research* (4th ed., pp. 1–19). Thousand Oaks, CA: Sage.

Descartes, R. (2006). *A discourse on the method of correctly conducting one's reason and seeking truth in the sciences* (I. Maclean, Trans.). Oxford, UK: Oxford University Press. (Original work published 1637)

Dewey, J. (2000). *Experience and nature* (Rev. ed.). Mineola, NY: Dover. (Original work published 1925)

Diamond, N. (1996). Can we really speak of internal and external reality? *Group Analysis, 29,* 302–323.

Dickson-Swift, V., James, E., Kippen, S., & Liamputtong, P. (2008). Researching sensitive topics: Qualitative research as emotion work. *Qualitative Research, 9,* 61–79.

Dickson-Swift, V., James, E., Kippen, S., & Liamputtong, P. (2009). Risk to researchers in qualitative research on sensitive topics: Issues and strategies. *Qualitative Health Research, 18,* 133–144.

Dilthey, W. (1977). *Descriptive psychology and historical understanding*. The Hague, Netherlands: Martinus Nijhoff. (Original work published 1894)

Donmoyer, R. (2008). Tacit knowledge. In L. M. Given (Ed.), *The SAGE encyclopedia of qualitative research methods* (pp. 862–863). Thousand Oaks, CA: Sage.

Douglass, B. G., & Moustakas, C. E. (1985). *Heuristic inquiry: The internal search to know*. Detroit, MI: Center for Humanistic Studies.

Ellingson, L. L. (2006). Embodied knowledge: Writing researchers' bodies into qualitative health research. *Qualitative Health Research, 16,* 298–310.

Ellingson, L. L. (2008). Embodied knowledge. In L. M. Given (Ed.), *The SAGE encyclopedia of qualitative research methods* (pp. 245–246). Thousand Oaks, CA: Sage.

Emerson, L. (2002). *The experience of parental suicide: A heuristic inquiry*. Unpublished doctoral dissertation, The Union Institute Graduate School, Union Institute and University, Cincinnati, OH.

Erickson, F. (1985). *Qualitative methods in research on teaching* (Occasional Paper No. 81). East Lansing: Michigan State University, Institute for Research on Teaching.

Erickson, F. (2011). A history of qualitative inquiry in social and educational research. In N. K. Denzin & Y. S. Lincoln (Eds.), *The SAGE handbook of qualitative research* (4th ed., pp. 43–59). Thousand Oaks, CA: Sage.

Erickson, F., Florio, S., & Buschman, J. (1980). *Fieldwork in educational research* (Occasional Paper No. 36). East Lansing: Michigan State University, Institute for Research on Teaching.

Eunson, B. (2015). *Communicating in the 21st century* (4th ed.). Queensland, Australia: John Wiley & Sons.

Figley, C. R. (2002). Compassion fatigue: Psychotherapists' chronic lack of self-care. *Psychotherapy in Practice, 58,* 1433–1441. doi: 10.1002/jclp.10090

Finlay, L. (2002). Outing the researcher: The provenance, process, and practice of reflexivity. *Qualitative Health Research, 12,* 531–545.

Finlay, L. (2005). "Reflexive embodied empathy": A phenomenology of participant-researcher intersubjectivity. *The Humanistic Psychologist, 33,* 271–292.

Finlay, L. (2008). A dance between the reduction and reflexivity: Explicating the "phenomenological psychological attitude." *Journal of Phenomenological Psychology, 39,* 1–32.

Finlay, L. (2011). *Phenomenology for therapists: Researching the lived world.* West Sussex, UK: John Wiley & Sons.

Finlay, L. (2012). Unfolding phenomenological research process: Iterative stages of "seeing afresh." *Journal of Humanistic Psychology, 53,* 171–201.

Finlay, L., & Langdridge, D. (2007). Embodiment. In W. Hollway, H. Lucey, & A. Phoenix (Eds.), *Social psychology matters* (pp. 173–198). Maidenhead, UK: Open University Press.

Flick, U., von Kardorff, E., & Steinke, I. (2004). What is qualitative research? An introduction to the field. In U. Flick, E. von Kardorff, & I. Steinke (Eds.), *A companion to qualitative research* (pp. 3–12). Thousand Oaks, CA: Sage.

Fogel, A. (2009). *Body sense: The science and practice of embodied self-awareness.* New York, NY: W. W. Norton.

Forester-Miller, H., & Davis, T. E. (2016). *Practitioner's guide to ethical decision making* (Rev. ed.). Retrieved from https://www.counseling.org/knowledge-center/ethics/ethical-decision-making

Fossey, E., Harvey, C., McDermott, F., & Davidson, L. (2002). Understanding and evaluating qualitative research. *Australian and New Zealand Journal of Psychiatry, 36,* 717–732.

Frankel, M., & Sommerbeck, L. (2007). Two Rogers: Congruence and the change from client-centered to we-centered therapy. *Person-Centered & Experiential Psychotherapies, 6,* 286–295.

Freire, P. (1970). *Pedagogy of the oppressed.* New York, NY: Bloomsbury.

Gadamer, H. (2013). *Truth and method* (J. Weinsheimer & D. G. Marshall, Trans.). London, UK: Bloomsbury Academic. (Original work published 1960)

Galtung, J. (1996). *Peace by peaceful means: Peace and conflict, development and civilization*. Oslo, Norway: International Peace Research Institute.

Galtung, J. (2004). *Transcend and transform: An introduction to conflict work*. Boulder, CO: Paradigm.

Galtung, J. (2010). Peace studies and conflict resolution: The need for transdisciplinarity. *Transcultural Psychiatry, 47*, 20–32.

Garcia, J. G., Cartwright, B., Winston, S. M., & Borzuchowska, B. (2003). A transcultural integrative model for ethical decision making in counseling. *Journal of Counseling and Development, 81*, 268–277.

Gehart, D. R., Ratliff, D. A., & Lyle, R. R. (2001). Qualitative research in family therapy: A substantive and methodological review. *Journal of Marital and Family Therapy, 27*, 261–274.

Gendlin, E. T. (1962). *Experiencing and the creation of meaning*. New York, NY: Free Press of Glencoe.

Gendlin, E. T. (1981). *Focusing*. New York, NY: Bantam Dell.

Gendlin, E. T. (1996). *Focusing-oriented psychotherapy: A manual of the experiential method*. New York, NY: Guilford Press.

Gilligan, C. (1982). *In a different voice: Psychological theory and women's development*. Cambridge, MA: Harvard University Press.

Giordano, J., O'Reilly, M., Taylor, H., & Dogra, N. (2007). Confidentiality and autonomy: The challenge(s) of offering research participants a choice of disclosing their identity. *Qualitative Health Research, 17*, 264–275.

Giorgi, A. (2009). *The descriptive phenomenological method in psychology: A modified Husserlian approach*. Pittsburgh, PA: Duquesne University Press.

Giroux, H. A. (1982). *Theory and resistance in education: A pedagogy for the opposition*. Boston, MA: Bergin & Garvey.

Given, L. M., & Saumure, K. (2008). Trustworthiness. In L. M. Given (Ed.), *The SAGE encyclopedia of qualitative research methods* (pp. 896–897). Thousand Oaks, CA: Sage.

Glaser, B. G., & Strauss, A. L. (1965). *Awareness of dying*. New York, NY: Routledge.

Glaser, B. G., & Strauss, A. L. (1967). *The discovery of grounded theory*. Chicago, IL: Aldine.

Glesne, C. (2016). *Becoming qualitative researchers: An introduction* (5th ed.). Boston, MA: Pearson.

Gough, N. (2008). First-person voice. In L. M. Given (Ed.), *The SAGE encyclopedia of qualitative research methods* (pp. 352–353). Thousand Oaks, CA: Sage.

Green, C. (2012). *The wild writer: A heuristic inquiry into the ecological writer's experience of nature*. Unpublished master's thesis, Prescott College, Prescott, AZ.

Greening, T. (2015). Becoming authentic: An existential-humanistic approach to reading literature. In K. J. Schneider, J. Fraser Pierson, & J. F. T. Bugental (Eds.), *The handbook of humanistic psychology: Theory, research, and practice* (2nd ed., pp. 177–186). Thousand Oaks, CA: Sage.

Grosz, E. (1994). *Volatile bodies: Toward a corporeal feminism*. Bloomington: Indiana University Press.

Gschwend, T., & Schimmelfennig, F. (2007). Introduction: Designing research in political science—A dialogue between theory and data. In T. Gschwend & F. Schimmelfennig (Eds.), *Research design in political science: How to practice what they preach* (pp. 1–18). Basingstoke, UK: Palgrave Macmillan.

Guba, E. G. (1981). Criteria for assessing the trustworthiness of naturalistic inquiries. *Educational Resources Information Center Annual Review Paper, 29,* 75–91.

Guba, E. G., & Lincoln, Y. S. (1989). *Fourth generation evaluation*. Newbury Park, CA: Sage.

Guenther, K. M. (2009). The politics of names: Rethinking the methodological and ethical significance of naming people, organizations, and places. *Qualitative Research, 9,* 411–421.

Harding, S. (Ed.). (2004). *The feminist standpoint theory reader: Intellectual and political controversies*. New York, NY: Routledge.

Hays, D. G., & Wood, C. (2011). Infusing qualitative traditions in counseling research designs. *Journal of Counseling & Development, 89,* 288–295.

Heery, M. (2015). A humanistic perspective on bereavement. In K. J. Schneider, J. Fraser Pierson, & J. F. T. Bugental (Eds.), *The handbook of humanistic psychology: Theory, research, and practice* (2nd ed., pp. 535–548). Thousand Oaks, CA: Sage.

Heidegger, M. (2008). *Being and time* (J. Macquarrie & E. Robinson, Trans.). New York, NY: Harper Perennial Modern Classics. (Original work published 1927)

Heider, K. G. (1988). The Rashomon effect: When ethnographers disagree. *American Anthropologist, 90,* 73–81.

Heron, J., & Reason, P. (1997). A participatory inquiry paradigm. *Qualitative Inquiry, 3,* 274–294.

Hesse-Biber, S. N. (2008). Feminist research. In L. M. Given (Ed.), *The SAGE encyclopedia of qualitative research methods* (pp. 336–339). Thousand Oaks, CA: Sage.

Hesse-Biber, S. (2014). A re-invitation to feminist research. In S. N. Hesse-Biber (Ed.), *Feminist research practice: A primer* (2nd ed., pp. 1–13). Thousand Oaks, CA: Sage.

Hesse-Biber, S. N., & Leavey, P. (2006). *The practice of qualitative research*. Thousand Oaks, CA: Sage.

Hewitt, J. (2007). Ethical components of researcher-researched relationships in qualitative interviewing. *Qualitative Health Research, 17,* 1149–1159.

Hiles, D. R. (2008a). Axiology. In L. M. Given (Ed.), *The SAGE encyclopedia of qualitative research methods* (pp. 53–57). Thousand Oaks, CA: Sage.

Hiles, D. R. (2008b). Heuristic inquiry. In L. M. Given (Ed.), *The SAGE encyclopedia of qualitative research methods* (pp. 390-393). Thousand Oaks, CA: Sage.

Holt-Waldo, N. Y. (2011). *The lived experience of being a holistic nurse educator: A heuristic inquiry.* Unpublished doctoral dissertation, Capella University.

Holzman, L. (2011). Critical psychology, philosophy, and social therapy. *Register of Social Critical Theories.* Retrieved from http://eastsideinstitute.org/wp-content/uploads/2014/05/HumanStudiesFinal.pdf

Husserl, E. (2001). *Logical investigations* (J. N. Findlay, Trans.). London, UK: Routledge. (Original work published 1900)

Husserl, E. (1998). *Ideas pertaining to a pure phenomenology and to a phenomenological philosophy: First book* (F. Kersten, Trans.). Dordrecht, Netherlands: Kluwer Academic. (Original work published 1913)

James, W. (2009). *Essays in radical empiricism.* Charleston, SC: BiblioBazaar. (Original work published 1912)

Johanson, G., & Kurtz, R. (1991). *Grace unfolding: Psychotherapy in the spirit of the Tao-te ching.* New York, NY: Bell Tower.

Johnson, J. M. (2008). Existentialism. In L. M. Given (Ed.), *The SAGE encyclopedia of qualitative research methods* (pp. 319–322). Thousand Oaks, CA: Sage.

Johnson, R. (2015). Grasping and transforming the embodied experience of oppression. *International Body Psychotherapy Journal, 14,* 80–95.

Jones, S. R., Torres, V., & Arminio, J. (2006). *Negotiating the complexities of qualitative research in higher education: Fundamental elements and issues.* New York, NY: Routledge.

Kaiser, K. (2012). Protecting confidentiality. In J. F. Gubrium, J. A. Holstein, A. B. Marvasti, & K. D. McKinney (Eds.), *The SAGE handbook of interview research: The complexity of the craft* (pp. 457–465). Thousand Oaks, CA: Sage.

Kant, E. (1966). *Critique of pure reason.* Garden City, NY: Doubleday. (Original work published 1781)

Kim, J. (2016). *Understanding narrative inquiry: The crafting and analysis of stories as research.* Thousand Oaks, CA: Sage.

Kingsley, A. E. (1998). *Meaning, identity, and wellness: The experience of living and working in Australian nursing homes.* Unpublished doctoral dissertation, School of Occupational Therapy, Curtin University of Technology, Bentley, Perth, Western Australia.

Kohler Riessman, C. (2008). *Narrative methods for the human sciences.* Thousand Oaks, CA: Sage.

Krathwohl, D. R. (2009). *Methods of educational and social science research: The logic of methods* (3rd ed.). Long Grove, IL: Waveland Press.

Krippner, S. (2015). Research methodology in humanistic psychology in light of postmodernity. In K. J. Schneider, J. Fraser Pierson, & J. F. T. Bugental (Eds.), *The handbook of humanistic psychology: Theory, research, and practice* (2nd ed., pp. 335–350). Thousand Oaks, CA: Sage.

Kudeva, R. P. (2015). *Disenfranchised grief in postpartum women: A heuristic inquiry into women's lived experience of loss of the dreamed-of birth*. Unpublished doctoral dissertation, School of Social Policy and Practice, University of Pennsylvania, Philadelphia.

Kvale, S. (2002). *Dialogue as oppression and interview research.* Paper presented at the Nordic Educational Research Association Conference, Tallinn, Estonia.

Lamb, D. (2013). Promoting the case for using a research journal to document and reflect on the research experience. *Electronic Journal of Business Research Methods, 11*, 84–91.

Lather, P. (1991). *Getting smart: Feminist research and pedagogy with/in the postmodern.* New York, NY: Routledge.

Lawler, S. (2002). Narrative in social research. In T. May (Ed.), *Qualitative research in action* (pp. 242–258). Thousand Oaks, CA: Sage.

Leder, D. (1990). *The absent body.* Chicago, IL: University of Chicago Press.

Lederach, J. P. (2003). *The little book of conflict transformation: Clear articulation of the guiding principles by a pioneer in the field.* Intercourse, PA: Good Books.

Lee, S. M., Cho, S. H., Kissinger, D., & Ogle, N. T. (2010). A typology of burnout in professional counselors. *Journal of Counseling & Development, 88*, 131–138.

Lee, Y. O., & Lee, R. (2012). Methodological research on "sensitive" topics: A decade review. *Bulletin of Sociological Methodology, 114*, 35–49.

Legare, C. H., & Watson-Jones, R. E. (2016). The evolution and ontogeny of ritual. In D. M. Buss (Ed.), *The handbook of evolutionary psychology* (Vol. 2, 2nd ed., pp. 829–847). Hoboken, NJ: John Wiley & Sons.

Leiby, J. C. (2014). *Windows to the soul: A heuristic inquiry in the use of the eyes as portals to innate presence*. Unpublished doctoral dissertation, Sofia University, Palo Alto, CA.

Levine, S. (1991). *Guided meditations, explorations, and healings.* New York, NY: Anchor Books.

Levinger, M. (2013). *Conflict analysis: Understanding causes, unlocking solutions.* Washington, DC: United States Institute of Peace.

Liamputtong, P. (2007). *Researching the vulnerable: A guide to sensitive research methods.* Thousand Oaks, CA: Sage.

Lichtman, M. (2014). *Qualitative research in education* (4th ed.). Thousand Oaks, CA: Sage.

Lillrank, A. (2012). Managing the interviewer self. In J. F. Gubrium, J. A. Holstein, A. B. Marvasti, & K. D. McKinney (Eds.), *The SAGE handbook of interview research: The complexity of the craft* (pp. 281–295). Thousand Oaks, CA: Sage.

Lincoln, Y. S. (1995). Emerging criteria for quality in qualitative and interpretive research. *Qualitative Inquiry, 1,* 275–289.

Lincoln, Y. S., & Guba, E. G. (1985). *Naturalistic inquiry.* Newbury Park, CA: Sage.

Lincoln, Y. S., Lynham, S. A., & Guba, E. G. (2011). Paradigmatic controversies, contradictions, and emerging confluences, revisited. In N. K. Denzin & Y. S. Lincoln (Eds.), *The SAGE handbook of qualitative research* (4th ed., pp. 97–128). Thousand Oaks, CA: Sage.

Lumsden, K. (2013). "You are what you research": Researcher partisanship and the sociology of the underdog. *Qualitative Research, 13,* 3–18.

Madden, E. M. (2015). *The lived experience of being spiritual for an atheist.* Unpublished doctoral dissertation, Harold Abel School of Social and Behavioral Science, Capella University.

Manning, J., & Kunkel, A. (2014). Making meaning of meaning-making research: Using qualitative research for studies of social and personal relationships. *Journal of Social and Personal Relationships, 31,* 433–441.

Marzano, M. (2012). Informed consent. In J. F. Gubrium, J. A. Holstein, A. B. Marvasti, & K. D. McKinney (Eds.), *The SAGE handbook of interview research: The complexity of the craft* (pp. 443–457). Thousand Oaks, CA: Sage.

Maslow, A. H. (1943). A theory of human motivation. *Psychological Review, 50,* 370–396.

Maslow, A. H. (1956). Self-actualizing people: A study of psychological health. In C. Moustakas (Ed.), *The self* (pp. 160–194). New York, NY: Harper & Brothers.

Maslow, A. H. (1966). *The psychology of science.* New York, NY: Harper & Row.

Maslow, A. H. (1968). *Toward a psychology of being* (2nd ed.). New York, NY: Van Nostrand Reinhold.

Maslow, A. H. (1971). *The farther reaches of human nature.* New York, NY: Penguin.

Maslow, A. H. (1976). Creativity in self-actualizing people. In A. Rothenberg & C. R. Hausman (Eds.), *The creativity question* (pp. 86–92). Durham, NC: Duke University Press.

Maxwell, J. A. (2013). *Qualitative research design: An interactive approach* (3rd ed.). Thousand Oaks, CA: Sage.

McGettigan, T. (2008a). Agency. In L. M. Given (Ed.), *The SAGE encyclopedia of qualitative research methods* (pp. 15–16). Thousand Oaks, CA: Sage.

McGettigan, T. (2008b). Truth. In L. M. Given (Ed.), *The SAGE encyclopedia of qualitative research methods* (pp. 897–901). Thousand Oaks, CA: Sage.

McGinn, M. K. (2008). Researcher-participant relationships. In L. M. Given (Ed.), *The SAGE encyclopedia of qualitative research methods* (pp. 768–772). Thousand Oaks, CA: Sage.

Mende, J. (2005). The poverty of empiricism. *Informing Science Journal, 8,* 189–210.

Merleau-Ponty, M. (2013). *Phenomenology of perception* (D. A. Landes, Trans.). London, UK: Routledge. (Original work published 1945)

Merleau-Ponty, M. (1968). *The visible and the invisible* (A. Lingis, Trans.). Evanston, IL: Northwestern University Press. (Original work published 1964)

Mertens, D. M. (2014). *Research and evaluation in education and psychology* (4th ed.). Thousand Oaks, CA: Sage.

Miller, P. (2008a). Social justice. In L. M. Given (Ed.), *The SAGE encyclopedia of qualitative research methods* (pp. 822–826). Thousand Oaks, CA: Sage.

Miller, P. (2008b). Validity. In L. M. Given (Ed.), *The SAGE encyclopedia of qualitative research methods* (pp. 910–911). Thousand Oaks, CA: Sage.

Miller, T. (2015). *Shared trauma and resiliency among military mental health veterans: A heuristic inquiry.* Unpublished doctoral dissertation, College of Social and Behavioral Sciences, Walden University.

Miller-Day, M. (2012). Toward conciliation: Institutional review board practices and qualitative interview research. In J. F. Gubrium, J. A. Holstein, A. B. Marvasti, & K. D. McKinney (Eds.), *The SAGE handbook of interview research: The complexity of the craft* (pp. 495–509). Thousand Oaks, CA: Sage.

Minichiello, V., & Kottler, J. A. (2010). The personal nature of qualitative research. In V. Minichiello & J. A. Kottler (Eds.), *Qualitative journeys: Student and mentor experiences with research* (pp. 1–9). Thousand Oaks, CA: Sage.

Moran, D. (2000). *Introduction to phenomenology.* London, UK: Routledge.

Moreira, V. (2012). From person-centered to humanistic-phenomenological psychotherapy: The contribution of Merleau-Ponty to Carl Rogers's thought. *Person-Centered & Experiential Psychotherapies, 11,* 48–63.

Morrow, S. L. (2007). Qualitative research in counseling psychology: Conceptual foundations. *The Counseling Psychologist, 35,* 209–235.

Morstyn, R. (2010). How the philosophy of Merleau-Ponty can help us understand the gulf between clinical experience and the doctrine of evidence-based psychotherapy. *Australian Psychiatry, 18,* 221–225.

Moss, D. (2015). The roots and genealogy of humanistic psychology. In K. J. Schneider, J. Fraser Pierson, & J. F. T. Bugental (Eds.), *The handbook of humanistic psychology: Theory, research, and practice* (2nd ed., pp. 3–18). Thousand Oaks, CA: Sage.

Moustakas, C. E. (1961). *Loneliness*. Englewood Cliffs, NJ: Prentice-Hall.

Moustakas, C. (1981). *Rhythms, rituals, and relationships*. Detroit, MI: Center for Humanistic Studies.

Moustakas, C. (1990). *Heuristic research: Design, methodology, and applications*. Newbury Park, CA: Sage.

Moustakas, C. (1994). *Phenomenological research methods*. Thousand Oaks, CA: Sage.

Moustakas, C. (2015). Heuristic research: Design and methodology. In K. J. Schneider, J. Fraser Pierson, & J. F. T. Bugental (Eds.), *The handbook of humanistic psychology: Theory, research, and practice* (2nd ed., pp. 309–319). Thousand Oaks, CA: Sage.

Norum, K. E. (2008). Artifacts. In L. M. Given (Ed.), *The SAGE encyclopedia of qualitative research methods* (pp. 26–27). Thousand Oaks, CA: Sage.

Oancea, A. (2014). Ethics in social science research. In K. F. Punch, *Introduction to social science research: Quantitative and qualitative approaches* (3rd ed., pp. 35–56). Thousand Oaks, CA: Sage.

Oeye, C., Bjelland, A. K., & Skorpen, A. (2007). Doing participant observation in a psychiatric hospital: Research ethics resumed. *Social Science and Medicine, 65*, 2296–2306.

Olesen, V. (2011). Feminist qualitative research in the millennium's first decade: Developments, challenges, prospects. In N. K. Denzin & Y. S. Lincoln (Eds.), *The SAGE handbook of qualitative research* (4th ed., pp. 129–146). Thousand Oaks, CA: Sage.

Orb, A., Eisenhauer, L., & Wynaden, D. (2001). Ethics in qualitative research. *Journal of Nursing Scholarship, 33*(1), 93–96.

Ortlipp, M. (2008). Keeping and using reflective journals in the qualitative research process. *Qualitative Report, 13*, 695–705.

Packer, M. (2011). *The science of qualitative research*. New York, NY: Cambridge University Press.

Paley, J. (2008). Empiricism. In L. M. Given (Ed.), *The SAGE encyclopedia of qualitative research methods* (pp. 256–261). Thousand Oaks, CA: Sage.

Palys, T. (2008). Purposive sampling. In L. M. Given (Ed.), *The SAGE encyclopedia of qualitative research methods* (pp. 698–699). Thousand Oaks, CA: Sage.

Patton, M. Q. (2002). *Qualitative research and evaluation methods* (3rd ed.). Thousand Oaks, CA: Sage.

Patton, M. Q. (2008). Evaluation criteria. In L. M. Given (Ed.), *The SAGE encyclopedia of qualitative research methods* (pp. 302–304). Thousand Oaks, CA: Sage.

Patton, M. Q. (2015). *Qualitative research and evaluation methods* (4th ed.). Thousand Oaks, CA: Sage.

Perez, L. (2013). *The perspectives of graduate students with visual disabilities: A heuristic case study*. Unpublished doctoral dissertation, College of Education, University of South Florida, Tampa.

Pilisuk, M., & Joy, M. (2015). Humanistic psychology and ecology. In K. J. Schneider, J. Fraser Pierson, & J. F. T. Bugental (Eds.), *The handbook of humanistic psychology: Theory, research, and practice* (2nd ed., pp. 135–147). Thousand Oaks, CA: Sage.

Pogge, S. M. (2013). *The experience of living with chronic illness: A heuristic study*. Unpublished doctoral dissertation, Department of Psychology and Philosophy, College of Arts and Sciences, Texas Woman's University, Denton.

Poland, B. D. (2008). Transcription. In L. M. Given (Ed.), *The SAGE encyclopedia of qualitative research methods* (pp. 885–887). Thousand Oaks, CA: Sage.

Polanyi, M. (1958). *Personal knowledge: Towards a post-critical philosophy*. Chicago, IL: University of Chicago Press.

Polanyi, M. (1966). *The tacit dimension*. Chicago, IL: University of Chicago Press.

Polanyi, M. (1969). *Knowing and being*. Chicago, IL: University of Chicago Press.

Polkinghorne, D. E. (1988). *Narrative knowing and the human sciences*. Albany: State University of New York Press.

Polkinghorne, D. E. (2015). The self and humanistic psychology. In K. J. Schneider, J. Fraser Pierson, & J. F. T. Bugental (Eds.), *The handbook of humanistic psychology: Theory, research, and practice* (2nd ed., pp. 87–104). Thousand Oaks, CA: Sage.

Pontecorvo, C. (2007). On the conditions for generative collaboration: Learning through collaborative research. *Integrative Psychology and Behavioral Science, 41*, 178–176.

Ponterotto, J. G. (2005). Qualitative research in counseling psychology: A primer on research paradigms and philosophy of science. *Journal of Counseling Psychology, 52*, 126–136.

Porter, M. (2010). Researcher as research tool. In A. J. Mills, G. Durepos, & E. Wiebe (Eds.), *Encyclopedia of case study research* (pp. 809–811). Thousand Oaks, CA: Sage.

Preissle, J. (2008). Ethics. In L. M. Given (Ed.), *The SAGE encyclopedia of qualitative research methods* (pp. 274–278). Thousand Oaks, CA: Sage.

Rainer, T. (2004). *The new diary: How to use a journal for self-guidance and expanded creativity*. New York, NY: TarcherPerigee.

Rapport, A. (2017). Cognitive approaches to foreign policy analysis. *Oxford research encyclopedia of politics*. Retrieved from http://politics.oxfordre.com/view/10.1093/acrefore/9780190228637.001.0001/acrefore-9780190228637-e-397?print=pdf

Ratts, M. J., Singh, A. A., Nassar-McMillan, S., Butler, S. K., & McCullough, J. R. (2016). Multicultural and social justice counseling competencies: Guidelines for the counseling profession. *Journal of Multicultural Counseling and Development, 44*(1), 28–48.

Ray, D. C., Hull, D. M., Thacker, A. J., Pace, L. S., Swan, K. L., Carlson, S. E., & Sullivan, J. M. (2011). Research in counseling: A 10-year review to inform practice. *Journal of Counseling & Development, 89,* 349–359.

Ray, M. A. (1994). The richness of phenomenology: Philosophic, theoretic, and methodologic concerns. In J. M. Morse (Ed.), *Critical issues in qualitative research methods* (pp. 117–133). Thousand Oaks, CA: Sage.

Ricoeur, P. (1976). *Interpretation theory: Discourse and the surplus of meaning.* Fort Worth: Texas Christian University Press.

Rogers, C. R. (1961). *On becoming a person: A therapist's view of psychotherapy.* Boston, MA: Houghton Mifflin.

Rogers, C. R. (1969). *Freedom to learn: A view of what education might become.* Columbus, OH: Merrill.

Rogers, C. R. (1980). *A way of being: The founder of the human potential movement looks back on a distinguished career.* Boston, MA: Houghton Mifflin.

Rogers. C. R. (1985). Toward a more human science of the person. *Journal of Humanistic Psychology, 24,* 7–24.

Rolef Ben-Shahar, A. (2010). The relational turn and body-psychotherapy, I. From ballroom dance to five rhythms: An introduction to relational psychoanalysis and psychotherapy. *United States Association for Body Psychotherapy Journal, 9,* 41–49.

Rolef Ben-Shahar, A. (2011). The relational turn and body-psychotherapy, II. Something old, something new, something borrowed, something blue: Individual selves and dyadic selves in relational body psychotherapy. *United States Association for Body Psychotherapy Journal, 10,* 59–68.

Romanyshyn, R. (2007). *The wounded researcher: Research with soul in mind.* New Orleans, LA: Spring Journal.

Salk, J. (1983). *Anatomy of reality.* New York, NY: Columbia University Press.

Sandelowski, M. (2008). Member check. In L. M. Given (Ed.), *The SAGE encyclopedia of qualitative research methods* (pp. 502–503). Thousand Oaks, CA: Sage.

Sandstrom, K. L., Martin, D. D., & Fine, G. A. (2006). *Symbols, selves, and social reality: A symbolic interactionist approach to social psychology and sociology.* Los Angeles, CA: Roxbury.

Saumure, K., & Given, L. M. (2008). Rigor in qualitative research. In L. M. Given (Ed.), *The SAGE encyclopedia of qualitative research methods* (pp. 796–797). Thousand Oaks, CA: Sage.

Schensul, J. J. (2008). Methodology. In L. M. Given (Ed.), *The SAGE encyclopedia of qualitative research methods* (pp. 517–522). Thousand Oaks, CA: Sage.

Schwandt, T. A. (1996). Farewell to criteriology. *Qualitative Inquiry, 2,* 58–72.

Seligman, L., & Reichenberg, L. W. (2014). *Theories of counseling and psychotherapy: Systems, strategies, and skills* (4th ed.). Boston, MA: Pearson.

Serlin, I. A., & Criswell, E. (2015). Humanistic psychology and women: A critical-historical perspective. In K. J. Schneider, J. Fraser Pierson, & J. F. T. Bugental (Eds.), *The handbook of humanistic psychology: Theory, research, and practice* (2nd ed., pp. 27–40). Thousand Oaks, CA: Sage.

Smith, D. E. (1990). *The conceptual practices of power: A feminist sociology of knowledge.* Boston, MA: Northeastern University Press.

Smith, E. W. L. (1985). *The body in psychotherapy.* Jefferson, NC: McFarland.

Smith, J. A. (2004). Reflecting on the development of interpretative phenomenological analysis and its contribution to qualitative research in psychology. *Qualitative Research in Psychology, 1,* 39–54.

Soccio, D. J. (2013). *Archetypes of wisdom: An introduction to philosophy* (8th ed.). Boston, MA: Wadsworth-Cengage Learning.

St. Pierre, E. A. (2013). The appearance of data. *Cultural Studies v Critical Methodologies, 13,* 223–227.

Stebbins, R. A. (2008). Serendipity. In L. M. Given (Ed.), *The SAGE encyclopedia of qualitative research methods* (pp. 815–816). Thousand Oaks, CA: Sage.

Strauss, A., & Corbin, J. (1998). *Basics of qualitative research.* Thousand Oaks, CA: Sage.

Sultan, N. (2014). *From darkness, beatitudes.* Georgetown, KY: Finishing Line Press.

Sultan, N. (2015). *A heuristic inquiry of the embodied experiences of body psychotherapists in the therapeutic encounter.* Unpublished doctoral dissertation, Department of Counseling and Human Services, St. Mary's University, San Antonio, TX.

Sultan, N. (2017a). Embodied self-care: Enhancing awareness and acceptance through mindfulness-oriented expressive writing self-disclosure. *Journal of Creativity in Mental Health.* http://dx.doi.org/10.1080/15401383.2017.1286277

Sultan, N. (2017b). Embodiment and the therapeutic relationship: Findings from a heuristic inquiry. *Journal of Humanistic Counseling, 56,* 180–196. doi: 10.1002/johc.12052

Taylor, E. I., & Martin, F. (2015). Humanistic psychology at the crossroads. In K. J. Schneider, J. Fraser Pierson, & J. F. T. Bugental (Eds.), *The handbook of humanistic psychology: Theory, research, and practice* (2nd ed., pp. 19–25). Thousand Oaks, CA: Sage.

Todres, L. (2007). *Embodied enquiry: Phenomenological touchstones for research, psychotherapy and spirituality.* London, UK: Palgrave Macmillan.

Toma, J. D. (2011). Approaching rigor in applied qualitative research. In C. F. Conrad & R. C. Serlin (Eds.), *The SAGE handbook for research in education: Pursuing ideas as the keystone of exemplary inquiry* (2nd ed., pp. 263–280). Thousand Oaks, CA: Sage.

Tulku, T. (1987). *Love of knowledge.* Oakland, CA: Dharma.

van den Hoonaard, D. K. (2008). Marginalization. In L. M. Given (Ed.), *The SAGE encyclopedia of qualitative research methods* (pp. 492–496). Thousand Oaks, CA: Sage.

van Manen, M. (1990). *Researching lived experience: Human science for an action sensitive pedagogy.* London, ON: Althouse.

van Wijngaarden, E., van der Meide, H., & Dahlberg, K. (2017). Researching health care as a meaningful practice: Toward a nondualistic view on evidence for qualitative research. *Qualitative Health Research.* https://doi.org/10.1177/1049732317711133

Vygotsky, L. (1978). *Mind in society: The development of higher psychological processes.* Cambridge, MA: Harvard University Press.

Wallas, G. (1976). Stages in the creative process. In A. Rothenberg & C. R. Hausman (Eds.), *The creativity question* (pp. 69–73). Durham, NC: Duke University Press.

Wertz, F. (2005). Phenomenological research methods for counseling psychology. *Journal of Counseling Psychology, 52,* 167–177.

Wertz, F. J. (2015). Humanistic psychology and the qualitative research tradition. In K. J. Schneider, J. Fraser Pierson, & J. F. T. Bugental (Eds.), *The handbook of humanistic psychology: Theory, research, and practice* (2nd ed., pp. 259–274). Thousand Oaks, CA: Sage.

Westland, G. (2015). *Verbal and non-verbal communication in psychotherapy.* New York, NY: W. W. Norton.

Whatley, R. J. (2015). *Pulling the arrows out of our hearts: An heuristic inquiry into the lived experience of internalized racism of African American women.* Unpublished doctoral dissertation, Institute of Transpersonal Psychology, Palo Alto, CA.

Woldt, A. L., & Toman, S. M. (2005). Prologue-forward. In A. L. Woldt & S. Toman (Eds.), *Gestalt therapy: History, theory, and practice* (pp. ix–xiv). Thousand Oaks, CA: Sage.

Yontef, G. (2005). Gestalt therapy theory of change. In A. L. Woldt & S. M. Toman (Eds.), *Gestalt therapy: History, theory, and practice* (pp. 81–100). Thousand Oaks, CA: Sage.

Index

Abram, David, 2, 48, 73
Active listening, 126–127
Active perspective taking, 82
Advocacy, 167
Agency, 167–168
Alternative explanations, 183
American Counseling Association *Code of Ethics*, 212, 221–222
Anthropology, 33
A posteriori knowledge, 63
Applications
   in conflict transformation, 235–236
   in counseling, 236–238
   description of, 230–231
   in education, 231–232
   in health care, 234–235
   in political science and government, 232–234
   in psychotherapy, 236–238
A priori knowledge, 63
Artifacts, 19, 32, 134–136, 195
Art journals, 85
Arts-based narrative inquiry, 34
Asymmetrical relationships, 165
Attitudes, 169–171
Authenticity, 37
Authentic movement, 124
Autobiographical narrative inquiry, 34
Autoethnography, 4
Autonomy, 212, 214
Axiology, 43, 54, 57–58

Being, ways of, 48, 77, 168
Beliefs, 169–171
Beneficence, 212, 214
Betweenness, intersubjectivity and, 66

Biases, 169–171
Biographical narrative inquiry, 34
Body–mind duality, 74
Body∞mind∞spirit∞world, 199, 231
Body psychotherapy, 91, 112, 133–134, 137, 166, 168
"Body-sense of meaning," 72
Bohm, David, 161, 177–178
Bracketing
   definition of, 18
   description of, 65
   purpose of, 18
Bradbury, Ray, 121, 122
Bricolage/bricolaging
   definition of, 29
   of feminist research with heuristic inquiry, 36–37
   of grounded theory with heuristic inquiry, 32
   of narrative research with heuristic inquiry, 34–35
Brute data, 47
Buber, Martin, 4, 42, 65–66
Burnout, 225–226

Carnal knowledge, 48
Cartesian dualist thinking, 64
Categorical thinking, 148
Cause–effect relationships, 232
Charmaz, Kathy, 30
Client-centered psychotherapy, 167
Client-centered theory, 159
Code of ethics, 211–213, 221
Coding, in grounded theory, 31
Cognitive theory, 233
Collaboration

281

with co-researchers, 189
in heuristic evaluation, 188
relationship and, 70
Communication
  with co-researchers, 214
  nonverbal, 35, 129, 133
Compassion fatigue, 225–226
Compensation, 216, 224
Composite depiction, 99
Composite depictions, 152–153
Confidentiality, 215–216, 224, 248–249
Confirmability, 181–182, 209
Confirmation bias, 170
Conflict, 163–165
Conflict management, 235
Conflict resolution, 235
Conflict transformation, 235–237
Congruence, 67
Consciousness, 73
Constructivist grounded theory, 31
Consultation, in ethical research, 228
Co-researcher(s)
  artifacts from, 134–136, 195
  co-construction process with, 57
  collaboration with, 189
  communication with, 214
  definition of, 159
  demographic characteristics of, 115, 201
  empowerment of, 189
  exclusion criteria for, 116
  in feminist research, 37
  heuristic manuscript inclusion of, 195
  identification of, 112
  inclusion criteria for, 116
  inviting of, 115–120
  in narrative research, 35
  as participants, 37
  in qualitative research, 51, 54
  rapport with, 118–120
  relational approaches to, 166
  relational boundaries with, 218–220, 224

  relaxation-oriented exercise with, 126
  researcher and, 56, 72, 114
  rights of, 113
  risks and benefits for, 113
  sampling considerations for, 115–118
  securing of, 115–120
  selection of, 115–120
  thank-you messages, 130
  trust with, 118–120
  as vulnerable populations, 112
Counseling, 236–238
Countertransference, 127–128, 219
Cover letter, 207, 244–246
Creative synthesis phase, 95, 99, 154–155
Credibility, 180–181, 208
Cultural sensitivity, 130
Curiosity, 102

Data analysis
  content and context in, 146–147
  description of, 145
  discipline during, 149, 151
  heuristic manuscript description of, 196
  holistic approach to, 145
  literature review and, 109
  procedures for, 145–146
  purpose of, 146
  themes identified from. *See* Themes, from data analysis
Databases, 110
Data collection
  description of, 122–123
  detachment in, 47
  in grounded theory, 30
  heuristic manuscript description of, 196
  interviews for. *See* Interview/interviewing
  literature review before, 109
  in narrative research, 33, 35
  in qualitative research, 50
  stopping of, 140

Data organization and management
  description of, 140
  immersion∞incubation∞reflexivity, 140–141
  verbatim transcripts, 141–144
Decision-making model, ethical, 221–222, 228
Demographic information form, 247
Dependability, 181, 208–209
Descriptive/empirical approach, to phenomenological research, 25
Developmental learning theory, 53
Dialogue, 161. *See also* Self-dialogue
Dialoguing, 128
Discipline, in data analysis, 149, 151
Discourse, 13
Discussion section, of heuristic manuscript, 196–197
Dissonance, 164
Dualistic Cartesian mind-over-body method, 26

Ecology, phenomenology and, 73
Education, 231–232
Embodied knowing, 88
Embodied perceptual phenomenology, 27
Embodied reflexivity, 169
Embodied relational interviewing, 124–130
Embodied relational listening, 126–127
Embodied relational transcription, 142–143
Embodied relational writing, 198–205
Empathy, 67, 75, 160
Empirical
  empiricism versus, 48
  heuristic inquiry as empirical process, 46–50
Empirical research
  definition of, 48
  forms of, 46–47
Empiricism
  definition of, 47, 63
  empirical versus, 48
  radical, 49–50
Empowerment, 167–168
Empty chair experiment, 82–84
Epistemology, 43, 54, 56–57
Époché, 64
Ethical dilemmas
  emergent types of, 220–224
  informed consent, 214–217
  relational boundaries with co-researchers, 218–220
  researcher competence, 220
  research methodology and design, 217–218
  transparency, 220
Ethics
  core principles and codes of, 211–213, 221
  decision-making model, 221–222, 228
  definition of, 211
Evaluation, heuristic. *See* Heuristic evaluation
Exclusion criteria, for co-researchers, 116
Exemplary portraits, 99, 153–154
Exercises
  embodied relational writing, 204–205
  emergent ethical dilemmas in heuristic research, 224
  empty chair experiment, 82–84
  finger labyrinth, 38–40
  needs self-assessment, 101
  personal dilemmas, 175
  reflexive journal, 175
  self-assessment, 101
  six-step exercise for clearing an inner space, 93–94
  subjectivity–objectivity continuum, 49
  values, 171
  ways of being, 77
  ways of knowing, 77
Existentialism, 65
Existential phenomenology, 73
Experiencing, 67, 72
Experiential learning, 158–160

Experiential time, 11
Explication phase, 95, 98–99
Exploratory research, 52. *See also* Qualitative research
External audit/review, 183
External experiences, 66

Feedback, 189, 203
Felt meaning, 67, 72
Felt sense, 72
Feminist research, 36–37
Fidelity, 212
Findings section, of heuristic manuscript, 196
Finger labyrinth exercise, 38–40
First-person active voice, 198–199
First-person approach, to phenomenological research, 25
Focusing, 72, 91–94
Freire, Paulo, 158, 160

Gendlin, Eugene, 4, 42, 67, 72–73, 91, 158
Generic content and forms, 114–115
Gestalt cycle of awareness, 102
Goodness, 179–180
Grosz, Elizabeth, 74
Grounded theory
 bricolaging of, with heuristic inquiry, 32
 coding in, 31
 constant comparison in, 30
 constructivist, 31
 data collection in, 30
 description of, 9
 features of, 30–31
 hierarchical structure used by, 31
 origins of, 30
 as qualitative approach, 31
Guided Meditations, Explorations, and Healings, 96

Health care, 234–235
Hermeneutic/interpretive approach, to phenomenological research, 25

Heuristic, 3
Heuristic approach
 description of, 12–13
 engagement in external processes, 13
 flexibility of, 21–22
 humanistic psychology origins of, 30
Heuristic evaluation
 collaborative approach to, 188
 confirmability in, 181–182, 209
 credibility in, 180–181, 208
 criteria for, 180–182
 dependability in, 181, 208–209
 description of, 113
 goodness in, 179–180
 interactive approach of, 179
 primer on, 178
 purpose of, 187, 190
 reflexive leadership in, 189–190
 rigor in, 179–180
 as shared experience, 187–188
 strategies for, 182–183
 transferability in, 181, 208
 trustworthiness in, 179–180
Heuristic inquiry
 autobiographical basis of, 18
 characteristics of, 3–7, 32, 184–186
 conflict transformation applications of, 235–237
 definition of, 3, 14, 210
 discourse in, 13
 education applications of, 231–232
 features of, 10–15
 focus of, identifying with, 81–85
 health care applications of, 234–235
 history of, 2–8
 informal engagement of, 239–240
 limitations of, 19–21
 narrative research versus, 34
 perspectives of, 26–27
 phenomenology versus, 26, 28, 60
 political science and government applications of, 232–234
 processes and phases of. *See* Heuristic phases; Heuristic processes

purpose of, 9–10
  as qualitative research, 50–53
  schematic diagram of, 28
  summary of, 14–15
  tacit knowing in, 14
  theories influencing, 4
  transformation in, 13
Heuristic interviewing, 68. *See also* Interview/interviewing
Heuristic manuscript
  abstract of, 193
  authenticity in, 198
  components of, 192–198
  conclusions and future directions section of, 197–198
  co-researchers in, 195
  cover letter with, 207
  creativity in, 203
  data collection and analysis section of, 196
  discussion section of, 196–197
  embodied relational writing of, 198–205
  findings section of, 196
  first-person, active voice in, 198–199
  introduction section of, 194
  keywords in, 193–194
  limitations section of, 197
  literature review section of, 194–195
  materials and procedure section of, 195–196
  method section of, 195
  overview of, 191–192
  perspectives in, 200
  rationale for study included in, 194
  revision of, 203
  as shared experience, 205
  social justice promotion in, 205–207
  tables in, 200
  themes in, 202
  theoretical framework of, 194
  title of, 193
  tone of, 198, 206
  topic of inquiry in, 194
  transparency, accuracy, and truthfulness in, 202–203
  writing of, 207–209
Heuristic phases
  application of, 99–100
  creative synthesis, 17, 95, 99
  explication, 17, 95, 98–99
  illumination, 17, 95, 97–98
  immersion, 17, 95–96
  incubation, 11, 17, 95–97
  initial engagement, 17, 94–95
  summary of, 17, 95
Heuristic processes
  description of, 13, 17–19, 75, 79–81
  focusing, 17, 91–94
  functioning of, 81
  identifying with the focus of inquiry, 17, 81–85
  indwelling, 17, 90–91
  internal frame of reference, 17, 92, 94
  intuition, 17, 89–90
  self-dialogue, 17, 85–87
  summary of, 17
  tacit knowing, 14, 17, 71, 87–89
Heuristic research
  definition of, 71
  evaluation of. *See* Heuristic evaluation
  history of, 2–8
  internal pathways in, 4
  limitations of, 19–20
  location of self within, 172
  non-objective nature of, 19–20
  open-ended, 140
  open-endedness of, 21
  purpose of, 129
  schematic diagram of, 15
  studies of, 9–10
Heuristic study
  co-researchers, 112–113
  evaluation of. *See* Heuristic evaluation
  generic content and forms, 114–115
  guidelines for, 114
  informed consent for. *See* Informed consent

institutional review board proposal, 111–114
integrity of, 182, 184–186
methods and procedures in, 112
preparing for, 111–120
purpose statement for, 112
relational boundaries with co-researchers, 218–220
researcher competence, 220
research methodology and design, 217–218
research question for. *See* Research questions
topic of inquiry. *See* Topic of inquiry
transparency, 220
Hierarchy of needs, 69–70
Highly subliminally known, 87
Human agency, 167
Humanistic psychology, 4, 30, 66, 69
Husserl, Edmund, 42, 61, 63–65, 73

I–It, 4, 65
Illumination phase, 13, 95, 97–98
Immersion
 in literature, 110
 as phase, 11, 20, 95–96, 122
Immersion∞incubation∞reflexivity, 140–141, 151
Inclusion criteria, for co-researchers, 116
Incubation phase, 11, 95–97, 122, 149
Individual depiction, 98
Individual depictions, 151–152
Inductive research. *See* Qualitative research
Indwelling, 19, 90–91
∞ symbol, xvi, 74
Informal conversational interview, 131–132
Informed consent
 autonomy in, 214
 benefits, 216–217
 compensation, 216
 confidentiality, 215–216
 ethical concerns, 214–217
 form for, 112, 248–249
 in institutional review board proposal, 112
 oral, 249
 risks, 217
Initial engagement phase, 10–11, 94–95
Institutional review board proposal, 111–114
Intentionality, 64
Intercorporeality, 73, 75
Internal experiences, 66
Internal frame of reference, 92, 94
Interpretative phenomenological analysis approach, to phenomenological research, 25
Interpretivism, 53
Intersubjectivity
 betweenness and, 66
 definition of, 65, 73, 160
 I–Thou, 87, 225
 as liminal space, 161
 resonance and, 160
Interview/interviewing
 authentic movement after, 124
 countertransference in, 128
 data collection through, 65, 123–134
 embodied relational, 124–130
 flow disruptions in, 131
 informal conversational, 126, 131–132
 location for, 133
 methods of, 133
 microskills in, 128
 narrative, 35
 open-ended approach to, 132
 person-centered approaches in, 128
 preparation for, 123–124, 256–257
 purpose of, 131
 questions in, 125
 recording of, 256–257
 semi-structured, 115, 131
 silence in, 129
 structure considerations for, 131–133

time considerations for, 131–133
transference in, 128
Interview meeting, 250
Intuition, 89–90, 233
Inverted perspective, 84
Invitation letter, 244–246
I-Thou, 4, 65–66, 73, 87, 130, 219

James, William, 49
Journal(s)
reflexive, 106, 136, 169, 173–174
researcher, 136–139
self-dialoguing uses of, 85–87
Justice, 212

Kafka, Franz, 229
Kant, Emmanuel, 50
Keywords, 193–194
Knower, 56
Knowing
embodied, 88
embodied ways of, 48, 71
tacit, 14, 71, 87–89, 239
Knowledge
a posteriori, 63
a priori, 63
co-construction of, 57
development of, 71
exploratory research view of, 53
in illumination phase, 97
incubation of, 11
intuition as, 89
perception as source of, 75
personal nature of, 42
sources of, 27
tacit, 4
Kurosawa, Akiro, 163

Labyrinths, xv–xvi, 7–8, 38–40
Language, 191
Learning, experiential, 158–160
Levine, Stephen, 96
Lifeworld approach, to phenomenological research, 25

Limitations section, of heuristic manuscript, 197
Listening, active, 126–127
Literary-based narrative inquiry, 34
Literature review
databases for, 110
description of, 108–109
in heuristic manuscript, 194–195
information sources identified through, 108
key words in, 110
process of, 110
purpose of, 110
timing of, 109
Lived experience, xvi, 4
Living experience, xvi, 4
Living manuscript, 199
Loneliness, 30
Loneliness, 2

Manuscript
heuristic. *See* Heuristic manuscript
qualitative research, 59
Marginalization, 52, 57, 167
Maslow, Abraham
description of, 4, 42, 66, 69–70
hierarchy of needs for, 69–70
Materials and procedure section, of heuristic manuscript, 195–196
Meaning-making, 174–176, 188
Member checking, 183
Merleau-Ponty, Maurice, 4, 24, 27, 42, 62, 73–75, 194
Methodology, 43, 54, 58
Microskills, 128
Moral judgments, 221
Moustakas, Clark, xiv, 2–3, 11, 14–15, 21, 26, 60–61, 70, 76, 89, 117, 230, 236

Narrative research
bricolaging of, with heuristic inquiry, 34–35
data collection in, 33, 35
features of, 33–34

heuristic inquiry versus, 34
stories in, 33
Needleman, Jacob, 104
Needs self-assessment exercise, 101
Negative explanations, 183
Nonmaleficence, 212
Nonverbal experience, 14
Nonverbals/nonverbal
    communication, 35, 129, 133

Objective reality, 50
Observation, 47
On Becoming a Person: A Therapist's View of Psychotherapy, 68
On Dialogue, 161
Ontology, 43, 54–56
Open-ended relational probing and prompting, 258–259
Outliers, 56

Paradigm, 43
Paradigm wars, 46
Pedagogy of the Oppressed, 160
Peer debriefing, 183
Perception
    as intuition, 75
    knowledge from, 75
Perceptual phenomenology, 27
Perls, Friedrich, 191
Personal dilemma, 175
Personal narratives, 176
Person-centered psychotherapy, 66
Perspective taking, 82, 84–85
Phenomenology
    approaches to, 25
    definition of, 60
    description of, 24–25
    ecology and, 73
    embodied perceptual, 27
    existential, 73
    heuristic inquiry versus, 26, 28, 60
    Husserl's work with, 63–65, 73
    origins of, 61

perceptual, 27
researcher in, 61–62
Philosophers
    Abraham Maslow, 4, 42, 66, 69–70
    Carl Rogers, 42, 66–69, 72, 128, 158–159
    Edmund Husserl, 42, 61, 63–65, 73
    Eugene Gendlin, 4, 42, 67, 72–73, 91, 158
    Martin Buber, 4, 42, 65–66
    Maurice Merleau-Ponty, 4, 24, 27, 42, 62, 73–75
    Michael Polanyi, 4, 42, 70–71, 74
Philosophical assumptions
    axiology, 43, 54, 57–58
    description of, 42–43
    epistemology, 43, 54, 56–57
    methodology, 43, 54, 58
    ontology, 43, 54–56
    rhetoric, 43, 54
    types of, 43
Polanyi, Michael, 4, 42, 70–71, 74
Political science and government, 232–234
Post-positivism, 49, 53–54
Power, 165–167
Privacy, 215
Private speech, 54
Privilege, 165–167
Prolonged engagement, 183
Proust, Marcel, 157–158
Psyche, 13
Psychotherapy
    description of, 4
    empathy in, 67
    heuristic inquiry applications in, 236–238
    person-centered, 66
Purpose statement, 112
Purposive sample, 19

Qualitative research
    co-researcher in, 51, 54
    data collection in, 50

definition of, 50
disciplines that use, 51
evaluation of, 187
grounded theory. *See* Grounded
  theory
heuristic inquiry as, 50–53
intersubjectivity in, 161
manuscripts, 59
phenomenology, 24–29
researcher in, 51
social constructivist paradigm use
  of, 60
studies utilizing, 51–52

Radical empiricism, 49–50
Rapport, 118–120
Rashomon, 163
Rashomon effect, 163–165
Reduction, 62
Reflective journaling, 136
Reflexive journaling, 136, 169,
  173–174
Reflexive leadership, 189–190
Reflexive-relational approach, to
  phenomenological research, 25
Reflexivity
  description of, 59–60, 166,
    168, 183
  embodied, 169
  holistic approach to, 169
  journal as tool for, 173–174
  purpose of, 18
  reduction and, 62
  researcher engagement through,
    222–223
Relational boundaries with
  co-researchers, 218–220, 224
Relationality
  agency, 167–168
  conflict, 163–165
  description of, 158–159
  empowerment, 167–168
  experiential learning, 158–160

power and privilege, 165–167
social justice, 167–168
Relationships
  asymmetrical, 165
  collaboration and, 70
  I–It, 65
  I–Thou, 4, 65
Relaxation-oriented exercise, 126
Remembrance of Things Past, 158
Researcher(s)
  artifacts from, 134–136
  competence of, 220
  co-researcher and, 56, 72, 114
  experience of, 27
  in feminist research, 36
  in grounded theory, 31
  initial engagement with topic by,
    10–11
  journals from, 136–139
  in narrative research, 33–34
  in phenomenology, 61–62
  in qualitative research, 51
  reflexive engagement of, 222–223
  rights of, 113
  role of, 113, 172–173
  well-being of, 225–228
Research paradigms
  post-positivism, 53–54
  social constructivism. *See* Social
    constructivism
  types of, 53–54
Research partners. *See also*
  Co-researcher(s)
  compensation for, 216
  conflict with, 164
  confusion by, 20
  definition of, 159
  engagement with, 125
  in feminist research, 37
  in narrative research, 35
  pseudonyms for, 118
  recruiting of, 115–120
Research problem, 111

Research questions
  being, relating, and knowing through, 12
  characteristics of, 106–108
  description of, 11
  examples of, 108
  facets for interacting with, 26
  formulating of, 105–109
  literature review after formulation of, 109
  roadblocks in defining or refining of, 20
  themes organized according to, 149
Research question–theory continuum, 43–44
Research team, xv
Resiliency, 238
Resonance, 160
Rhetoric, 43, 54, 58–60
Rigor, 179–180
Rituals, 123–124
Rogers, Carl, 42, 66–69, 72, 128, 158–159
Romanyshyn, Robert, 62

Sampling/sample
  co-researcher selection through, 115–118
  size of, 117–118
Saturation, 117–118
Scientific inquiry, 64
Self-actualization, 22, 66, 70, 216
Self-assessment exercise, 101
Self-awareness, 170
Self-care, 227
Self-dialogic technique, 66
Self-dialogue, 85–87, 166
Self-disclosure
  description of, 85, 87, 167, 172
  in interviews, 127
Self-exploration, 13, 85
Self-reflection, 13
Self-research, 4, 27

Self-searching technique, 66
Semi-structured interview
  description of, 115, 131
  sample protocol for, 251–255
Sensory experience, 47
Sensory∞kinesthetic experience, 26, 225
Shared reality, 163
Shared trauma, 238
Silence, 129
Situational analysis, 31
"Sleeping-on-it" phase, 96
Snowball sampling, 31
Social action and change, 21
Social constructivism
  axiological assumptions, 57–58
  characteristics of, 54
  description of, 49, 53
  epistemological assumptions, 56–57
  methodological assumptions, 58
  ontological assumptions, 54–56
  qualitative research uses of, 60
  rhetorical assumptions, 58–60
Social constructivist, 5
Social justice, 35, 167–168, 205–207
Sociology, 33
Stories, 33
Stress, 124
Subjectivity, 47, 50
Subjectivity–objectivity continuum, 49, 219

Tables, 200
Tacit knowing, 14, 71, 87–89, 239
Tacit knowledge, 4
Thank-you messages, 130
Themes, from data analysis
  composite depictions, 152–153
  creative synthesis, 154–155
  deciphering of, 147–149
  exemplary portraits, 153–154
  explication of, 151–155
  in heuristic manuscript, 202

identification of, 150
illumination of, 149
individual depictions, 151–152
organizing of, 149
Theoretical foundations, 42–43
Theory. *See also specific theory*
    benefits of, 45
    competent practice and, 46
    description of, 42–46
    heuristic inquiry, 4
    research question–theory continuum, 43–44
    roles of, 43
Thick description, 183
Tip-of-the-tongue phenomenon, 97
Title, of manuscript, 193
Topic of inquiry
    awareness of, 105–108
    being, relating, and knowing through, 12
    in heuristic manuscript, 194
    identification of, 105
    internal location of, 18
    journaling of, 138
Transcription, 142–144
Transferability, 181, 208

Transference, 127–128, 219
Transparency, 220
Triangulation, 183
Tropper, Jonathan, 78
Trust, 118–120
Trustworthiness, 179–180

Unknown known, 87

Values, 169–171
van Manen, Max, 61
Veracity, 212
Verbatim transcripts, 141–144
Vicarious trauma, 225–226
Visible and the Invisible, The, 75
Visual-based narrative inquiry, 34
Vulnerable populations, 112
Vygotsky, Lev, 53–54

Wallas, Graham, 17
Ways of being, 77
Ways of knowing, 48, 71, 77
Wellness, 234
Would-be knower, 56
Wounded Researcher: Research With Soul in Mind, The, 62

Printed in Great Britain
by Amazon